The Addiction-Prone
Personality

LONGITUDINAL RESEARCH IN THE SOCIAL AND BEHAVIORAL SCIENCES
An Interdisciplinary Series

Series Editors:
Howard B. Kaplan, *Texas A&M University, College Station, Texas*
Adele Eskeles Gottfried, *California State University, Northridge, California*
Allen W. Gottfried, *California State University, Fullerton, California*

The Addiction-Prone Personality

Gordon E. Barnes
University of Victoria, Victoria, British Columbia, Canada

Robert P. Murray and **David Patton**
University of Manitoba, Winnipeg, Manitoba, Canada

Peter M. Bentler
University of California, Los Angeles, California

and

Robert E. Anderson
University of New Mexico, Albuquerque, New Mexico

Kluwer Academic / Plenum Publishers
New York, Boston, Dordrecht, London, Moscow

Library of Contress Cataloging-in-Publication Data

The addiction-prone personality / Gordon E. Barnes ... [et al].
    p. cm. -- (Longitudinal research in the social and behavioral sciences)
    Includes bibliographical references and index.
    ISBN 0-306-46249-4
    1. Substance abuse--Etiology. 2. Personality. I. Barnes, Gordon E., 1943- II. Series.

RC564 .A287 2000
616.86'071--dc21

99-053617

ISBN 0-306-46249-4

©2000 Kluwer Academic / Plenum Publishers, New York
233 Spring Street, New York, New York 10013

http://www.wkap.nl/

10 9 8 7 6 5 4 3 2 1

A C.I.P. record for this book is available from the Library of Congress

Preface

The production of this book represents a culmination for me of some 25 years of interest in the field of personality and substance use and abuse. In choosing the field of substance use and abuse for the focus of our research, all of the investigators collaborating in this research have been sustained by the awareness that the work we are doing has an important purpose. Substance abuse continues to have enormous impacts on individuals and families, and prevention and treatment approaches developed to date have not always been as successful as we would hope to see. New advances in our fundamental understanding of the causal mechanisms involved in the development of addiction may be necessary to advance our success in developing new forms of prevention and treatment for alcohol and drug abuse.

The work in this book builds on the work of numerous previous investigators who have been drawn to investigate this topic. As you will notice in the extensive reference list, there have been hundreds of articles published on this topic. Although each of these references has added a small piece to our understanding of the relationship between personality and alcohol abuse, the majority of these studies have been done on clinical samples and often involved no control groups or poorly matched control groups. Several important previous longitudinal investigations have been conducted, but these investigations have usually not included general population samples or comprehensive personality test batteries. The current investigation is also unique in that a clinical sample is also included and compared with the general population sample, and an adoption study was conducted to examine the environmental factors associated with the development of the Addiction-Prone Personality.

The conceptual and methodological focus for this book has been influenced by many mentors. My interest in the areas of personality, substance abuse, and structural equation modeling were nurtured while studying with Paul Kohn at York University. An interest and appreciation for the importance of conducting research in the general population was developed while taking a course on psychiatric epidemiology with Alexander Leighton. An appreciation for the importance of the life span approach to research, and the importance of parenting in the development of the individual was developed while I was teaching in the Family Studies Department at the University of Manitoba.

The completion of the project has involved the cooperation of numerous collaborators, some of whom are included as coauthors of the book. Bob Murray and I have shared an interest in substance abuse epidemiology for some 20 years, and Bob has added expertise in conducting survey research to the research team. I was first introduced to Peter Bentler while attending a workshop on structural equation modeling at the International Congress of Psychology in Acapulco. Subsequently, I spent some time studying with Peter at UCLA while on sabbatical and fortunately was able to persuade him to join our research team to provide methodological expertise in structural equation modeling and longitudinal research. David Patton is a former graduate student and has played an active part in all phases of the research starting with the data collection in Manitoba and continuing through to the completion of the data analysis. Rob Anderson is also a former student who has played a large role in analyzing the data for this project and completing the chapters on the clinical study.

The three studies described in this book and the completion of this book were supported by funding from a variety of sources. The Winnipeg Health and Drinking Survey was funded by the National Health Research and Development Program of Health Canada as part of the National Alcohol and Drug Strategy. The clinical study described in this book was conducted with the support of the Alcoholism Foundation of Manitoba and was funded by the Manitoba Health Research Council. The Vancouver Family Survey was funded by the National Health Research and Development Program. Peter Bentler's participation in this project was facilitated by grant DA01070 from the National Institute on Drug Abuse. Rob Anderson's participation in this research was made possible by the financial support he received from the Alcohol and Drug Programs Division of the British Columbia Ministry of Health and the British Columbia Health Research Foundation.

The analysis and dissemination of the results from the Winnipeg Health and Drinking Survey described in this book have been greatly enhanced by the large number of graduate students who have participated in the research, including Len Greenwood, Reena Sommer, Shaila Khan, Lana Feinstein, Maureen Rodrique, Carole Beaudoin, and Christine Kreklewetz. Data collection for the Vancouver Family Survey was accomplished through the assistance of the Health Promotion Centre at the University of British Columbia, under the direction of Lawrence Green. Anne George provided the project management for this study, and her good nature and competence in managing this difficult task is much appreciated.

The completion of this book required a considerable amount of effort by secretarial and other support staff. The bulk of this work was completed by Caroline Green and Katherine Woodhouse. Throughout the completion of all three of these studies, Terry Perkins has been involved as an interviewer and data analyst, and in drawing the structural equation models. Terry's agreeableness and conscientiousness in completing all of these tasks has been very much appreciated. The assistance of Elizabeth Houck in editing and proofreading was very helpful.

Rob Anderson would like to thank all of those who gave him encouragement and inspiration along the way. This includes the other authors of the book; his loving parents and sister; and the growing number of people with addiction-prone personalities who, after having directly experienced the isolation and degradation of active addiction, now offer each other ongoing support in recovery fellowships like Narcotics Anonymous and Alcoholics Anonymous.

The completion of the three studies described in this book placed a large burden on all of the participants in this research. Two of the studies were longitudinal in nature, and the other study required participation by three family members. All of the studies involved completing questionnaires and interviews that were lengthy and complex. We would like to express our sincerest thanks to all of the respondents who made this work possible by taking the time to participate in this research.

Although the completion of the three research studies—and production of this book—has been a lengthy and difficult task, it has been a process that produced many enjoyable moments along the way. Whether these moments included working on proposals late at night, analyzing data in various locations ranging from the University of Manitoba to the University of Victoria and UCLA, or attending conferences to present our findings all over the world, the process has been enhanced by the warm relationships enjoyed with colleagues and students who have worked on this project.

Gordon E. Barnes

Contents

PART IV. SUBGROUPS OF ALCOHOLICS

PART V. THE PREALCOHOLIC PERSONALITY

PART VI. CONCLUSIONS

I

INTRODUCTION

1

Introduction

In the years that have elapsed since the publication of the review article by Barnes (1979) on the alcoholic personality, dramatic developments have occurred in the fields of both personality and alcohol abuse. Although there was a time when personality traits had fallen into disfavor because of the alleged low correlations between personality traits and actual behavior, this trend has currently been reversed for several reasons. Now it is recognized that low correlations between personality and behavior may be attributable at times to unreliable measures of behavior rather than the lack of validity of personality traits. Where reliable estimations of behavior are achieved through aggregation, the correlations between personality and the aggregated measures of behavior have generally been much higher (Epstein, 1979; Rushton, Brainerd & Pressley, 1983). As an illustration of this principle, the correlations between a personality scale score and drinking behavior in a group of subjects on a given day may be fairly low, but if the drinking behavior were observed and recorded over a period of thirty days, the correlation is likely to be much higher. Relationships between personality risk factors and alcohol abuse can also be enhanced by using latent variable structural equation modeling techniques (e.g., Earleywine, Finn & Martin, 1990). Recent research has also tended to show that biologically based individual differences or temperaments are relatively stable from early childhood on (Buss & Plomin, 1984; Caspi & Silva, 1995), that neonatal temperament is linked with molecular genetic structure (Ebstein, Levine, Geller et al., 1998), and that personality characteristics are particularly stable in adulthood (McCrae & Costa, 1984). In one particular study (Costa, McCrae, & Arenberg, 1980), it was noted that the median test–retest correlation for 10 personality traits over a twelve year period was .74.

In addition to the growing evidence that personality traits are fairly stable,

new evidence is also accumulating to show that there is a biological basis underlying the primary personality characteristics (Cloninger, 1987a; Zuckerman, 1989).
Research on samples of twins (e.g., Eysenck, 1990; Macaskill, Hopper, White, &
Hill, 1994) has shown that a substantial proportion of the reliable variance in the
primary personality characteristics of Extraversion, Neuroticism, and Psychoticism
can be explained by genetic variance. Recent research has shown an association
between molecular genetic structure and personality. Ebstein and Belmaker (1997)
found an association between the dopamine D4 receptor and novelty seeking as
measured by the TPQ (Cloninger, 1987b). These results were replicated by Benjamin (Benjamin, Li, Patterson et al., 1996) in research employing the NEO-Five
Factor Inventory where associations were found between high extraversion and
low conscientiousness on the NEO and the presence of long alleles of D4DR
exon III. A significant association was also found between this genetic pattern
and a calculated measure of novelty seeking. By carefully analyzing sibling data,
Benjamin et al. (1996) were able to show that population factors such as ethnicity
could not account for this genetic transmission. Results confirmed that associations within the same families were apparent between the genetic structure and
novelty seeking. Benjamin et al.(1996) point out that genetic variation does not
explain all of the variance in novelty seeking and that their discovery accounts
only for 10% of the genetic variance in the transmission of novelty seeking. They
suggest that several other genetic locii that predict novelty seeking will eventually be identified. In fact recent research by Blum et al. (in press) confirms the
prediction having found an association between the A1 of D2 allele, or the so-
called alcohol or reward-seeking gene and novelty seeking.

     Research on twins reared apart has confirmed that the genetic influence on
personality is just over 40%. Even the trait self-concept, which one would think
might be more strongly affected by environmental influences, also has a strong
genetic component (e.g., Hur, McGue, & Iacono, 1998). If major personality dimensions are stable and biologically based, then the chances that these factors
may be causally related to alcoholism is also enhanced. Recent evidence from
both twin studies (e.g., Jang, Livesley, & Vernon, 1995; Kaij, 1960; Kendler,
Heath, Neale, Kessler, & Eaves, 1992; Koopmans & Boomsma, 1986; Murray,
Clifford, & Gurling, 1983; Pickens et al., 1991; Prescott, Hewitt, Heath, Truett,
Neale, & Eaves, 1994; Romanov, Kaprio, Rose, & Koskenvuo, 1991) and adopted
out studies (e.g., Goodwin, Schulsinger, Hermansen, Guze, & Winokur, 1973;
Cloninger, Bohman, & Sigvardsson, 1981) has established a likely association
between genetic factors and alcoholism, found that the genetic aspect is particu-
larly relevant to the type of alcoholism associated with physical dependence
(Goodwin, 1985), and shows up more strongly in older samples (Koopmans &
Boomsma, 1996).

     More recently, a new avenue of research has been established stemming
from developments in the field of molecular genetics. Blum et al. (1990) reported

that the A1 allele of the dopamine receptor gene occurred with a much higher frequency in the DNA of brain samples taken from alcoholics following autopsy than in a comparison sample. This particular receptor was chosen because of the important role of the dopaminergic system in alcohol-related behaviors. Blum et al. (1990) cautioned that their results would have to be replicated because of failures in the past to replicate molecular genetic findings linking particular loci of inheritance with neuropsychiatric disorders. In a recent review of the research in this area, Gelernter, Goldman, and Risch (1993) concluded that the body of data collected to date did not support an association between the A1 Allele of D2 and alcoholism. However, Gelernter et al. (1993) did not employ scientifically approved meta-analytic procedures to combine the results of different studies. In our own reanalysis of this data (Barnes, Patton, & Sharp, unpublished manuscript), using standard meta-analytic procedures, as advocated by Rosenthal (1984), we found that the overall pattern of results supported an association between the A1 D2 Allele and alcoholism ($p < .001$, overall). The magnitude of this effect was $r = .15$ when all studies were combined, and somewhat stronger ($r = .23$) when studies not screening alcoholics from their control groups were excluded. A recent review of this literature by Lawford et al. (1997) supported the association between the A1 Allele and severe alcoholism and also highlighted the importance of using nonalcoholic controls.

Because it is not possible to inherit alcoholism per se (if one was never exposed to alcohol and never drank, it would be impossible to become an alcoholic no matter what the predisposition), the search has been going on to identify potential biological markers of alcoholism (see Schuckit, 1987), which would make people susceptible to alcoholism once they began drinking. Noble, Blum, Ritchie, Montgomery, & Sheridan (1991) have examined some of the possible mechanisms through which the A1 allele might act to affect alcoholism by examining the association between this allele and receptor binding characteristics. In their book called *Alcohol and the Addictive Brain*, Blum and Payne (1991) articulate the theory that individuals who are vulnerable to alcohol suffer from abnormally low levels of dopamine and a lower ability to bind dopamine receptors in the reward part of the brain. This condition produces a supersensity in the reward center of the brain so that anything that increases the amount of dopamine available in the brain, including alcohol, can produce strong feelings of well-being. The appeal of their theory to psychologists is that their results are consistent with a lot of what is known about the psychology of addictive behaviors and sensation-seeking behavior in general. The results showing that the A1 allele is associated with cocaine dependence (Noble et al., 1993), cigarette smoking (Comings et al., 1996; Noble et al., 1994), and polysubstance abuse (Smith et al., 1992) add another important piece to the puzzle.

Recently Noble and co-workers have established linkages between the A1 allele and other risk factors for alcoholism, including P300 latency (Noble et al.,

1994), reduced visuospatial performance (Berman & Noble, 1995), and novelty seeking (Noble et al., in press). Research has also confirmed an association between the A1 allele and hyperactivity, another important risk factor for alcoholism (Miller & Blum, 1996). Perhaps what Blum and Payne (1991) have discovered is not so much the gene for alcohol abuse but the gene for reward-seeking or sensation-seeking behavior. In fact Miller & Blum have started to use the term reward deficiency syndrome to describe this condition. Zuckerman (1987) now postulates that sensation seeking is associated with a desire for stimulation in the reward center of the brain. Biologically based dimensions of individual difference seem to rate serious consideration as possible factors that could be inherited and play a causal role in risk for alcoholism.

Progress in our understanding of the relationships between personality characteristics and alcohol abuse has been spurred on by research in several different areas. New longitudinal studies conducted by Cloninger, Sigvardsson, & Bohman (1988) and by Hagnell, Lanke, Rorsman, & Ohman (1986) have been particularly important in illuminating the relationship between personality characteristics and alcohol abuse. These projects will be described in more detail in the next chapter. In brief, however, it can be noted that Cloninger, Sigvardsson, & Bohman (1988) found a twentyfold difference in the risk of alcohol abuse in adulthood predicted by childhood personality characteristics. In a similar vein, Hagnell et al. (1986) reported that subjects with high-risk personalities in 1957 were more than twelve times as likely to develop alcoholism 15 years later than those with low-risk personalities. In another longitudinal investigation by Labouvie and McGee (1986), the sample was studied between the ages of 12 and 21. Here again personality seemed to predict the development of alcohol and substance abuse, "adolescents who proceed early and quickly to heavier levels of use tend to score lower on achievement, cognitive structure and harm avoidance and, at the same time, higher on affiliation, autonomy, exhibition, impulsivity and play" (p. 292). In analyses based on the same data set, Bates and Labouvie (1995) reported that high impulsivity and disinhibition (i.e., sensation seeking) were associated with high-risk developmental trajectories for alcohol use and problems.

Several recent longitudinal investigations have confirmed the importance of personality in measuring subsequent alcohol abuse even when personality is assessed at a very young age. Pulkkinen and Pitkanen (1994) studied 196 males and 173 females at ages 8, 14, and 26. In their male subjects, problem drinking was predicted by higher aggression and lower anxiety, prosociality, and school success at age 8. For females, higher anxiety and lower school success at age 8 were associated with more problem drinking in adulthood. Masse and Tremblay (1997) examined the association between temperament assessed at ages 6 and 10 and the onset of alcohol and substance abuse assessed at ages 11, 12, 13, 14, and 15. The large-scale, well-conducted study provided impressive evidence for the linkage between personality and alcohol and substance abuse. High novelty seeking and low harm avoidance were associated with early developing alcohol and substance misuse even when personality was assessed as early as age 6. In another large and well-conducted study, Caspi et al. (1997) found that personality measures as early as age 3 could be used to predict health-risk behavior (including alcohol abuse) patterns at age 21. Children who later developed healthrisk behavior patterns were described as "undercontrolled" at age 3.

There are few longitudinal studies examining the association between personality and alcohol abuse where positive findings have not been reported. One paper where a positive association between personality and alcohol abuse was not reported was the study reported by Vaillant and Milofsky (1982). In this research, data from the Glueck and Glueck (1950, 1968) inner city youth study were reported. The original sample for this study was not a random sample, but was comprised of reform school youth who had at the age of 14 not been charged with delinquency. In the Vaillant and Milofsky (1982) paper, a report was made of a follow-up study conducted on this sample at age 47. This is an important study because it involves such a long period between the original data collection and follow-up. In their description of the results of this study, Vaillant and Milofsky (1982) argued that their results did not support an association between personality and the development of alcoholism. This conclusion was subsequently challenged by Zucker and Lisanskey Gomberg (1986), who argued that some of the personality factors examined in this study, such as "oral dependency" have not been given much credence in the personality and alcohol abuse literature. On the other hand, Zucker and Lisanskey Gomberg (1986) note that within the Vaillant and Milofsky data, antisocial behavior in adolescence, which they regard as part of personality, played an important role in predicting adult alcoholism.

Another longitudinal investigation where positive findings were not reported was in the study reported by Schuckit, Klein, Twitchell, and Smith (1994). Several factors in the design of this study worked against finding significant results. The exclusion of patients with personality disorders would certainly restrict the range of personality scores in this sample and reduce the potential for finding significant results. It is not surprising in a way that when you control for personality, personality does not predict alcohol abuse. Although the study used the Eysenck questionnaire, it did not include a recent version of the EPQ test, so the P dimension was not included in the study, nor were there any measures of sensation seeking. The sample size in this study was also too small to detect the effects that they were looking for. For example, the study included the MacAndrew Alcoholism Scale (MacAndrew, 1965), but data were available for only 62 subjects on this test and subsequent alcoholism diagnoses. The results comparing alcoholics and non-alcoholics on the MAC test were almost significant ($p < .08$) and would almost certainly have been significant with a larger sample size.

Recent developments in the drug abuse field are also consistent with the position taken in this book. In a major new book (Glantz & Pickens, 1992) containing a series of articles describing longitudinal studies predicting the transition from drug use to drug abuse, Glantz and Pickens (1992) concluded that "drug use appears to be more a function of social and peer factors, whereas abuse appears to be more a function of biological and psychological processes" (p. 9). Recent longitudinal research by Jessor, Donovan, and Costa (1991) lends further support for this contention. In their cross-sectional research, Jessor et al. (1991) found strong support for the role of the perceived environment in predicting substance abuse. In their longitudinal analyses using structural equation modeling, however, no support for the role of the perceived environment was observed. Personality characteristics were the major factors associated with predicting the risk of problem behaviors, including alcohol abuse, in their longitudinal analyses. This perspective is also being supported by recent research in the field of childhood temperament. Dobkin, Tremblay, Masse, and Vitaro (1995), for example, found that children who were disruptive at age 6 (e.g., more fighting, hyperactivity, etc.) were more likely to report getting drunk and using drugs at age 13. Longitudinal analyses suggested that personality may also affect substance abuse indirectly by affecting the selection of deviant peers. Longitudinal research by Brook, Whiteman, and Finch (1992) has also supported an association between childhood aggression and adolescent drug use and delinquency. Tubman and Windle (1995) also found that individuals who display a pattern of continuous difficult temperament were more vulnerable to abuse alcohol and other substances.

Support for the importance of the personality domain in predicting the development of drug abuse can also be derived from research employing the use of risk factors. In their study of concurrent and predictive risk factors for drug use among 994 adolescent 10th-12th graders, Newcomb, Maddahian, and Bentler (1986), for example, found that a scale composed of ten different risk factors was reliably associated with several types of alcohol and drug use. They also reported that the risk factors significantly predicted increased drug use across a one-year period, controlling for initial levels of use. The risk factors included poor self-esteem and sensation seeking.

In another longitudinal study employing a risk factor approach, Scheier, Botvin, and Baker (1997) examined the role of a set of psychological risk factors that included behavioral undercontrol, depression/anxiety, locus of control, and self-esteem. Their results confirmed the importance of psychological factors in predicting an increase in alcohol problems. In this research, the magnitude of the psychological set in predicting the development of alcohol abuse was comparable to that of social influences.

Recent longitudinal research in the field of personality disorders also supports the importance of personality in prospectively predicting risk for alcohol and substance abuse. In one such investigation, Kwapil (1996) investigated the importance of psychosis-prone traits and nonconformity in predicting substance abuse ten years later. Their results confirmed the importance of both psychosis proneness and nonconformity in predicting the development of substance abuse disorders. In another longitudinal study examining the relationship between personality disorders and substance abuse in adolescents over a three-year period, Johnson, Bornstein and Sherman (1996) found support for the relationship between the prevalence of personality disorders and the occurrence of substance use over time.

Another important source of evidence contributing to our understanding of the relationship between personality characteristics and alcohol abuse has been the research on high-risk individuals. In the past ten years, numerous studies have been conducted on high-risk individuals, as defined in various ways, but generally based on whether the person has had a family history of alcohol abuse. This important research, which has now been conducted on such characteristics as stimulus augmenting reducing, field dependence (Hennecke, 1984), anxiety and tension reduction (see Finn & Pihl, 1987; Finn, Zeitouni, & Pihl, 1990; Pihl, Peterson & Finn, 1990), and minimal brain dysfunction (e.g., Tarter, Hegedus, Goldstein, Shelly, & Alterman, 1984) has improved our understanding of the most likely causal direction between these risk factors and abuse. Before this research, it was uncertain which of these characteristics came as a result of drinking and which characteristics may have been caused by drinking. This research will also be described in more detail in the sections that follow.

Another important area of research that has contributed toward our understanding of the relationship between personality and alcohol abuse has been the research on alcoholic personality types. At the time I (Barnes) wrote my review article in 1979, I did not include a review of the various possible subtypes of alcoholic personalities. This omission has led some of the people who read the original review to conclude that I was somehow trying to argue that there was a single alcoholic personality type. That was not my belief or intention at that time. The main problem I had in reviewing the cluster analytic studies searching for the subtypes of alcoholic personality was that this literature seemed to be producing results that did not seem to be very consistent or easily compared across studies. The studies also seemed to be producing too many different possible subtypes to be credible. Recent research (Dush & Keen, 1995) has shown that the number of subtypes of alcoholics identified in MMPI research on clinical samples is not stable over time and probably capitalizes on transient withdrawal symptoms.

Results from the adopted out research conducted by Cloninger, Bohman, and Sigvardsson (1981) and the longitudinal research by Cloninger, Sigvardsson, and Bohman (1988) provide strong support for the validity of the two major classifications of alcoholics that differ according to personality characteristics. Cloninger (1987a) describes the neurotic or Type 1 alcoholic as low on novelty seeking, high on harm avoidance, and high on reward dependence. This type of alcoholism is associated with later onset, more guilt, and less frequent history of fighting and arrests. This type of alcoholic is motivated to drink for tension relief and is milieu limited. In other words, this type of alcoholism occurs only in environments that are conducive to heavy drinking. Type 2 alcoholics are described by Cloninger (1987a) as high on novelty seeking, low on harm avoidance, and low on reward dependence. They are characterized by an earlier onset of drinking and frequent fighting and arrests. This type of alcoholism is associated with lower levels of serotonin, dopamine, and metabolites. Persons with this type of alcoholism are expected to be at greater risk regardless of the environment, and this form of alcoholism is limited to males.

Support for the Cloninger classification system described above has been provided by several studies. Von Knorring, Palm, and Andersson (1985) examined the relationship between treatment outcome and subtypes of alcoholism in 30 alcoholics receiving treatment and 39 ex-alcoholics. Their results showed that drug use and criminal involvement were more common in Type II alcoholics. There was also a higher percentage of Type II alcoholics in the ex-alcoholic group suggesting that Type II alcoholics were perhaps able to control their drinking more easily or had matured out of alcoholism. The hypothesized association between a family history of alcoholism and antisocial behavior in association with alcoholism in men has also been supported (Frances, Timm, & Bucky, 1980; Glenn & Parsons, 1989). Further, Donovan and Marlatt (1982) identified five clusters in their sample of Driving While Impaired Offenders. Three of these groups were high on risk taking, corresponding to Cloninger Type II alcoholics, and the two other groups were low on risk taking, corresponding to Cloninger Type I alcoholic.

Further support and clarification for the concept of two main alcoholic personality types comes from the research and writing by MacAndrew (1979, 1980, 1983). In this work, MacAndrew (1979) indicates that 85% of the alcoholics that are identified by the MacAndrew Alcoholism Scale are Primary Substance abusers. These are individuals who are high on Extraversion and high on Neuroticism and whom Eysenck (1978) would call secondary sociopaths (MacAndrew, 1979). According to MacAndrew (1980), the other 15% of alcoholics, who are not as readily identified by the MacAndrew Scale, are low on extraversion and high on neuroticism. As noted by MacAndrew (1983), both of these groups are characterized by emotional tension and depression. Because of the strong findings cited above indicating that there are likely at least two major subtypes of alcoholism, there is a chapter in this book assigned to examining the possible subtypes of alcoholism in the general population and in a clinical sample of alcoholics.

To discuss the relationships between personality characteristics and alcohol abuse it is necessary to describe the perspective on personality structure that one is adopting. In the review by Barnes (1979) of the alcoholic personality literature, a taxonomy of alcoholic personality characteristics was provided. This taxonomy was based on what was known about personality structure at that time. The four primary traits that were listed included (1) stimulus augmenting-reducing, (2) ego strength, (3) neuroticism, and (4) field dependence. Current factor analytic studies on personality structure (Digman & Inouye, 1986; McCrae & Costa, 1985a, 1985b, 1987, 1989; Noller, Law, & Comrey, 1987; Watson, 1989; Zuckerman, Kuhlman, & Camac, 1988) suggest that there are between three and seven major personality dimensions. The three main personality dimensions described by the Eysencks (Eysenck, Eysenck, & Barrett, 1985) which include Introversion-Extraversion, Neuroticism, and Psychoticism have been repeatedly found in factor analytic studies, have been observed in different cultures (Barrett & Eysenck, 1984), and have been linked in the literature with biological underpinnings (see Zuckerman, 1989).

The stimulus augmenting-reducing dimension described in the Barnes (1979) review corresponds to the dimension of Introversion-Extraversion. Stimulus reducers characterized by Petrie (1967) are similar to extraverts described by the Eysencks (Eysenck et al., 1985) as sociable, lively, active, assertive, sensation-seeking, carefree, dominant, surgent, and venturesome. Augmenters or introverts are lower on all of these characteristics. Augmenters as hypothesized by Petrie (1967) are more susceptible to becoming alcoholic because of the desirable stimulus-reducing effect that they receive from alcohol.

The second dimension described in the Barnes (1979) taxonomy of alcoholic personality characteristics was Neuroticism. High N scorers are characterized by the Eysencks (1985) as anxious, depressed, high on guilt feelings, low on self-esteem, tense, irrational, shy, moody, and emotional. This dimension emerges consistently in the factor analytic research using both self-reports and peer ratings. In the alcoholic personality literature, high anxiety has frequently been found in association with alcoholism and alcohol is presumed to have tension-reducing properties.

The third dimension in the Barnes (1979) taxonomy of alcoholic personality characteristics was called Ego Strength. Current research suggests that the characteristics which were listed under this characteristic, including, low frustration tolerance, impulsivity, etc., might more be associated with what the Eysencks have called high Psychoticism. High P scorers have been characterized by the Eysencks (Eysenck & Eysenck, 1985) as aggressive, cold, egocentric, impersonal, impulsive, antisocial, unempathic, creative, and tough-minded. The opposite pole of this dimension, which seems to emerge more in factor analytic studies of normals using peer ratings, includes the characteristics of Agreeableness and Conscientiousness.

Although McCrae and Costa (1987) have argued that their data support a five-factor model and that the factors for Agreeableness and Conscienciousness should stand alone, others are not as convinced (see Zuckerman, 1989). The characteristics of Agreeableness and Conscientiousness proposed by McCrae and Costa, although promising, are not as well established as independent personality dimensions. Ultimately the determination of whether there are two factors or one factor that make up the domain of the Psychoticism dimension will not be decided by factor analysis alone, but by the ability of the different models to predict behaviors. Eysenck (1992) has maintained that factor analysis is a good slave but a poor master. For the purposes of this investigation, we have started from the position that Ego Strength, or what McCrae and Costa call conscientiousness, are similar constructs and have retained this term. We are also employing the term of Psychoticism for the component of this domain that is comprised of impulsive and antisocial characteristics.

The fourth alcoholic personality characteristic described in the Barnes (1979) review of the alcoholic personality literature was described as Field Dependence-Independence. This dimension includes aspects of intelligence and cognitive style and probably overlaps a bit with what McCrae and Costa have called culture. Zuckerman et al. (1988) indicated that "we agree with Eysenck that intelligence or its noncognitive aspects should not be considered a basic personality dimension" (p. 103). Other reviewers of the concept of the alcoholic personality have not included this dimension in their reviews. (e.g., Nathan, 1988). In the Barnes (1979) theory of the alcoholic personality, this concept formed an integral part of the original model. Field-dependent individuals as originally described by Witkin (Witkin, Dyk, Faterson, Goodenough, & Karp, 1962) are hypothesized to be more vulnerable to becoming alcoholics than field-independent persons.

In the Barnes (1979) review of the alcoholic personality literature, a distinction was made between clinical and prealcoholic personality characteristics The term clinical alcoholic personality was used to describe the characteristics of alcoholics that discriminate them from normals and other clinical groups, and the term prealcoholic was used to describe the characteristics that predict the onset of alcoholism. This distinction will be retained in the current research.

Although there have been hundreds of studies conducted on the relationships between personality characteristics and alcohol abuse, there is still considerable debate regarding the role of personality characteristics in predicting alcohol abuse. Part of the problem lies in the fact that the majority of studies of this topic have been cross-sectional comparing clinical samples of alcoholics with poorly matched controls. Pihl and Spiers (1978), for example, estimated that 93% of all studies relating personality factors to alcoholism were done on clinical samples of alcoholics using either no control groups or poorly matched control groups. It would obviously be much more desirable to do prospective research using longitudinal samples. Although a few studies of this kind that have been conducted (e.g., Block, 1971; Caspi et al., 1997; Cloninger, Sigvardsson, & Bohman, 1988; Hagnell et al., 1986; Jones, 1968; Kammeier, Hoffman, & Loper, 1973; Labouvie & McGee, 1986; Masse & Tremblay, 1997; McCord, 1972; Pulkkinen & Pitkanen, 1994; Robins, 1966; Tubman & Windle, 1995; Vaillant & Milofsky, 1983), many of them were not designed to predict the risk of alcoholism. Because of this factor, these studies do not usually contain comprehensive measures of the constructs that have been found to discriminate alcoholics in clinical samples from nonalcoholics in a general population sample.

The most desirable alternative for examining the relationships between personality characteristics and alcohol abuse would be a large longitudinal study beginning with a comprehensive personality assessment before alcohol consumption had begun. Because alcoholism may not occur for a long time following initial consumption of alcohol, this type of research is not very practical. An alternative research strategy, which guided the current research project, is to take a two-year slice in the life span for subjects in different age groups and follow the relationships between personality and alcohol abuse over this period. With this type of research design, it is possible to examine the cross-sectional associations between personality and alcohol abuse at one time, and then to examine the longitudinal relationships between these characteristics and drinking in different age groups. In this way, for example, it might be possible to examine the relationships between a personality construct such as field dependence and alcohol abuse at time 1, and then to examine whether the relationship between personality at Time 1 with alcohol abuse at Time 2 is stronger than the relationship going in the opposite direction (see Figure 1.1). By examining these relationships using three different age groups, it will be possible to determine whether this relationship is constant throughout the life span or varies at different points in the life span.

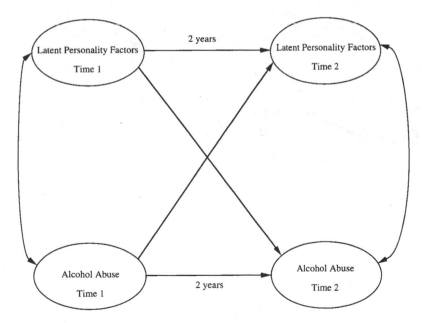

Figure 1.1. Personality and alcohol abuse: longitudinal design.

To examine the longitudinal associations between personality and alcohol abuse, the technique of structural equation modeling using latent variables is ideally suited. This technique was used successfully in the research by Newcomb and Bentler (1988) to model the factors present in adolescence that are associated with drug use and related problems in early adulthood. The proposed personality model that will be used to predict alcohol abuse in the present study is presented in Figure 1.2. Based on our review of the alcoholic personality literature, which is described in the next chapter, we predicted that alcohol abuse would be associated with more Extraversion, more Neuroticism, lower Ego Strength, more Psychoticism, and more Field Dependence. Because not all alcohol abuse is associated with these characteristics, additional analyses are planned to examine possible subtypes of alcohol abusers.

Although longitudinal prospective research may be the ideal strategy for

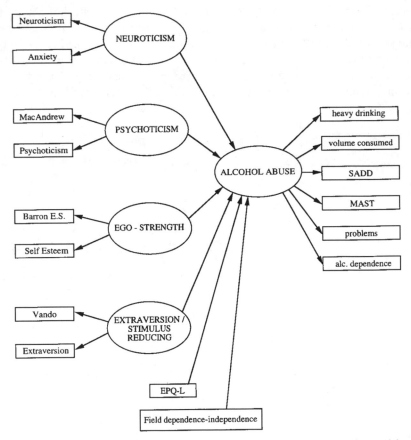

Figure 1.2. Hypothesized personality and alcohol abuse structural equation model.

examining the associations between personality characteristics and alcohol abuse, much can also be learned from examining the personality characteristics of clinical samples of alcoholics. In their landmark research on the social origins of depression, Brown and Harris (1978) established a classic design for studying psychopathology. If a particular variable predicts psychopathology in the general population, this particular predictor should also discriminate a clinical group from a matched general population comparison group. For example, if field dependence predicts alcohol abuse in the general population and discriminates clinical alcoholics from a matched comparison sample, this would provide strong evidence for the association between field dependence and alcoholism. Results become particularly interesting when inconsistent patterns emerge. For example, field dependence might discriminate clinical alcoholics from the comparison sample but not be a predictor of alcohol abuse in the general population. This pattern of results would suggest that field dependence is more likely to predict who goes for treatment than who develops alcoholism.

The addition of a clinical sample to our program of research also provided an opportunity to compare the personality traits of people addicted to different types of drugs. Research has tended to show that alcohol and drug use tend to co-occur in both clinical and nonclinical samples (Jang, Livesley, & Vernon, 1995; Miller, Guttman, & Chawla, 1997). Genetic studies have found common genetic factors underlying the risk of alcohol and drug problems (Grove et al., 1990; Jang et al., 1995; Koopmans, van Doornen, & Boomsma, 1997; Swan, Carmelli, & Cardon, 1997). Personality traits are logical possible factors to account for the underlying vulnerability to addiction. Research by Jang et al. (1995) and Swan et al. (1997) has also shown that there may be separate genetic factors that are specific to different types of substance misuse. Therefore it is possible that there might also be personality differences between alcohol abusers and drug addicts.

Longitudinal data on clinical samples may also be important. Do the same personality variables that predict a worsening of alcohol symptoms in the general population also predict who has a poor prognosis for treatment. Research conducted to date on this topic suggests that individuals with a co-occurring personality disorder such as Antisocial Personality Disorder may have a poorer prognosis in treatment (see Fals-Stewart and Lucente,1994). Alcoholism scales such as the MacAndrew Alcoholism Scale have also shown some potential for predicting treatment outcome (Little and Robinson, 1989).

In the past, efforts to develop a measure of the "alcoholic" personality have met with mixed success. These efforts have been based primarily on using the item pool of the MMPI (e.g., MacAndrew, 1965). In this project, an effort will be made to develop a measure of the "prealcoholic personality" by selecting items from a broader item pool. The criteria chosen for item selection will be (1) significant association with a family history of alcohol abuse, and (2) significant association with the person's own current abuse. The prealcoholic personality measure will be developed and validated in a general population sample and then cross-validated in the clinical sample.

If in fact there is a prealcoholic personality that predisposes an individual to become an alcoholic, it is important to know what the environmental factors are that contribute to the development of the "prealcoholic personality." Not much research is available on the development of the prealcoholic personality, and most of the research in the personality development area fails to control for genetic confounds (Reiss, 1995; Rowe, 1994). In this book, a large general population family data set will be used to provide further data on the reliability and validity of the newly developed prealcoholic personality test. The Vancouver Family Survey contains a large sample of biological and adoptive families and includes data on perceptions of the family environment from three different family members. This data set will be used to test the possible role of the family environment in the development of the prealcoholic personality.

2

Personality and Alcohol Abuse

1. Extraversion–Introversion

As discussed earlier, most if not all factor analytic studies of personality scales and ratings produce a dimension that lines up with the Extraversion–Introversion dimension. A summary of the characteristics associated with this dimension and the expected relationships between these characteristics and the two different forms of alcoholism is presented in Table 2.1. Type I or dysthymic alcoholics are expected to score lower on measures of extraversion and related characteristics. Type I alcoholics are expected to be low sensation seekers, low scorers on the MacAndrew Alcoholism Scale, stimulus augmenters, to score higher on sensitivity to pain, to show pain reduction in response to alcohol, and to score higher on hypochondriasis and guilt. Type II alcoholics are expected to display the opposite pattern of results on these dimensions. In the general population, it is anticipated that the relationship between Extraversion–Introversion will generally be positive (i.e., extraverts report more alcohol abuse) because Type II or extraverted alcoholics are supposed to account for approximately 80% of the cases of alcoholism (MacAndrew, 1980).

1.1. Clinical Alcoholic Personality Research

1.1.1. Trait Measures

1.1.1a. Eysenck Personality Questionnaire. Research with alcoholics employing the Eysenck E scale has generally found no significant differences between alcoholics and normals (Calaycay & Altman, 1985; Edwards, Hensman,

Table 2.1. The Extraversion–Introversion Dimension and Alcoholic Personality Types

Characteristic	Type I alcoholic (dysthymic)	Type II alcoholic (secondary psychopath)
Trait measures		
Reducer–augmenter	Augmenter	Reducer
Extraversion	Introvert	Extravert
Novelty Seeking	Low	High
Hypochondriasis	High	Low
Guilt	High	Low
MacAndrew Scale	Low	High
State measures		
Kinesthetic Figural Aftereffect	Augmenter	Reducer
Averaged Evoked Response	Augmenter at low intensity/ Reducer at high intensity	Reducer
Pain tolerance	Low	High
Alcohol response	Reduces sensitivity to pain	Does not reduce sensitivity to pain

Hawker, & Williamson, 1966; Hallman, von Knorring, Edman, & Oreland, 1991; Keehn, 1970; Limson, Goldman, Roy, & Lamparski, 1991; Rankin, Stockwell, & Hodgson, 1982; Shaw, MacSweeney, Johnson, & Merry, 1975; Vogel, 1961) or between alcoholics and depressed patients (Shaw et al., 1975). These results are not too surprising in view of the work by Cloninger (1987a) and MacAndrew (1979, 1980, 1983) suggesting that subjects at both extremes of the Extraversion–Introversion dimension are those who are most at risk for alcoholism. One other study (Rosenthal, Edwards, Ackerman, Knott, & Rosenthal, 1990) compares alcoholics and other drug addicts with each other and EPQ norms. In this study, the addicts scored higher than the normal group on the Eysenck E, N, and P scales. In the analyses for this article, however, the authors seemed to have gotten the means on two of the Eysenck Scales reversed. The means on the Extraversion dimension seem to have gotten confused with the means on the P dimension. In their report the authors give much higher scores on the P dimension than ever reported before in the literature and unrealistically low scores on the E Scale, suggesting that a transposing of the data has occurred. The data are still interpretable, however, because the addicts score lower on both of these dimensions than the controls. Problems arise, however, when the authors compare the drug abuse groups because results are not the same for the P and E dimensions, and the authors get their results confused.

Although the data based on clinical samples does not provide much support for an association between Extraversion and alcohol abuse, it is possible that there might be a slight positive correlation between Extraversion and alcohol abuse in the general population because extraverted alcoholics, it is hypothesized are more common than introverted alcoholics (MacAndrew, 1980). It also seems possible that extraversion would be more highly correlated with drinking in younger samples. Cloninger (1987a) has predicted that early onset alcohol abuse will be predicted by high novelty seeking and low harm avoidance, traits that are associated with higher extraversion (Cloninger & Svrakic, 1994). A series of recent studies has provided support for an association between extraversion and alcohol use particularly in younger samples. In the study employing the younger sample, Hopper, White, Macaskill, Hill, and Clifford (1992) studied the relationship between the junior EPA Scale scores and alcohol consumption in a large sample of Australian twin pairs aged 11–18. Extraversion was positively correlated with alcohol consumption in this study. In a college aged sample, La Grange, Jones, Erb, and Reyes (1995) also found positive correlations ($r = .298$ in males, $r = .361$ in females) between extraversion and drinking. In another study employing a college sample ($n = 100$), Martsh & Miller (1997) found that extraversion predicted alcohol consumption, binge drinking and alcohol problems better than other personality scales, including Spielberger's state/trait anxiety scales and state/ trait anger expression scales. In another twin study employing a large adult female sample, the relationships between EPQ Scale scores and problem drinking and alcohol abuse were examined (Prescott, Neale, Corey, & Kendler, 1997). The sample in this study included 2,163 white women in the 17–55 age range. Extraversion was positively associated with alcohol problems and abuse in this sample and made a significant contribution in logistic regression equations to predict alcohol problems and abuse when many other factors were controlled. In another large study ($n = 557$), Sher, Bylund, Walitzer, Hartmann, and Ray-Prenger (1994) tested a young male sample and found that extraversion contributed positively in predicting alcohol consumption which in turn was related to alcohol abuse.

1.1.1b. NEO Five-Factor Inventory. The 240-item NEO Inventory (Costa & McCrae, 1992) comes in both a self-report form (form S) and an observer rating form (form R). A 60-item version of the self-report version of the test is also available. In a recent study, Martin and Sher (1994) used the short version of the NEO-PI, the NEO-FFI (Costa & McCrae, 1992), to examine the association between DSM-III defined alcohol abuse and personality in a young adult sample. Their results did not support any association between the NEO Extraversion Scale and alcohol abuse. Gotham, Sher, and Wood (1997) also used the short version of the NEO and found no significant correlations between extraversion and frequency of intoxication in their college age sample. In our own research using a large general population family survey and multiple measures of alcohol consumption and abuse, no significant correlations between alcohol consumption measures and NEO short-form Extraversion Scale scores were observed in either our parent sample or in their offspring. The Extraversion Scale had some significant correlations with measures of alcohol abuse, particularly among sons where correlations were significant with the frequency of getting drunk and CAGE Scale scores (Mayfield, McLeod, & Hall, 1974). The longer version of the NEO would probably be preferable in this type of research because the short version of the NEO PI contains only one item from the Excitement-Seeking Facet Scale and no items from the Impulsivity Facet Scale. In one study where the longer version of the NEO was employed, Musgrave-Marquart, Bromley, and Dalley (1997) also failed to find significant correlations between extraversion and alcohol consumption.

1.1.1c. MMPI. MacAndrew Alcoholism Scale: As noted in my earlier reviews (Barnes, 1979; Barnes, 1983), the MacAndrew Alcoholism Scale has generally been quite successful in discriminating alcoholics from other psychiatric patients. In his own review of this topic, MacAndrew (1980) indicated that the scale had a mean accuracy rate of about 85% in identifying alcoholics in 11 studies reviewed. As noted in my earlier review (Barnes, 1983) the MacAndrew (1965) scale was generally less successful in discriminating alcoholics from other drug users. The psychological meaning of the scale has also been somewhat problematic. High MacAndrew Scale scorers have been described in various studies as impulsive (Burke, 1983; Moore, 1984; Schwartz & Graham, 1979), interpersonally shallow (Schwartz & Graham, 1979), rebellious (Finney, Smith, Skeeters, & Auvenshire, 1971; Moore, 1984), immature (Lachar, Berman, Grisell, & Schooff, 1976), and aggressive (Moore, 1984).

In a recent review article on the personality correlates of the MacAndrew Alcoholism Scale, Allen (1991) concluded that

> high MAC patients could be characterized as less inhibited, more prone to act out against social standards, more self-confident, and more willing to admit problems, than are low MAC patients. (p. 63)

Recent research confirms the association between the MAC Scale and a latent variable called Behavioral Inhibiton (Earleywine et al., 1990) or behavioral undercontrol (Sher, Walitzer, Wood, & Brent, 1991). The MAC Scale is also significantly correlated with the Zuckerman Novelty Seeking Scale (Earleywine & Finn, 1991).

MacAndrew himself (1980) favors the description provided by Finney et al. (1971) of high MAC scorers as:

> High scorers . . . seem to be bold, uninhibited, self-confident, sociable people who mix well with others. They show rebellious urges and resentment of authorities. They tell of carousing, gambling, playing hookey and generally cutting up. Yet . . . they are drawn to religion.

In summarizing his interpretation of the meaning of his scale, MacAndrew (1980) concludes that "the evidence that the Mac Scale is tapping E+ and not E- could scarcely be more persuasive" (p. 157). According to MacAndrew, the 85% of the alcoholics, who correctly identified by his scale, fit the E+N+ quadrant of secondary sociopathy. Empirical work by MacAndrew (1980) confirmed that the alcoholics who are not successfully identified by his test were Dysthymic or Type I alcoholics. Confirmation that the MacAndrew Scale measures a type of alcoholism that has an early onset and is associated with other sociopathic behavior, including criminal behavior and drug use, is provided in the research conducted by Rathus, Fox, and Ortins (1980). In this study, the abbreviated version of the MacAndrew Scale successfully predicted alcohol abuse but was also predictive of criminal behavior and marijuana use. Further clarification of the meaning of the MacAndrew Alcoholism Scale is provided in the research conducted by Sher et al. (1994). In this research the facet scales of the MacAndrew Alcoholism Scale were employed, and it was noted that these scales tended to weigh on three factors, including antisociality, extraversion, and negative affectivity. These results suggest that the MacAndrew Scale taps into high P, high N, and high E. All three of these factors were important in predicting alcohol and drug use in the Sher et al. (1994) research.

1.1.1d. Zuckerman Sensation-Seeking Scale. Sensation seeking is generally considered by Eysenck to be related to extraversion (Eysenck & Eysenck, 1985). More recently, Zuckerman et al. (1988) reported results suggesting that sensation seeking might more appropriately fit the Psychoticism dimension. In the original formulation of the Zuckerman theory, sensation seeking, it was hypothesized, is associated with the optimum level of arousal theory. In this version of the theory, heavy alcohol consumption was not viewed as particularly rewarding for sensation seekers. In the reformulation of the theory, however, Zuckerman (1987) now considers that sensation seeking is associated with a desire for stimulation in the reward center of the brain. Alcohol is another drug that seems to meet this need and sensation seeking may be a predisposing trait for alcoholism.

It is interesting to note that although the relationship between sensation seeking and drug use in general is one of the most frequently replicated findings in the drug abuse field (Zuckerman, 1987), hardly any studies look at the sensation-seeking characteristics of alcoholics. In the research that has been done, results have supported a relationship between sensation seeking and alcoholism. Kilpatrick, Sutker, and Smith (1976) reported that alcoholics differed from nondrinkers on all of the sensation-seeking scales but differed from other drinkers only on the boredom susceptibility scale. Alcoholics were higher on boredom susceptibility. These results were supported in an older sample of alcoholics and controls (age 55+) Kilpatrick, McAlhany, MCurdy, Shaw, & Roitzch, (1982) where alcoholics scored higher than controls on both boredom susceptibility and disinhibition.

Although most of the studies that examined the correlations between sensation seeking and alcohol consumption have been carried out in high school or university age samples (Zuckerman, 1987), at least a couple of studies examined this relationship in adult samples. Marvel and Hartmann (1986) reported a relationship among three measures of sensation seeking (total sensation seeking, experience seeking, and disinhibiton) and frequency of alcohol use in U.S. Navy officers. The Stacy, Newcomb, and Bentler (1991) results suggest a somewhat stronger association between sensation seeking and liquor consumption than other forms of alcohol consumption in their adult sample.

Sensation seeking is also associated with problems resulting from drinking. Within an alcoholic sample, Malatesta, Sutker, and Treiber (1981) reported that the frequency of public drunkeness was related to sensation seeking. Stacy et al. (1991) also observed that sensation seekers reported a higher frequency of driving while impaired behavior. Zuckerman has recently developed a new short version sensation-seeking scale as part of the Zuckerman Kuhlman Personality Questionnaire. An investigation of the association between this scale and alcohol and drug use in a high-risk adolescent sample has recently been completed (Simon, Stacy, Sussman, & Dent, 1994). Results confirmed that sensation seeking was strongly predictive of alcohol abuse in this high-risk sample. Of particular note was the finding that sensation seeking was more strongly predictive of alcohol use within the Latino sample. These findings are interesting and suggest that sensation-seeking options selected by adolescents may be determined by both culture and underlying personality.

The Disinhibition (DIS) Subscale of the Zuckerman measure is most strongly predictive of alcohol use and abuse (Zuckerman, 1994). In a recent study by La Grange et al. (1995) conducted in a college age sample, the DIS was more strongly associated with alcohol use in both males and females than any of the other sensation-seeking subscales. Recently, the question of possible criterion contamination in this relationship due to alcohol-related items in the DIS has been investigated by Darkes, Greenbaum, and Goldman (1998). Their results show that elimination of alcohol-related items from the DIS reduces, but does not totally eliminate, the relationship between this scale and alcohol involvement (measured by a latent variable).

1.1.1e. Cloninger Tridimensional Personality Questionnaire. Research by Cloninger (1987a, b) is also relevant to understanding the relationship between sensation seeking and alcohol abuse. Cloninger (1986) postulated that there are three relevant personality dimensions for predicting the two different kinds of alcoholism, novelty seeking, harm avoidance, and reward dependence. Type 1 alcoholics who are late onset alcoholics are characterized by low novelty seeking, high harm avoidance, and high reward dependence. Type 2 alcoholics who are early onset alcoholics are characterized by high novelty seeking, low harm avoidance, and low reward dependence. Cloninger (1987b) developed a questionnaire called the Tridimensional Personality Questionnaire (TPQ) to assess these three personality dimensions. Cloninger's scales do not line up very well with the Eysenck and McCrae and Costa personality factors. There is some extraversion content in both the Cloninger Novelty Seeking (high E) and Harm Avoidance (low E) Scales, for example. The Novelty-Seeking scale of the TPQ is closely linked with the concept of sensation seeking and, according to Cloninger, is associated with low basal firing rates for dopaminergic neurons and greater sensitivity to dopamine when it is released. Preliminary efforts to validate the TPQ by Earleywine, Finn, Peterson, and Pihl (1992) found some evidence for the reliability and convergent validity of the TPQ , but some problems with the factor structure. The Novelty-Seeking Scale correlated with other measures of sensation seeking (Zuckerman scales) and behavioral undercontrol (MMPI MacAndrew Scale, CPI Socialization Scale) in the expected manner. The measures did not conform, however, to the expected three-factor structure where novelty seeking and harm avoidance overlap. The only scale that was significantly associated with alcohol abuse was the Novelty Seeking Scale. Recently, Cloninger and his colleagues (Cloninger, Sigvardsson, Przybeck, and Svrakic, 1995) have examined the association between TPQ Scale scores and alcohol use and abuse patterns in a large U.S. general population sample ($n = 1019$). Results confirmed that novelty seeking was predictive of alcohol use and of alcohol problems and that this relationship occur primarily in the younger age group.

Two studies have looked at the relationship between TPQ Scale scores and alcohol abuse in psychiatric samples. Bulik, Sullivan, McKee, Weltzin, and Kaye (1994) looked at TPQ scale scores in alcohol-abusing versus nonabusing women and found higher TPQ Novelty Seeking Scale scores in the alcohol-abusing women. Van Ammers, Sellman, and Mulder (1997) looked at the relationship between TPQ Scale scores and alcohol and substance abuse in a sample of schizophrenics. Higher TPQ Novelty-Seeking scores were associated with higher lifetime and current prevalence for alcohol abuse in this sample. Several significant correlations between novelty seeking and other forms of substance abuse were also reported.

To date, most of the research with the new Cloninger scales has been with high-risk samples, and not much research has been done with adult alcoholics. In one study that was conducted comparing alcoholics with a small control sample, Limson and colleagues (Limson et al., 1991) reported that alcoholics scored higher on the TPQ Novelty-Seeking Scale than controls. In another small study comparing alcoholics and nonalcoholics with no family history of alcoholism, Whipple and Noble (1991) found higher TPQ novelty scores in the alcoholic sample.

1.1.1f. Stimulus Augmenting–Reducing. According to the theory first put forth by Petrie (1967), alcoholics are supposed to be stimulus augmenters. Petrie hypothesized that, because of their greater sensitivity to pain, stimulus augmenters would benefit more from the effects of alcohol than stimulus reducers. The methods for measuring augmenting–reducing employed by Petrie (1967) were pain tolerance level and the Kinesthetic Figure Aftereffect (KFA). These techniques measure the state of augmenting–reducing. The only trait measure of this concept developed to date is the Vando (1969) Reducer–Augmenter Scale (RAS).

The Vando R-A Scale is a paper and pencil test that was developed to measure stimulus augmenting–reducing. The scale was originally derived by selecting items that discriminated between individuals who were high and low on pain tolerance. The scale was described by Vando (1969) as having a split half reliability of .89 and a three month test-retest reliability of .89. The original validity data on this scale, as reported by Vando (1969), were outstanding based on high correlations with pain tolerance ($r = .83$) and other validity criteria. Other information on the reliability and validity of this scale is available in a review by Barnes (1985b).

Two studies that examined the relationship between stimulus reducing–augmenting, as measured by the Vando (1969) Scale, and alcoholism were reported in an article by Barnes (1980). In both of these studies, alcoholics scored in the direction of being stimulus augmenters relative to controls, but these differences disappeared when age differences were controlled. These findings suggest that the stimulus-augmenting characteristic of clinical alcoholics could perhaps be simply a function of age and/or drinking history. A different pattern emerged when stimulus augmenting–reducing was examined in relation to problem drinking in a sample of teenagers (Barnes, 1985a). Problem drinkers in this sample were stimulus reducers. Although these findings were somewhat surprising to me (Barnes) at the time, because they were inconsistent with Petrie's theory, they are readily interpretable according to the new work by Cloninger (1987a) and MacAndrew (1979, 1980, 1983). Type II problem drinking or secondary sociopathy drinking is more likely to have an earlier onset. Samples of young problem drinkers are more likely to contain a higher percentage of Type II drinkers.

1.1.2. State Measures

Although Extraversion is generally regarded as a trait rather than a state, other measures of this construct can be viewed in state versus trait terminology. In particular, the augmenter–reducer dimension can be viewed in these terms (Barnes, 1976). Measures of augmenting-reducing that could be considered state measures and that have been used with alcoholics include (1) kinesthetic figural aftereffect, (2) average evoked response, and (3) pain tolerance.

1.1.2a. Stimulus Intensity Modulation and Alcohol Use. In her original work on stimulus intensity modulation, Petrie (1967) hypothesized that alcoholics would tend to be augmenters because of the beneficial reducing effect that they would receive from alcohol. Presumably augmenters are operating under a somewhat higher than optimum level of stimulation. Alcohol reduces this level of stimulation to a more comfortable level. To test the hypothesis that alcoholics are stimulus augmenters, Petrie administered the Kinesthetic Figural Aftereffect task to 15 alcoholics and compared their scores with a group of 33 students. The results confirmed the hypothesis that alcoholics were stimulus augmenters in relation to the control group. In fact no stimulus reducers were found in the alcoholic group. The alcoholic group consisted of three subjects who were stimulus bound, six who were moderates, and six who were augmenters. These results need to be interpreted cautiously because Petrie (1967) never made any attempt to control for demographic differences between the alcoholic and control groups. Age in particular is an important demographic characteristic that is positively associated with stimulus augmenting and needs to be controlled in research on stimulus intensity modulation and alcoholism (Barnes, 1980).

Stimulus intensity modulation differences between alcoholics and controls have also been examined in studies using the Average Evoked Response (AER) method to measure the style of augmenting–reducing. In one such study, Von Knorring (1976) compared the AERs of alcoholic normals and psychiatric patients. Von Knorring (1976) found that alcoholics tended to be augmenters to a greater extent than both the normal and psychiatric patient groups. Although there were demographic differences between the groups in the Von Knorring (1976) study, he was able to argue that these demographic differences could have worked only against finding significant results.

In two other studies employing the AER, results have been found similar to those reported by Von Knorring (1976). Coger, Dymond, Serafetinides, Lowenstam, and Pearson (1976) compared AER scores for two groups of alcoholics (stabilized, undergoing withdrawal) and found that the alcoholic groups showed a significantly greater tendency toward stimulus augmenting than a comparison group of normals. Buchsbaum and Ludwig (1980) tested groups of 12 male alcoholics and 12 male controls and also found that alcoholics tended to be augmenters on the AER compared with the control group. Here again, however, demographic differences between alcoholics and controls were not controlled.

Although research seems to suggest that alcoholics are indeed augmenters, as hypothesized by Petrie (1967), it would be simplistic to assume that all alcoholics are stimulus augmenters, and Petrie's theory does not require this. In an alcoholic sample, Ludwig, Bendfeldt, Wikler, & Cain (1978) did not find that all alcoholics were augmenters on the AER. Ludwig, Cain, & Wikler (1977) did find, however, that subjects who were stimulus augmenters on the AER were significantly more likely to work for and consume alcohol in an experimental task. This finding suggests that even within the alcoholic population, subjects who are augmenters might be more strongly addicted than subjects who are not augmenters.[1]

Further research is required to examine the relationship between state measures of augmenting–reducing and the Cloninger (1987a) alcoholic types. Subjects who are Type I or Dysthymic alcoholics should be stimulus augmenters, as hypothesized by Petrie (1967). It is less clear, however, what to expect for Type II alcoholics. The secondary sociopaths might normally be expected to be stimulus reducers, a characteristic that has been frequently associated with criminal behavior and drug use (Barnes, 1985b). On the other hand, it is possible that the long-term effects of alcohol might change a stimulus reducer into a stimulus augmenter or at least make them appear so during withdrawal.

1.1.3. Alcohol Effects

Alcohol seems to have the effect of changing peoples positioning on the Introversion–Extraversion dimension. Keehn (1970) asked subjects to complete the Eysenck questionnaire as they would when they were drinking and as they would when they were sober. Results indicated that subjects scored higher on the Extraversion Scale in the drinking instructional set than in the normal instructional set.

Similar results have been observed on the augmenting–reducing dimension. Petrie (1967) observed that subjects who were augmenters on the KFA task moved in the direction of becoming stimulus reducers after drinking alcohol. Research in the area of averaged evoked responses has been consistent in suggesting that alcohol reduces cortical arousal. Alcohol has been shown to lower somatosensory evoked responses (Salamy & Williams, 1973), visual evoked responses (Lewis, Dustman, & Beck, 1970; Spilker & Calaway, 1969), auditory evoked responses (Fruhstorfer & Soveri, 1968; Gross, Begleiter, Tobin, & Kissin, 1966; Wolpaw &

---

[1] Although the results described above appear consistent, these results need to be interpreted with some caution. In particular, the findings that alcoholics are augmenters, as measured by the AER procedure, must be regarded with caution. Research by Lukas (1987) suggests that some investigators are using the terms augmenter in a different manner than originally proposed by Petrie (1967). At high levels of stimulation, subjects who are stimulus augmenters will start to reduce as protective inhibition comes into play. At that time, subjects who appear to be stimulus reducers in terms of their AER slopes measured at the vertex are in fact only state reducers as opposed to trait reducers. These state reducers who are actually trait augmenters will be lower in sensation seeking. This has led to some confusion in the sensation-seeking literature. Some investigations argue that augmenters are sensation seekers (see Zuckerman, Murthaugh & Siegel, 1974), and others (see Barnes, 1985b, Davis, Cowles & Kohn, 1982; Dragutinovich, 1986; Petrie, 1967; Sales, 1971) argue that reducers are sensation seekers. Both positions are technically correct in that under special limited procedures with the AER, stimulus augmenting correlates with sensation seeking. In general, however, when other measures of state augmenting or reducing such as the KFA or strength of the nervous system measures are employed or when a trait measure of augmenting reducing is employed, reducers are sensation seekers.

Henry, 1978) and to increase pain tolerance (Brown & Cutter, 1977; James, Duthie, Duffy, McKeag, & Rice, 1978). In at least one study the differential effects of alcohol on augmenters and reducers were examined. In testing Petrie's theory, Buchsbaum and Ludwig (1980) tested groups of twelve male alcoholics and an equal number of control subjects. They found that alcohol produced a stimulus-reducing effect for the alcoholics, who also tended to be augmenters. This effect was strongest at the highest levels of stimulation.

1.2. Prealcoholic Personality

1.2.1. Longitudinal Studies

Longitudinal and high-risk studies are the two major types of studies that are relevant in determining the possible causal direction of the relationship between personality and alcohol abuse. Several longitudinal studies are relevant for examining the relationship between the personality dimension of Introversion–Extraversion and related characteristics and alcoholism. Not many of these investigations have employed standard personality test batteries such as the EPQ or NEO. In one recent investigation, Gotham, Sher, and Wood (1997) used the NEO to predict the change in the frequency of drinking for college students as they matured and left school. In the univariate analyses, Extraversion at year four in the study was not significantly associated with the frequency of intoxication at year seven. In the multivariate analyses, however, a significant interactive effect that involved the Extraversion Scale emerged. Extraverts who were frequently getting intoxicated at year four were more likely to continue this pattern at year seven.

Several other longitudinal investigations examined the association between temperament measures of constructs related to Extraversion and alcohol use patterns. In a Swedish longitudinal study for example, Cloninger, Sigvardsson, and Bohman (1988) examined the relationship between childhood characteristics assessed at eleven years of age and adult alcohol abuse at age 27 in a sample of 431 subjects. Results showed that the risk of alcohol abuse was increased the most in individuals who were high on novelty seeking (extraverts) and low on harm avoidance as children. These results are consistent with the hypothesis that Type II alcoholism is related to and possibly caused by personality traits associated with sensation seeking. This study did not allow an adequate examination of the possible personality precursors of Type I alcoholism because the subjects were not old enough at the second testing to have reached the age at risk for this type of alcoholism. In an interesting attempt to replicate this study, Masse and Tremblay (1997) constructed scales measuring the Cloninger constructs based on teacher ratings at age 6 and 10 and then used these ratings to predict the early onset (age 11–15) of alcohol use, cigarette smoking, and other drug use. Their findings showed that high novelty seeking and low harm avoidance, as assessed as early as age 6, were predictive of early onset substance use. These findings are very important in demonstrating that personality traits, even as assessed at a very young age by independent observers, are predictive of early onset alcohol and drug use. Another recent longitudinal investigation by Killen et al. (1996) looked at the relationship between temperament and the onset of drinking in 9th grade California high school students. They found that low fear and high sociability, as measured by the EAS (Buss & Plomin, 1984), predicted the onset of drinking. These results are consistent with Cloninger's theory and the research just described.

Several recent additional longitudinal studies confirm the relationship between sensation seeking and substance abuse. Using structural equation techniques, Newcomb and McGee (1991) found a significant association between sensation-seeking characteristics in the high school period and licit drug use in early adulthood. Teichman, Barnea, and Ravav (1989) studied a large sample of adolescents in a one-year longitudinal study and also found general support for the longitudinal effects of sensation seeking on substance abuse. Pedersen (1991) studied students aged 16–18 over a span of 20 months and found that the Disinhibition Scale at Time 1 predicted alcohol abuse at Time 2. In a similar study, Bates, Labouvie, and White (1986) tested 584 adolescents aged 15–18 and again three years later. The Disinhibition Scale score at Time 1 was predictive of the frequency and quantity of alcohol use at Time 2. Changes in Disinhibition scores were also important with subjects who showed an increase in their Disinhibition scores between Time 1 and Time 2 and reported more alcohol use at Time 2. In a more recent publication (Bates & Labouvie, 1995) on this study, results were reported over a longer time span of six years. Results seemed to follow a similar pattern and sustained levels of Disinhibition needs were found in association with higher intensity of alcohol use.

1.2.2. High-Risk Studies

There are now several studies on high-risk samples that are relevant to the issue of whether the Extraversion–Introversion dimension alters a person's risk for alcoholism. Only one of these studies has found significant results. Sher and McCrady(1984) found that male sons of alcoholics had higher Extraversion scores than male sons of nonalcoholics. In a small study, Whipple and Noble (1991) did not find any difference in Extraversion scores for their young sample of sons of alcoholic fathers in comparison with controls. In a larger study by Martin and Sher (1994) using the NEO Five-Factor Inventory, similar results were reported, and no significant differences in Extraversion scores were found in comparisons between children of alcoholics and nonalcoholics. Martin and Sher (1994) did, however, find a difference between the children of alcoholics and children of nonalcoholics on the Five-Factor Openness to Experience Scale, and children of alcoholics scored higher on this measure. In one other study of the children of alcoholics, Berkowitz and Perkins (1988) compared the personality characteristics of the late adolescent and young adult children of alcoholics with their peers and observed no significant difference in their scores on sociability. In a larger study, Sher et al. (1991) also found no differences between Extraversion scores of adult children of alcoholics and adult children of nonalcoholics. Sher et al. (1991) did find a significant difference on the MacAndrew Alcoholism Scale, and children with alcoholic fathers scored higher than those without alcoholic fathers. These results differ from the results of an earlier smaller study by Sher and McCrady where no significant differences in MAC Scale scores were observed between offspring of alcoholics versus nonalcoholics. The higher MacAndrew Scale scores in children of alcoholics was also reported by Svanum and McAdoo (1991) in their large study ($n = 639$) of alcoholics with and without family histories of alcoholism.

Several studies have used a high-risk design to examine the relationship between sensation seeking and alcoholism. In a study using the Zuckerman scales, Finn, Earleywine, and Pihl (1992) looked at sensation-seeking characteristics of alcoholics with a multigenerational history of alcoholism, a unigenerational history, or no history of alcoholism. The alcoholics with a multigenerational history of alcoholism scored highest on the Zuckerman experience-seeking scale.

Sensation seeking seems to be a particularly strong predictor of alcohol abuse in younger samples. In a study of alcohol and other substance abuse in a high school sample, Andrucci, Archer, Pancoast, and Gordon (1989) conducted regression analyses using MMPI scales and the Zuckerman sensation-seeking scale to predict adolescent alcohol use. Sensation seeking was the only significant personality predictor of alcohol abuse in this sample. Recently, Zuckerman (1994) and Andrew and Cronin (1997) argued that the intensity of experience rather than the novelty of experience is most important in predicting alcohol use. Research by Andrew and Cronin (1997) using the Zuckerman sensation-seeking scale and the Arnett (1994) measure of sensation seeking that includes an intensity of sensation scale confirmed the importance of the intensity dimension in predicting adolescent alcohol abuse.

Several high risk studies on sensation seeking have also been conducted using the Cloninger TPQ questionnaire. In four of these studies, children of alcoholics did not differ from children not having an alcoholic parent on the TPQ novelty-seeking scale (Peterson, Weiner, Pihl, & Finn, 1991; Schuckit, Irwin, & Mahler, 1990; Whipple & Noble, 1991; Zaninelli, Porjesz, & Begleiter, 1992). All of these studies used fairly small samples. In a more comprehensive investigation using a large sample of subjects with paternal alcoholism ($n = 252$) and controls ($n = 237$), Sher et al. (1991) did find higher scores on Novelty Seeking and other characteristics associated with behavioral undercontrol in children of alcoholics. They reported that the behavioral undercontrol factor also contributed significantly in predicting alcohol involvement.

In the one high-risk study that has been conducted on stimulus reducing–augmenting, Hennecke (1984) examined the level of augmenting–reducing in a sample of teenage children of alcoholics and controls using the KFA task. Results showed that the children of alcoholics were augmenters to a greater extent than was found in the control sample. In fact, there were no stimulus reducers at all found in the sample of alcoholic children. These results are somewhat surprising in the light of the Cloninger (1987a) theory. If there are two types of alcoholics that differ in novelty seeking (extraversion), then there should also be two different types of children of alcoholics, an augmenter group and a reducer group. It is possible, however, that Hennecke (1984) drew the alcoholic sample from an older clinical sample that contained primarily Type I alcoholics. Then, their children would be expected to be augmenters. High-risk studies on the children of alcoholics are important, but future research in this area needs to address the issue of the two different types of alcoholism. Predictions from this theory suggest that the children of alcoholics might be more extreme in their extraversion, novelty seeking and augmenting–reducing scores than their peers.

2. Psychoticism

The dimension that is being called psychoticism in this chapter might also be called anti-social personality, or if described in terms of its opposite pole, agreeableness. A summary of the characteristics associated with this dimension and the expected relationships between these characteristics and the two different forms of alcoholism are summarized in Table 2.2. Type II alcoholics, or secondary psy-

Table 2.2. The Psychoticism Dimension and Alcoholic Personality Types

Characteristic	Type I alcoholic (dysthymic)	Type II alcoholic (secondary psychopath)
Trait measures		
Psychoticism	Low	High
Psychopathic deviate (Pd)	Low	High
Hostility	Low	High
Impulsivity	Low	High
Frustration tolerance	High	Low
Behavioral measures		
Antisocial behaviors	Low	High
Criminal activity	Low	High
Cognitive functioning		
Minimal brain dysfunction (Hk-Mbd)	Low	High

chopaths, are expected to score higher on measures such as the Eysenck P Scale, the MMPI Pd Scale, and the Kallin Antisocial Behavior Scale. Other characteristics related to high psychoticism that are expected to occur in Type II alcoholics include: (1) impulsivity and (2) low frustration tolerance. Hostility could be considered part of the P dimension but could also be associated with the Neuroticism dimension because of the association between anxiety and anger (see Buss & Plomin, 1984). The Psychoticism dimension is not commonly viewed in terms of trait versus state distinctions the way that Neuroticism has been considered. In the present review, the behavioral manifestations of the Psychoticism dimension, including incidents of antisocial behavior, will be considered in the place of state measures. Because of the absence of research examining state-related changes along this dimension under the influence of alcohol, this section will be relatively abbreviated.

2.1. Clinical Alcoholic Personality Research

2.1.1. Trait Measures

2.1.1a. Eysenck Personality Questionnaire.   The P dimension is a relatively new addition to the Eysenck questionnaire and hence has not yet been included in much research on alcohol abuse. High scorers on the Eysenck P dimension have been described as aggressive, cold, egocentric, impersonal, impulsive, antisocial, unempathic, creative, and tough-minded (Eysenck et al., 1985). In one study of this kind where the P dimension was included, Rankin et al. (1982), reported that alcoholics scored higher on the P scale than controls. These results are made more impressive by the fact that the study controlled for the possible effects of age differences between alcoholics and controls. In the Rosenthal et al. (1990) study, substance abusers as a whole, including alcoholics, scored higher on the P Scale than on EPQ norms. In a recent study employing a small sample, Limson et al. (1991) failed to find a significant association between the Psychoticism Scale and a diagnosis of alcoholism. In another study, also using a small sample, Hallman et al. (1991) failed to find a significant difference on the P Scale between alcoholics and controls in their female sample.

In studies involving nonclinical samples, the P dimension is related to drinking and alcohol problems. Hopper et al. (1992) used the junior EPQ to predict drinking in a sample of young (aged 11–18) Australian twins, and the P scale had a significant effect on the occurrence of drinking in the young sample. In a college age sample, La Grange et al. (1995) found that P correlated moderately with the frequency of alcohol consumption in males ($r = .276$) and a little less so for females ($r = .180$). In our own research with a sample of 245 male college students (Barnes, Greenwood, & Sommer, 1990), we found that the P dimension was not significantly correlated with the amount of alcohol consumed but did correlate significantly with alcohol problems.

2.1.1b. MMPI. The relationship between the Pd scale and alcoholism has been reviewed by Barnes (1983) and others (see Graham & Strenger, 1988). This research has consistently shown that alcoholics can be discriminated from normals on the basis of their elevated Pd profiles and that the Pd scale is less useful in discriminating alcoholics from other psychiatric groups. More research is required to examine the relationship between the Pd scale and the different types of alcoholism as described by Cloninger (1987a). Cluster analytic research with the MMPI, described earlier in this chapter, has generally shown that there are different clusters of alcoholics, and some groups are higher on the Pd scale than others. Cluster analytic research with the MMPI is problematic, however, because of the overlap in MMPI items used in the different scales.

Age differences in the pattern of MMPI scores of male alcoholics also confirm the importance of the different types of personality profiles associated with alcoholism. Penk, Charles, Patterson, Roberts, Dolan, and Brown (1982) compared the personality characteristics of alcoholics classified into five different age groups: 30 or younger, 31–40, 41–50, 51–60, and 61+. Younger alcoholics scored higher on the Ma, Sc, and Pd scales of the MMPI. This profile corresponds with the Type II alcoholic. Older alcoholics reported more health concerns and had higher Hs and Hy scale scores. This is more likely to reflect a pattern of stimulus augmenting common in Type I alcoholics. It is possible to interpret these cross-sectional differences in personality in a number of ways. Differences could reflect personality changes with aging and drinking history. The lower Pd Scale scores in the older group could be the results of the aging process and/or the effects of their long drinking history. On the other hand, it is possible that more of the Type II alcoholics develop problems earlier, come into the treatment system earlier, and contribute to the higher Psychoticism profile in the younger sample.

Recent research using the MMPI suggests that the elevated 4–2 profile commonly found in alcoholics also occurs in cocaine addicts (Johnson, Tobin, & Cellucci, 1992) and gamblers (Ciarrocchi, Kirschner, & Fallik, 1991). This finding has important implications for understanding the mechanisms underlying alcohol abuse. These results are consistent with sensation-seeking theory (Zuckerman, 1987) and with the new results showing that the same genetic pattern that occurs in alcoholics is also found in drug addicts (Noble et al., 1993; Smith et al., 1992).

2.1.1c. California Psychological Inventory. A personality scale that is also measuring something similar to the Psychoticism Scale is the Gough (1969) Socialization Scale on the California Psychological Inventory (CPI). This scale was designed to measure social maturity. Low scorers are characterized as rebellious, ostentatious, and defensive (Gough, 1969). Earleywine et al. (1990) consider that this scale is a measure of behavioral inhibition. In a recent monograph on the CPI, Gough (1994) reported that the mean value on the CPI Socialization Scale for three samples of male alcoholics ranged between 22 and 24. Comparable scores were reported in studies by Kadden, Litt, Donovan, and Cooney (1996) with a mean of 23.52 and Cooney, Kadden, and Litt (1990) with a mean of 24.58. As noted by Kadden et al. (1996), these scores are in the bottom half of the scores reported for the CPI Socialization Scale. The CPI Socialization Scale also predicts stress-response dampening in response to alcohol (Levenson, Oyama, & Meek, 1987; Sher & Levenson, 1982). In two studies using college males (Earleywine & Finn, 1991; Earleywine, Finn, & Martin, 1990), significant correlations between the Socialization Scale and the amount of alcohol consumed were reported, and higher Socialization Scale scores were associated with lower alcohol consumption. Mayer (1988) also found a strong association between the CPI Socialization Scale and alcohol misuse in their adolescent sample. The CPI Socialization Scale was included in a recent large-scale study on substance use by males in their early twenties (Sher et al., 1994). In this investigation, the Socialization Scale weighted on a latent factor called antisociality. This latent factor predicted both alcohol consumption and abuse as measured by the MAST.

2.1.1d. NEO Five-Factor Inventory. The NEO scale that comes closest to the Eysenck Psychoticism Scale is the Agreeableness Scale. In the Martin and Sher (1994) study examining the association between this scale and alcohol abuse disorder, results supported an association between low agreeableness and alcohol abuse. In the research by Musgrave-Marquart et al. (1997) predicting alcohol consumption frequency, the Agreeableness Scale had the highest correlation with alcohol consumption ($r = .25$), with low agreeableness associated with higher consumption. In the research by Gotham et al. (1997) predicting continuation of heavy drinking following college, the NEO agreeableness correlated significantly with heavy drinking measures concurrently during college. In our own research (Anderson, Barnes, Patton, & Perhins, 1999) where the NEO has been used to predict a variety of alcohol consumption and abuse measures in parents and their offspring, high agreeableness has been correlated with lower alcohol consumption in fathers, sons, and daughters but not in mothers. One possible interpretation for this pattern is that women in this cohort drink less due to greater social restraints against women drinking in the past. This could have attenuated the relationship between personality and drinking.

2.1.1e. Other Measures. Interesting contributions toward understanding the relationship between personality and alcoholism have been coming from Sweden in recent years (see Rydelius, 1983a, 1983b). In this research, Rydelius put forward the hypothesis that

Among teen-agers there is a group (predominantly boys) which develops alcohol abuse in combination with drug abuse and criminality. Their biological parents are known for alcohol abuse, mental problems, and emotionality, and their upbringing situation was very poor. This group shows early aggressive acting out behavior, lack of control of impulses, restlessness and difficulties in concentration, but not anxiety of the introvert type. (p. 369)

This description clearly agrees with the description of the Type II alcoholic given earlier. Research by Rydelius (1983a) on a sample of 1000 eighteen-year-old boys from the general population in the Stockholm area supported this hypothesis. Alcohol consumption was correlated with psychologists' ratings for the boys. Results showed that alcohol consumption was correlated with acting out, irritability, restlessness, and difficulties in concentration. Boys who were high alcohol consumers were also characterized by inner tension, discomfort, and problems in the area of emotional contact with others. A more in-depth study of the personality characteristics of 47 high alcohol consumers and 48 nonconsumers was reported by Rydelius (1983b). These subjects were given the Karolinska Hospital Personality Inventory (KSP). Significant differences between groups occurred on 13 of the 15 scales. High consumers were characterized by higher values on measures of anxiety, indirect and verbal aggression, irritability and suspicion, impulsivity, and monotony avoidance. These descriptions are consistent with the personality profile of the Type II alcoholic.

2.1.2. Clinical Diagnoses

Although the number of studies that examined the relationship between the MMPI scales and alcoholism has declined in recent years, several studies have examined the relationship between antisocial personality characteristics (ASP) and alcoholism in either general population or clinical samples. In a general population study on the association between ASP and alcoholism, Nestadt, Romanoski, Samuels, Folstein, and McHugh (1992) reported a strong "dose response" connection between ASP and alcoholism. In the Epidemiologic Catchment Area (ECA) study (Regier et al., 1990), the prevalence for ASP diagnoses for respondents who have alcohol disorders was 14.3%. In the numerous studies that have examined the prevalence of ASP in clinical samples of alcoholics, most studies have found a much higher prevalence of ASP than the 1.5% prevalence found in the general population by Nestadt et al. (1992). In a systematic review of the literature on the relationship between personality disorders and substance abuse, Verheul, van den Brink, and Hartgers (1995) summarized the data on the prevalence of ASP in alcoholics for 16 studies. The range for ASP varied from 1 to 52% with a median of 18%. Obviously the range of comorbidity can vary greatly in clinical studies because assessment techniques vary greatly and samples are not representative. The best way to determine the comorbidity is through general population research such as the ECA study. The estimated comorbidity of ASP in alcohol disorders of 14.3% found in the ECA study is fairly close, however, to the median of 18% reported by Verheul et al. (1995) in their review of clinical studies. Alcoholics with ASP comorbidity are also characterized by earlier onset and a more rapid course (Liskow, Powell, Nickel & Penick, 1991), heavier consumption (Hesselbrock, 1991) and more symptoms/problems (Hesselbrock, 1991; Liskow et al., 1991) than alcoholics who do not have ASP comorbidity.

Another method for establishing the association between alcoholism and antisocial personality disorder is to examine the prevalence of antisocial personality disorder in a given population and then determine the prevalence of alcoholism among the subjects with or without antisocial personality disorder. This procedure was employed in a study by Lewis, Rice, and Helzer (1983). A total of 412 subjects presenting for psychiatric assessment were screened for antisocial personality disorder. Much higher percentages of alcoholism were observed on clients who had antisocial personalities than in both male (68% versus 26%) and female (30% versus 6%) controls. Furthermore, the antisocial alcoholics were younger, and the age of onset of heavy drinking occurred earlier for this group. These results are consistent with the description of the Type II alcoholic given earlier.

2.1.3. Antisocial Behaviors

The association between alcoholism and antisocial behaviors is well established on the basis of several different types of research. First, the incidence of antisocial behaviors is higher in alcoholic samples than in control samples. Hewett and Martin (1980), for instance, reported that the incidence of antisocial behaviors, adult criminal behaviors, work instability, legal difficulties, and incarcerations was higher in their alcoholic sample than in their control sample. These differences occur despite the type of environment present. In a retrospective recall study of the early childhood behaviors of adopted alcoholics and controls, Goodwin (Goodwin, Schulsinger, Hermansen, Guze, & Winokur, 1975) reported that adopted alcoholics more commonly showed (1) below average school performance, (2) hyperactivity, and (3) truant and antisocial behavior, compared with controls. They also reported being more aggressive, impulsive and disobedient in their youth than control children who were also adopted.

Another type of data that supports the association between alcohol use and antisocial behavior is the high rates of alcoholism frequently observed in prison populations. Rates of alcoholism in prison populations are commonly in the 50% range for both males (see Barnes, 1980) and females (see Martin, Cloninger, & Guze, 1982). The association between alcohol consumption patterns and particular crimes such as rape (Johnson, Gibson, & Linden, 1978) and homicide (Haberman & Baden, 1978; Trott, Barnes, & Dumoff, 1981) are also well established.

Still another source of data that supports the association between alcohol abuse and criminal behavior is the research on teen-age drinking. In particular, the research testing the Jessor problem behavior theory (Donovan & Jessor, 1985; Donovan, Jessor, & Costa, 1988; Jessor et al., 1991) has supported the association between drinking and other problem behaviors. This association has also been supported in the Swedish research conducted by Rydelius (1983a) which also showed a significant association between alcohol consumption and minor criminal offenses. In our own Canadian research testing an expanded version of the Jessor problem behavior model, we also observed high rates of alcohol problems in a delinquent sample (Vulcano & Barnes, 1986) and strong associations between problem drinking and other deviant behaviors in nondeliquent samples. Further support for the association between alcoholism and antisocial behaviors can be derived from longitudinal research. This research will be discussed in the prealcoholic personality portion of this section.

2.1.4. Cognitive Functioning

An interesting avenue of research on the relationship between cognitive functioning associated with antisocial behavior and alcoholism has been developed by Ralph Tarter and his colleagues (Tarter, Hegedus, & Gavaler, 1985; Tarter, McBride, Buonpane, & Schneider, 1977). They proposed a relationship between a childhood history of Minimal Brain Dysfunction (Hk-Mbd), often associated with antisocial behavior and alcoholism. Tarter et al. (1985) have argued that hyperactivity has a causal link with alcoholism based on research findings in the following areas:

1. Alcoholics have a history of childhood hyperactivity.
2. Alcoholics frequently suffer from attention deficit disorder.
3. Hyperactive adolescents are more likely to abuse alcohol than their peers.
4. Longitudinal studies show an association between childhood hyperactivity and alcoholism.
5. Hyperactive children are more likely to have biological fathers, but not adoptive fathers who suffer from alcoholism.

In their original research, Tarter et al. (1977) found that primary alcoholics could be discriminated from other psychiatric patients and normal controls on the basis of their history of childhood Hk-Mbd symptoms. Primary alcoholics also scored significantly higher on the history of Hk-Mbd symptoms than secondary alcoholics. Tarter reported in a separate article (1977) that childhood Hk-Mbd symptoms were associated with alcoholics' scores on the essential–reactive continuum and alcoholics who scored in the essential alcoholic direction had higher HK-Mbd scores. The high childhood Hk-Mbd alcoholics were also characterized by more severe alcoholic deterioration, more marital conflict associated with drinking, and more drinking for self enhancement and mood change. These findings, along with the results by Tarter, McBride, Buonpane, & Schneider (1977) showing higher MacAndrew Scale scores associated with childhood Hk-Mbd symptoms, suggest an association between childhood Hk-Mbd and Type II alcoholism.

Support for the association between childhood Hk-Mbd symptoms and alcoholism has been provided by the research conducted by Hewett and Martin (1980) and Workman-Daniels and Hesselbrock (1987). Hewett and Martin (1980) observed that alcoholics differed from controls in both their scores on the MMPI Pd scale and a variety of other measures of antisocial behavior and in their history of developmental difficulties. In particular, they reported that alcoholics and prison addicts were characterized by more difficulties relating to learning, sleep and restlessness. In a similar vein, Workman-Daniels and Hesselbrock (1987) replicated the findings by Tarter et al. (1977) that showed greater childhood Hk-Mbd symptoms in alcoholics than in nonalcoholics. Higher Hk-Mbd scores were associated with poorer cognitive performance on other measures of cognitive functioning, including the WAIS Digit Span and Verbal IQ subscales and the Wechsler Memory Test. Further evidence for the theory proposed by Tarter et al. (1985) can be found in the research by Wood, Wender, and Reimehr (1983) showing that alcoholics frequently suffer from attention deficit disorder, and in the research by Blowin, Bornstein, and Trites (1978) and Mendelson, Johnson, and Stewart (1971) showing that hyperactive adolescents are more likely than their peers to abuse alcohol.

The finding by Tarter et al. (1977) that Hk-Mbd symptoms are associated mainly with primary rather than secondary alcoholism has been replicated in a study by De Obaldia, Parsons, and Yohman (1983). De Obaldia et al. (1983) also reported that primary alcoholics performed more poorly on other cognitive tasks such as the Shipley Abstracting Age and Conceptual Quotients and the Raven's tests. In another related study, De Obaldia and Parsons (1984) reported results supporting the stability and validity of alcoholics reports of childhood HK-Mbd symptoms. Alcoholics were tested for their recall of Hk-Mbd at the beginning and at the end of treatment. Results showed that alcoholics were very consistent ($r = .93$) in the number of Hk-Mbd symptoms reported during approximately six weeks. Alcoholic self-reports were also quite highly correlated with parent reports of the alcoholic's childhood symptoms ($r = .62$), but not with sibling reports.

2.2. Prealcoholic Personality

2.2.1. Longitudinal Research

A number of longitudinal studies have now been conducted on the relationship between the P dimension and alcoholism. These studies have been quite consistent in demonstrating a relationship between antisocial behaviors and personality characteristics during childhood and alcoholism in early and later adulthood. In the first of these studies, Robins, Bates, and O'Neal, (1962) compared the childhood characteristics of alcoholics tested at a children's mental health clinic as children with the characteristics of other children tested at the clinic. The results showed that the alcoholic sample as children was characterized by a higher frequency of antisocial behavior in their records. In a similar type of study, Jones (1968) examined the childhood characteristics of problem drinkers identified in the Oakland Growth Study. Results indicated that the problem drinkers were more undercontrolled and impulsive as children than comparison groups at the same age level.

Further support for the prediction that high P personality characteristics in young adulthood are associated with risk of alcoholism is provided in research conducted by Loper, Kammeier, and Hoffmann (1973). In this research, Loper et al. (1973) compared the MMPI scale scores of 32 prealcoholic male subjects who later became alcoholic with 148 of their male classmates who did not become alcoholic. The prealcoholics scored significantly higher than their classmates on the F, Pd, and Ma scales of the MMPI. Loper et al. (1973) concluded from their results that prealcoholics, although not grossly maladjusted, showed a tendency to be impulsive, nonconforming, and gregarious.

More recently, ten new longitudinal studies have been completed on this topic (af Klinteberg, Anderson, Magnusson, & Stattin, 1993; Brook et al., 1992; Cloninger, Sigvardson, & Bohman, 1988; Dobkin et al., 1995; Gotham et al., 1997; Hagnell et al., 1986; Huesman & Eron, 1992; Kwapil, 1996; Pulkkinen & Pitkanen 1994; Rydelius, 1981). All of these studies support the relationship between P dimension characteristics and alcohol abuse. Rydelius (1981) looked at a general sample of Swedish children who were from either alcoholic or control families followed over time. The study used extensive materials collected via interviews and social indicators. Antisocial behaviors occurred in association with temperance registrations at a very early age. Longitudinal analyses revealed that the childhood characteristic of aggression was predictive of later temperance registrations.

In the report by Hagnell et al. (1986), results were reported for the Lundby Psychiatric Epidemiology Study. In this study, adults were followed during the course of 15 years. Alcoholism in the second wave of interviews was predicted on the basis of personality traits and clinical diagnoses, as assessed at the first interview. Results showed that a diagnosis of psychopathy at the first interview was associated with later problems of alcohol abuse. Results also showed a relationship between personality and alcohol abuse. Subjects who were characterized as subsolid (i.e., impulsive or high P scorers) and neurotic were at an increased risk of alcoholism of around 15 times compared to those who did not have these characteristics. Subjects who had the lowest risk of developing alcoholism possessed subvalidity in combination with psychosomatic symptoms. They were described as quiet, retiring persons. These results are consistent with the hypothesis that high P scores are associated with the development of Type II alcoholism.

Research by Cloninger, Sigvardson, and Bohman (1988) is also relevant for establishing the possible association between childhood characteristics and later development of alcoholism. In the Swedish research they describe, children were given detailed psychological assessments at age 11 and followed up at age 27. They hypothesized that "high novelty-seeking, low harm avoidance and low reward dependence, as seen in anti-social personalities, are expected to be predominant in early-onset alcohol abusers" (p. 498). Their results supported the hypothesis, in that the risk for alcoholism was increased by some twentyfold in subjects who had traits associated with an antisocial personality.

In another recently completed longitudinal study, af Klinteberg and colleagues (af Klinteberg et al., 1993) examined the relationships between hyperactivity in childhood (teachers' ratings at age 6) and alcoholism and violent offending in subjects aged 15–24. This study was impressive in that it involved a large number of subjects ($n = 540$), the sample comprised almost all of the children in a grade six cohort of a community, the data on hyperactivity levels were based on teacher ratings, and the adult data were based on public records for alcoholism, drunkenness, and violent offending. The data are taken from very different sources with no possible contamination due to response set or experimenter effects. No one knew at the time the teacher ratings were taking place that they would be used to predict alcoholism. The results supported a relationship between hyperactive behavior in childhood and subsequent alcohol problems, and 33% of hyperactive children had subsequent alcohol problems. This rate was more than three times higher than the rate in subjects who were not hyperactive at age six. The results also confirmed a configuration that childhood hyperactivity is associated with subsequent alcohol problems and violent offending in the same individuals.

Another facet of the Psychoticism dimension that has been studied longitudinally in relation to drug use, including alcohol use, has been aggressiveness. Huesman and Eron (1992) reported that peer ratings of aggressiveness at age 8 were correlated with driving while intoxicated at age 30 ($r = .24$, P, .001, $n = 322$). In a similar vein, Pulkkinen and Pitkanen (1994) followed a male sample from age 8 to 26 and found that aggression at age 8 is associated with problem drinking at age 26. In another longitudinal study beginning at a young age, Dobkin et al. (1995) looked at boys' disruptive behavior at age six, which included hyperactivity and fighting, in relation to children's characteristics at age 12 and substance abuse and deviance at age 13. Although this sample was still very young for the development of alcohol problems, fighting and hyperactivity at age 6 correlated with getting drunk at age 13. Brook et al. (1992) looked at the association between childhood aggression, assessed in the 5–10 year old age range and drug use in the 15–20 year age. The results also supported an association between childhood aggressiveness and adolescent drug use. In another longitudinal investigation spanning 33 years, Drake and Vaillant (1988) reported that school behavioral problems were predictive of alcohol abuse 33 years later. These studies are similar in nature and provide impressive consistency in relating aggressiveness and antisocial behavior in early childhood to the development of substance abuse problems later on.

Longitudinal research in young adult samples has also confirmed an association between antisocial behavior and the development of alcohol dependence. Harford and Parker (1994) employed data from the New York longitudinal study to show a relationship between antisocial behavior and alcohol dependence assessed nine years later. The results also showed that this relationship was not explained by other factors such as social class.

Low agreeableness seems to be another characteristic linked with the P dimension that is associated with the development of heavy drinking. Gotham et al. (1997) found that low agreeableness in year four of their study was significantly correlated with the frequency of intoxication three years later ($r = -.25$).

Recently, a new longitudinal study by Kwapil (1996) examined two additional important facets of the Psychoticism dimension, psychosis-prone thinking (e.g., perceptual aberration and magical thinking) and nonconformity-impulsivity in relation to the development of alcohol abuse problems. In this study, a high-risk sample and a control group were identified by screening a large sample of college students. The sample was followed up ten years later and assessed for the occurrence of substance abuse problems (DSM-III-R) during the ten year interval. The results indicated that although 12% of the control sample had experienced alcohol abuse problems, 30% of the nonconforming group and 22% of the psychosis-prone individuals had experienced these problems. These results are interesting in that they seem to support the possible importance of two facets of the P dimension, psychosis-prone thinking and non-conformity, as possible risk factors for alcohol abuse.

Longitudinal research on various facets of the P dimension and the development of alcohol abuse has been very consistent in establishing a relationship between these constructs. This pattern was recently confirmed in another longitudinal study (Caspi et al., 1997) that measured temperament as early as age 3. In this study, Caspi et al. (1997) reported that having an undercontrolled temperament at age 3 was predictive of health risk behaviors, including alcohol abuse, at age 21.

2.2.2. High-Risk Studies

If there is a type of alcoholism in which antisocial personality characteristics plays a causal role, then evidence of these characteristics should be present in the families of alcoholics and particularly primary alcoholics. A number of studies have investigated this association in a number of different ways. One strategy involved looking at alcoholics in treatment, measuring the presence of antisocial personality, and relating this to their family histories of alcoholism. In one study of this kind, Hesselbrock, Hesselbrock, and Stabenau (1985) reported that antisocial personality occurred for 71% of their alcoholics with a bilineal history of alcoholism, and rates for clients with one alcoholic parent or no alcoholic parent ran closer to 50%. Alcoholics with antisocial personalities reported an earlier age of onset for alcohol problems and more psychosocial consequences of alcohol misuse. These characteristics are consistent with the description of the Type II alcoholic given by Cloninger (1987a).

In a type of study similar to that described above, Glenn and Parsons (1989) compared men who had a positive family histories for alcoholism with those who did not have positive family histories for alcoholism on outcomes associated with hyperactivity. The results showed that subjects with family histories of alcoholism had more symptoms of attention deficit disorder, conduct disorder, and learning disorders. In a study employing a very large sample ($n = 7,064$) of military men in treatment for alcoholism, Frances, Timm, and Bucky (1980) also obtained positive results. Alcoholics with family histories of alcoholism had more severe alcohol symptoms, more antisocial behavior, worse academic performance, and poorer employment records than alcoholics with no family history of alcoholism.

In one study of this kind, the results were somewhat less positive. Harwood and Leonard (1989) conducted a study on 123 Driving While Impaired offenders. In this sample some 45% had a positive history of alcoholism. They did not find any difference in the prevalence of youthful antisocial behaviors in the two groups (FH+ vs. FH-). The nature of this sample could explain the absence of this effect. The DWI offender group would be likely to contain a disproportionate number of Type II alcoholics, and the base rate for antisocial behavior would be quite high in the sample as a whole. This would make it unlikely that differences in the prevalence of youthful antisocial behavior would occur on the basis of family history. They did report, however, that offenders with youthful antisocial behavior were younger when they first experienced intoxication and received higher scores on the Alcohol Dependence Scale. They also reported that there was a very low perceived ability to control alcohol among subjects with both a family history of alcohol abuse and a history of youthful antisocial behavior.

In two other studies, the strategy employed has been to obtain adult children of alcoholics in the general population and compare them with their peers for characteristics of the P dimension. In one study of this kind, Berkowitz and Perkins (1988) compared 83 children of alcoholics with 347 of their peers and obtained no difference in impulsivity scores. In another study, however, Knop, Teasdale, Schulsinger, and Goodwin (1985) compared the high-risk children of alcoholics with low-risk children and did obtain a number of differences. The high-risk sample had more grade repeats, more referrals to school psychologists, were rated by their teachers as being more impulsive, and had lower verbal proficiency. In this study, the authors plan to conduct a follow-up of the subjects to determine whether the subjects who have the greatest amount of problems as children also have the highest risk of developing alcohol problems.

A couple of studies on adult children of alcoholics also examined the association between a family history of alcoholism, on the one hand, and Psychoticism and related characteristics, on the other. In a study employing a large alcoholic sample, Svanum and McAdoo (1991) found higher elevations of most MMPI Scales for adult children of alcoholics, including higher Pd and MAC Scale scores. In a study employing a college freshman sample, Sher et al. (1991) found higher Psychoticism, Pd, and Impulsivity scores in adult children of alcoholics. Martin and Sher (1994) examined the agreeableness scores in adult children of alcoholics versus controls and reported lower agreeableness scores in their sample of adult children of alcoholics.

Another strategy for establishing the association between P characteristics and alcoholism has been to take children with identified problems such as hyperactivity and then examine their family history for the prevalence of problems such as alcoholism. In one study of this kind, Morrison and Stewart (1971) investigated the family history of 59 hyperactive children and 41 control children. They found twice as much alcoholism in the families of the hyperactive children as in the control children. In a similar type of study, Cantwell (1972) also examined the family history of hyperactive children and controls with similar results. The families of hyperactive children contained a higher prevalence of alcoholism, sociopathy and hysteria.

The results of the above research are generally consistent with the hypothesis that there is a type of alcoholism associated with antisocial characteristics that also runs in families. Future research might shed even further light on this relationship if more careful attention is given to the type of alcoholism occurring in parents. Primary or Type II alcoholism is expected to be associated with antisocial behaviors, Hk-Mbd, impulsivity, etc., in children, whereas secondary or Type I alcoholism is not.

3. Neuroticism

The dimension of personality called neuroticism consistently emerges as a basic trait related to alcohol use. Neuroticism refers to a lack of emotional stability, is associated with suspiciousness and shyness, and is often accompanied by feelings of anxiety, tension, and sometimes depression.

It is a common intuition that drinking reduces tension or relieves anxiety. Many people have a couple of drinks before social occasions to "loosen up." Historically, one of the classic explanations of alcoholism focused on the motivational consequences of this need or drive to reduce tension. Jellinek (1945) suggested that the complexities and frustrations of social life create tension that may be relieved in the short term by alcohol consumption. Consequently, alcohol becomes a conditioned reinforcer because of the reduction of this aversive state of tension (Conger, 1956). This tension reduction theory of alcoholism has had a profound impact on research into alcohol use (Wilson, 1988). Therefore, a brief summary of the theory is required.

Tension reduction theory makes two basic testable postulates. First, alcohol will reduce tension. Second, a state of anxiety will motivate alcohol use. Animal and human studies of the first postulate are generally inconclusive (Cappell & Greely, 1987; Sher, 1987). There are some contexts in which alcohol does indeed reduce tension. However, the linear effect is mediated by a number of other factors, including the amount of alcohol consumed, expectations about the effect of alcohol, and the social context in which alcohol is consumed.

A current incarnation of anxiety reduction theory is the stress-response dampening model (Sher, 1987). It is a "pared-down" tension reduction hypothesis that focuses on the reinforcing effects of alcohol in adverse or stressful situations. The basic postulate of the model is that individuals who experience stress-response dampening effects are more likely to consume greater amounts of alcohol in stressful situations. There is some evidence that alcoholics are especially prone to this effect. For example, problem drinkers receive greater stress reduction from alcohol than nonproblem drinkers (Eddy, 1979), and are more likely to increase their consumption when stressed (Miller, Hersen, Eisler, & Hilsman, 1974). In a study of prealcoholic males, Sher and Walitzer (1986) found greater stress reducing effects for these subjects than for subjects at low risk (on the basis of their MMPI MacAndrews Scale scores). Additionally, subjects with a positive family history (who are also at increased risk) had greater tension reduction after consuming small doses of alcohol (Schuckit, Engstrom, Alpert, & Duby, 1981) than subjects without positive family histories. In sum, these studies suggest that people at risk may be more susceptible to the tension reducing effects of alcohol.

Not all of the data are entirely consistent with the tension reduction hypothesis, and a number of mediating factors affect the relationship between alcohol use and tension reduction. It is likely that differences within alcoholic samples influence the stress-dampening response to alcohol. In terms of Cloninger's typology, the Type I loss of control alcoholic would be more likely to find alcohol reinforcing due to its antianxiety effects. Type II alcoholics, who are unable to abstain from drinking, it is hypothesized, find alcohol more positively reinforcing because of its stimulant effects. However, the data are not consistent in this regard, because Robyak, Floyd, and Donham (1982) found that alcoholics who drank continuously reported drinking to reduce anxiety more so than heavy bingers. Nevertheless, a fairly large body of literature that suggests under most conditions a reduction in tension or anxiety is one of the short-term effects of moderate doses of alcohol. Furthermore, this effect appears most prominently in individuals who are predisposed toward alcoholism on the basis of their personalities or their family histories.

3.1. Clinical Alcoholic Personality Research

If negative mood states such as anxiety and depression are motivational for alcohol consumption, then individuals who are chronically higher on these characteristics might be expected to be higher consumers of alcohol and develop more alcohol problems, including alcoholism. The following section reviews the association between trait measures of neuroticism and alcohol abuse.

3.1.1. Trait Measures

3.1.1a. MMPI. On the MMPI, the most relevant scales for determining elevations in neuroticism are the Neurotic Triad scales (Hs, D, Hy) and the Anxiety Derived scale (A). Several reviews of the alcoholic personality literature (e.g., Barnes, 1979; Barnes, 1983; Graham & Strenger,1988) have looked at the association between these scales and alcoholism. In the review by Barnes (1983), it was concluded that alcoholics score higher than nonalcoholic controls on the Neurotic Triad and depression in particular. Alcoholics were also reported to be higher than controls on the Anxiety Derived scale in at least one study (Ballard, 1959). Alcoholics seem to score lower on the Neurotic Triad scales than other psychiatric patients (Barnes, 1983), score more in the depressed range than prisoners (Barnes, 1983), and score higher in the neurotic direction than other addictive groups. In their review of the MMPI and alcoholism literature, Graham and Strenger (1988) also found support for an association between the MMPI Depression (2) Scale and alcoholism. They concluded that "Very consistent data have suggested that the mean profile for alcoholics is characterized as a 42 two-point code type" (p. 198).

Most of the recent literature on the MMPI has examined the relationship between MMPI alcoholism scales and alcohol abuse or looked for possible subtypes of alcoholism. The literature in these two areas will be discussed later in this book in the sections that deal with these issues. In one recent small sample study examining the MMPI Scale scores of alcoholics and controls, Limson et al. (1991) found that their alcoholics scored higher than controls on the D Scale and the A Scale. Although no significant differences between alcoholics and controls were reported on the HS and Hy Scales, the control sample was very small in this study ($n = 15$). In another recent MMPI study examining depression scores in alcoholics, Elwood (1993) found that 20% of his sample qualified as depressed on the SCID diagnoses but that only half of these subjects had elevated MMPI depression scores, suggesting that this scale underestimates the amount of depression in alcoholics.

Recent research has suggested that it may be very difficult to distinguish alcoholics from closely related clinical groups, including cocaine addicts (Johnson et al., 1992) and gamblers, (Ciarrocchi et al., 1991) on the basis of MMPI Scale scores alone. Johnson et al. (1992) compared the MMPI profiles of alcoholics and cocaine addicts and found that they are virtually identical, except possibly that alcoholics were a little more introverted. Brown and Fayek (1993) compared a small sample of alcoholics with a small group of clients who were addicted to both alcohol and cocaine. The alcohol group displayed the familiar 2–4–7 profile pattern and generally showed no differences from the alcohol and cocaine group on the Neurotic Triad scales. Ciarrocchi et al. (1991) reported that alcoholics were also virtually identical to gamblers in their MMPI profiles, even when the gamblers with alcohol problems were separated from the gambler group.

3.1.1b. Eysenck Personality Questionnaire. A number of studies have compared alcoholics with nonalcoholics on the EPQ Neuroticism dimension. Both male and female alcoholics have significantly higher EPQ-N scale scores than the norms for the scale (Ogden, Dundas, & Bhat, 1989). Current alcoholics in outpatient treatment were "markedly more neurotic" than a matched nonalcoholic sample (Calaycay & Altman, 1985). Limson et al. (1991) also compared EPQ-N scores of male alcoholic inpatients with a small inpatient control group and reported higher N scores in their alcoholic sample. A comparison of alcoholics, who were currently attending A.A. and therefore presumably in remission, with alcoholics who did not attend, suggests that those in remission are less neurotic (Hurlburt, Gade, & Fuqua, 1984). In sum, studies that have compared current alcoholics with former alcoholics and the general population suggest that the former have higher EPQ-N scores. The High N scores occurring in alcoholics are as high or higher than N scores in other types of substance abusers. Rosenthal et al. (1990) compared the N scores of alcoholics and other types of substance abusers with EPQ norms and found that the N scores were higher in substance abusers than in the EPQ normative sample. The EPQ N Scale scores of alcoholics were among the highest in the various substance abuse groups.

Cross-sectional comparisons of current alcoholics in treatment with reformed alcoholics or normals are very limited in terms of identifying cause and effect. High EPQ-N may simply be a consequence of a lifetime of alcohol abuse. Nevertheless, high neuroticism seems to be characteristic of clinical alcoholics.

Recent general population research with the EPQ has been important in showing that the relationship between Neuroticism and alcohol consumption and abuse also holds up in the general population. In the research by Sher et al. (1994) on a large sample of young adult male volunteers, for example, the EPQ N Scale weighted on a negative affectivity latent factor that contributed significantly in predicting alcohol consumption and abuse in structural equation modeling analyses. Although this study was restricted to a male sample, another recent study has tested this relationship in a female sample. Prescott et al. (1997) looked at predictors of alcohol problems and dependence in a large female adult twin sample. The N Scale was significantly associated with alcohol problems and made an important contribution in multivariate analyses predicting alcohol problems while controlling for other factors. Furthermore, within the sample of problem drinkers, Neuroticism seemed to play an important role in predicting alcohol dependence symptoms.

A couple of general population studies have not found a relationship between the Eysenck N scale and alcohol measures. These studies have focused on alcohol consumption measures only and employed younger samples. Thus Hopper et al. (1992) used the junior EPQ to predict alcohol consumption in their young (11–18) twin sample and found no relationship between EPQ-N Scale scores and alcohol consumption. La Grange et al. (1995) also found that the N score was unrelated to alcohol consumption in their college sample.

3.1.1c. Cloninger TPQ. In their review of the research on the TPQ, Howard, Kivlahan, and Walker (1997) concluded that the evidence supporting Cloninger's theory with respect to the relationship between harm avoidance and alcohol abuse was much less conclusive than the evidence pertaining to the association between novelty seeking and alcohol abuse. At the time of their review, only a couple of studies compared alcoholics and nonalcoholics and the sample sizes in these studies were too small to be very useful (e.g., two studies by Limson et al., 1991 and Simonsson, Berglund, Oreland, Moberg, & Alling, 1992 contained only 15 control subjects each). One other study by Wills, Vaccaro, and McNamara (1994) examined the relationship between TPQ Scales and substance abuse in general in a sample of 7th and 8th graders. The results supported the Cloninger theory in that low harm avoidance was associated with substance use in this young sample.

Only one study examined the association between harm avoidance and alcohol abuse in an adult general population sample (Cloninger et al., 1995). In that study, Cloninger et al. (1995) examined the association between harm avoidance and alcohol use and abuse in different age groups in their large general population sample. The results showed that high harm avoidance was associated with alcohol abuse in older subjects. The pattern tended to be in the oppposite direction in the younger sample where low harm avoidance was associated with abuse, but these correlations were not significant.

Two studies have looked at the relationship between harm avoidance and alcohol abuse in nonalcoholic clinical samples. Bulik et al. (1994) found no relationship between harm avoidance and alcohol abuse in their sample of bulimic women, and Van Ammers et al. (1997) found no relationship in their schizophrenic sample.

3.1.1d. Institute for Personality & Ability Testing (IPAT). Another anxiety measure that has been used to compare alcoholics and controls is the IPAT anxiety measure. For example, Lundin and Sawyer (1965) found that IPAT anxiety was related to the frequency of drinking and intoxication but was not related to the quantity of alcohol consumed. Subjects who drank more frequently or who became intoxicated more frequently had higher trait anxiety on the IPAT. Rosenberg (1969) found that alcoholics generally scored higher than nonalcoholics, and within the alcoholic sample young alcoholics (under 30 years of age) had much higher IPAT anxiety scores than older alcoholics. Again, this finding is useful because it suggests that the higher level of trait anxiety is a precursor to alcoholism.

3.1.1e. 16 PF. The Sixteen Personality Factor Questionnaire also has an anxiety scale that has been used to compare drinkers with nondrinkers. Fuller (1966) found that alcoholics had a 16 PF profile very similar to that of a mixed group of neurotics. On the 16PF, alcoholics also have a unique response pattern, and their profiles indicate higher apprehension and tension (Cattell, Eber, & Tatsuoka 1970; Gross, 1971). Ross (1971) also got a high correlation between alcoholics' and neurotics' profiles on the 16PF, although again, not all of the literature is consistent (see Golightly & Reinehr, 1969). Last, alcoholics' 16PF profiles differ from other drug users in that the former are more apprehensive and less independent or self-sufficient (Ciotola & Peterson, 1976).

3.1.1f. NEO Five-Factor Inventory. A newer personality inventory that contains a neuroticism scale is the NEO Five-Factor Inventory (Costa & McCrae, 1992). Martin and Sher (1994) examined the relationship between the NEO Inventory and DSM IIIR alcohol diagnoses in a college age sample. Their results supported a relationship between neuroticism and a diagnosis of alcoholism. Of interest also was their finding that remitted alcoholics scored more like the nonalcoholic group, suggesting either that neuroticism scores go down once alcoholism problems disappear or that low neuroticism subjects have an easier time quitting. Gotham et al. (1997) found that the FFI Neuroticism Scale was not significantly associated with the frequency of intoxication in men but was significantly associated in women. Musgrave-Marquart et al. (1997) reported that the FFI-N scale was not associated with alcohol consumption in their sample, but results were not reported separately by gender. In our own research (Anderson et al., in press), the FFI-N scale was found to be predictive of alcohol abuse in mothers and fathers but not as strongly among their sons and not at all among daughters. The results in these analyses are somewhat consistent with Cloninger's (1987a) theory and suggest that it is wise to consider age and gender groups separately when looking at personality and alcohol use and abuse relationships.

3.1.1g. Other Anxiety Measures. Alcoholics also score higher than nonalcoholics on the Taylor Manifest Anxiety Scale (Belfer, Shader, Carroll, & Harmatz, 1971), and the most severe cases of alcoholism report the highest anxiety (Ross, 1973). Hire (1978) found in a sample of college students, that those who drank had higher trait anxiety as measured by Spielberger's scale. Significant differences between alcoholics and controls on the anxiety scales of the Swedish personality measure (KSP) have also been reported (Von Knorring, Von Knorring, Smigan, Lindberg, & Eldholm, 1987). Von Knorring et al. (1987) also reported that Type II alcoholics scored higher on somatic anxiety than Type I alcoholics.

3.1.2. Clinical Diagnoses

3.1.2a. Anxiety. One means of examining the relationship between alcoholism and anxiety is to evaluate their cooccurrence. Alcoholics and nonalcoholics have been compared on clinical diagnoses that are related to neuroticism, such as anxiety disorders and depression. Some studies have examined the prevalence of anxiety disorders in alcoholics in treatment; others focus on the level of alcohol use in anxiety and phobic patients. From both research directions, there is evidence of considerable overlap in diagnoses.

Studies of alcoholics in treatment suggest that high levels of anxiety are present when these individuals first report for treatment. Mullaney and Trippett (1979) reported that about one-third of their alcoholic sample of 102 subjects had severe phobias, usually agoraphobia or a social phobia, and an additional one-third had less severe phobias. Bowen, Cipywnyk, D'Arcy, and Keegan (1984) found that about 44% of their inpatient alcoholic sample was also diagnosed as having anxiety disorders. Likewise, Ross, Glaser, and Germanson (1988) found that about half of the alcoholics that they assessed (141 of 279) also met the criteria for a lifetime generalized anxiety disorder. A recent report found that 50% of male alcoholics in treatment reported at least one panic attack in the past year, and 28% met DSMIII criteria for a panic disorder (Norton, Malan, Cairns, Wozney, & Broughton, 1989). Somewhat lower prevalence rates (e.g., of the order of 25%) of anxiety disorders among alcoholics have been reported by other researchers (Hesselbrook et al., 1985; Smail, Stockwell, Canter, & Hodgson, 1984; Weiss & Rosenberg, 1985). In contrast to the above results, Schuckit, Irwin, and Brown (1990) reported that a history of panic disorder was relatively uncommon (4%) in their sample of male veterans with a diagnosis of primary alcoholism. Most of the subjects in this study (98%) did report experiencing one or more symptoms of anxiety during withdrawal.

Other studies have also looked at the degree of alcohol use and the prevalence of alcoholism in patients being treated for anxiety disorders. Quitkin and Rabkin (1982) reviewed four studies that had found high rates of alcoholism in patients with panic attacks. High proportions of alcoholics have been found in a number of small sample studies (e.g., 17/61, or 28% in Reich & Chaudry, 1987; 4/11, or 36% in Thyer et al., 1986; 7/15, or 46% in Turner, Beidel, Dancy, & Keys, 1986). In other studies the percentages are not quite so high. For example, Schneier, Martin, Leibowitz, Gorman, and Fyer (1989) found that 16 of 98 (16.3%) outpatient social phobics met research criteria for a lifetime alcoholism diagnosis, although this percentage is likely an underestimate because current alcoholics were excluded from the sample. In an inpatient psychiatric population, Murray et al. (1984) found that 13% of anxious or phobic patients fell into their "heavy drinking" category (more than 8 drinks a day for the year before admission).

Cross-sectional evaluation of the co-occurrence of alcoholism and anxiety disorders suggests that the two are related. Two equally valid postulates can be made. Feelings of high anxiety can lead to alcohol use to decrease the symptoms, or excessive alcohol use produces social problems that increase personal anxiety. It is unclear whether alcohol use precedes high anxiety or whether trait anxiety precipitates alcohol use. The notion of "self-medication" (using alcohol to reduce anxiety symptoms) has received some empirical support from studies that have measured the time of onset of the various disorders. Schneier et al. (1989) found that 15 of 16 of their social phobics with alcoholism reported that the social phobia preceded the onset of alcoholism. However, their data may be suspect because the mean age of onset of the social phobia was 10.4 years of age. Bibb and Chambless (1986) reported a 21% prevalence rate of alcoholism in patients who have agoraphobia with panic attacks, and agoraphobics without panic attacks are much less likely to have an alcoholism diagnosis (Quitkin & Rabkin, 1982). In the Bibb and Chambless (1986) study more than 90% of the alcoholic agoraphobics reported that they used alcohol for self-medication.

Studies of alcoholics in treatment have also evaluated the onset of anxiety disorders to determine the temporal and therefore causal sequence. A number of studies have reported that a large percentage of alcoholics with panic attacks report that their alcohol abuse is a consequence of their anxiety disorder (see Cox, Norton, Swinson, & Endler, 1990, for a review of these data). Forty-two percent of alcoholics with phobias report that their anxiety preceded their alcoholism. Furthermore, it would appear that patients with anxiety disorders *and* alcoholism have more severe anxiety than phobic patients without alcoholism, which led Cox et al. (1990) to suggest that there may be two types of anxious alcoholics, those whose phobias precede their abuse and those whose alcoholism preceded their anxiety problems. Such a conception is consistent with Cloninger's Type I and Type II distinction, where the Type I alcoholic is more prone to alcoholism due to a preexisting anxious personality. For these persons, alcohol is reinforcing because of its antianxiety effects. MacAndrew (1981) has made a similar distinction between what he calls primary and secondary alcoholics. Primary alcoholics are alcoholics who score high on the MMPI MacAndrew's Scale and began drinking early in life. Secondary alcoholics, alcoholics who are low on the MAC Scale, are "neurotics who just happen to drink too much." The implication is that secondary alcoholics have a preexisting personality disorder that includes neurotic characteristics that may predispose them toward drinking problems. Results by Schuckit et al. (1990) cited earlier support the contention that primary alcoholics may be relatively lower in anxiety than anticipated. In a follow up study of their sample, Brown, Irwin, and Schuckit (1991) reported that although state anxiety symptoms were elevated in 40% of their sample of primary alcoholics at admission, for most clients these symptoms had returned to the normal range after the first two weeks of treatment.

Although more than half of the alcoholics in treatment report symptoms of anxiety that preceded the onset of drinking, these retrospective results need to be interpreted cautiously. It is plausible that this is an attribution designed to protect the self. Rather than assume responsibility for the consequences of excessive drinking, it may be a psychologically defensive posture to state that the reason one drinks is a high level of anxiety.

3.1.2b. Depression. Clinical depression is another psychiatric diagnosis that may be considered a manifestation of a neurotic personality. In a general population survey, Weissman and Myers (1980) found that almost three-quarters of the respondents who had been given an alcoholism diagnosis also met the criteria for an additional diagnosis, usually depression. In a sample of older psychiatric patients, Speer and Bates (1992) reported that 11.1% of their sample had co-occurring major depression and alcoholism, and another 22.2% had co-occurring alcoholism, personality disorder, and major depression. As in the anxiety literature, many studies of hospitalized alcoholics have found higher levels of depression in their samples than in comparable general population samples. For example, Cadoret & Winokur (1972) found that 41% of primary alcoholics also had depressive syndromes. Sex differences in rates of depression for alcoholics have also been reported. Female alcoholics have more symptoms of depression and higher prevalence of depressive disorders than their male counterparts (Schuckit, 1987).

A number of studies have examined the lifetime prevalence of psychiatric disorders in alcoholics admitted for treatment. Bedi and Halikas (1985) found that 43% of females and 29% of male alcoholics in treatment met the criteria for major affective disorders during their lifetimes. Penick, Powell, Liskow, Jackson, and Nickel (1988) found that the most frequently co-occuring disorder was depression (25.7%), and the depressive symptoms were not simply due to the distress of hospitalization for alcoholism treatment. Similar findings were reported by Elwood (1993) where 20% of the sample qualified as depressed on the SCID and only about one-quarter of these cases were judged to be alcohol induced. In another study of alcoholics that utilized three different self-report measures of depression, Tamkin et al. (1987) reported that 55% was considered depressed on the basis of the response to the MMPI, 22% was moderately or severely depressed on the Beck Depression Inventory, and 28% was mild to severely depressed on the Geriatric Depression Scale (Tamkin, Carson, Nixon, & Hyer, 1987). Ross et al. (1988) found that 22.6% of alcoholics who did not have other drug disorders had suffered a major depressive episode, and an additional 13.4% reported dysthymia. Bowen et al. (1984) reported that 46% of their alcoholic sample had suffered major depressive episodes. Shaw, Donley, Morgan, and Robinson (1975) found self-reported depression in 98% of their alcoholic sample. Powell, Penick, Othmer, Bingman, and Rice (1982) found that 42% of their large sample ($n = 565$) of male alcoholics was also diagnosed as depressed and the presence of an additional diagnosis predicted earlier onset of problem drinking. Further, persons who had *only* an alcoholism diagnosis (i.e., other drug addictions were excluded) were more likely to have a later onset of problem drinking and fewer first-degree relatives with a history of alcohol abuse than persons with multiple addictions. These people fit the description of the Type I alcoholic proposed by Cloninger (1987a).

There is a large body of evidence that alcoholism is associated with depression in addition to anxiety. As with the anxiety literature, it is important to identify whether the alcoholism preceded the depression or vice versa. In the Powell et al. (1982) study, additional diagnoses (i.e., depression and anxiety) tended to precede or coincide with the onset of alcohol abuse. On the other hand, Bowen et al. (1984) reported that alcoholism tended to precede the onset of depression. When Ross et al. (1988) examined the age of onset of the disorders in their alcoholic and substance abuse samples, they found that signs of antisocial personality preceded the onset of alcoholism in almost all cases. Abuse of alcohol and other drugs was more likely to follow anxiety disorders and major depression. Again, this may be an attributional phenomenon to lessen responsibility for drinking.

In a study that examined the effects of major depression and antisocial personality on the course of alcoholism, Hesselbrock, Hesselbrock, and Workman-Daniels (1986) interviewed more than 300 alcoholics in treatment and found that the alcoholics with antisocial personality disorders (Cloninger's Type II) had an accelerated course of alcoholism. Hesselbrook et al. (1986) compared alcoholic patients with a history of depression to those with no history of depression and found that there were no differences in the age of onset of alcoholism in the two groups, which led them to conclude that depression does not affect the natural history of alcoholism.

The conflicting results in terms of the temporal sequence of alcohol and depression may simply reflect the heterogeneous nature of alcoholism. There is probably no single "alcoholic personality." Therefore, a number of characteristics must be taken into account simultaneously. Cloninger's Type I and Type II distinctions may be helpful for disentangling the relationships between alcoholism and personality characteristics. The Type I alcoholic is more neurotic which may contribute to the alcoholism. Type I alcoholics have a later onset of drinking and may find that alcohol is reinforcing due to its tension-reducing effects. This type of alcoholism may be more of a response to the presence of an affective disorder. Type II alcoholism has an earlier onset and may be associated with the characteristics of the antisocial personality (e.g., childhood misbehavior, fighting and other criminal behavior). For these persons, alcohol is reinforcing due to its stimulant effects. From this perspective, the association of alcoholism and other psychiatric disorders can be explained by the underlying personality characteristics. These characteristics are neurobiologically determined and are likely influenced by genetic, inheritable means.

3.1.3. State Measures

3.1.3a. Alcohol Effects on Neuroticism. The discussion of role strain and high neuroticism in clinical alcoholics has highlighted the fact that there are a number of unique characteristics of alcoholics in treatment. A conceptual problem is created, however, by the fact that chronic alcoholism probably has a profound impact on state anxiety. The short-term impact of alcoholism on neuroticism will be examined next.

Much of the literature on alcohol's effect on neuroticism has compared alcoholics' and nonalcoholics' responses to alcohol in experimental settings. Chronic alcoholics increase their alcohol consumption following an interpersonal stressor, compared to nonalcoholics (Miller et al., 1974). A number of studies have also demonstrated that there are greater reductions in state anxiety for problem drinkers than nonproblem drinkers following a moderate dose of alcohol (e.g., Abrams & Wilson, 1979; Eddy, 1979).

In the section on tension reduction theory, the data reviewed suggested that some individuals are at greater risk for alcoholism on the basis of their personality and that these individuals also experience greater tension reduction after drinking. In a study of drinking and personality in college students, Brown and Munson (1987) found that students with high trait anxiety were more likely to expect positive changes from drinking than students with low trait anxiety. Sher and Levenson (1982) found that individuals at risk on the basis of their MAC Scale scores had greater cardiovascular reduction to stress when they consumed alcohol, compared to the low-risk group. Furthermore, the high-risk group reported less distress in the stress condition than the low-risk group. Unfortunately, a subsequent study (Sher & Walitzer, 1986) did *not* support the hypothesis that stress-dampening effects due to alcohol are moderated by prealcoholic personality (MAC Scale scores) or by expectancies about alcohol's effects. In the most recent study in this series of investigations, Sher et al. (1994) did find individual differences in the stress-dampening effect. Low MAO subjects showed a greater stress-dampening effect. Low MAO was associated with the Antisociality latent factor in this research, but not with the Negative Affectivity or Extraversion dimensions. These results suggest that the stress-dampening effects of alcohol do not apply to those who are highest on the N dimension but rather to those who are highest on the P or Antisociality dimension.

Other experimental studies of alcohol effects have failed to find that alcohol reduces phobic anxiety or avoidant behavior (e.g., Cameron, Liepman, Curtis, & Thyer, 1987; Thyer & Curtis, 1984). However, due to ethical considerations, the levels of alcohol used in experimental studies are usually very low, with a concomitant reduction in the power to find actual differences if they really do exist.

3.2. Prealcoholic Personality

Studies of prealcoholic neuroticism can be divided into three general types. The first type of study is the longitudinal study in which trait neuroticism is measured prior to signs of alcoholism or alcoholics are followed up after treatment. Such studies are time-consuming, expensive, and difficult to conduct, yet, are better able to identify causal relationships than cross-sectional comparisons. The second type of study is a high-risk study. In this type of research, an at risk group, such as the children of alcoholic parents, are evaluated and compared with the children of nonalcoholics. Children of alcoholics or individuals with high MAC Scale scores are followed for a number of years. Therefore, early differences between those who become alcoholic and those who do not can be examined without the confound of current alcohol-related problems. Cross-sectional studies of young and old alcoholics are also useful for elucidating characteristics of old alcoholics that are common to young alcoholics and are therefore probably *not* a consequence of alcohol usage.

3.2.1. Longitudinal Studies

In contrast with the cross-sectional studies that show a positive association between neuroticism and alcohol abuse, a number of longitudinal studies have shown the reverse pattern of results with low neuroticism or low harm avoidance predicting alcohol abuse. In the longitudinal study by Cloninger, Sigvardsson, and Bohman (1988), for example, they found that childhood high novelty seeking and low harm avoidance were most strongly predictive of early onset alcohol abuse. In another study predicting early onset substance abuse, including alcohol abuse, Masse and Tremblay (1997) also found that low harm avoidance is predictive of early onset substance abuse. In a one-year longitudinal study employing a different temperament measure (e.g., the Buss & Plomin (1984) EAS), Killen et al. (1996) reported that low fear was associated with the initiation of drinking. High harm avoidance, as measured by the PRF, also played a role in the Labouvie and McGee (1986) longitudinal research. Harm avoidance figured into their analyses as one of the safe attributes associated with a lower risk for developing substance abuse. In the research described above, low harm avoidance was predictive of early onset alcohol and substance abuse problems. In at least one other study, a somewhat different pattern of results was reported. Caspi et al. (1997) reported that high negative emotionality at age 18 was predictive of alcohol dependence at age 21 in their large New Zealand general population sample. In one of the few longitudinal investigations involving an older alcoholic sample, results did not support any association between neuroticism-related personality traits measured by the MMPI and the development of alcoholism. In this research conducted by Kammeier et al. (1973) and Loper et al. (1973), alcoholics did not differ from their college freshman classmates on any of the Neurotic Triad scales.

Recent research by Pulkkinen and Pitkanen (1994) suggests that the relationship between anxiety and alcohol abuse may be fairly complex. Their results showed an association between signs of social anxiety in early childhood (age 8) and alcohol problems at age 26 in females. A different pattern emerged, however, for males where higher social anxiety at age 14 was associated with lower problem drinking at age 26. Gotham et al. (1997) also found a slight positive association between the NEO FFI-N scale at year four in their college sample and the frequency of intoxication in females three years following graduation.

Longitudinal research conducted to date has not provided a clear picture regarding the relationship between symptoms of neuroticism and the development of alcohol abuse. Some evidence suggests that low neuroticism or more specifically low harm avoidance may be associated with early onset alcohol and drug abuse. The evidence is much less clear on the issue of later developing alcohol abuse where very few longitudinal studies have been conducted.

Several longitudinal studies have been conducted in clinical samples examining the changes in anxiety and other neurotic characteristics following treatment. Research has been consistent in showing improvement on the D scale of the MMPI following treatment (Barnes, 1983). Not all signs of depression disappear following treatment, however. McMahon and Davidson (1986) looked at symptoms of depression in an inpatient sample of alcoholics at intake and after six weeks of treatment. They reported that approximately two-thirds of their alcoholics suffered from significant levels of depressive symptoms at intake. McMahon and Davidson (1986) reported that approximately half of their depressed alcoholics were still depressed after six weeks of treatment. Anxiety also declines in alcoholics following treatment (Brown et al., 1991).

3.2.2. High-Risk Studies

There is growing evidence that the children of alcoholic parents are at increased risk of alcoholism regardless of whether they are raised by their biological parents or nondrinking foster parents. In a study of adolescent delinquents, Tarter et al. (1984) compared sons of alcoholics with the sons of nonalcoholics on the MMPI. The former group had higher scores on scales 1, 2, and 3 (the "Neurotic Triad"), supporting the notion of a predisposition toward affective disorders in this group. More recently, Knowles and Schroeder (1990) compared male college students with positive families history of alcoholism ($n = 199$) to those with negative family histories ($n = 601$) on the MMPI. The students whose family history was positive were significantly higher on depression and organic symptoms (one of the Wiggins content scales) and replicated the findings of significant elevations on the Neurotic Triad. In a study of female children of male alcoholics, Benson and Heller (1987) found that the daughters of alcoholic and problem drinking fathers were more depressed and neurotic than the daughters of nonproblem drinking fathers. The highest levels of depression and neuroticism were found in daughters where both parents were alcoholic or problem drinkers. In contrast with these results, Martin and Sher (1994) did not find any differences on the NEO Five-Factor Neuroticism Scale in their comparisons involving adult children of alcoholics and nonalcoholics.

Moos and Billings (1982) looked at emotional problems in three groups of children; children of relapsed alcoholics, children of recovered alcoholics, and the children of control families. Compared with the other two groups, the children of relapsed alcoholic fathers were more depressed and anxious, which led the authors to suggest that the effects of parental alcoholism can be reduced or reversed when the parents successfully control their drinking. Children whose parents were no longer alcoholic had depression and anxiety scores that were similar to control children.

In a study taking a somewhat different approach, Schuckit et al. (1995) looked at the rates of anxiety-related diagnoses in the relatives of alcoholics. Schuckit et al. (1995) reasoned that if alcoholism and major anxiety disorders shared a common genetic basis, the rates of anxiety disorders would be higher in the close relatives of alcoholics than in the general population. The results did not support a common genotypic theory, and the prevalence of anxiety-related disorders in the close relatives of alcoholics was not very high (e.g., 3.4% for panic disorder, 1.4% for agoraphobia, 2.3% for social phobia, and 1.4% for obsessive compulsive disease).

The high-risk approach has also been used to experimentally evaluate the tension-reduction hypothesis. For example, Finn and Pihl (1988) identified three levels of risk based on the presence of alcoholism in the father and the paternal grandparent. Moderate risk subjects had alcoholic fathers but no alcoholism in the paternal grandparent, and high-risk subjects had both alcoholic fathers and alcoholic paternal grandparents. When tested in an experimental setting, the high-risk group showed the greatest cardiovascular reactivity to a signaled stressor. After they consumed a moderate amount of alcohol, this reactivity was reduced to a level comparable to the other two groups. An experimental study with nonalcoholic students at risk of alcoholism on the basis of their family histories, personalities, or both, found that alcohol's capacity to attenuate the physiological reaction to both a social stressor and a shock was most pronounced in the high-risk group compared to a group with neither of these factors (Levenson et al., 1987).

The effects of an alcoholic parent on the development of antisocial personality have been well documented in the previous section. In addition to these effects, there are higher levels of neuroticism in both the male and female children of alcoholics. Parental alcoholism may predispose these individuals to the anxiety-reducing effects of alcohol, that is, alcohol may be more reinforcing for these persons. Furthermore, although children of alcoholics report feeling emotionally distant from their parents, they are likely to learn a similar pattern of coping with life stress.

3.2.3. Cross-Sectional Studies of Young Heavy Drinkers

A number of cross-sectional studies have related alcohol use in college students with their neuroticism, as measured by the EPQ. In a British sample, Orford, Waller, and Peto (1974) found that high neuroticism was associated with increased drinking and with problems related to drinking, especially in females. Other studies have also found that high neuroticism and trait anxiety are associated with drinking in college and with a higher level of problems associated with excessive alcohol use (e.g., Parker, 1975). The evidence of high neuroticism in young heavy drinkers is useful because high neuroticism in older alcoholics may simply reflect the consequences of a lifetime of alcohol abuse. The demonstration of elevated neuroticism in persons *before* they become alcoholic suggests that this personality characteristic may be a precursor of difficulties with alcohol.

In an effort to determine whether young alcoholics differed from the description of the old alcoholic that was prevalent in the literature, Rosenberg (1969) administered the EPQ (or the EPI as it was known) and the IPAT anxiety scale to a sample of young alcoholics (aged less than 30). The younger alcoholics were more likely than older alcoholics (over 30) to have fathers who drank heavily, or were alcoholic themselves. The young alcoholics had a much higher total anxiety score on the IPAT and were beyond the 96th percentile for their age group. On the EPI, both alcoholic groups were significantly higher in neuroticism than the sample upon which the scale was developed, and the young alcoholics were significantly more neurotic than the older ones. This suggests that neuroticism is a factor predisposing to alcoholism.

In another study that examined MMPI differences between young and old alcoholics, Delatte and Delatte (1984) found a significant correlation between age and Goldberg's index of neuroticism versus psychoticism. Younger alcoholics were more like sociopaths (antisocial personality), whereas the older alcoholics tended more toward neuroticism. In a study of young males who were heavy drinkers (on average), Leonard and Blane (1988) found that those who were socially anxious were more likely to think that alcohol produces positive change than males who were low in social anxiety. Therefore, socially anxious males should find alcohol's effects more reinforcing than nonanxious males.

4. Ego Strength

If you were to ask the man in the street what is the main personality characteristic that is associated with alcoholism, you might expect the anwer in return to be something like "The alcoholic is a person who is lacking in will power or character." In psychological terms this trait comes closest to what Freud characterized as a weak versus a strong ego. The concept of ego strength does not seem to have played a dominant role in trait theory. This may be changing currently, however, as the Five-Factor model of personality structure (Costa & McCrae, 1992) gains in popularity. In this personality model, the construct of Conscientiousness or Will comprises one of the big five major personality constructs. This domain of personality is comprised of the facets of competence, order, dutifulness, achievement striving, self-discipline, and deliberation.

In the earlier theory and research by Barnes (1979,1980,1983) on the alcoholic personality, the domain of ego strength was comprised of characteristics associated with both agreeableness and conscientiousness in the Five-Factor model of personality. In particular, antisocial and high P characteristics were combined with characteristics linked with conscientiousness under the rubric of Ego Strength. In this study we will be considering the P and Ego-Strength dimensions as separate dimensions. Although this agrees more closely with the Five-Factor model of personality, the acceptance of this model is by no means universal (Eysenck, 1991). The structural equation modeling technique employed in the current research will allow examining different measurement models in the personality domain.

Although there are many different ways of conceptualizing and measuring the concept of Ego Strength, the perspective adopted herein is that a strong ego is comprised of several important ego functions, including (1) a sense of reality of the world and of the self, (2) regulation and control of drives, affects, and impulses, (3) object relationships, and (4) control of stimulation (e.g., stimulus barrier). These functions are part of the set of 12 ego-functions identified by Bellak, Hurvich, and Gediman (1973). In the section that follows, the evidence supporting an association between Ego Strength and related characteristics, on the one hand, and clinical alcoholism, on the other, will be reviewed. Evidence related to the issue of whether these characteristics can be considered "prealcoholic" characteristics is also examined.

4.1. Clinical Alcoholic Personality Research

4.1.1. Trait Measures

4.1.1a. MMPI. The Barron (1953) Ego-Strength Scale (Es) is a 68-item test that was originally developed to measure preparation for therapy and high ego strength is expected to be associated with better outcome during therapy. Items on the scale relate to personal adequacy, ability to cope, moral position, phobias and anxiety, religious attitude, and physical functioning (Graham, 1987). Scores on the Es have also been found positively correlated with intelligence, education, and masculine role identification (Tamkin & Klett, 1957; Holmes, 1967). The majority of studies that have compared alcoholics and controls on the MMPI have not included comparisons on the Ego-Strength Scale. In two studies where this comparison has been made (Barnes, 1980; Spiegel, Hadley, & Hadley,1970), the Ego-Strength Scale has performed very well in discriminating alcoholics from other groups. Spiegel et al. (1970) found that the Es Scale was the best measure in their study for discriminating alcoholics from normals and other psychiatric patients. Barnes (1980) also found that the Ego-Strength Scale was the best personality measure in this study for discriminating alcoholics from normals and for discriminating alcoholic prisoners from other prisoners. In a more recent study using a very small control group ($n = 15$), Limson et al. (1991) did not find any significant difference between alcoholics and controls on the Es Scale. The Es Scale does not appear to be any more useful than other MMPI scales for discriminating cocaine addicts from alcoholics (Johnson et al., 1992).

4.1.1b. 16 PF. In the research on the 16 PF, alcoholics have consistently scored lower on the Cattell factor C measuring emotional versus mature (Barnes, 1983). In an early study comparing alcoholics and controls (DePalma & Clayton, 1958), for example, the greatest difference between alcoholics and controls occurred in this factor. DePalma and Clayton (1958) concluded that emotional immaturity was at the core of the alcoholic personality and that an alcoholic's personality seemed to be governed by the pleasure principle rather than the reality principle.

4.1.1c. NEO Five-Factor Inventory. In the Martin and Sher (1994) study, the relationship between the NEO Five-Factor Conscientiousness Scale and alcohol abuse disorders was examined. Results supported an association between alcohol abuse and conscientiousness, and alcohol abusers scored lower on conscientiousness than nonalcohol abusers. Remitted alcoholics in this sample had scores that were intermediate.

4.1.1d. Self-Esteem. Self-esteem refers to a positive or negative attitude toward the self (Rosenberg, 1965). According to Rosenberg (1965), equivalent terms would be "self-acceptance" or "self-satisfaction." Individuals with low self-esteem are more likely to appear depressed and report higher proportions of psychosomatic symptoms and physiological indicators of anxiety, such as nervousness, insomnia, and headaches. Persons of high self-esteem do not necessarily think they are superior to others but express feelings that they are "good enough" (Rosenberg, 1965).

A number of studies have compared the self-esteem of the alcoholics with that of nonalcoholics. Generally speaking, alcoholics have lower self-esteem (Berg, 1971; Charlampous, Ford, & Skinner, 1976; Gross & Alder, 1970; Sandahl, Lindberg, & Bergman, 1987), a finding that is consistent for both males (Allen, 1969) and females (Beckman, 1978). Gross and Alder (1970) found that the mean Tennessee Self-Concept Scale score for 140 male alcoholics was significantly lower than the norms for the scale. Furthermore, the differences were consistent across all 10 aspects of the scale, suggesting that alcoholics' low self-concept is a general perception and is not limited to one or two specific components of self-esteem. In nonalcoholics, self-esteem is positively associated with heavy drinking (Beckman & Bardsley, 1981), although the data are not consistent (e.g., Ratliff & Burkhart, 1984; Richman & Flaherty, 1990). Most of the studies reviewed by Brennan, Walfish, and Aubuchon (1986) found that heavy drinking was influenced by self-esteem, although the strength of the relationship was attenuated by a number of other factors. For example, the relationship is stronger in females than males, is stronger in high SES black males than low SES black males, and is stronger in high SES subjects generally.

Labouvie (Labouvie, 1987; Labouvie & McGee, 1986) attempted a developmental explanation of self-esteem and alcohol and drug use based on Lazarus' model of stress and coping. Because the intuitive notion that people drink to reduce stress is not logical in the long term (i.e., additional physical and psychological stresses are created by heavy alcohol use), Labouvie suggests that personality characteristics may be associated with poor coping behaviors. Specifically he reports data suggesting that adolescents with weak egos are more likely to use emotion-focused coping rather than problem-focused coping. As a consequence of the heightened desire to reduce the impact of stressful events, these individuals are more likely to use alcohol and drugs. Because adolescence is a time of change and stress, teenagers with weak egos are at greater risk of using alcohol to cope.

4.1.1e. Sex-Role Identity and Adjustment. Sexual disorders have often been reported in alcoholic men (Whalley, 1978). Although it may often be a consequence of treatment (Schiavi, 1990), the percentage of alcoholics reporting impotence and sexual dysfunction is remarkably high. For some, impotence may be a direct consequence of heavy drinking, for example, through alcohol's disruption of regular sleep patterns, and for others impotence may be due to the toxic effects on neurological processes. A third possibility is that both impotence and alcoholism reflect some preexisting personality problem, low self-esteem, sexual anxiety, or feelings of inadequacy (Schiavi, 1990).

Sexual disorders may reflect problems with sex-role identity. The characterization of the male alcoholic as lacking in masculinity has been used to reinforce the notion that alcohol is a substitute for sexual activity in these persons. Low levels of masculinity in male alcoholics have been observed (Parker, 1959). Parker suggests that the conflict created by low masculinity in a society that expects a masculine role from men leads to tension and anxiety that is treated by drinking. In a study of prealcoholic college students, Parker (1969) found that subjects with higher alcohol consumption levels had greater divergence between latent and manifest masculinity scores, that is, the anxiety and tension created by a highly incongruent sex disposition was correlated with heavier drinking. Although these experiments are cross-sectional and therefore causal statements are less valid, the data do suggest that there is additional sex-role strain in alcoholic men.

Studies of sexual identity in alcoholic women have focused more on deviance from role norms and its relationship to drinking. Parker (1972) found that female alcoholics, compared with moderate drinkers, had less feminine sex role preferences and more feminine emotional responses. Similarly, Wilsnack (1973) found that female alcoholics were more masculine than nonalcoholics on measures of unconscious gender identity but were more consciously feminine ("hyperfeminine"). Scida and Vannicelli (1978) reported a positive relationship between sex-role conflict and problem drinking. Conscious sexual identity and unconscious gender identity were both positively associated with problem drinking. These data did not suggest that any particular sex-role stance (i.e., females with a more masculine orientation than a normative sample) is associated with drinking, rather the *degree* of conflict is the critical factor. In a review of sex-role conflict and alcoholism in women, Beckman (1975) points out that unconscious masculine tendencies are also prevalent in women who are successfully coping with their careers. The implication is that this conflict does not need to produce alcoholism. The relationship between alcoholism in women and their sex-role identification is unclear, and a number of equivocal findings are due to ignoring complex sets of interacting variables (Lundy, 1987).

4.1.2. Clinical Diagnoses

The clinical diagnosis that is probably most closely associated with low ego strength is the borderline personality disorder. The borderline personality condition is found quite commonly in conjunction with alcohol abuse and other forms of substance abuse. Verheul et al. (1995) reviewed seven studies in alcoholic samples and found that the range for diagnoses of borderline conditions ranged from 4–66% with a median of 21%. The other way of estimating comorbidity for these disorders has been to find a sample of borderline personality cases and look at the prevalence of alcohol abuse in this sample. In a general population sample of borderline cases, Swartz, Blazer, George, and Winfield (1990) reported that the prevalence of alcohol abuse and dependence was 21.9%. In a clinical study of borderline cases (Zanarini, Gunderson, & Frankenburg, 1989), the prevalence of alcohol abuse /dependence was much higher (66%).

4.1.3. Alcohol Effects on Self-Concept.

Studies of the short-term effects of ingesting alcohol have shown that, for alcoholics, self-concept improves after drinking, whereas the same is not true for social drinkers (Berg, 1971). Social drinkers' self-esteem scores shifted toward a less favorable view of the self after drinking. Studies of the development of alcohol abuse in adolescents suggest that the user's expectation that alcohol will enhance self-esteem may be a useful predictor of abuse (Chassin et al., 1981). According to a social learning perspective (Abrams & Niaura, 1987), adolescents with low self-esteem are prone to using alcohol to cope, progressively isolate themselves from those with adequate coping skills and associate with peers who have similar skill deficits, engage in delinquent behaviors, and develop distorted, positive expectancies about alcohol's effect. This "reciprocally determined social selection process" contributes to the downward spiral that becomes alcoholism.

4.2. Prealcoholic Personality

4.2.1. Longitudinal Studies

There have not been any classical longitudinal studies designed to directly test the relationship between ego strength and alcoholism. At least two longitudinal studies were designed to test the relationship between personality charcteristics and problem behaviors, including alcoholism, that are relevant for assessing the effects of ego strength on alcohol abuse. In the longitudinal research by Jessor et al. (1991), subjects were initially tested in high school or in college and then followed up in young adulthood. Their results showed that personality characteristics during adolescence were generally more important than the perceived environment at the time in predicting long-term risk of alcohol abuse and other problem behaviors. In particular, some measures of variables relating to ego strength were significant predictors whereas others were not. Self-esteem, for example, did not prove to be an important predictor in the longitudinal analyses. Personal controls against problem behaviors on the other hand were strongly predictive of subsequent problem behaviors, and lower intolerance of deviancy and less religiosity were associated with later development of problem behaviors, including alcohol abuse. A low value on academic achievement was also predictive of subsequent alcohol problems for both men and women. The results in the longitudinal research conducted by Labouvie and McGee (1986) have been consistent with these findings. Self-esteem did not play a role in predicting alcohol and drug use in their longitudinal study. High need for achievement, however, did play a role as one of their "safe" personality characteristics. In a study involving a shorter time frame (one year), Killen et al. (1996) also found that self-esteem did not predict the onset of drinking.

Another type of longitudinal study has examined the changes in aspects of ego strength, such as self-esteem, in alcoholics after treatment. Gross (1971), for example, measured self-concepts in alcoholics before and after a sixty-day treatment program. Most means increased, indicating healthier functioning, although only 2 of 10 were statistically significant. White and Porter (1966) found a negative correlation between the length of sobriety and self-esteem. The longer the period of sobriety, the more favorable view the alcoholic has of the self. Another two-year follow-up study of the drinking habits of 300 alcoholic inpatients was conducted by Sandahl et al. (1987). These investigators found that there were significant improvements in several measures of ego strength, including monotophobia, impulsivity, and self esteem during the two-year recovery period. Improvements in alcohol states were associated only with positive changes in self-esteem (Sandahl et al., 1987). This result was especially true for female subjects. Subjects with unfavourable outcomes (defined as daily drinking or weekend bingeing at follow-up) had lower self-esteem at first examination two years earlier. Further, improvements in drinking states were associated with improvements in self-esteem. Successful treatment for alcoholism is associated with improvements in self-esteem.

4.2.2. High-Risk Studies

In the Martin and Sher (1994) study, the scores of high-risk adult children of alcoholics were compared with the scores of other low-risk adults on the Conscientiousness Scale of the NEO. Results supported an association between a family history of alcohol abuse and lower Conscientiousness Scale scores.

Most of the high-risk studies that are relevant for determining the relationship between ego strength and alcohol abuse have focused on the self-esteem variable. Generally speaking, the children of alcoholic parents have lower self-esteem and poorer self-concepts than children from nonalcoholic families (Baraga, 1977; O'Gorman, 1975; Rearden & Markwell, 1989). Berkowitz and Perkins (1988) reported that the children of alcoholics report greater self-deprecation than their peers and that the effect was greater for females. In a self-report survey of both male and female children of alcoholics, both genders reported higher levels of self-deprecation than children of nonalcoholic parents (Berkowitz & Perkins, 1988). For females, the high self-deprecation seems to be due to the effect of an alcoholic father because daughters of alcoholic mothers did not differ from daughters of nonalcoholic mothers. Other reports on the self-esteem levels of the children of alcoholics are now available. Rearden and Markwell (1989) looked at drinking problems in college students and found that the children of alcoholics had significantly lower self-concepts.

Werner (1986) conducted a longitudinal study of the children of alcoholics and found that by age 18, 30% were delinquent, and 25% had "serious mental problems." Self-esteem consistently emerged as a good predictor of those who did or did not develop serious coping problems in adolescence. Werner (1986) suggested that a high level of self-esteem in early adolescence may help to protect the children of alcoholics from developing the usual problems associated with this group. Bennett, Wolin, and Reiss (1988) compared 6- to18-year-old children from alcoholic families with children from nonalcoholic families. The former were lower on the Pier–Harris self-concept scale in addition to a number of cognitive and emotional variables. Unfortunately, these results are tenuous because the alcoholic families had lower occupational status and lower family income than the comparison group. Nevertheless, high self-esteem in childhood may help prevent problems from occurring in children who would be most likely to develop problems due to their parent's drinking. Many children of alcoholics do not become alcoholic, and a positive self-concept may be an important component of resiliency.

Not all of the data are consistent with the notion that children of alcoholics have lower self-esteem. Clair and Genest (1987) did not find differences in depression or self-esteem between children with alcoholic fathers and children from nonalcoholic homes. Similarly, Churchill, Broida, and Nicholson (1990) did not find differences between children of alcoholics and nonalcoholics on either self-esteem or locus of control. In a study of premedical students, there was no correlation between alcohol-related problems and self-esteem, although patterns of parental affectivity were correlated with alcohol problems (Richman & Flaherty, 1990). The main problem with the Richman and Flaherty (1990) study is that the sample was young medical students (likely a restricted range of high self-esteem) who may be too young to have developed the alcohol problems tapped by the MAST. This final point is substantiated by their data; half of the items were not endorsed by *any* female subjects.

Research on young problem drinkers is also relevant for determining the potential role of ego strength in predicting alcohol abuse. In our own research (Barnes, 1985a), young problem drinkers did not differ significantly from nonproblem drinkers on the Baron Ego-Strength Scale. Another study (Yanish & Battle, 1985) of young heavy drinkers found differences in self-esteem. Yanish and Battle (1985) did not find that adolescent depression was predictive of alcohol use but did find that self-esteem predicted both alcohol use and depression. In young male college students, higher neuroticism and low self-esteem were associated with wine and cocktail drinking. There was no relationship between self-esteem and alcohol use for female college students in this study.

5. Field Dedpendence–Independence

Witkin, Karp, and Goodenough (1959) first described field dependence as a perceptual style that may be related to alcoholism. Field dependence is the tendency to rely on either internal or external referents in making perceptual judgments. Field-dependent persons show less differentiation in social perception and interaction, whereas field independence is associated with greater perceptual differentiation and fewer dependency problems in interpersonal relationships. Early studies tended to rely on judgments of body position in space (the Body Adjustment Test) or on judgment of the verticality of an illuminated line within an illuminated box (the Rod and Frame Test). More recent research on field dependence has employed a paper and pencil measure, the Embedded Figures Test (EFT), that requires subjects to find simple shapes hidden within more complex patterns.

5.1. Clinical Alcohol Personality Research

Witkin et al. (1959) compared alcoholics in treatment with psychiatric controls and normals and found that the alcoholics were more field-dependent on all three measures. A number of subsequent studies have supported this distinction between alcoholics and non-alcoholics (Bailey, Hustmyer & Kristofferson, 1961; Goldstein & Chotlos, 1965; Karp, Poster, & Goodman, 1963; Rhodes, Carr, & Jurji, 1968; Robertson, Fournet, Zelhart, & Estes, 1987). However, other studies have failed to support the hypothesis that alcoholics are more field dependent (Hayes, Schwarzbach, Schmeier, & Stacher, 1975; Jones & Parsons, 1972). The results of a meta-analysis of data prior to 1980 support the suggestion that alcoholics are indeed more field-dependent than nonalcoholics (Barnes, 1979), but it is likely that field dependence is a more important characteristic in certain alcoholic groups than others (e.g., low SES, Barnes, 1980).

There are two competing explanations for the relationship between field dependence and alcoholism. The first postulates that field dependence is a factor predisposing to alcoholism (e.g., Karp, Witkin, & Goodenough, 1965). The second suggests that field dependence is a consequence of extensive alcohol abuse (e.g., Tarter & Edwards, 1986). Two bodies of literature have been used to compare and evaluate these competing hypotheses. First, studies of the stability of field dependence in alcoholics in treatment may demonstrate whether field-dependence scores change as alcohol status changes. Second, if alcohol abuse causes cognitive deterioration, of which field dependence is an example, then we should expect to find that field dependence is associated with the length or severity of alcoholism and that field dependence is associated with other cognitive deficits in alcoholics. However, failure to find stability of posttreatment field dependence or finding an association between measures of field dependence and cognitive performance in alcoholics does not necessarily suggest that field dependence is a consequence of alcohol abuse because both types of studies begin with alcoholics in treatment, who may be a unique subsample of all alcoholics.

Studies of the stability of field dependence in alcoholics have produced mixed results. Some reports suggest that alcoholics become less field-dependent after remaining abstinent for a short period of time (Chess, Neuringer, & Goldstein, 1971; Goldstein & Chotlos, 1965; Lafferty & Kahn 1986), others have found that alcoholics who remain abstinent are on average as field dependent as drinking alcoholics (Jacobson, Pisani, & Berenbaum, 1970; Karp et al., 1965). Unfortunately, studies of alcoholics who remain in treatment are clouded by the fact that alcoholics who drop out of treatment are more field-dependent than those who remain in treatment (Calsyn, Roszell, Walker, & O'Leary, 1983; Erwin & Hunter, 1984). Assuming that treatment dropouts do not remain abstinent, it is likely that they have a more severe manifestation of the disorder. Studies that have demonstrated changes in field dependence may be testing subjects who have less severe alcohol problems.

Whether field dependence scores remain stable immediately after drinking has also been investigated experimentally. In a study of nonalcoholic college students, field dependence increased only in the drinking group (Kristofferson, 1968). Karp et al. (1965) did not find that alcohol influenced performance on the BAT or the RFT in a sample of alcoholics. However, performance on the EFT was significantly slower, resulting in scores indicating greater field dependence. These authors attribute this finding to decreased concentration that follows alcohol use and suggest that this effect may be more pronounced for alcoholics.

The second body of literature has examined the relationship between field dependence and the severity or chronicity of alcohol abuse. Correlations between the length of alcohol abuse and field dependence have been contradictory. In a sample of older alcoholics, Steiger, Negrete, and Marcil (1985) found that field dependence was positively correlated with the number of years of drinking, the quantity of alcohol drunk daily, and problems associated with drinking (alcohol dependence). These authors concluded that field dependence is, in part, a consequence of the progressive neural damage caused by alcohol abuse. If this is true, then one should expect to find that field dependence is associated with the degree of cognitive impairment found in heavy drinkers. In a study that examined field dependence and cognitive impairment during treatment for alcoholism, Lafferty and Kahn (1986) found a moderate correlation with the degree of cognitive impairment. In contrast, Bergman, Holm, and Agren (1981) compared two groups of alcoholics, one that had a greater degree of intellectual impairment than the other, and did not find differences between the two groups on field dependence as measured by a modified RFT. Pisani, Jacobson, and Berenbaum (1973) found a significant positive correlation between field dependence and brain damage in chronic alcoholics, but this correlation was reduced to a nonsignificant level once the effects of age were controlled. This brings us to an important point. Scores on the EFT are influenced by both age and education. Younger people and those who are more educated score higher, reflecting field independence. Therefore, it is important to consider the age of the sample being tested. Bergman et al. (1981) tested groups whose mean ages were 52 and 56. Steiger et al.'s (1985) mean age was 47.6 and Lafferty and Kahn's (1986) sample averaged 40.6 years of age. Bergman's groups had been drinking on average for more than 30 years, and the alcoholics in the other two studies had been drinking excessively for about 15 years (±0.3). The relatively younger alcoholics, who have been drinking for a much shorter time, may be more able to recover from the debilitating effects of drinking, whereas Bergman's sample seems to be severely chronic and may be suffering from irreversible cognitive impairment. Regardless, comparing young and old alcoholics' scores on the EFT. is not appropriate unless the scores are transformed to reflect age differences.

It may also be useful to speculate about the motivation to perform the field dependence test. From a subjective point of view, it appears like a test of ability. Because the individual is required to find hidden figures, there is a correct and an incorrect response. Furthermore, it is a timed test. To do well requires that each part be completed within five minutes. It may not be the goal of alcoholics in treatment to look like they are healthy or functioning at an optimal level. Therefore, their motivation to do the task quickly may be reduced. Lack of motivation will produce low scores that will be scored as field-dependent. Furthermore, it is also possible that field-dependent alcoholics are more likely to seek treatment than field-independent alcoholics.

5.2. Prealcoholic Personality

Longitudinal studies of field dependence prior to the onset of alcoholism are nonexistent. Therefore, only high-risk studies will be reviewed.

5.2.1. High-Risk Studies

Recent studies have examined field dependence in the children of alcoholics, although the amount of research is small. In response to doubts about the etiological role of field dependence in alcoholism, Hennecke (1984) compared children aged 10–12 at high risk of alcoholism, because of the presence of an alcoholic father, with children of nonalcoholic parents. Although stimulus augmenting was premorbid to alcoholism, there were no group differences in field dependence. However, the mean scores for the subjects in the Hennecke study were around 90 seconds per item, which is much faster than the norms provided by Witkin, Oltman, Raskin, and Karp (1971). It is unclear why these children would be so much better at finding the hidden figures. Tarter and Edwards (1986) found support for the consequence hypothesis by comparing the sons of alcoholics (mean age 12.4 years) with the sons of depressed fathers and nonalcoholic controls using a portable rod and frame apparatus. Again, there were no group differences, leading them to suggest that field dependence is *not* a risk factor in alcoholism. A similar pilot study of adult sons of alcoholics (Schuckit & Penn, 1985) found no difference in men at risk, compared to controls. In sum, these data are unanimous in suggesting that individuals at risk of developing alcoholism on the basis of positive family histories do not differ in field dependence from individuals at lower risk.

The results of these studies are less damaging to the "predisposing trait" theory than might be inferred. Although the children of alcoholics are more at risk of developing the disorder, fully 75% of them will remain abstinent from alcohol or will have no drinking related problems. Because these subjects are included in the high-risk group, they reduce the probability of finding differences between groups. A more convincing demonstration would be to compare the children of alcoholics who subsequently become alcoholics with those who do not. Consequently, longitudinal research is required to adequately resolve the issue of field dependence as a precursor or consequence of alcoholism.

6. Summary

In this chapter, the extensive literature on the association between major personality dimensions and alcohol abuse has been reviewed. On the Extraversion dimension, results have shown there is not much evidence supporting an association between extraversion, as measured by the Eysenck Scale or similar measures, and alcoholism. Extraversion is, however, related to drinking in younger samples. There are also facets of the Extraversion dimension that are measured by scales such as the MacAndrew Alcoholism Scale and various sensation-seeking scales that are related to alcoholism.

In the Psychoticism domain, results have been fairly consistent in showing an association between Psychoticism and associated characteristics and clinical alcoholism. In particular, alcoholics have consistently scored differently from controls on measures of this construct, including the MMPI Pd Scale and the NEO Agreeableness Scale. An association between alcoholism and Antisocial Personality disorder has also been consistently reported in the literature reviewed. In the longitudinal and high-risk studies, the association between this dimension and alcoholism is more strongly substantiated than for any of the other major personality domains.

In the Neuroticism domain, there is consistent data supporting the association between clinical alcoholism and neuroticism. In particular, alcoholics score higher on a variety of scales that measure anxiety and related constructs such as the MMPI Neurotic Triad, the Eysenck N Scale, and the NEO-N Scale. An association between alcoholism and anxiety disorders and depression has also been frequently reported in the literature. The evidence in support of the Neuroticism domain as a prealcoholic personality characteristic is somewhat less conclusive. Longitudinal data on this issue is inconclusive. Some high-risk studies, however, suggest that adult children of alcoholics and young problem drinkers may score higher on Neuroticism and that high-risk subjects may be more vulnerable to the tension-reducing effects of alcohol.

In the Ego-Strength domain there is consistent evidence supporting an association between clinical alcoholism and low Ego Strength. In particular, alcoholics score lower than controls on such measures as the Barron Ego-Strength Scale, Cattell's factor C, and the NEO Conscientiousness Scale. Some evidence suggests that alcoholics may have lower self-esteem and more problems with sex-role identity than nonalcoholics. Not much relevant data is available for establishing whether or not low Ego Strength is a prealcoholic characteristic. In the Jessor research (Jessor et al., 1991), the results of their longitudinal analyses supported an association between personality and problem behavior, including drinking. In particular, some of their measures in the personality domain associated with lower drinking, including more personal controls, more religiosity, and higher achievement striving, are consistent with the characteristics associated with higher Ego Strength.

In the Field Dependence-Independence domain there is consistent data to support an association between this characteristic and clinical alcoholism. There are no longitudinal data available, however, to test whether the field dependence that is characteristic of alcoholics in treatment is also a prealcoholic characteristic. The high-risk studies have been consistent in not showing any association between a high-risk status and more field dependence.

II

THE WINNIPEG HEALTH
AND DRINKING SURVEY

3

Methodology

1. Objectives

1. To describe the sampling, response, and measurement instruments of Wave 1 and Wave 2 of the Winnipeg Health and Drinking Survey.
2. To describe sample respresentativeness and the differences between Wave 1 and Wave 2 samples and measures.

The Winnipeg Health and Drinking Survey (WHDS) is a longitudinal panel survey using a life-span approach to the relationship between personality and substance use. A stratified random sample of noninstitutionalized adult residents of Winnipeg was drawn from the records of the Manitoba Health Services Commission (MHSC), which is the provincial medicare insurance body. The strata were by age group (18–34, 35–49, 50–65) and gender. From this sample, a total of 2,761 introductory letters was required to produce a sample that included a minimum of 200 subjects in each age/sex group. Within 1 to 3 weeks of this initial letter, attempts were made to contact the respondents by telephone.

2. Wave 1

2.1. Eligibility

Of the original sample, 336 (8.1%) were ineligible because they had

1. moved out of the city ($n = 166$ or 49.4% of ineligible),
2. could not read or write English well enough to understand the questions ($n = 155$ or 46.1% of ineligible), or

3. were currently institutionalized or had died (n = 15 or 4.5% of ineligible).

Usually eligibility was determined over the telephone, but occasionally interviews were terminated once the interviewer realized that the respondent could not understand the procedures or questions.

2.2. Finding the Sample

Of the original sample, 885 (32.1%) could not be contacted initially by telephone. Therefore, they went into the "tracking system." This system required that an interviewer go to the home at various times of the day to contact the respondent in person. A minimum of three attempts were made, a maximum of 11, and an average of 5. Neighbors were checked in an effort to establish that this was the correct address for the particular name.

If we could still not find the person at this address, the name and date of birth were given by MHSC to the provincial motor vehicle licensing bureau. This bureau provided the most recent known address of the person's driver's license which was used to verify the address that we had, to identify that the person had moved out of the city, or to indicate whether the person's address was unknown (i.e., the person did not have a valid driver's license within the past few years). New addresses were followed up, but if the respondent still could not be reached, the name was sent to a credit bureau for address verification. These procedures enabled us to contact an additional 439 possible respondents (49.6% of the unable to contact group). Of these, 178 (41%) were interviewed, 156 (35.7%) refused to be interviewed, and the rest (n = 105, 23.9%) were ineligible, usually because they had moved out of the city.

Prior to 1984, Manitoba Health (the medicare system from whom we received the sample list) reimbursed patients after a physician visit. However, an administrative change to reimbursement of physicians resulted in a reduction in the motivation for individuals to keep the insurance plan up to date with current address information. Checks were made payable directly to physicians, rather than payable as reimbursement to patients, who had already paid the physician. As a result, the sample list may have become slightly out of date and resulted in the larger than anticipated incidence of "unable to find" individuals.

2.2.1. Response Rates

A total of 446 potential respondents was not found using any of the tracking procedures. This represents 14.9% of the original sample. Two response rates for each of the six age by gender cells in the sample have been calculated. The first rate is the ratio of completed interviews to the number who were eligible *and* found. The overall ratio is 64.3% with a slightly higher ratio for women than for men (65.3% vs 63.6%). The second rate is the percentage of completed interviews in each group of those eligible to participate in the survey. This ratio is 45.7% for the total sample. This second percentage is lower because it includes potential subjects, whom we could not find, in the denominator of the equation. This estimate is a likely worst case scenario, as it includes potentially ineligible subjects in addition to potential refusals.

Although the final participation rate of 64.3% of those found or contacted appears lower than desirable, compared to other surveys of drinking (e.g., Herd, 1994), this rate is reasonable given the demanding nature of the project (i.e., the voluntary commitment to an hour and a half interview). Every effort was made to maximize participation rates. Subjects who initially refused were recontacted by the most effective interviewer. Although most chose to remain nonparticipating, a small number ($n = 24$) was convinced of the importance of participation and agreed to be interviewed. Further efforts to minimize the refusal rate were undertaken by comparing the participation rates of the different interviewers. Those with low rates were not retained.

A total of 1257 respondents completed the interview and the self-report personality measures. Six subjects refused to give their dates of birth and are therefore excluded from some analyses because categorization into various age and gender groups was used for the stratification.

2.2.2. Refusal Rates by Each of the Six Age/Gender Cells

A summary of the response rates for each age and gender cell are presented in Table 3.1. Two trends emerged. It was more difficult to find the younger subjects and more difficult to get the older subjects to participate. We were unable to find

Table 3.1. Subject Participation by Demographic Characteristics

	Sample drawn	Unable to find	Ineligible	Refused	Interviewed
Men	501	142	53	95	211
18–34		28.3%	10.6%	19.0%	42.1%
Women	511	119	57	88	247
18–34		23.3%	11.2%	17.2%	48.3%
Men	478	85	52	132	209
35–49		17.8%	10.9%	27.6%	43.7%
Women	393	37	48	104	204
35–49		9.4%	12.2%	26.5%	51.9%
Men	414	40	57	125	192
50–65		9.7%	13.8%	30.2%	46.6%
Women	456	23	69	160	204
50–65		5.0%	15.1%	35.1%	44.7%

about a quarter of the younger subjects, and about one third of the older subjects refused to participate.

2.3. Sample Description

The demographic characteristics of the sample are reported in some detail to evaluate whether the sample is representative of Winnipeg and/or Canadians as a whole. This is done by comparing the characteristics of the 1257 respondents from Wave 1 with the 1988 Canadian Census and with the 1988 Winnipeg Area Survey (WAS). The WAS is an annual survey of randomly selected households in Winnipeg conducted by the Department of Sociology at the University of Manitoba. The Canadian Census information is provided in both the Canada Yearbook (1992) and through Statistics Canada.

The demographic characteristics of the WHDS sample are shown in Table 3.2. The sample is primarily married (71.5%), white (92%), many have taken their education beyond high school (50.7%), and report a relatively high family income (e.g., 57.6% report a family income of more than $35,000). Comparison of the WHDS sample with Statistics Canada information and the WAS on major demographic variables is shown in Table 3.3. Where comparisons cannot be made (if categories across the different surveys are not comparable), they have been omitted.

2.3.1. Age

Recall that stratification along age and gender lines was undertaken. Thus there is no reason to assume that the age and gender breakdown of the sample is representative of the city or of the country in general. Overall, women in the sample were slightly younger than men (39.5 years versus 42.5 years). In attempting to get equal cell sizes for our age strata, we undersampled young respondents and oversampled older respondents, compared to the 1986 Canadian Census information.

2.3.2. Gender

Although the original target was to have 600 men and 600 women participate in the WHDS, we have slightly more, 615 men and 645 women. This was done in anticipation of having a more difficult time locating these individuals at the follow-up two years later. However, as can be seen in Table 3.3, the ratio of men to women is very close to the Winnipeg population ratio.

Table 3.2. Percentage of Respondents in Various Demographic Groups by Gender

	Men (n = 615)	Women (n = 642)	Total (n = 1,257)
Age (in years)	42.5	39.5	40.6
Marital status			
Single	21.3	17.9	19.6
Married	72.7	70.4	71.5
Divorced	1.0	3.4	2.2
Widowed	5.0	8.3	6.7
Education			
Some grade school	1.8	2.6	2.2
Grade school	3.6	3.3	3.4
Some high school	19.0	19.9	19.5
High school	22.0	26.2	24.1
Some college	26.5	25.4	25.9
University graduate	15.9	16.5	16.2
Some post-graduate	3.6	3.6	3.6
Master's or doctorate	7.6	2.5	5.0
Family Income			
< $10,000	3.4	4.4	3.9
$10,000–$19,999	5.2	9.6	7.5
$20,000–$34,999	20.9	24.3	22.7
$35,000–$49,999	25.4	21.8	23.5
$50,000+	40.5	28.0	34.1
Refused or missing	1.5	2.9	2.2
Don't know	3.1	8.9	6.0
Employment status			
Working full time	75.0	42.1	58.2
Working part time	3.6	20.6	12.3
Unemployed	4.4	5.0	4.7
Student	6.2	5.4	5.9
Homemaker	0	18.7	9.7
Retired	8.3	6.4	7.3
Other	2.6	1.9	2.2
Religious preference			
Catholic	25.9	32.4	29.3
Protestant	39.0	43.4	41.2
Jewish	2.4	3.0	2.7
Other	12.1	10.6	11.3
None	20.6	10.6	15.5
Ethnicity			
White	92.5	91.6	92.0
Black	1.6	0.8	1.2
Asian	3.7	4.2	4.0
Native	1.1	1.9	1.5
Other	1.0	1.6	1.3

Table 3.3. Percentage of Each Sample by Demographic Characteristics[a]

		Canadian Census		
	Canada	Winnipeg	WAS	WHDS
Men	47.4	48.4	43.1	48.9
Women	52.6	51.6	56.9	51.1
Age group				
20–24	13.3		12.4	11.2
25–34	25.2		27.6	23.0
35–44	19.0		21.0	21.7
45–54	13.0		13.4	19.0
55–64	12.9		12.6	22.2
Marital status				
Single		27.9	23.3	19.6
Married		61.3	59.5	71.5
Div/sep		3.7	10.8	6.7
Widowed		7.1	6.1	2.2
Education				
Jr. high or less			25.3	25.1
Complete high school			20.8	24.1
Some Univ./college			33.8	25.9
University grad			16.5	16.2
Some postgrad			3.9	8.6
Family income				
Don't know			11.1	6.0
Refused/missing			10.0	2.2
Under $10,000		7.2	9.0	4.2
$10–20,000		15.3	12.9	8.2
$20–35,000		27.9	32.4	24.7
$35–50,000		25.4	20.2	25.6
Over $50,000		24.2	25.5	37.1

[a]WHDS groups have been categorized differently from the previous table to facilitate comparison with the other surveys. For example, the percentages of respondents with particular family income is adjusted to exclude the refused and "don't know" category; to be consistent with the W.A.S.

2.3.3. Marital Status

In the WHDS, 71.5% of the sample was married or currently living with a partner. The comparable figure from the WAS is 59.5%. In the 1988 WAS, the percentage divorced was 4.9%. An additional 5.9% was separated. The WHDS sampled 84 divorced and separated people (6.7% of the total sample). The WHDS includes a higher proportion of married people and a lower proportion of divorced individuals than the WAS and Statistics Canada census information. The difference between the WHDS and the WAS is likely to be due to sampling differences. The WAS interviewers went door-to-door, looking for respondents in a neighborhood, within a specific age group and gender. The WHDS sampled persons from the provincial medical insurance records and looked for specific individuals. Divorced and recently separated people may be more difficult to find using insurance records, as they are more likely to have moved since they last updated their medical file. We also oversampled younger respondents.

2.3.4. Ethnicity and Racial Origins

British and French are the most common ethnic groups in Canada and represent 34% and 24% of the population, respectively (Statistics Canada, 1986 Census). The French community is clustered primarily in Quebec. Only 4.9% of the Manitoba population is considered of French ethnic origin. In the WHDS, 6.7% was classified as French Canadian, a figure that is quite comparable with census information on Winnipeg. A summary of the respondents' self-reported racial designations is summarized in Table 3.2. The sample is primarily white (92%). About 3% of Canadians has aboriginal origins. In the WHDS, 1.5% ($n = 19$) of the sample reported "native" as their race. Including parent's cultural background resulted in an additional 1.3% of the WHDS classified as of aboriginal origin. This figure approximates the national and provincial percentages.

2.3.5. Language

English is the mother tongue for 62% of Canadians and French is the mother tongue for 25% of the population. The proportion of French-speaking individuals is much lower in Manitoba (5% according to the 1986 Statistics Canada figures), and the WHDS reflects this. Seventy-four and one-tenth percent report English as their first language, 4.7% report French as their first language, and 21.2% report neither.

2.3.6. Religion

The most recent statistics for religious affiliation in Canada are based on quite dated 1981 national data. Forty-seven percent of Canadians was Catholic, 41% was Protestant, 1.2% was Jewish, and 7.3% report no religious affiliation. Eastern Orthodox and other non-Christian religions account for the remainder. The data from the WHDS indicate 29.3% Catholic, 41.2% Protestant, 2.7% Jewish, and 15.5% with no religious affiliation; 11.3% report "other." The higher proportion of respondents who reported no religious affiliation is consistent with more recent national trends.

2.3.7. Education

According to the Census, slightly less than half of the Winnipeg population aged between 20–64 graduated high school. This figure is half a percentage point below the national average. Educational level in the WHDS was very similar to that obtained using quite a different sampling procedure (i.e., the WAS). In both Winnipeg surveys, slightly more than 25% of the samples had not completed high school. According to the Census, 82% of Canadian adults completed at least grade 9, whereas 94% of the WHDS sample had at least some high school. The high level of education in the WHDS may be explained by two factors. First, the upper age limit cutoff used in the sampling for the WHDS was 65 years old. Subjects were not sampled beyond age 65. The Statistics Canada data indicate that a high proportion of the 18% of the population who had not completed high school were over 55. Additional support for the suggestion that the upper age limit cutoff increased the mean education level in the WHDS is that the older age group (49–65) was less educated than the other groups ($F(2,1251) = 18.3$, $p < .001$). It is likely that, had we sampled beyond age 65, the average level of education would have declined. Second, one of the criteria for participation in the WHDS was the ability to read and understand English. Unlike the Statistics Canada methodology, which collects data via telephone, respondents in the WHDS were required to complete some of the forms themselves, which required English fluency. Despite this, the level of education is reasonably comparable with the WAS, even though 13% of the WAS was over 65 years of age. The slightly higher than average level of education is not a problem for the present analyses, unless educational level affects the relationship between personality and addictions.

The WHDS sample is a relatively representative cross section of Manitobans and is quite representative of Canadians, with the following qualifications. The respondents in the WHDS are more educated than the national average, but this may be due to the eligibility requirements (ability to read English and age under 65). The WHDS sample also had a higher income level than the average for Winnipeg, which is probably due to the fact that people without residences and those who move frequently would not have been interviewed, based on the sampling procedure.

2.4. Measures

2.4.1. Personality

Personality characteristics were assessed via self-report. The personality questionnaire battery included the revised version of the Eysenck Personality Questionnaire (EPQR, Eysenck, Eysenck and Barrett, 1985); two research scales from the MMPI, Ego Strength (Barron, 1953) and the MacAndrews Scale (MAC;

MacAndrew, 1965); the Vando Reducer–Augmenter Scale (R-A; Barnes, 1985b; Vando, 1969); the trait subscale of the State-Trait Anxiety Inventory, (STAI-T; Spielberger, Gorsuch, & Lushene, 1970); the Rosenberg (1965) Self-Esteem Inventory, and a test designed to measure field dependence/independence, the Group Embedded Figures Test (GEFT; Witkin et al., 1971). The constructs measured by these tests are defined as follows:

1. EPQ Psychoticism (P) This is a genetically based dimension that reflects aggressiveness, hostility, and characteristics that are "normal" aspects of what in the more extreme would result in a clinical diagnosis of "psychosis." Antisocial behaviors and impulsivity are characteristics of people with high P scores.
2. EPQ Extraversion (E) The primary component of extraversion is sociability. The extrovert is a carefree, easy-going person who is usually quite optimistic, whereas the introvert is a quite retiring person who appears reserved and cautious.
3. EPQ Neuroticism (N) A highly neurotic person is anxious, frequently worries, is moody, and is often depressed. Overly emotional, the neurotic may react strongly to a variety of stimuli. The low N individual may be called "stable" and is usually even-tempered and controlled.
4. EPQ Lie (L) The L scale was developed to measure the tendency to "fake good." This scale also measures some stable personality characteristic of dissimulation. Persons who score high on L may be socially naive and are likely trying to make a good impression on the tester.
5. Ego strength (ES) Originally developed to identify patients who would respond well to brief psychotherapy, a high score on this scale reflects self-confidence and security, a lack of psychopathology, and a person who is effective in dealing with others.
6. MacAndrew Scale (MAC) The MAC discriminates alcoholics from nonalcoholics, and a high score indicates greater probability of alcohol or other substance abuse.
7. Vando Reducer-Augmenter Scale (R-A) Consistent with Petrie (1967), Vando suggests that the augmenter–reducer dimension reflects a continuum of styles for handling stimulation. People who score high on the scale (reducers) have greater pain tolerance and may feel chronically understimulated. Augmenters score low on the scale, are low in pain tolerance, and avoid high intensity stimulation. Reducers seek out such stimulation and are more extraverted than augmenters.
8. Trait Anxiety (TA) The TA scale measures symptoms of general anxiety. The Spielberger trait anxiety measure is a widely used index of anxiety phenomena used in "normal" populations. Trait anxiety refers to a stable individual difference in anxiety proneness. High scores on

the scale indicate a greater likelihood of responding with increased anxiety in interpersonal situations that may pose some threat to self-esteem.

9. Self-Esteem (SE) As defined by Rosenberg, self-esteem is a positive attitude toward the self. Persons with high self-esteem respect themselves, consider themselves worthy, and are self-satisfied.

10. Field-Dependence/Independence This concept is measured by the Group Embedded Figures Test (GEFT). The GEFT is a perceptual test that measures, in the strictest sense, the extent of competence at perceptual disembedding. This competence reflects a cognitive style that is characteristic of a broader dimension of personal functioning, psychological differentiation. Subjects able to perform the test well are called field-independent, are not likely to have problems in dependence in relationships, and are likely to have developed a strong sense of separate identity.

2.4.2. Alcohol Use Measures

There is some confusion in measuring in alcoholism research that stems from a lack of consensus about what is being measured (Babor, 1990; Murray, Barnes & Patton, 1994). As a result, rather than being tied to one theoretical approach and therefore restricted by measurement limitations, we have selected a variety of measures from clinical work, sociological approaches, and psychological approaches.

Alcohol use and alcoholism were measured by four instruments. Consumption was measured with the Volume-Variability Index (Cahalan & Cisin, 1968; Room, 1972). This instrument contains twelve questions and measures the quantity and frequency of wine, beer and liquor consumption during the past month. This enables computing the number of ounces of ethanol per day consumed if we assume drinks contain 0.6 oz. of ethanol for beer and spirits and 0.64 oz. for wine. For each of wine, beer, and liquor, it also asks about the frequency of consuming eight or more drinks at a sitting, the variability or binge drinking aspect.

Also based on the work of Cahalan and Room (1974), a measure of the problems associated with alcohol use was adopted. They included being drunk for more than one day in a row, instances of heavy drinking, symptoms due to alcohol use, problems with controlling drinking, spousal complaints about drinking, problems at work due to drinking, problems with police due to drinking, health problems due to drinking, and accidents due to drinking.

Alcohol dependence was measured by the short version of the Alcohol Dependence Data Schedule (SADD) (Raistick, Dunbar, & Davidson, 1983). This scale is based on the construct of the alcohol dependence syndrome developed by Edwards (1986; Edwards & Gross, 1976) which is primarily a physiological definition of dependence. This emphasis is reflected in the items.

Alcoholism was measured by the short form of the Michigan Alcoholism

Screening Test (SMAST) (Pokorny, Miller, & Kaplin, 1972), a test intended to screen individuals in the general population and one which has been widely used in other studies. This instrument has proven as effective as the longer version in screening for alcoholism (Selzer, Vinokur, & Rooijen, 1975). A lifetime diagnosis of alcohol abuse or dependence was obtained from the National Institute of Mental Health Diagnostic Interview Schedule Version III Revised (DIS III-R) (Robins, Helzer, Cottler, & Goldring, 1989). This measure provides a diagnosis that is consistent with the American Psychiatric Association's definition of alcohol abuse that emphasizes impairment in occupational and social functioning.

3. Wave 2

3.1. Wave 2 Procedures

A summary of some initial project results was sent to participants about six months after the completion of interviewing. To maximize the response rate at Wave 2, those who had responded to Wave 1 were contacted by phone about one and a half years after their first interview. The purpose of the call was to verify that they could be reached and to confirm that we had a current telephone number and address.

Participants were then contacted two years after their first interview, and a second interview was scheduled. The target date was the second anniversary of their first interview, and a window was defined as the interval of time from 23 months to 25 months after. The goal was to conduct the second interview in this window, with the result that we initially proceeded to try to establish an appointment closer to the 23 month end of the window. At the Wave 2 contact, participants were again contacted by letter about a week in advance of the phone call. Then the phone scheduler, who was not one of the interviewers, would establish an appointment for an interview in the participant's home or, occasionally, in some other place acceptable to the participant. Because the interviewers were newly hired for Wave 2, participants were not interviewed by the same person who had interviewed them at Wave 1. Participants who could not be contacted by telephone were sought through the contact people whose names had been given at Wave 1. Participants whose precontact letters had been returned by the post office and people whom we otherwise had no success in reaching were identified to the Motor Vehicle License Bureau and/or the Manitoba Health Services Commission (where we had obtained the original list) and/or were sought in the city directory.

Eventually we were able to reinterview 988 of the original 1257 Wave 1 respondents, 96% of these in window. Less than 10% ($n = 121$) refused to participate the second time, 57 could not be found, and 83 were known to have moved out of town. Eight participants were no longer available, four had died, and four were in institutions.

3.2. Materials in Wave 2

The questionnaires used in Wave 2 were the same as those in Wave 1 with the following exceptions. Self-report health questions were asked only in Wave 2 (e.g., "Have you ever had any heart trouble?"). Questions about illness and the death of people close to the participant were asked only in Wave 2.

The DIS-III-R questions were asked in their proper format and all in one section in Wave 2. In Wave 1, these questions were scattered throughout, arranged according to their similarity to other questions from other scales. This also meant that the answer format of the questions changed depending on where they were located in the survey.

In Wave 1, a series of questions concerning family of origin was asked. Participants were asked about the number and potential alcohol abuse of their biological brothers, sisters, aunts, and uncles. In addition, each subject completed the parental MAST for both mother and father. To avoid being redundant, these questions were dropped at Wave 2.

Given the two-year time span between waves, a number of questions were included in Wave 2 regarding changes in personal and spousal employment, changes in personal marital status, and changes in the number of people living in the participant's household during the two years of the study.

Only in Wave 1 were participants asked questions concerning religious preference, parents' religion, primary language spoken in the family of origin (for respondent and for parents), country of birth (respondents' and parents'), cultural affiliation (respondents' and parents'), racial affiliation, and the size of the place where the participant grew up.

Only in Wave 1, participants were asked to identify their relationship to each person living in their household and that person's age, sex, and employment status. All Wave 1 personality scales were included in Wave 2.

4. Comparison of Reinterviewed Participants with Those Not Reinterviewed

To illustrate the characteristics of the subset of respondents who completed interviews in the second wave, Table 3.4 shows the demographic characteristics of (A) those who completed Wave 1, (B) the characteristics at Wave 1 of those participants who would complete Wave 2, and (C) the Wave 2 characteristics of Wave 2 participants. Men and women in columns B compared with those in columns A reflect the differences between Waves 1 and 2 but on the same set of Wave 1 variables. This comparison directly addresses the differences between Wave 1 and Wave 2 samples. Any analysis of change that uses repeated measures and therefore requires nonmissing data from both waves will use data from columns B and C.

Table 3.4. Percentage of Respondents in Various Demographic Groups by Gender, Comparing Wave 1, the Wave 1 Responses of Wave 2 Participants, and Wave 2 reponses

	A. Wave 1 responses		B. Wave 2 Subset of Wave 1 responses		C. Wave 2 responses	
	Men (n = 615)	Women (n = 642)	Men (n = 476)	Women (n = 506)	Men (n = 476)	Women (n = 506)
Age (in years)	42.5	39.5	42.6	40.8		
Marital status						
Single	21.3	17.9	19.7	18.0	15.8	15.8
Married	72.7	70.4	74.2	71.2	77.6	72.9
Divorced	1.0	3.4	1.3	3.4	2.3	3.6
Widowed	5.0	8.3	4.8	7.5	4.4	7.7
Education						
Some grade school	1.8	2.6	1.1	1.8	1.3	0.8
Grade school	3.6	3.3	3.2	2.4	1.3	2.6
Some high school	19.0	19.9	17.4	19.6	18.3	18.8
High school	22.0	26.2	21.2	26.1	21.4	27.2
Some college	26.5	25.4	28.2	25.9	26.3	24.8
University grad.	15.9	16.5	17.2	17.2	18.9	19.4
Some postgraduate	3.6	3.6	3.4	4.2	4.8	3.8
Master's/doctorate	7.6	2.5	8.4	3.0	7.8	2.6
Family Income						
< $10,000	3.4	4.4	2.4	4.4	2.8	3.8
$10,000–$19,999	5.2	9.7	4.6	9.5	5.4	12.0
$20,000–$34,999	21.0	24.3	21.4	27.6	16.1	22.6
$35,000–$49,999	25.4	21.8	27.2	26.0	23.7	26.5
$50,000+	40.5	28.0	44.4	32.5	52.0	35.0
Employment status						
Working full time	75.0	42.1	74.8	42.7	75.4	43.9
Working part time	3.6	20.6	4.0	20.4	2.3	19.4
Unemployed	4.4	5.0	3.4	4.3	1.7	4.0
Student	6.2	5.4	5.9	6.1	5.9	4.4
Homemaker	0	18.7	0	18.8	0	17.8
Retired	8.3	6.4	9.0	5.7	10.9	7.5
Other	2.6	1.9	2.7	2.0	3.8	3.2
Religious preference						
Catholic	25.9	32.4	25.7	31.7		
Protestant	39.0	43.4	40.8	43.2		
Jewish	2.4	3.0	2.9	3.6		
Other	12.1	10.6	10.3	1.6		
None	20.6	10.6	20.2	1.6		
Ethnicity						
White	92.5	91.6	94.7	92.7		
Black	1.6	0.8	1.1	0.6		
Asian	3.7	4.2	3.2	3.6		
Native	1.1	1.9	1.1	1.6		
Other	1.0	1.6	0	1.6		

To maximize the indication of any differences between those Wave 1 participants who were reinterviewed in Wave 2 and those who were not, the data in columns B were compared with data from the cases from column A that were *not* present in column B, aggregating men and women together. ANOVA was used to compare differences between means of continuous measures. The number of respondents in the various categories of marital status, employment status, and ethnicity were compared across the groups with chi-square tests. There is no difference between the two groups on age ($F(1,1250) = .31$, n.s.), however, people who were reinterviewed are more educated ($F(1,1255) = 23.7, p < .001$) and have a higher family income ($F(1,1151) = 16.8, p < .001$). There is no difference on employment status ($\chi^2_{(2)} = 2.87.$, ns), gender ($\chi^2_{(1)} = 0.21$, ns), marital status ($\chi^2_{(3)} = 3.26$, ns), or race ($\chi^2_{(1)} = 5.59$, ns). It may be that those with lower income are more likely to have moved in the two-year interval. Although efforts were made to contact respondents who had moved (including calling relatives and friends and searching for new addresses through the motor vehicle licensing bureau), they may be more difficult to track down. Less educated people may also have been more skeptical about participating in scientific research, that is, they may have been less able to understand the overall significance of the first wave of the study and may have been less willing to invest more time in the project.

Differences between reinterviewed and not reinterviewed respondents in personality were compared with ANOVA. The means and standard deviations are presented in Table 3.5. People who were not interviewed twice are lower in ego strength ($F(1,1223) = 14.4, p < .001$), higher on the EPQ-L ($F(1,1223) = 7.94, p < .01$), higher on the EPQ-P ($F(1,1223) = 19.67, p < .001$), are more field-dependent ($F(1,1223) = 9.26, p < .01$), higher on the MacAndrew Scale ($F(1,1223) = 10.68, p < .001$), and are more trait anxious ($F(1,1223) = 5.45, p < .01$).

Differences between participants reinterviewed and not reinterviewed on the primary alcohol variables are shown in Table 3.6. The two subsamples are similar

Table 3.5. Means and Standard Deviations on Personality Measures

	Reinterviewed		Not reinterviewed	
	Mean (SD)		Mean (SD)	
EPQ-P	3.86	(2.78)	4.65	(3.14)
EPQ-E	13.82	(4.96)	14.38	(4.57)
EPQ-N	10.32	(5.41)	10.16	(5.59)
EPQ-L	9.6	(4.39)	10.6	(4.85)
Ego strength	45.06	(6.03)	43.49	(5.93)
MacAndrew Scale	21.45	(3.86)	22.27	(3.88)
Self-esteem	33.12	(4.54)	32.63	(4.53)
Field dependence	8.23	(5.18)	7.06	(5.57)
Trait anxiety	35.06	(8.41)	36.39	(8.64)
Vando augmenter–reducer	21.61	(9.03)	22.39	(9.29)

Table 3.6. Comparison of Respondents Who Were Reinterviewed with Those Who Were Not on Alcohol Use, Dependence, and Alcoholic Diagnosis[a]

	Reinterviewed ($n = 982$)		Not reinterviewed ($n = 275$)	
Oz. of ethanol per day	.50	(.98)	.71	(1.78)
DIS-III-R lifetime diagnosis of abuse or dependence	1.25	(.71)	1.34	(.75)
Ten-item MAST score	1.21	(3.58)	2.08	(4.94)*
Alcohol dependency (SADD)	1.43	(2.39)	2.27	(4.85)*
Sum of problems due to alcohol	.75	(1.51)	1.19	(2.23)*
More than eight drinks per occasion	28%		32%	
Drunk more than one day in a row	4%		7%	

[a]Comparisons were made with t-tests for independent samples in the case of continuous variables and χ^2 tests for categorical variables. Significant comparisons are indicated with *, $p < .01$. The effect size indices (ω^2) for the three significant variables were .012 for the MAST, .018 for the SADD, and .017 for the sum of problems.

in volume of alcohol consumed, lifetime DIS-III-R diagnosis of abuse or dependence, and the reports of two indices of drinking pattern: the consumption of more than eight drinks per occasion and being drunk more than one day in a row. The subsample not reinterviewed scored higher on the 10-item MAST, the alcohol dependence scale (SADD), and the sum of problems due to alcohol.

4.1. Logistic Regression Analysis of Nonresponse

To consider the effect of nonresponse in a multivariate fashion, multiple logistic regression models were estimated for those Wave 1 respondents who responded to Wave 2 versus those who did not. Men were considered separately from women. Two sets of independent variables were entered separately. The demographic variable set included age, married status, educational status, and categories of income. The alcohol variable set included the DIS-III-R score, drinking of more than eight drinks per occasion, the number of ounces of ethanol consumed per day, the 10-item MAST score, the alcohol dependence score, total problems due to alcohol, and the MacAndrew Scale of the MMPI.

We were interested in whether the alcohol set of variables would improve the model created with the demographic variables, that is, once the difference between those who responded to Wave 2 and those who did not was characterized by demographic variables, would the addition of alcohol variables improve the description. We were particularly interested to see that Wave 2 respondents and nonrespondents were not significantly differentiated by their use and the consequences of alcohol.

In the models of men's data, the demographic model was significant ($\chi^2(4) = 21.9$, $p < .001$) and the improvement in the model from adding in the block of alcohol variables was not significant ($\chi^2(7) = 5.7$, $p = .57$). Educational status and income made significant contributions to the demographic model ($p < .01$ and $p = .01$), but none of the alcohol variables made significant contributions to the combined model.

In the models for women, the demographic model was of marginal significance ($\chi^2(4) = 8.3, p = .08$), and the addition of alcohol variables did not significantly improve the model, although the improvement in the model approached significance ($\chi^2(7) = 13.4, p = .06$). No variable made a significant contribution to the combined model.

We concluded that respondents and nonrespondents, whether male or female, were not significantly differentiated by alcohol variables when the models were adjusted by demographic characteristics.

5. Summary

The survey obtained its sample from what was then the Manitoba Health Services Commission and conducted 1257 initial interviews which were generally representative of other studies of Winnipeg. The study used broadly accepted procedures for contacting and interviewing participants and contained standardized measures of alcohol consumption, alcohol dependence, personality, and other constructs. For the measurement of personality, multiple measures of similar constructs were typically used.

Two years later a second survey was conducted with many (78.6%) of the same participants. Differences in the content of the measures are described. A detailed analysis of the differences between Wave 1 and Wave 2 participants is provided. People who were reinterviewed are more educated, have higher incomes, and have lower indicators of involvement with alcohol. The personality differences are also described. The differences between those who responded to Wave 2 versus those who did not were described by both univariate and multivariate models.

4

Prevalence

1. Objectives

1. To compare the prevalence of alcohol consumption and dependence reported by the Winnipeg Health and Drinking Survey with the results of other major surveys.

2. To describe in detail the prevalence of consumption levels, pattern, problems, and dependence, adjusted by demographic characteristics.

The Winnipeg Health and Drinking Survey (WHDS) was designed to incorporate widely used definitions of alcohol consumption and dependence. This enables comparison of our survey results with those in other jurisdictions to confirm the validity of our measurements. Published data on consumption and on dependence in the adult general population in 1989/90 when we collected our Wave 1 data are shown in Tables 4.1 to 4.3. A National Alcohol and Other Drugs Survey was conducted in 1989 by Health and Welfare Canada, and it serves as a primary comparison source for alcohol consumption (Eliany, Giesbrecht, Wellman, & Wortley, 1992). U.S. national surveys have been conducted by the Alcohol Research Group (ARG) in Berkeley, CA, and the National Institute on Alcohol Abuse and Alcoholism (NIAAA) in Bethesda, MD. The West North Central region in the 1984 ARG survey (loosely equivalent to the U.S. Midwest) has been selected as a comparison to our results (Hilton, 1991). Although their territory is geographically different from ours, our measures of consumption are largely modeled on theirs. The Midwest Region of the NIAAA 1992 National Longitudinal Alcohol Epidemiologic Survey (NLAES) was also selected for comparison to our results. This survey includes measures of alcohol use and DSM-IV alcohol dependence. Bland, Orn, and Newman (1988) conducted a community study of

Table 4.1. Percent Current Drinkers in the WHDS Compared to Other Surveys Comparable in Time and Population

Survey	Source	Year	Population	Percent current drinkers
1. WHDS		1989/90	Winnipeg ages 18–65	87.7
2. NADS	Eliany et al. (1992)	1989	Manitoba ages 15+	79
3. ARG	Hilton (1991)	1984	U.S. West North Central ages 14+	80
4. NLAES	Grant (1997)	1992	U.S. Midwest ages 18+	N/A
5. Bland	Bland et al. (1988)	1983/86	Edmonton ages 18+	N/A

psychiatric disorders, including alcohol abuse/dependence in Edmonton. The definition they used was based on the DSM-III rather than the DSM-III-R used in our study.

The prevalence of current drinkers in the WHDS is higher than in the other community surveys shown in Table 4.1. This discrepancy may have as much to do with our truncation of the age distribution to focus on the years where drinking is more prevalent, rather than on other differences intrinsic to geography.

Although researchers in major surveys use predominantly similar questions, their definitions of what constitutes heavy drinking, for example, often pose frustration in attempts to compare results. Drinking behavior is complex, of course, and each report highlights those aspects that its authors select as important. In Table 4.2, the listed definitions are only vaguely comparable. In this context, the WHDS definition is indicative of more extreme behavior. Our question wording does not permit a closer comparison to the other surveys. The WHDS did not have a question about 5+ drinks at a sitting. Two of these comparison studies included the estimation of DSM abuse or dependence, as shown in Table 4.3.

Considering definitional and demographic differences among these three studies, we regard these prevalence estimates as sufficiently similar to represent confirmation of our procedures. That said, we proceed to describe the Winnipeg prevalences in more detail. Our pattern of display is modeled on a report of alcohol use in Canada by Kellner (1997). Each alcohol use attribute (for example, the occurrence of lifetime abstainers in Table 4-4), has a calculated odds ratio for its occurrence (Kellner used risk ratios). Then with the sample broken down by a

Table 4.2. Percent of Current Drinkers Who Report Heavy Drinking by Some Definition in the Year Preceding the Survey

Survey	Definition of heavy drinking	Frequency	Percent heavy drinkers
1. WHDS	8+ drinks at a sitting	Once a week or more	5
2. NADS	5+ drinks per occasion	6+ times in the past year	26
3. ARG	5+ drinks at a sitting,	once a week or more	16

Table 4.3. Prevalence of Lifetime Alcohol Abuse or Dependence among Adults in Winnipeg, the U.S., and Edmonton

Survey	Definition of abuse or dependence	Percent of men	Percent of women
1. WHDS	DSM-III-R	23.3	7.6
4. NLAES for total U.S.	DSM-IV dependence	18.6	8.4[a]
5. Bland et al.	DSM-III	29.3	6.7

[a]The NLAES gives odds ratios by region but not prevalence. The odds ratio for lifetime dependence is 1.12 (1.02–1.25) for the Midwest vs the South.

standard set of demographic characteristics, the odds ratio for the occurrence of the attribute is calculated for each demographic subset separately. Adjusted odds ratios are provided by logistic regression analyses. In a given table (for example, Table 4.4), the odds ratio of, say, 18–34 year olds versus all others for being lifetime abstainers is adjusted by each of the other demographic characteristics in the table. In practice, this involves a logistic model including 18–34 year olds and $n - 1$ levels of the other demographic descriptors as covariates and lifetime abstainer status as the outcome variable. The adjusted odds ratio from such a model is the antilog of the regression coefficient for 18–34 year olds.

Adjusted odds ratios are sometimes quite different from unadjusted odds ratios. Where sample size is small or where the odds ratio does not differ much from 1.0, the adjusted odds ratio may not be significant. These nonsignificant odds ratios are shown in the tables but should not be interpreted as carrying useful information.

From Table 4.4, then, lifetime abstainers are much more likely to be female, older, to use a language at home that is other than English, French, Ukrainian or German, and to be a current nonsmoker. In this table, as it happens, the adjusted odds ratios lead to the same general conclusions as the unadjusted odds ratios.

Table 4.5 describes those who report themselves as former drinkers versus others in the sample. Former drinkers tend to be characterized by a low (less than secondary) educational level. Survey participants where incomes between are $35,000 and $50,000 are less likely than others to be former drinkers. No other demographic characteristics led to significant odds ratios.

Table 4.6 describes the prevalence of light drinkers (0.05 to 0.57 ounces of ethanol per day) in the sample. Women who are current drinkers are more likely to be in the light category, as are married respondents. No other demographic characteristics distinguish those who report light drinking.

Table 4.7 describes medium (between 0.58 and 1.49 ounces of ethanol per day) drinkers. Men have higher odds than women of being medium drinkers. In a dichotomy, the odds ratio for one category is the reciprocal of the odds ratio for the other category. On no other demographic variable are the odds ratios signifi-

Table 4.4. Lifetime Abstainers Versus the Rest by Sex, Age, Language, Marital Status, Education, Income, and Smoking Status

Variable/Category	n	Percent	Odds ratio	Adjusted odds ratio
Overall	1257	4.1		
Sex				
Male	615	1.3	0.18	.15[a]
Female	642	6.7	5.45	6.67[a]
Age				
18–34	450	2.2	0.42	0.43
35–49	401	3.0	0.65	0.68
50–65	406	7.1	2.90	2.70[b]
Language				
English	931	2.3	0.23	.30[a]
French	59	5.1	1.28	1.10
Ukrainian	49	4.1	1.01	.62
German	72	11.1	3.32	2.15
Other	146	11.6	4.17	3.91[a]
Marital status				
Single	246	2.8	0.64	1.88
Married/Equivalent	872	4.8	2.11	1.01
Widowed	28	3.6	0.87	.64
Divorced/Separated	84	1.2	0.27	.28
Education				
Less than secondary	316	5.4	1.52	1.36
Secondary	303	3.3	0.76	.83
Some post-secondary	326	4.3	1.08	1.34
University degree	312	3.2	0.73	.62
Income				
<$20,000	143	3.5	0.95	.62
≥$20,000 and <$35,000	285	4.6	1.38	.95
≥$35,000 and <$50,000	296	4.7	1.47	1.80
≥$50,000	429	2.3	.52	.55
Current smoker				
Yes	347	0.3	.05	.07[b]
No	910	5.5	20.0	1.43[b]

[a]$p < .001$; [b]$p < .01$.

cantly different from 1, meaning, for example, in describing medium drinkers versus others, that young, middle, and older aged respondents did not differ significantly in their odds of having this attribute.

Table 4.8 differentiates heavy (> 1.49 ounces of ethanol per day) from other categories of drinkers. Again, not many of the demographic covariates distinguish attributes of this group. The sex attribute is associated with a very high odds ratio, however. Men are four times as likely as women to be heavy drinkers. With respect to marital status, single respondents are twice as likely as other drinkers

Table 4.5. Former Drinkers Versus the Rest by Sex, Age, Language, Marital Status, Education, Income and Current Smoking Status

Variable/ Category	n	Percent	Odds ratio	Adjusted odds ratio
Overall	1257	8.3		
Sex				
Male	615	9.4	1.35	1.44
Female	642	7.2	0.74	0.69
Age				
18–34	450	4.7	0.43	0.50
35–49	401	8.7	1.09	1.26
50–65	406	11.8	1.90	1.30
Language				
English	931	8.1	0.90	1.22
French	59	11.9	1.53	1.27
Ukrainian	49	10.2	1.27	0.95
German	72	13.9	1.87	1.30
Other	146	4.8	0.53	0.45
Marital status				
Single	246	5.7	0.62	0.86
Married/ Equivalent	872	8.4	1.04	1.07
Widowed	28	7.1	0.85	0.52
Divorced/ Separated	84	13.1	1.75	1.26
Education				
Less than secondary	316	14.6	2.59	2.09[a]
Secondary	303	5.0	0.51	0.63
Some postsecondary	326	6.7	0.75	0.79
University degree	312	6.7	0.75	0.83
Income				
<$20,000	143	12.6	1.77	1.83
≥$20,000 <$35,000	285	10.5	1.48	1.35
≥$35,000 <$50,000	296	4.1	0.40	0.41[a]
≥$50,000	429	7.9	0.95	0.97
Current Smoker				
Yes	347	8.1	0.96	0.83
No	910	8.4	1.04	1.20

[a] $p < .01$.

to drink heavily. Married respondents are less than half as likely as other respondents to drink heavily.

Table 4.9 describes drinkers of 8 or more drinks at a sitting, once a year or more compared to other drinkers. The criterion of eight or more drinks is a high level compared to most other surveys, so that more extreme behavior is required in our study for individuals to be counted. The criterion of once a year or more is less stringent than in most other studies, so that individuals in whom this behavior is quite rare are still counted. These comparisons are evident from Table 4.2.

Table 4.6. Light Drinkers Versus Other Current Drinkers by Sex, Age, Language, Marital Status, Education, Income and Current Smoking Status

Variable/ Category	n	Percent	Odds ratio	Adjusted odds ratio
Overall	1102	43.4		
Sex				
Male	549	36.6	0.58	0.55[a]
Female	553	50.1	1.74	1.81[a]
Age				
18–34	419	44.6	1.09	1.21
35–49	354	42.4	0.94	0.88
50–65	329	42.9	0.97	0.95
Language				
English	835	43.4	1.00	1.01
French	49	42.9	0.98	0.95
Ukrainian	42	45.2	1.08	1.10
German	54	46.3	1.13	1.21
Other	122	41.8	0.93	0.89
Marital status				
Single	225	38.2	0.77	0.68
Married/Equivalent	757	45.7	1.36	1.75[a]
Widowed	25	32.0	0.61	0.56
Divorced/Separated	72	33.3	0.63	0.55
Education				
Less than secondary	253	41.1	0.89	0.88
Secondary	278	40.6	0.86	0.81
Some postsecondary	290	44.8	1.08	1.09
University degree	281	46.6	1.19	1.25
Income				
<$20,000	120	40.0	0.85	0.93
≥$20,000 <$35,000	242	46.7	1.19	1.31
≥$35,000 <$50,000	270	40.4	0.84	0.79
≥$50,000	385	44.7	1.08	1.06
Current Smoker				
Yes	318	44.0	1.04	1.15
No	784	43.1	0.96	0.87

[a]$p < .001$.

Note that our frequency is once a year or more in Table 4.9 and once a week or more in Table 4.2. The result in Table 4.9 is that a third of our participants qualify for designation as drinkers of eight or more drinks at a sitting. Those included range from individuals who frequently abuse alcohol to those who lose control at a wedding reception once a year. Accompanying this somewhat unique definition are quite a number of highly significant covariates.

In Table 4.9, men are six times as likely as women drinkers to report eight or more drinks at a sitting. Eighteen to 34 year olds are three times as likely as other age groups combined to report this pattern of drinking, and 50 to 65 year olds are

Table 4.7.–Medium Drinkers Versus Other Current Drinkers by Sex, Age, Language, Marital Status, Education, Income and Current Smoking Status

Variable/Category	n	Percent	Odds ratio	Adjusted odds ratio
Overall	1102	22.6		
Sex				
Male	549	25.9	1.45	1.51[a]
Female	553	19.3	0.69	0.66[a]
Age				
18–34	419	23.9	1.12	1.12
35–49	354	24.0	1.13	1.11
50–65	329	19.5	0.77	0.79
Language				
English	835	23.8	1.36	1.27
French	49	20.4	0.87	0.93
Ukrainian	42	23.8	1.07	1.24
German	54	13.0	0.50	0.53
Other	122	18.9	0.78	0.80
Marital status				
Single	225	24.4	1.14	1.01
Married/Equivalent	757	21.8	0.87	0.84
Widowed	25	24.0	1.08	1.41
Divorced/Separated	72	26.4	1.25	1.44
Education				
Less than secondary	253	20.9	0.88	0.97
Secondary	278	24.8	1.18	1.18
Some postsecondary	290	22.4	0.99	0.94
University degree	281	22.1	0.96	0.91
Income				
<$20,000	120	20.8	0.88	0.90
≥$20,000 <$35,000	242	20.2	0.83	0.82
≥$35,000 <$50,000	270	23.3	1.05	1.03
≥$50,000	385	24.4	1.17	1.19
Current Smoker				
Yes	318	23.3	1.06	0.99
No	784	22.3	0.95	1.01

[a]$p < .01$.

about a third as likely as other age groups to report it. Those respondents who speak English at home are twice as likely as others to report eight or more drinks at a sitting. Germans, somewhat surprisingly, are about a quarter as likely as other drinkers to report doing so. In Manitoba, a high proportion of those using the German language are Mennonites and Hutterites. Both of these groups have fairly strict religious objections to the liberal use of alcohol.

Married drinking participants are half as likely as those with other marital statuses to report eight or more drinks at a sitting, whereas single drinkers are somewhat less than twice as likely to report it. Drinking more than eight drinks

Table 4.8. Heavy Drinkers Versus Other Current Drinkers by Sex, Age, Language, Marital Status, Education, Income and Current Smoking status

Variable/ Category	n	Percent	Odds ratio	Adjusted odds ratio
Overall	1102	20.1		
Sex				
Male	549	30.1	3.81	4.03[a]
Female	553	10.1	0.26	0.25[a]
Age				
18–34	419	21.2	1.13	0.85
35–49	354	18.1	0.83	0.90
50–65	329	20.7	1.06	1.32
Language				
English	835	20.2	1.05	0.96
French	49	18.4	0.89	1.0
Ukrainian	42	11.9	0.53	0.54
German	54	18.5	0.90	0.85
Other	122	23.0	1.21	1.38
Marital status				
Single	225	29.8	1.99	2.24[a]
Married/Equivalent	757	16.6	0.53	0.42[a]
Widowed	25	16.0	0.75	1.05
Divorced/Separated	72	26.4	1.47	2.06
Education				
Less than secondary	253	21.3	1.11	1.13
Secondary	278	21.6	1.13	1.22
Some post-secondary	270	20.0	1.00	0.96
University degree	281	17.4	0.80	0.76
Income				
<$20,000	120	21.7	1.12	0.99
≥$20,000 <$35,000	242	19.0	0.92	0.85
≥$35,000 <$50,000	270	20.0	1.00	1.12
≥$50,000	385	20.3	1.02	1.00
Current Smoker				
Yes	318	22.3	1.21	1.15
No	784	19.1	0.82	0.87

[a]$p < .001$.

characterizes those with low (less than secondary) education, whereas those with one or more university degrees are less likely than others to report it. Finally, smoking tends to co-occur with reports of eight or more drinks.

Current drinkers who have problems related to their use of alcohol are described in Table 4.10. The definition of problems that was used included mention of any of the following: being drunk for more than one day in a row; having eight or more drinks at a sitting; drinking enough to get high or tight; having symptoms due to alcohol use (drink first thing in the morning, take a few quick drinks before going to a party, sneak drinks, tend to drink more when by oneself, take a drink to

Table 4.9. Drinkers of Eight or More Drinks at a Sitting Once a Year or More Versus Other Drinkers by Sex, Age, Language, Marital Status, Education, Income and Current Smoking Status

Variable/ Category	n	Percent	Odds ratio	Adjusted odds ratio
Overall	1102	33.1		
Sex				
Male	549	47.4	3.84	6.22[a]
Female	553	19.0	0.26	0.16[a]
Age				
18–34	419	48.7	3.08	3.19[b]
35–49	354	28.8	0.75	0.83
50–65	329	17.0	0.31	0.35[a]
Language				
English	835	37.5	2.48	2.15[a]
French	49	22.4	0.57	0.60
Ukrainian	42	19.0	0.46	0.68
German	54	11.1	0.24	0.26[b]
Other	122	22.1	0.54	0.63
Marital status				
Single	225	56.0	3.40	1.74[b]
Married/Equivalent	757	25.9	0.36	0.50[a]
Widowed	25	24.0	0.63	1.26
Divorced/Separated	72	40.3	1.39	2.02
Education				
Less than secondary	253	34.4	1.08	1.67[b]
Secondary	278	40.3	1.52	1.43
Some postsecondary	290	38.3	1.36	1.16
University degree	281	18.6	0.40	0.36[a]
Income				
<$20,000	120	39.2	1.33	0.99
≥$20,000 <$35,000	242	36.0	1.16	1.00
≥$35,000 <$50,000	230	31.5	0.89	0.92
≥$50,000	385	31.2	0.85	1.12
Current Smoker				
Yes	318	46.5	2.27	1.91[a]
No	784	27.7	0.44	0.52[a]

[a]$p < .001$; [b]$p < .01$.

get rid of a hangover, blackouts); problems with control (staying drunk when there is an important reason to stay sober, drink until passing out, have kept on drinking when promised yourself not to, thought really ought to cut down drinking, and found that you couldn't); problems with spouse (worry or complain about your drinking, drinking created problems between you and spouse or other near relative); problems at work (lost a job because of drinking, got into trouble at work because of drinking); problems with police (arrested for drunk driving, any other kind of trouble with the law); health problems (did the doctor ever tell you

Table 4.10. Current Drinkers Reporting Any Problems Due to Alcohol in the Past Wear by Sex, Age, Language, Marital Status, Education, Income and Current Smoking Status

Variable/ Category	n	Percent	Odds ratio	Adjusted odds ratio
Overall	1102	29.6		
Sex				
Male	549	38.8	2.47	3.11[a]
Female	553	20.4	0.41	0.32[a]
Age				
18–34	419	41.1	2.39	1.89[a]
35–49	354	24.9	0.71	0.81
50–65	329	20.1	0.50	0.64
Language				
English	835	31.1	1.38	1.03
French	49	28.6	0.95	1.11
Ukrainian	42	26.2	0.84	1.29
German	54	18.5	0.53	0.63
Other	122	25.4	0.79	1.01
Marital status				
Single	225	50.2	3.15	2.00[a]
Married/ Equivalent	757	23.0	0.38	0.49[a]
Widowed	25	32.0	1.12	1.62
Divorced/ Separated	72	34.7	1.29	1.50
Education				
Less than secondary	253	29.6	1.00	1.04
Secondary	278	35.3	1.42	1.32
Some postsecondary	290	30.7	1.07	0.97
University degree	281	22.8	0.63	0.73
Income				
<$20,000	120	41.7	1.86	1.38
≥$20,000 <$35,000	242	32.2	1.19	1.04
≥$35,000 <$50,000	270	26.3	0.81	0.85
≥$50,000	385	26.0	0.76	0.89
Current Smoker				
Yes	318	42.1	2.25	2.05[a]
No	784	24.5	0.45	0.49[a]

[a]$p < .001$.

that drinking was having a bad effect on your health); or accidents (an accident or injury of some kind either at work, at home, on the street or some place else). This definition of problems due to alcohol is so inclusive that 30% of our sample of drinkers reported at least one instance in the past year.

In Table 4.10, men are three times as likely as women to report problems due to alcohol. The young age category is nearly twice as likely to report problems as other categories. Single individuals are twice as likely as others to report alcohol problems, whereas married individuals are half as likely. It is interesting that education and income do not appear to be related to the odds of experiencing problems with alcohol. Finally, smokers are twice as likely as nonsmokers to report problems with alcohol.

Table 4.11 reports the odds of a lifetime diagnosis of alcohol abuse or dependence by the various demographic characteristics. The definition was obtained from the DSM-III-R by using the DIS-III-R interview schedule (Robins et al., 1989). Men are 4.5 times more likely to be diagnosed in the general population

Table 4.11. Participants Estimated To Have a Lifetime Diagnosis of Alcohol Abuse or Dependence by Sex, Age, Language, Marital Status, Education, Income and Current Smoking Status

Variable/ Category	n	Percent	Odds ratio	Adjusted odds ratio
Overall	1257	15.3		
Sex				
Male	615	23.3	3.67	4.55[a]
Female	642	7.6	0.27	0.22[a]
Age				
18–34	450	22.0	2.17	1.77[b]
35–49	401	14.2	0.88	1.00
50–65	406	8.9	0.43	0.51[b]
Language				
English	931	17.9	2.63	2.13[b]
French	59	18.6	1.29	1.61
Ukrainian	49	12.2	0.77	1.05
German	72	2.8	0.15	0.18
Other	146	4.1	0.21	0.25[b]
Marital status				
Single	246	27.6	2.73	1.70
Married/ Equivalent	872	11.8	0.45	0.59[b]
Widowed	28	21.4	1.53	2.55
Divorced/ Separated	84	15.5	1.02	1.04
Education				
Less than secondary	316	15.8	1.06	1.32
Secondary	303	16.5	1.13	0.97
Some postsecondary	326	16.3	1.11	0.94
University degree	312	12.5	0.74	0.86
Income				
<$20,000	143	22.4	1.72	1.49
≥$20,000 <$35,000	285	16.1	1.09	1.04
≥$35,000 <$50,000	296	14.5	0.93	0.98
≥$50,000	429	14.2	0.88	0.91
Current smoker				
Yes	347	24.5	2.43	2.07[a]
No	910	11.8	0.41	0.48[a]

[a]$p < .001$; [b]$p < .01$.

than are women. This difference, based on adjusted odds ratios, is greater than the difference in raw prevalence rates between men and women but is quite consistent with Bland et al.'s (1988) results reported in Table 4.3. Other differences are reasonably consistent with the prevailing understanding. The young are more likely to be diagnosed than other ages; the old are less likely to be diagnosed. This downward gradient with age, observable in our raw prevalence results as well, is ironic in a diagnostic indicator that ought in principle to be cumulative with increasing age. Also in Bland et al.'s 1988 report, the trend is generally downward with increasing age. Bland et al. suggest that the selective removal of older cases due to mortality and changing social phenomena of recent years such that currently older alcoholics may have had less access to alcohol when they were younger than currently young alcoholics (a cohort effect), may help explain this counterintuitive trend.

English speakers are twice as likely to be diagnosed alcoholic as those who speak other languages, for reasons that are unknown. Those in the "other" language category are only 25% as likely to be alcoholic. This result appears to be consistent with the performance of the "other" language respondents in Table 4.4, who are four times as likely as others to be lifetime abstainers. Married respondents are less likely than others to be diagnosed. As with alcohol problems, education and income appear to make no difference to diagnosis, and current smoking is strongly related. Smokers are twice as likely to be DSM-III-R positive with respect to alcohol.

In Chapter 3, Table 3.4, we described the demographic characteristics of Wave 1 and Wave 2 participants. During a 2-year interval, shifts appeared in the demographic profile of even those people who responded to both waves. There were fewer single men and women, and correspondingly more were married. More were both widowed and divorced.

Men and women who responded to both waves ($n = 982$) are compared in Table 4.12 for prevalence of drinking status and consequences of drinking. Some of these differences may be due to actual differences in status, but some are likely due to forgetting, to respondent bias, and to minor changes in question response scale wording. In Wave 2 versus Wave 1, there are a few less men and women who reported the intermediate category of drinking (0.58–1.48 oz. per day), and a few more reported that they did not drink during the past year. The reports of consumption of eight or more drinks at a sitting are infrequent and consistent from Wave 1 to Wave 2. Reports of some problems were also consistent from Wave 1 to Wave 2. The exceptions were staying drunk more than one day in a row, problems with spouse and accidents which decreased in both genders, and loss of control which increased in both genders.

Table 4.12. Prevalence of Drinking Status and Consequences of Drinking at Wave 1 and 2 among 982 Respondents, in Percent

Drinking history	Wave 1		Wave 2	
	Men	Women	Men	Women
Never drank alcohol	1.3	5.7	1.9	5.3
Drank but not in the past year	9.5	7.1	11.6	13.4
Drank < 0.58 oz. per day	40.3	61.7	41.3	58.8
Drank 0.58–1.49 oz. per day	22.7	17.4	18.3	14.2
Drank > 1.49 oz. per day	26.3	8.1	26.9	8.3
Drank ≥ 8 drinks per occasion in the past year	5.5	1.6	3.8	2.0
Problems with drinking				
Stayed drunk more than one day in a row	8.6	3.0	3.4	1.4
Instances of heavy drinking	5.3	2.1	6.0	2.7
Symptomatic drinking	17.0	7.3	16.6	9.1
Loss of control	8.0	5.3	12.4	6.1
Problems with spouse	25.2	8.1	17.2	4.5
Problems at work	4.0	0.6	3.4	0.2
Problems with police	0.8	0.0	0.8	0.0
Health problems	32.8	41.7	13.4	17.2
Accidents due to drinking	3.4	6.9	14.1	17.4
Total	476	506	476	506

2. Summary

As closely as can be ascertained, the prevalence of consumption of alcohol and of dependence correspond well with other studies that used comparable measures. Adjusted odds ratios were calculated in detail. Lifetime abstainers are more likely to be female, older, to use a language other than English or another European one at home, and not to smoke cigarettes. Heavy drinkers, on the other hand, tend to be single men. Drinkers of eight or more drinks at a sitting tend to be young, English-speaking, single, smoking men. Drinkers with evidence of dependence tend to be young, English-speaking, not married, smoking men.

5

Personality and Alcohol Abuse Results

In this chapter the relationship between personality and alcohol use and abuse is investigated in the general population data set described in the previous chapter. The main objectives in this chapter are described here:

1. Objectives

1. Examine the pattern of correlations between personality and the various measures of alcohol consumption problems and abuse. Based on the literature review presented in Chapters 1 and 2, it was anticipated that higher alcohol use and abuse would be associated with higher psychoticism, more extraversion/stimulus reducing, higher neuroticism, lower ego-strength, and more field dependence.
2. Develop structural equation models to test the longitudinal relationship between latent personality factors and latent alcohol use and abuse factors. For these analyses, it was anticipated that personality dimensions asssociated with prealcoholic traits, such as psychoticism, would predict the development of alcohol abuse.
3. Examine the stability of the personality and alcohol use and abuse relationship across gender and age groups.
4. Develop structural equation models examining the relationship between alcohol abuse and changes in personality in the longitudinal data set. For these analyses, it was anticipated that alcohol abuse over time might contibute to the development of clinical alcoholic traits such as higher neuroticism.

The primary methodology used in these analyses is that of linear structural equation modeling, which has become social and behavioral science's most successful methodology for specifying and evaluating causal hypotheses, especially with nonexperimental data. In a cross-sectional anaysis, a typical model is the confirmatory factor analysis model that attempts to explain the interrelationships among the observed data variables on the basis of hypothesized latent variables or factors. In this type of measurement model, it is presumed that the factors and errors of measurement generate the observed variables. With longitudinal data, the direction of the causal flow across time makes possible stronger models with specified directions of causal flow among the latent variables. In general, a model consists of a set of hypotheses about the influences of sets of variables and hypothesized latent factors on other variables or latent factors. These hypotheses can be represented visually in a path diagram, such as are used in this book, or equivalently, as a series of simultaneous regression equations with covariance specifications among independent variables. These provide the technical means for estimating the parameters of a model, the standard errors of those parameter estimates, and goodness of fit statistical tests for evaluating the plausibility of the model. Automatic means of translating a diagram into equations for model testing are provided with EQS for Windows (Bentler & Wu, 1995), which was used for the analyses in this book.

Good introductions to structural equation modeling are given by Dunn, Everitt, and Pickles (1993), Byrne (1994), Hoyle (1995), Mueller (1996), Schumacker and Lomax (1996) and, as part of a popular text on multivariate statistics, by Ullman (1996). Austin and Calderon (1996) provide an annotated bibliography of the field. In preliminary models, we use the standard maximum likelihood (ML) method based on the normality assumption. This always provides excellent parameter estimates, but statistical tests may be distorted when data are nonnormal. Bentler and Dudgeon (1996) and Yuan and Bentler (1997) review statistical issues and alternatives for obtaining good inferences, especially with data that contain badly distributed variables. We accept the ML estimates but in final models also make extensive use of two features of EQS, the Satorra–Bentler (1994) chi-square statistic, which is the most reliable statistic for evaluating models with nonnormal data (e.g., Hu, Bentler, & Kano, 1992; Curran, West, & Finch, 1996), and robust standard errors that correct for nonnormality. Although significance tests on parameter estimates are done in the original metric of the variables, we typically describe results based on the corresponding standardized solution in which all variables have unit variance. This is appropriate because most variables have arbitrary scales, and the results are easier to interpret: path coefficients represent standardized regression coefficients.

The models that we estimate are based on a large number of variables whose interrelationships are to be explained by models containing relatively few parameters. For example, a model with 35 variables has 630 variances and covariances to be modeled. If a parsimonious model contains about 100 free parameters, it will have a very large number (over 500) degrees of freedom. Because every degree of freedom implies a potential way to be incorrect in precisely modeling the 630 data points, it is inevitable that in such large models even the most well thought-out model will contain sources of misspecification. Thus a strict null hypothesis model test is unreasonable in such a case: "It is more realistic, however, to assume that the model yields a fairly good approximation but does not fit exactly in the population" (Browne & Arminger, 1995, p. 195). As a result, the chi-square test of model fit should be considered primarily a guide to model quality and not a strict test. Even if a strict test were available, there is strong reason to believe that the proposed test statistics will not behave according to the nominal chi-square distribution with such large degrees of freedom and with sample sizes of about 1000 subjects. As noted by Yuan and Bentler (in press),

> Outside the standard linear model, the distributions of most goodness of fit test statistics are approximated by chi-square distributions. However, these approximations can be very poor, especially when the models have very large degrees of freedom. This problem occurs even for fairly large samples. In covariance structure analysis, which is usually used for high dimensional data analysis, this problem is serious.

Thus, we interpret the chi-squares in a relative sense and augment our model evaluation with fit indexes that transform the chi-square values into a more meaningful 0–1 metric. Among the many alternative indexes that have been proposed, the Comparative Fit Index (Bentler, 1990), which assesses fit by comparing the current model to a baseline model of uncorrelated variables, remains a good choice (Hu & Bentler, 1995). It will be used extensively.

2. Analytical Strategy

The first step in developing of these models involved examining the data distributions. In addition to age and gender, ten personality scales, seven alcohol use measures for Time 1 and Time 2, and five variables related to family drinking history were used in the data analyses. A summary of the statistical characteristics of these variables is presented in Table 5.1. To facilitate the structural equation modeling, a number of transformations were performed on these variables to produce a set that would not be extremely different in their distributions. The variables measuring the percentages of in-laws, siblings, and grandparents with drinking problems and their ages were divided by 10 to yield a manageable score range. Occupational classifications were derived from the Statistics Canada Occupational Classification Index, and the code obtained was also divided by ten.

The second stage of the data analyses involved computing correlations between the Time 1 personality measures and the Time 1 alcohol measures. The

Table 5.1. Characteristics of Variables Used in the Structural Model (after Data Imputation and Transformations)[a]

	Mean	No. of items	Range	SD	Skew	Kurtosis
Age[a]	4.18	1	1.8–6.7	1.33	.04	−1.17
Gender	.49	1	0–1	.50	.04	−2.00
Socioeconomic indicators						
Education	13.26	1	6–20	2.85	.30	.29
Income	3.77	1	.5–5	1.27	−.88	−.12
Occupation	8.14	1	1–16	4.10	.04	−1.17
Family background						
Mother's MAST	.39	13	0–11	1.38	4.75	24.46
Father's MAST	1.60	13	0.12	2.82	1.97	3.04
Sibs alc.[b]	1.29	1	0–10	2.67	2.22	4.02
Inlaws alc.[b]	1.10	1	0–10	1.62	2.38	6.28
Gprts alc.[b]	.77	1	0–10	1.62	3.37	13.70
Personality measures						
EPQ-E	13.94	23	0–23	4.87	−.32	−.53
EPQ-P	4.04	34	0–17	2.88	.95	1.05
EPQ-N	10.29	24	0–24	5.44	.32	−.58
EPQ-L	9.82	21	0–21	4.50	.19	−.70
Field dep.	7.98	25	0–18	5.31	.14	−1.15
R-A scale	21.77	54	3–47	9.04	.40	−.54
Ego strength	44.38	67	22–59	5.96	−.48	.23
Self-esteem	33.03	10	10–40	4.52	−.44	.48
Trait anx.	35.35	20	20–69	8.45	.72	.47
MacAndrew	21.10	54	8–36	4.03	.27	.38
Alcohol measures - time1						
Heavy drinking	.32	3	0–39	2.33	12.10	177.19
Get drunk	.65	1	0–30	1.97	9.28	121.90
Oz./day	.55	1	0–15.8	1.21	7.61	77.92
Maxever[b]	1.09	1	0–9.7	1.01	2.39	9.88
MAST	.84	13	0–13	1.76	3.06	10.92
SADD	1.61	15	0–38	3.11	4.47	33.93
DSM symptoms	1.92	9	0–9	2.41	1.31	.75
Probhist	1.51	14	0–14	2.46	2.20	4.94
Alcohol measures - time2						
Heavy drinking	.24	3	0–30	1.64	10.51	142.96
Get drunk	.69	1	0–30	2.94	7.96	71.43
Oz./day	.52	1	0–16.4	1.08	7.64	88.47
MAST	1.01	1	0–5	.64	1.29	5.13
SADD	.83	13	0–19	2.07	3.51	15.35
DSM symptoms	.84	15	0–9	1.58	2.39	6.17
Problems	.34	9	0–11	.99	4.30	24.70

[a]*Education* is years of education; *income* is in $10,000 units; *occupation* is based on the Statistics Canada occupational classification index; *mother's MAST* and *father's MAST* are the respondents' report of parents' drinking on the short MAST; *sibs.alc., inlaws alc.*, and *gprts alc.* are the proportion of known siblings, biological aunts and uncles, and biological grandparents who have had problems with alcohol; *heavy drinking* refers to the number of days month when more than 8 glasses of beer, wine, and/or liquor were consumed; *get drunk* refers to the number of days/month when

results of these correlational analyses are presented in Table 5.2. These correlations, along with the standard deviations in Table 5.1, represent the data to be modeled.

The next step in the data analyses involved testing the hypothesized structural equation model. These analyses were conducted in several stages. Preliminary confirmatory factor analyses using EQS and maximum likelihood estimation procedures were conducted within each level of the model (I. Sociodemographics, II. Personality, III. Time 1 Alcohol Measures, IV. Time 2 Alcohol Measures) to establish measurement models at each level in the analysis. Modifications of the hypothesized measurement models were guided by theory and empirically by using the Lagrange Multiplier and Wald tests. After modifications were made to the preliminary measurement models, the full structural equation model for Wave 1 was produced in the following manner.

1. The hypothesized factor to factor paths and factor to variable paths were entered, and the resulting model was evaluated.
2. The Lagrange Multiplier and Wald tests were used along with the theory to modify the structure.
3. Possible correlated error paths were tested using the Lagrange Multiplier test, and where these paths seemed appropriate theoretically, they were added.
4. Maximum likelihood robust statistics were computed. Robust statistics adjust the maximum likelihood standard errors and test statistics for violation of the assumption of distributional normality.
5. Gender was removed from the model, and separate analyses were conducted within gender to determine whether the relationships were stable across gender.
6. Then the stability of the model was tested across the three age groups (18–35, 36–49, 50–65).
7. After the models testing the prediction that personality would predict alcohol use and abuse were examined, the reverse models in which alcohol measures were used to predict Time 2 Personality were explored.

---

subject became intoxicated; *oz./day* represents ounces of absolute alcohol consumed per day on average; *SADD* refers to alcohol dependency as measured by the short form of the Alcohol Dependency Data questionaire; *MAST* refers to the 13-item Michigan Alcoholism Screening Test,; *maxever* reflects the largest number of drinks ever consumed in one day; *DSM symptoms* is a variable that reflects level of severity in terms of dependence symptoms; *probhist* refers to lifetime prevalence of negative consequences due to drinking; *problems* refers to negative consequences due to drinking between the two waves of data collection.
*b*These items were rescaled by dividing the scores by 10.

Table 5.2. Correlations Between Wave 1 Personality and Drinking Measures (WHDS Wave 1 Sample)

Variable	$r(t_1, t_2)$	HEAV_DRK	GET_DRNK	Ethanol	Maxever	DSMSX	SADD	RMAST13	PROB-HIST
EPQE	.82	.11	.12	.12	.21	.18	.11	.08[b]	.12
VANDO	.85	.13	.18	.19	.41	.33	.24	.13	.24
MAC	.70	.21	.19	.18	.29	.32	.23	.28	.33
EPQ-P	.68	.17	.18	.13	.23	.30	.25	.22	.25
EPQ-L	.81	-.07[a]	-.08[b]	-.06[a]	-.23	-.28	-.19	-.14	-.22
EGOST	.74	-.09[b]	-.03[c]	.02[c]	.13	-.05[c]	-.11	-.11	-.09[b]
EPQ-N	.80	.11	.09[b]	.05[c]	.04[c]	.20	.21	.18	.21
Esteem	.69	-.08[a]	-.09[b]	-.05[c]	.01[c]	-.11	-.12	-.14	-.14
Anxiety	.78	.14	.11	.09[b]	-.01[c]	.14	.18	.15	.15
GEFT	.76	-.05[c]	.02[c]	-.01[c]	.11	.05[c]	.01[c]	-.04[c]	.02[c]

[a] $p < .05$.
[b] $p < .01$.
[c] not significant; all others are significant at the $p < .001$ level.

The first stage in developing the longitudinal model was to test the original Wave 1 model on the reduced longitudinal sample. Then the Wave 1 structural model was used as the basis for developing the longitudinal model, and alcohol use and problems at Time 2 were added as a fourth level in the model. This model was modified using procedures similar to those described before. Then the model was tested for stability across age groups by running a multiple group model and testing the constraints that the measurement and structural paths were the same across all three age groups.

3. Results

3.1. Correlational Analyses

The results in Table 5.2 show that extraversion is positively correlated with all of the alcohol measures at Time 1 and the highest correlation occurs with the maximum ever consumption variable. The Reducer–Augmenter Scale showed a similar, but somewhat stronger pattern of correlation with the alcohol measures. The Ego-Strength Scale was weakly negatively correlated with alcohol abuse measures but had a significant positive correlation with the maximum amount of alcohol ever consumed. Self-esteem was also negatively correlated with all of the alcohol abuse measures but was not significantly correlated with average ethanol consumption or maximum ever consumed. The Eysenck P Scale and the MacAndrew Alcoholism Scale were both significantly correlated with all of the alcohol measures, and high scores were associated with high alcohol consumption and abuse. The Neuroticism Scale was positively correlated with alcohol abuse measures but not with alcohol consumption measures. Trait Anxiety followed this same pattern, except for a weak positive correlation with average ethanol consumption. The Group Embedded Figures Test was not significantly correlated with any of the alcohol measures, except for a weak positive correlation with the maximum amount of alcohol ever consumed. High scorers on the Lie Scale reported fewer symptoms and problems associated with alcohol abuse, lower consumption levels, and differed marginally in the amount of alcohol they reported consuming. The correlational patterns between personality characteristics and alcohol measures are generally consistent with our hypotheses with the notable exception that field dependence (the Group Embedded Figures Test) was not correlated very strongly with the alcohol measures.

3.2. Structural Equation Models

The final structural equation model for the overall sample is presented in Figures 5.1 to 5.4. Paths not shown on the diagram are summarized in Table 5.3. Al-

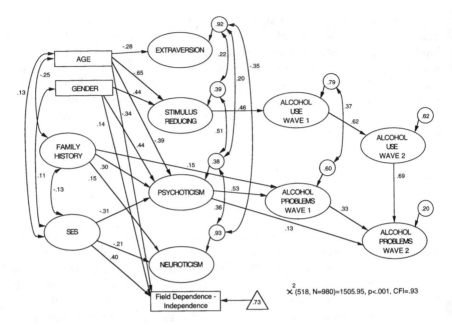

Figure 5.1. Structural equation longitudinal model: relationships among demographics, personality, and drinking.

though there is only one model, different components of the model are shown in separate figures for ease of presentation and discussion of results. Although the model fits the data quite well with a Comparative Fit Index (CFI, Bentler, 1990) of .93, the chi-squared value was still fairly high and significant (X^2 (518, n = 980) = 1505.95, p < .001). The ML-adjusted robust statistic yielded a Satorra–Bentler scaled chi-squared value of 1140.60. Although this value is still significant, the chi square to degrees of freedom ratio is now very close to the 2 to 1 ratio which we consider acceptable for a sample of this size. To test whether this

Table 5.3. Paths Not Shown on Any Diagram for the General Population Longitudinal Model

	MAC	EPQL	EGOST	EPQN	Maxever	RMAST13
Age	.35					.13
Gender				−.12	.23	
SES		−.35	.30			
Stimulus reducing					.20	
Alcohol problems						

[a]Correlated error paths (Heav_drk to Hev_drk2 = .26; Ethanol to Ethanol2 = .46; Probhist to RMAST13 = .48) also not shown on diagrams.

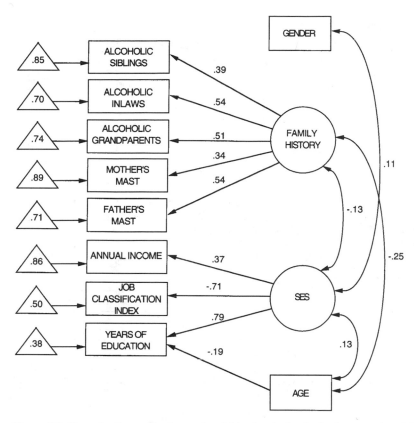

Figure 5.2. Factor loadings of background variables for the longitudinal structural model.

model applied equally well to both men and women, the gender effect was removed from the equation, and a two-sample model was run by gender. The results showed that although there were significant differences between gender
models (X^2 (55) = 202.35, $p < .001$), the fits of the constrained and unconstrained
models were close (.90 versus .91), and all major structural paths were similar for
both males and females.

In Figure 5.2 the relationships for the sociodemographic component of the
model are shown, including family history of alcohol abuse. As noted above, in
this and subsequent figures, standardized parameter estimates are shown for ease
of interpretation, though all significance tests were based on the unstandardized
solution.

The personality component of the structural model is shown in Figure 5.3.

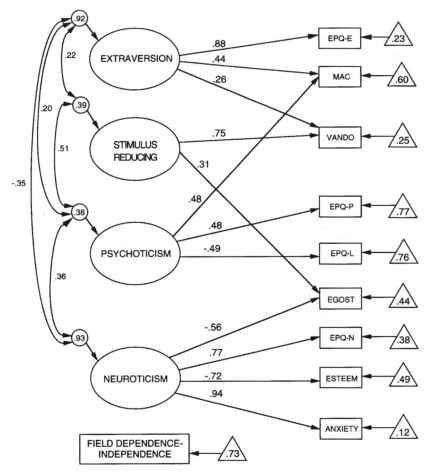

Figure 5.3. Factor loadings of personality variables for the longitudinal structural model.

For the most part, this model conformed to expectations. The three major Eysenck dimensions of Extraversion, Psychoticism, and Neuroticism formed latent variables. The Ego-Strength latent variable that was hypothesized, however, did not emerge as expected. Instead, both the Ego-Strength and Self-Esteem measured variables loaded heavily on the Neuroticism factor along with Eysenck's Neuroticism Scale and Trait Anxiety. Aside from Neuroticism, the latent variable that had the next strongest relationship with Ego Strength was much more strongly associated with the Vando Reducer–Augmenter Scale. Therefore, it was called the Stimulus-Reducing factor. The Lie Scale ended up being an indicator of Psychoticism, supporting an interpretation of this measure as an indicator of social conformity.

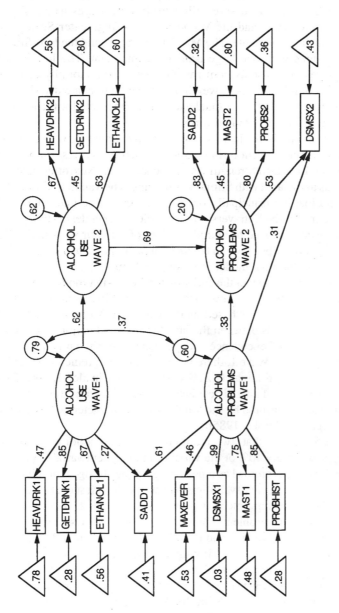

Figure 5.4. Factor loadings of alcohol variables for the longitudinal structural model.

Several personality variables other than Ego Strength were also functions of more than one latent variable. A factorially complex measurement structure was not surprising to us, and we were willing to allow measures such as Ego Strength, the MacAndrew Scale, and the Vando Reducer–Augmenter Scale to weigh on more than one latent variable. The MacAndrew Scale and the Ego-Strength Scale are not measures with one large principal component. The low reliabilities of these measures in this study confirms that these are factorially complex scales. By allowing complex scales to weigh on more than one latent variable, it is possible to improve the fit of the model and help compensate for the low reliabilities of the measures in their original form.

The MacAndrew Scale was positively associated with two latent factors, Extraversion and Psychoticism, and the strongest association was with Psychoticism. Low Ego Strength was associated with Neuroticism and high Ego Strength was associated with Stimulus Reducing. The Vando Reducer–Augmenter Scale, while loading principally on its own factor, also had a relatively minor positive loading on the Extraversion factor. Field Dependence-Independence as a measured variable proved to be independent of the four personality latent variables. The relationships between the alcohol factors and their indicators for Wave 1 and Wave 2 in the final model are shown in Figure 5.4.

The major pathways in the full structural equation model are shown in Figure 5.1, to which we return now. Secondary paths that were not in the original model and that were added based on the LaGrange Multiplier test are shown in Table 5-3. Correlations between the latent factors and major measured variables (Age, Gender, Field Dependence-Independence) are shown in Table 5.4. For the Alcohol Use factor at Wave 1, there is one significant predictor, Stimulus Reducing, that explains approximately 21% of the variance in alcohol use. This is given as 1.0 minus the standardized residual variance shown in the small circle. The stimulus reducer measured by the Vando scale is characterized by a high level of sensation seeking (Barnes, 1985b).

Figure 5.1 shows that two main predictors of alcohol problems at Wave 1 explain approximately 40% of the variance in this latent variable (1.0–.60 shown in the small circle, expressed as a percentage). The strongest predictor of alcohol problems at Wave 1 is the Psychoticism Factor, and high scores on this dimension are associated with more alcohol problems. At Wave 2, there are three major predictors of alcohol problems including: (1) Alcohol Use between waves, (2) Alcohol Problems at Wave 1, and (3) higher Psychoticism at Wave 1.

The effects of gender on drinking observed in this study are quite interesting. In Figure 5.1 there are no direct paths from gender to the main drinking latent variables. The effects of gender on drinking operate primarily through the personality characteristics of Stimulus Reducing and Psychoticism. Males are more inclined to score high on Stimulus Reducing and Psychoticism, and these characteristics in turn predict Alcohol Use and Alcohol Problems. It should be

Table 5.4. Correlations Among Latent Constructs and Major Measured Variables in Longitudinal Model[a]

	Age	Gend.	GEFT	Fam. Hist.	SES	Extra.	St. Red.	Psyc.	Neur.	Use W 1	Prbs W 1	Use W 2	Prbs W 2
Age	X												
Gend.	.00	X											
GEFT	-.29	.18	X										
Fam. Hist.	-.25	.00	.03	X									
SES	.13	.11	.37	-.13	X								
Extra.	-.28	.00	.08	.07	-.04	X							
St. Red.	-.65	.44	.26	.16	-.04	.31	X						
Psyc.	-.51	.41	.09	.44	-.35	.26	.71	X					
Neur.	-.06	-.02	-.07	.18	-.23	-.30	.03	.35	X				
Use W I	-.30	.20	.12	.07	-.02	.14	.46	.32	.02	X			
Prbs W I	-.31	.22	.05	.39	-.21	.15	.40	.60	.21	.44	X		
Use W II	-.18	.12	.07	.05	-.01	.09	.28	.20	.01	.62	.27	X	
Prbs W II	-.29	.21	.08	.21	-.12	.14	.41	.46	.12	.61	.59	.80	X

[a]Age=age of respondent; Gend.=gender; GEFT=group embedded figures test, a measure of field dependence; Fam. Hist.=family history of alcoholism; SES=socioeconomic status (based on education, income, and occupation); Extra.=extraversion; St. Red.=stimulus reducing; Psyc.=psychoticism; Neur.=neuroticism; Use W 1=alcohol use at wave 1; Prbs W 1=alcohol-related problems at wave 1; Use W 2=alcohol use at wave 2; Prbs W 2=alcohol-related problems at Wave 2.

noted, however, that not all of the effects of gender on drinking are mediated through personality. The results in Table 5.3 show that there is a significant direct path from gender to the maximum ever consumed variable (being female was associated with lower maximum levels of alcohol ever consumed).

The effects of Family History on Alcohol Use and Alcohol Problems observed here are also very interesting. The association between Family History and Alcohol Problems is explained partly by the association between Family History and Psychoticism. Subjects with a family history of alcohol problems are more likely to score high on Psychoticism, and high Psychoticism in turn predicts Alcohol Problems. There is also a direct path from Family History to Alcohol Problems. Subjects with a family history of alcohol abuse scored higher on the Alcohol Problems latent variable. Evidently not all of the effects of family history on drinking are mediated by personality.

The SES latent variable was associated only indirectly with alcohol factors. SES had a strong indirect effect on Alcohol Problems through its association with Psychoticism. Higher Psychoticism scores were observed in the lower SES subjects, and higher Psychoticism scores in turn predicted Alcohol Problems.

In the design of the WHDS, we proposed to examine the direction of the effects of personality and alcohol abuse in three different age groups, 18–34, 35–49, and 50–65, to approximate the effects that might be generated in a longer term project over this full period of the adult life span. We were also interested in testing the possible reverse model using alcohol use and abuse to predict changes in personality. A comparison of constrained versus unconstrained multiple sample models across the three age groups revealed significant differences (X^2 (124) = 837.71, $p < .001$) and a substantial decrement in the comparative fit of the constrained and unconstrained models (.83 versus .88). Although many of the structural paths were similar across all age groups, large differences in the measurement paths for the alcohol consumption factors across age groups necessitated running separate models within each age group. These results suggest that, although personality characteristics may have a large degree of stability over time, patterns of alcohol consumption vary substantially across different age groups. As age increases, commonality among the different measures of alcohol consumption decreases, and the distributions of drinking variables become more severely skewed and nonnormal.

In response to the analyses suggesting a poor fit of our overall model across the three age groups, separate models were developed within each age group. Modifications to the models were guided by the Lagrange and Wald tests to determine which paths needed to be added or dropped. Results of these analyses are presented in Figures 5.5 to 5.16 and Tables 5.3 to 5.7 where results are presented for each of the three age groups. These results show that the measurement paths for the demographic component of the model (Figures 5.6, 5.10, and 5.14) are comparable across groups except for a minor path between education and age

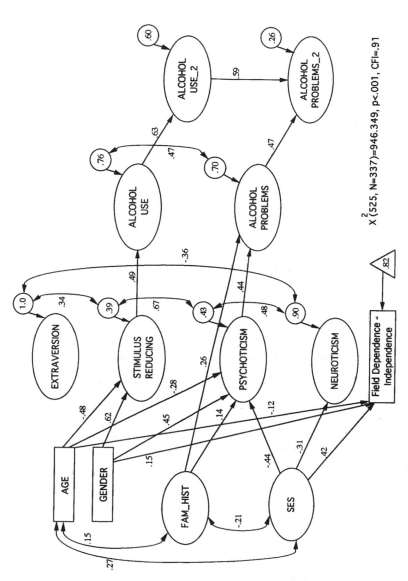

Figure 5.5. Structural equation longitudinal model: relationship between demographics, personality and drinking in the 18–34 age group.

$X^2 (525, N=337)=946.349, p<.001, CFI=.91$

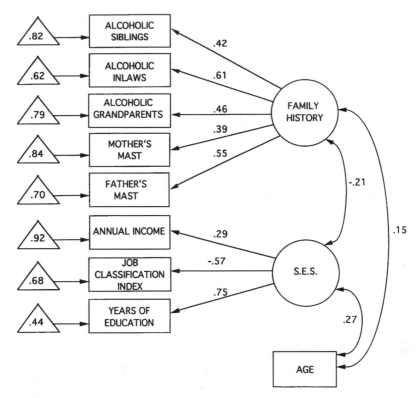

Figure 5.6. Factor loadings of background variables for the 18–34 age group in the longitudinal structural model.

which was significant only for the middle age group. Measurement paths for the personality factors (Figures 5.7, 5.11, and 5.15) were also consistent across the three age groups, though the residual correlation among stimulus-reducing and psychoticism factors was not significant only in the oldest age group. On the alcohol measures, the measurement paths varied somewhat in the different age groups (Figures 5.8, 5.12, and 5.16), and some of the heavy drinking or binge drinking measures contributed less to the alcohol factors in the older samples. It is also interesting and expected to note that alcohol use is much more stable in the older samples than in the youngest sample. Because of a different pattern of residual correlations among alcohol use and problems at Time 1, the demographic variables explain covariation between these two constructs differentially. In the young sample, this covariation is not all explained by its predictors, in the inter-

Table 5.5. Paths Not Shown on Any Diagram for the 18–34 Age Group[a]

	MAC	EPQL	EGOST	EPQN	Maxever	RMAST13
Age	.24					.09
Gender				−.17	.33	
SES		−.53	.36			

[a]Correlated error paths (Heav_drk to Hev_drk2 = .26; Ethanol to Ethanol2 = .42; Probhist to RMAST13 = .36) also not shown on diagrams.

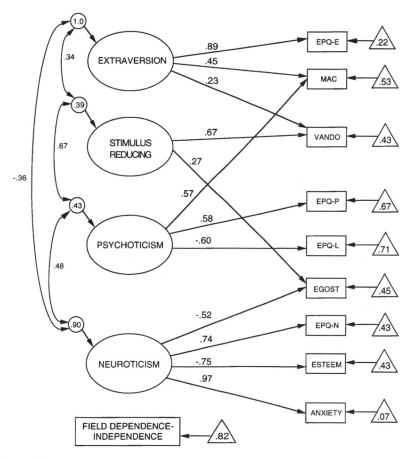

Figure 5.7. Factor loadings of personality variables for the 18–34 age group in the longitudinal structural model.

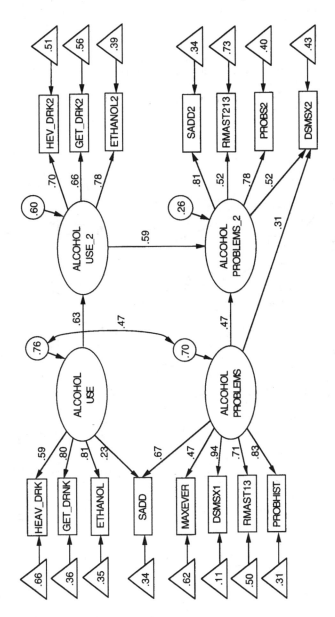

Figure 5.8. Factor loadings of alcohol variables for the 18–34 age group in the longitudinal structural model.

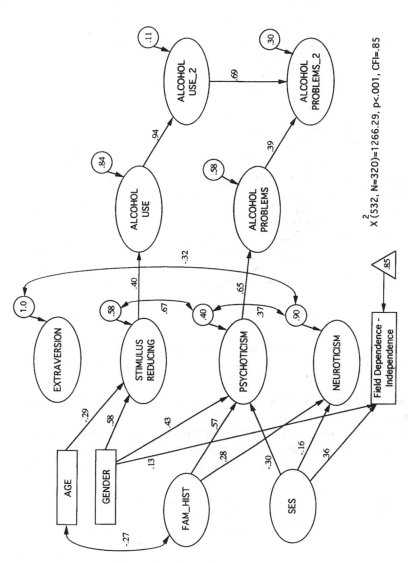

Figure 5.9. Structural equation longitudinal model: relationships among demographics, personality and drinking in the 35–49 age group.

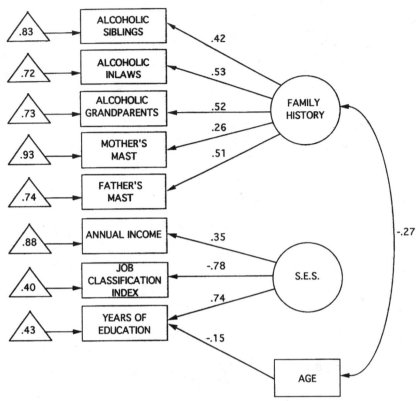

Figure 5.10. Factor loadings of background variables for the 35–49 age group in the longitudinal structural model.

mediate sample it is, and in the oldest sample there is an overprediction, and the residuals correlate negatively.

Major structural paths for the three different age groups are depicted in Figures 5.5, 5.9, and 5.13. These figures show that although there are some general consistencies in the structural paths across the three age groups, some differences

Table 5.6. Paths Not Shown on Any Diagram for the 35–49 Age Group[a]

	EPQL	EGOST	EPQN	Maxever	RMAST13
Age					.08
Gender			−.12	.28	
SES	−.34	.30			
Stimulus reducing				.19	

[a]Correlated error paths (Ethanol to Ethanol2 = .45; Probhist to RMAST13 = .40) also not shown on diagrams.

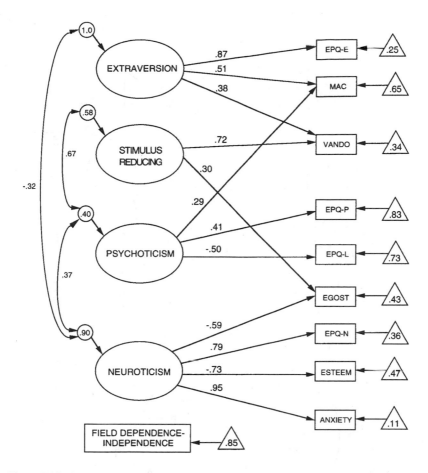

Figure 5.11. Factor loadings of personality variables for the 35–49 age group in the longitudinal structural models.

emerged as well. At the front end of the model, for example, the effects of family history are entirely mediated through the Psychoticism dimension in the two older samples, whereas this is not the case in the youngest age group. The effect of a family history of psychoticism was much weaker in the youngest sample than in the other two age groups. The effect of a family history of alcohol abuse on off-spring neuroticism occurred only in the oldest age group. In all three age groups, the primary pathways to addiction are maintained. Stimulus Reducing predicts consumption, and Psychoticism predicts problems. It is worth noting, however, that Stimulus Reducing or sensation seeking is a significantly stronger predictor of Alcohol Consumption in younger as opposed to older samples. In the older

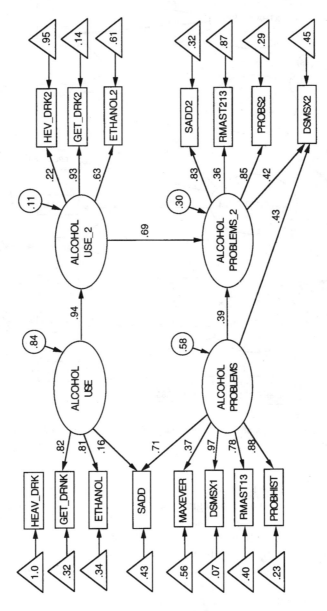

Figure 5.12. Factor loadings of alcohol variables for the 35–49 age group in the longitudinal structural model.

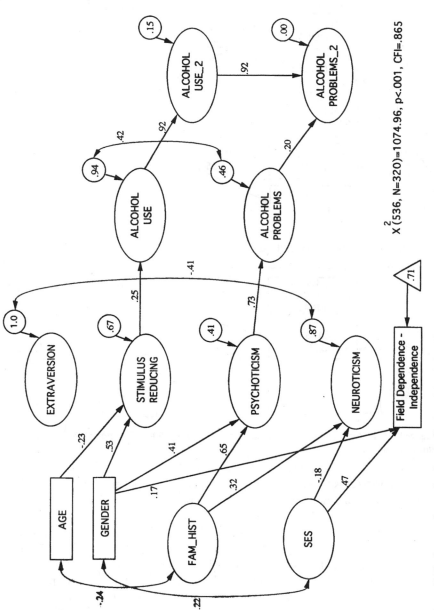

Figure 5.13. Structural equation longitudinal model: relationships among demographics, personality and drinking in the 50–65 age group.

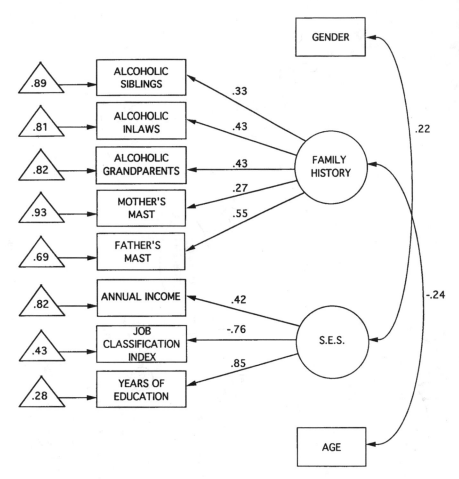

Figure 5.14. Factor loadings of background variables for the 50–65 age group in the longitudinal structural model.

samples, use seems to be very stable and becomes a stronger predictor of subsequent use, and current use becomes almost a perfect predictor of problems.

In the model described, personality is assumed to be causing changes in alcohol consumption and abuse. In this study, we also attempted to test a model predicting personality on the basis of earlier alcohol use and abuse, while controlling for personality at Wave 1. But these efforts met with limited success. Personality characteristics were extremely stable during the two-year period of the study (e.g., median test–retest correlations of .72). This made it virtually impossible to predict personality change. Nevertheless, a weak path from Alcohol Problems at Wave 1 to Psychoticism at Wave 2 occurred in this model. It is pos-

Table 5.7. Paths Not Shown on Any Diagram for the 50–65 Age Group[a]

	EPQL	EGOST	Maxever
Gender			.11
SES	−.22	.24	

[a]Correlated error paths (Ethanol to Ethanol2 = .68; Probhist to RMAST13 - .55) also not shown on diagrams.

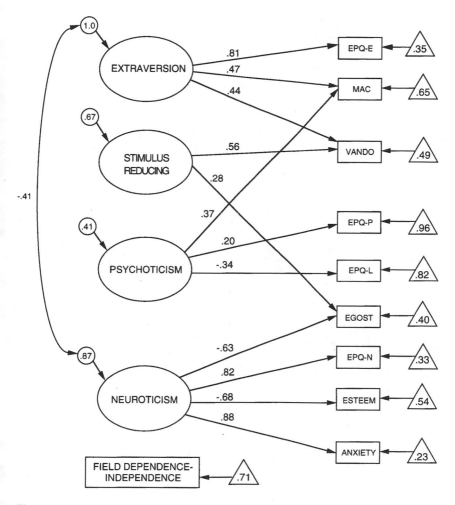

Figure 5.15. Factor loadings of personality variables for the 50–65 age group in the longitudinal structural model.

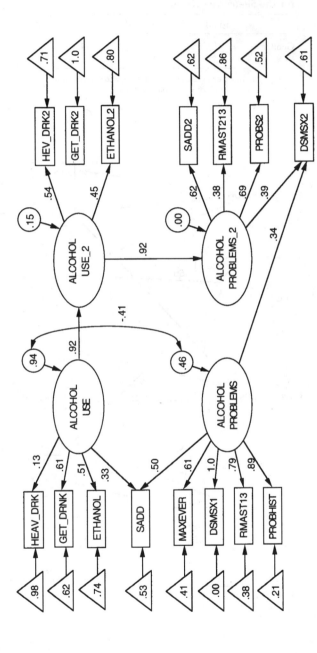

Figure 5.16. Factor loadings of alcohol variables for the 36–49 age group in the longitudinal structural model.

sible that, given a longer period of follow-up, more substantial influences of alcohol consumption patterns on personality will be detectable. A test of this hypothesis will be conducted when the third Wave of WHDS data are collected and analyzed. (See Figure 5.17 for the basic model without these reverse paths.) This will allow for a five-year time lag between Wave 2 and Wave 3 and a seven year time lag between Wave 1 and Wave 3.

4. Discussion

Prior to this study, there has not been much general population research on the association between personality and alcohol abuse. The Winnipeg Health and Drinking Survey is a unique study in many respects, and because of the longitudinal nature of the research, this survey makes a strong contribution to our understanding of the possible processes involved in developing of addiction to alcohol. Because the Winnipeg Health and Drinking Survey looked at alcohol abuse in a general population sample, the relationships that emerged between personality and alcohol abuse in this survey present a somewhat different picture than has typically emerged in studies employing clinical samples. For example, the relationship between field dependence and alcoholism is not a very important factor in our longitudinal study. This relationship has been repeatedly observed in clinical studies (Barnes, 1983). The fact that this relationship does not emerge in the general population research suggests that perhaps field dependence is a more important factor in predicting who will seek treatment or how they will respond to treatment than in predicting who will develop alcoholism.

In the clinical research and theorizing about addiction, tension reduction is frequently mentioned as an important factor in predicting addiction. In our longitudinal structural equation models, we did not find any paths from our neuroticism latent variable that predict alcohol use or abuse. We also examined major life events that occurred in the interval between our two points of data collection. These major life events were not predictive of alcohol abuse by themselves, in combination, or as moderating variables.

In the clinical research on addiction, alcoholics have generally been stimulus augmenters (Barnes, 1983). In our general population study alcoholics, were high on stimulus reducing, as measured by the Vando (1969) Scale. High scorers on the Vando (1969) Scale are characterized as sensation seekers (Barnes, 1985b). These results are consistent with Zuckerman's (1987) theory which suggests that alcoholics are high in sensation seeking. The results in the clinical literature may reflect (1) selection biases in these samples, (2) alcohol withdrawal effects, or (3) problems associated with the particular measures employed (e.g., some confusion exists in the augmenter–reducer literature regarding what constitutes an "augmenter" in the averaged evoked response procedure (see Davis et al., 1982)).

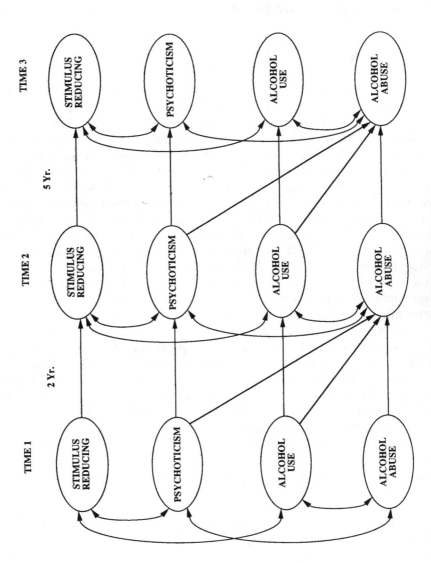

Figure 5.17. Wave III proposal design.

The results of our longitudinal analyses using structural equation modeling suggests that there are two primary pathways to alcohol abuse. These pathways apply in both men and women and across different age groups. In one of these pathways, people who are high in a dimension called psychoticism are at high risk of developing alcohol problems. These individuals have characteristics similar to those described by Cloninger when he talks about Type II alcoholics. These are individuals who are low on impulse control and are socially nonconforming. Their problems with alcohol abuse begin early and often occur in combination with other problems involving low impulse control. Our results showing this pathway are consistent with numerous other longitudinal studies that have shown a relationship between antisocial personality/behavior in early childhood and adult alcohol abuse (Barnes, 1983). This link is especially strong in the older age groups, where a family history of alcohol abuse is also a strong precursor of this relationship. It seems that the mediated effect of family history on alcohol problems, operating through psychoticism, takes time to develop.

The second pathway to alcohol abuse observed in our research leads from the personality trait of Stimulus Reducing to alcohol use, and then to alcohol abuse. This is an interesting pathway in that it seems as though individuals who start out with a healthy sensation-seeking appetite and relatively strong ego control may eventually become addicted to alcohol and suffer the harmful effects resulting from heavy consumption. This effect, of course, depends on age and gender, which are consistent predictors of stimulus reducing in all three models. Younger males are predicted to score highest on Stimulus Reducing.

Relationships between sensation seeking and the use of licit drugs including alcohol have been reported in numerous other studies (Jaffe & Archer, 1987; Newcomb & McGee, 1991; Zuckerman, 1983, 1987). Zuckerman (1987) has argued that the prealcoholic personality is characterized by extraverted, impulsive, and sensation-seeking traits rather than by anxiety. The theory of sensation seeking and drug abuse advocated by Zuckerman (1987) recognizes that reward seeking is the primary motivation behind sensation seeking and that alcohol stimulates the reward center of the brain much in the same way as other drugs. Three recent longitudinal investigations have supported this position (Cloninger, Sigvardsson, & Bohman, 1988; Masse & Tremblay, 1997; Newcomb & McGee, 1991). In the Newcomb & McGee (1991) research, sensation seeking predicted licit drug use (primarily alcohol use) in longitudinal analyses, as well as in cross-sectional analyses. Masse and Tremblay (1997) found that high novelty seeking at age six predicted the onset of substance use at age 11–15. Cloninger, Sigvardsson, and Bohman (1988) found that subjects who were high on novelty seeking at eleven years of age were at risk of alcohol abuse at age 27. In our own longitudinal analyses predicting Alcohol Use at Wave 2, however, we did not find any longitudinal paths from personality to Alcohol Use at Wave 2. The reason for this could be that we have included alcohol use in this analysis as a predictor at

Wave 1 and this is capturing most of the variance in predicting use at Wave 2. Our results also suggest that this relationship is strongest in the youngest age group and may be already well formed before the age at which our study began (age 18).

5. Summary and Conclusions

The first objective in this chapter was to examine the associations between personality and alcohol use and abuse patterns at Wave 1. The results of the correlational analyses were generally as anticipated. Personality measures that were more strongly linked with the "prealcoholic personality" included Stimulus-Reducing, Psychoticism, and the MacAndrew Alcoholism Scale. These were significantly correlated with most measures of alcohol consumption and abuse. Traits that are more strongly associated with the "Clinical Alcoholic Personality " such as low Ego Strength and high Neuroticism were more strongly correlated with measures of alcohol problems and abuse than consumption. The one major surprise in terms of the pattern of correlations was the weak association between field dependence and alcohol use and abuse. This relationship does not seem to have been examined previously in general population research, so the current investigation probably provides a more accurate estimate of this association than has been obtained in previous research.

The second objective in this investigation was to develop longitudinal structural equation models predicting Wave 1 and Wave 2 alcohol use and abuse. These analyses suggested that there are two major personality pathways predicting alcohol use and abuse. At Wave 1, Alcohol Use is strongly predicted by the Reducing–Augmenting factor and Alcohol Problems are strongly predicted by the Psychoticism latent factor. At Wave 2, Alcohol Problems are predicted primarily by consumption levels at Wave 1, and Psychoticism at Wave 1 also contributes. A Family History of Alcohol Abuse also plays an important role, and part of this prediction works through the Psychoticism dimension. The results of these analyses are consistent with previous longitudinal studies suggesting that psychoticism and sensation seeking are two of the primary dimensions associated with the development of alcohol and drug abuse.

The third objective in this investigation was to examine the stability of our structural equation models across age and gender. The results of the analyses conducted separately for males and females confirmed the importance of the personality pathways in predicting Alcohol Use and Problems for both genders. Prior research in the field of the relationship between personality and alcohol abuse has often failed to include females subjects, so the current investigation adds an important piece of knowledge to our understanding in this field. The results are also consistent with prior research by Barnes (1980) on the Clinical Alcoholic Personality which generally showed consistent results across gender. The structural equation models did not remain as stable across different age cohorts. The primary personality pathways seemed to remain, however, and the one major difference involving personality was a stronger link between the Reducing–Augmenting factor and Alcohol Use in the youngest cohort.

The final objective in this chapter was to examine the possible role of alcohol use and or abuse in predicting personality at Time II. The results of these analyses suggested that personality is very stable over the two-year period, and that a longer period of time might be required to detect any changes in personality resulting from alcohol use or abuse. For example, a weak (i.e., nonsignificant) association between alcohol abuse at Time 1 and P scale scores at Time 2 was evident in our data, and this trend might become stronger over a longer interval.

III

THE CLINICAL STUDY

6

Methodology of the Clinical Study

1. Introduction

The clinical study portion of the Winnipeg Health and Drinking Survey (WHDS) includes an add-on component intended to allow comparisons of demographic and personality differences between clinical substance abusers and individuals in the general population. The advantage of including data from a clinical sample is that independent variables that predict criterion variables of interest (e.g., alcoholism indicators) in the general population and discriminate clinical from general population groups can be isolated. Then, predictors of this sort can be interpreted as strong evidence for an overall relationship between the predictor and the criterion. For example, if it were found that field dependence predicts alcohol abuse in the general population and also discriminates clinical alcoholics from a matched comparison sample in the general population, then one would have stronger support for an association between field dependence and alcoholism than if field dependence discriminated alcoholics from a comparison sample, yet was not a predictor of alcohol abuse in the general population.

2. Description of the Clinical Treatment Program

Data gathered for the clinical portion of the WHDS was collected at the Alcoholism Foundation of Manitoba (AFM) programs at Winnipeg, Manitoba, in 1992. The AFM is a government-funded set of treatment programs designed to address the broadly defined problem of alcoholism, as it is likely to be manifested in a variety of individuals with differing treatment needs. As such, the AFM offers a variety of inpatient and outpatient programs, geared toward treating alcoholism *per se* and also the abuse of other substances.

All of the substance abusers who participated in the AFM clinical study were assigned to either residential or community-based treatment by the AFM. Residential treatment consisted of a treatment center offering a 21-day intensive program for men and another treatment center offering a 28-day intensive program for women. Criteria for admission to these programs were based on the individual's inability to remain drug-free, inability to function on a daily basis without using alcohol/drugs, inability to access community-based rehabilitation services in the home community, or an unstable or nonsupportive living environment. Community-based treatment consisted of 10 to 13 weeks of less intensive involvement. Admission to community-based treatment was limited to those who were deemed to have sufficient community resources and supports in place to maintain abstinence while living in the community.

Both residential and community-based treatment offered individual and group counseling sessions, lectures, film presentations, and discussion groups. Both also emphasized the establishment of links to various self-help and community groups/agencies for continued support during the rehabilitation process. Following treatment, clients were referred to aftercare services and encouraged to attend voluntarily.

Aftercare services offered by the AFM included ongoing group and individual counseling (on an outpatient basis). During counseling sessions, aftercare clients were given the opportunity to explore relapse issues, gain further support in problem solving (alcohol/drug-free), explore community supports that may not have been identified in primary treatment, and review family issues/concerns relative to support resources. Clients could remain in aftercare for as long as they felt necessary.

3. Procedure for Data Collection

All inpatient and outpatient groups were contacted for inclusion in the AFM study during their regular meeting sessions at the treatment center after their medical condition had stabilized (i.e., after they had completed detoxification, if necessary). The purpose of the study was explained to potential respondents in groups ranging in size from 3 to 15. They were told that this was a large study of the characteristics of substance abusers. They were informed that their responses would be grouped and compared with people not in treatment. Confidentiality and anonymity were assured, and all subjects were free not to participate without putting their treatment in jeopardy.

In the first wave of data collection, questionnaires were administered when consent was given. While the respondents were completing the questionnaires (in the group setting), a research assistant was present at all times to answer questions and ensure that questionnaires were filled out as completely and accurately as possible. For the follow-up, respondents were contacted by telephone, and the research assistant completed questionnaires based on oral responses. Data gathered at follow-up were not as extensive as at the initial interview; the chapter section on measures indicates which data were gathered at follow-up.

4. Sample Selection and Description

Only 3% refused to participate in the study. This high participation rate is probably due to the nonthreatening way in which the study was presented to the participants and due to the attitude of the treatment staff toward the project. Respondents were classified by the AFM according to whether they sought admission for problems due to alcohol only, drugs only, or alcohol and drugs. They were not given the DIS interview or any other screening test, such as the Michigan Alcoholism Screening Test (MAST; Pokorny, Miller, & Kaplin, 1972) because an alcoholism diagnosis was presumed if they were in treatment for alcohol-related problems, but they were given the Drug Abuse Screening Test (DAST; Skinner, 1982) and at the time of admission, were asked about their drug of choice. Alcohol consumption patterns in the months prior to treatment were also assessed.

Subjects who participated in the clinical study ($n = 420$) included all of the respondents who were classifiable into groups pertaining to the drug of choice (i.e., alcohol only, other drugs only, and alcohol as well as other drugs) based on their self-reported response to a question in which they were asked to select one of these three alternatives. Data from an additional 31 respondents had to be discarded because information regarding the drug of choice was not available. The final counts of respondents in each category included 270 abusers of alcohol only, 57 abusers of drugs other than alcohol only, and 93 abusers of alcohol and other drugs.

In the total clinical sample ($n = 420$), the mean age was approximately 38 years (SD = 10.9), and 72% was male. The sample was predominantly white (67%) but was also comprised of a large number of people of first nation (i.e., Native Indian) origin (22%); others in the sample were either black (1%) or classified themselves as "other" (10%). A majority of the sample (65%) was single (i.e., 37% never married, 25% divorced or separated, and 3% widowed), and the rest (35%) was married or equivalent. A total of 52% was either working (full or part time) or attending school (full or part time), 6% was homemakers, 5% was retired, 9% involved in "other" activities, and 28% was unemployed. On average, reported income was approximately $26,200 per year (SD = 17,400), and years of education were approximately 12 (SD = 2.7). A total of 61% was involved in the inpatient programs.

In terms of family history of alcohol abuse, the mean levels for percentage of siblings, in-laws, and grandparents who were considered alcoholic were 35% (SD = 38.7), 37% (SD = 34.9), and 12% (SD = 21.6), respectively. Mean levels for mothers' and fathers' 13 item MAST scores (as reported by the respondents) were 4.0 (SD = 3.2) and 3.6 (SD = 3.0), respectively.

At the six-month follow-up period, 71% (n = 297) was reinterviewed. The respondents who were reinterviewed at follow-up were more likely to be older, to have been married (or equivalent) at the time of initial interview, to be of higher average annual income, to have more years of education, and to have been working full time in the months prior to treatment. Those included in the follow-up were also less likely to be of first nation ancestry and reported lower percentages of in-laws who were alcoholic. Differences in many personality measures (but not in Extraversion, Neuroticism, Trait Anxiety, Ego Strength, GEFT, and Eysenck's Lie scale) and in alcohol-related problems at Wave 1, but not average ethanol consumption or heavy drinking, were also noted. Those not reinterviewed were typically more extreme in personality measures that were associated with alcoholism in the WHDS general population sample and reported having more alcohol-related problems in the months immediately preceding their participation in treatment. No differences were found in terms of gender, abuse of other substances prior to intake, or in terms of participation in residential versus community treatment. Those in the residential settings, however, were more likely to have participated in follow-up aftercare services that were offered as an optional adjunct to treatment.

5. Measures

5.1. Demographics

Demographic variables used in the analyses include age, gender, race, religious preference, marital status and socioeconomic status variables, including (1) yearly income level, (2) years of education, and (3) current employment status. Essentially, these are the same variables, as used in the WHDS general population sample, except for occupational classification. Although most of these demographics were assessed only once during the initial assessment, marital and employment status were also queried during follow-up to assess any changes.

5.2. Family History of Alcoholism

At the initial assessment, all respondents were asked to complete the 13-item MAST (Pokorny et al., 1972) with respect to the drinking behaviors of both their mothers and their fathers. In addition to the fathers' and mothers' MAST scores, variables indicating the percentage of siblings, in-laws, and grandparents, who were characterized as alcoholic by respondents, were created from the responses to questions about these different classes of family members.

5.3. Personality

At the first interview, personality characteristics were assessed via self-report. The personality questionnaire battery included the revised version of the Eysenck Personality Questionnaire (EPQ-R, Eysenck et al., 1985); two research scales from the MMPI, Ego Strength (Barron, 1953) and the MacAndrews Scale (MAC; MacAndrew, 1965); the Vando Reducer-Augmenter scale (VANDO; Barnes, 1985; Vando, 1969); the trait subscale of the State-Trait anxiety inventory (STAI-T; Spielberger et al., 1970); the Rosenberg (1965) Self-Esteem inventory; and a test designed to measure field dependence/independence, the Group Embedded Figures Test (GEFT; Witkin et al., 1971). The constructs measured by these tests are explained in Chapter 4.

5.4. Alcohol Measures

Three alcohol measures were used in both the initial assessment of drinking behavior and in the treatment follow-up. For the initial assessment, respondents were asked to consider the period of time "in the months prior to treatment." For the follow-up, six months after treatment ended, respondents were asked to consider the period of time since they completed treatment at AFM. All alcohol measures used in this study have been adapted from a series of questionnaires used by the Social Research Group at the University of California, Berkeley (Cahalan & Room, 1974).

The first of these drinking measures reflects the average daily amount of absolute alcohol that respondents reported drinking during the specified period. This measure was not the result of direct questioning. Rather it was calculated from the responses to questions pertaining to the frequency (in times per day/week/month) and quantity (in glasses) of alcohol consumed. The second alcohol measure pertains to instances of heavy drinking and is a composite variable that sums the responses to questions about the number of days per month that respondents had eight or more glasses of wine and/or beer and/or liquor at a sitting. For each class of alcohol, responses were coded to reflect the number of days in a month that they had eight or more drinks. In the composite variable, respondents who drank more types of alcohol heavily scored higher, as did respondents who reported more days per month drinking heavily. The third alcohol related measure is a composite variable that sums the number of positive responses to 15 questions concerning problematic drinking practices and negative consequences due to drinking.

5.5. Drug Measures

In addition to the alcohol measures above, respondents were given the Drug Abuse Screening Test (DAST; Skinner, 1982), and were asked, at the initial assessment, about their drug of choice. For the initial assessment, respondents were asked to consider the period of time "in the months prior to treatment." At follow-up, respondents were asked whether they used a variety of licit and/or illicit drugs "in the last six months." Licit drugs included aspirin or similar pain reliever; tranquilizers such as valium; diet pills or stimulants; antidepressants; or codeine, demerol, or morphine. Illicit drugs included marijuana or hash; cocaine or crack, LSD (acid), speed (amphetamines), or heroin. Although the responses pertaining to licit drug use were coded only in terms of "yes" or "no," responses involving illicit drug use were also coded in terms of frequency of use. Detailed analyses involving the patterns of licit and illicit substance use in the AFM clinical sample are beyond the scope of this book and will be published elsewhere.

7

Personality and Addiction in Clinical and General Population Samples

1. Objectives

In this chapter, the main objective is to combine the data from our general population and clinical samples to compare various groups in the clinical and general population samples. More specifically, the objectives are as follows:

1. To compare alcoholics in treatment with nonalcoholics in the general population. Although the bulk of the alcoholic personality literature consists of studies of this kind (e.g., estimated by Pihl and Spiers (1978) at more than 90%), studies have generally relied on convenience samples for comparisons rather than using more broadly representative comparison samples. In the past, investigators have generally not gone to the trouble of screening current alcoholics or remitted alcoholics from their comparison samples. In the current investigation, the current alcoholics and remitted alcoholics in the general population will be separated from the general population group and treated as distinct groups. Comparisons in these analyses will include female samples and will be conducted on a broad range of personality traits and on the family history of abuse. It is anticipated that clinical alcoholics will be characterized by a family history of alcohol abuse and clinical alcoholic personality traits, including higher neuroticism (including higher EPQ-N and Trait Anxiety and lower Ego Strength and Self-Esteem), higher psychoticism, and greater field dependence (i.e., lower GEFT scores).
2. To compare alcoholics in treatment with alcoholics in the general population. It has been estimated that only about 20% of alcoholics ever enter the formal treatment system (Sobell, 1994; Vaillant, 1983). There is not a

lot known about the personality differences between alcoholics who can function in the general population and those who decide to go for treatment. In this investigation, comparisons will be made of alcohol consumption and problem indicators as well as on family history of alcohol abuse and a broad range of personality traits. It is anticipated that alcoholics in treatment might be more extreme in their personality profiles, particularly in neuroticism-related characteristics.

3. To compare current alcoholics with former alcoholics. In the general population study, our data allow us to identify former alcoholics which then can be compared with current alcoholics in the general population and clinical samples. It is predicted that former alcoholics might score lower than current alcoholics on characteristics more strongly associated with the clinical condition of alcoholism such as neuroticism but may not differ as much on traits more closely linked with the prealcoholic personality such as Psychoticism and Stimulus Reducing.

4. To compare drug addicts with the general population. In our clinical sample there were groups of patients who were addicted to a combination of alcohol and drugs or only to drugs in addition to those who were addicted only to alcohol. This affords us an excellent opportunity to compare drug addicts with a general population sample on family history of alcohol abuse and on a wide range of personality characteristics. The literature on personality and addiction is characterized by two main types of research. The first type of research looks at the relationship between personality and drug use in student samples. The second type compares drug addicts with comparison groups (usually convenience samples) and suffers from the same problems as this branch of research in the alcoholism field in that these comparison samples are rarely representative. In this study, it is anticipated that when drug addicts are compared with the general population and demographic characteristics are controlled, the drug addicted population will score higher on P, Neuroticism and related characteristics, and stimulus reducing (e.g., higher Vando Scale scores).

5. To compare alcoholics with patients addicted to alcohol and drugs or only drugs. Comparisons will be made on the family history of alcohol abuse and on the full range of personality traits. This will provide valuable information on whether personality traits associated with alcoholism are similar or different from traits associated with drug addiction. Based on the prior literature, it is expected that drug addicts and polysubstance abuse scorers might be more extreme than alcoholics in their personality profiles, particularly on P and sensation-seeking related traits, such as stimulus reducing on the Vando Scale.

Before describing the methodology for the research presented in this chapter, it is necessary to review some of the literature with respect to the relationship between personality and drug addiction. The literature that is most relevant to the objectives in the current project compares drug addicts with normals and/or alcoholics on objective measures of personality such as the EPQ. Also relevant are studies that examine the comorbidity of Axis I disorders and Axis II disorders in substance-abusing samples. Studies that examine the personality correlates of substance abuse in adolescent samples or the longitudinal predictors of substance abuse are more relevant for determining prealcoholic or addiction-prone traits rather than clinical addict traits.

2. Comparison of Drug Abusers versus Nonabusers or Other Problem Groups on Personality Measures

2.1. EPQ

On the EPQ, addicts have been compared with comparison groups or EPQ norms in several studies. The results have generally been consistent in showing higher P and N Scale scores for addict groups (Gossop & Eysenck, 1983; Lodhi & Thakur, 1993; Teasdale, Seagraves, & Zacune, 1971). The results are less consistent with respect to Extraversion and only one study reported lower E Scale scores in addicts (Gossop & Eysenck, 1983). When Lie Scale scores have been considered, they are lower in addict groups (Gossop & Eysenck, 1983; Lodhi & Thakur, 1993; von Knorring, Oreland, & von Knorring, 1987) reflecting a lower concern for social conformity. In one study, however, comparing various types of drug users participating in San Francisco NA and AA programs, O'Connor, Berry, Morrison, and Brown (1995) did not find any significant differences among different types of drug abusers on the EPQ scales. They did not report that differences occurred on the Zuckerman Boredom Susceptibility Scale where alcoholics and marijuana users tended to score lower than heroin addicts, stimulant users, and polydrug users.

Results may vary somewhat depending on the cultural context of the drug abuse. Chinnian, Taylor, Subaie, Sugumar, and Jumaih (1994) compared heroin addicts with alcoholics and controls in a Saudi Arabian sample. Results showed that heroin users did not differ from controls on the Eysenck P or N Scales. Heroin users did, however, score higher than controls on the Lie Scale. This result is not consistent with findings in Western cultures. Alcoholics, on the other hand, did present a more consistent pattern, and alcohol abuse was found in association with high P or high N. In another study employing a young Icelandic sample, Sigurdsson and Gudjonsson (1996) administered the EPQ to a sample of 108 juvenile offenders and compared the scores of subjects, who were classified as drug users or frequent alcohol users with the other offenders. On the EPQ, the only significant difference occurred on the Lie Scale where drug users and frequent alcohol users scored lower than the other juveniles.

2.2. NEO

In a recent APA conference presentation, Quirk, McCormick, and Zegarra (1996) compared large samples of substance abusers addicted only to alcohol ($n = 251$), only cocaine ($n = 257$), cocaine and alcohol ($n = 525$), and cocaine, alcohol, and other drugs ($n = 517$). Their results showed that cocaine users scored the highest on Openness and Extroversion. Polysubstance users had the lowest scores on Agreeableness and Conscientiousness. All groups scored lower than McCrae and Costa norms for this scale, however. Cocaine users had somewhat lower N Scale scores than other clinical groups, although here again all groups scored higher than the McCrae and Costa norms for this scale. These results are consistent with the EPQ results described above in that low Agreeableness and Conscientiousness reflect higher P, so that again high P and high N are associated with addiction to alcohol and other drugs.

2.3. MCMI

On the MCMI, comparisons are usually made between different clinical groups rather than against an undisturbed normal sample. Five studies of this kind comparing addicts with other clinical groups are summarized in Table 7.1. One of these studies (Grilo, Fehon, & Walker, 1996) employed the adolescent version of the Millon test. In the three studies comparing addicts with other psychiatric inpatients (Campbell & Stark, 1990; Marsh, Stile, Stoughton, & Trout-Landen, 1988; Yeager, DiGiuseppe, Resweber & Leaf, 1992), some consistent findings occurred, and drug groups scored higher on the narcissistic and antisocial scales in all three studies. Yeager et al. (1992) interpret their results as indicating that substance abusers are motivated more by sensation seeking and a low tolerance for boredom than by the alleviation of symptoms of anxiety. Brown (1992) looked at MCMI scale scores of 50 inpatient substance abusers (including a mixed group of alcoholics and drug addicts). This study did not include a comparison group but relied on MCMI norms to report scale elevations. Brown (1992) concluded that 70% of the sample was suffering from "disorders of the self" which included the borderline and antisocial personality categories. In the one study comparing alcoholics and addicts, Craig, Vernis, and Wexler (1985) reported that drug addicts scored higher on the narcissistic personality and alcoholics scored higher on several other scales. In the adolescent study (Grilo et al., 1996), the substance abusers scored higher on unruly and forceful scales and lower on submissive, inhibited, and introverted characteristics.

2.4. MMPI

In an early review of the MMPI studies on heroin addiction, Craig (1979) reviewed 32 studies and reported that in almost every case heroin addicts had el-

Table 7.1. MCMI Comparisons Between Substance Users and Other Groups

Study	Addicts	Comparison groups	Results
Craig et al. (1985)	106 alcoholic inpatients	100 addicts	Alcoholics higher on avoidant, dependent submissive, schizotypal, borderline, paranoid. Drug addicts higher on narcissistic personality.
Marsh et al. (1988)	163 opiate addicts participating in methadone program	MCMI norms	In addition to scale elevation on drug abuse scale, addicts showed highest elevations on anxiety, narcissism, dysthymia, and antisocial personality.
Campbell & Stark (1990)	16 opiate, 16 amphetamine, 34 cocaine, 29 marijuana, all outpatients	Normative psychiatric	Drug groups higher on schizoid, narcissistic, antisocial, passive-aggressive anxiety, lower on schizotypal compulsive. Within drug groups, amphetamine users most schizoid, cocaine users least.
Yeager et al. (1992)	144 substance abusing inpatients	1000 psychotherapy outpatients	Substance abusing clients higher on hypomania, antisocialism, narcissism, schizoidism, paranoia, psychotic thinking, psychotic delusions. Clinical outpatients higher on anxiety, somatoform, dysthymia, borderline and compulsive scales.
Grilo et al. (1996)	44 adolescent inpatient substance use disorders	61 adolescent inpatients without substance use	Substance use disorders higher on unruly (antisocial), and forceful (sadistic), lower on submissive (dependent), inhibited (avoidant), introversive (schizoid).

evated Pd Scale scores that were in general two standard deviations above the mean. The second most common elevations occurred on the D and Ma Scales. These findings are consistent with the high P, high N pattern reported above. In studies comparing heroin addicts and alcoholics, Craig (1979) noted that higher Pd, Ma, and He Scale scores were common in heroin addicts. A summary of recent MMPI studies comparing addicts of one type or another with norms and alcoholics is presented in Table 7.2. These results in general support the earlier findings reviewed by Craig (1979). Johnson et al. (1992) found elevated D and Pd Scale scores in a cocaine addict sample, and Brown and Fayek (1993) found elevated D and Pd Scale scores in their alcohol and cocaine group. Marsh et al. (1988) also found elevated D and Pd Scale scores in their sample of opiate addicts. In an adolescent sample, Walfish, Massey, and Krone (1990) reported that

Table 7.2. MMPI Comparisons Between Substance Users and Other Groups

Study	Addicts	Comparison groups	Results
Spotts & Shontz (1983)	9 chronic cocaine users, 9 chronic amphetamine users, 9 chronic opiate users, 9 chronic barbiturate/sedative hypnotic users	9 nonusers	Nonusers lower on Hs, D, and Pt and higher on Ego Strength.
Marsh et al. (1988)	163 opiate addicts participating in methadone program	MMPI norms	Addicts had highest MMPI scale elevations on psychopathic deviate, depression, and hypochondriasis.
Walfish et al. (1990)	243 adolescent inpatients drug of choice: marijuana- 69% alcohol- 18% cocaine- 13%	MMPI norms	No difference in drug use groups. Pd only elevated scale (i.e., T score over 65).
Johnson et al. (1992)	44 cocaine inpatients; 44 alcohol inpatients	MMPI norms	No differences in MMPI scores. Both groups high in MAC Scale and low in Ego Strength, as well as elevated in D and Pd.
Greene et al. (1993)	29 alcoholic, 29 cocaine, 29 marijuana inpatients	400 psychiatric patients	Psychiatric patients higher on L, F, Pd Sc. Alcoholics lower than other substance dependent patients on most, except L and K scales.
Brown & Fayek (1993)	24 alcohol only, 33 alcohol and cocaine inpatients	MMPI norms	Both groups have T scores over 70 on D and Pd. Alcohol and cocaine group higher on F, Sc, Ma, A, MAC; lower on L, K, Es.

the only elevated scale was the Pd Scale. Spotts and Shontz (1983) conducted a detailed and well-controlled study comparing addicts of various kinds and controls, but their sample sizes were too small to have adequate statistical power for comparing groups. Thus they failed to find statistically significant differences among their groups on the Pd Scale, although results were in the expected direction. They did find that nonusers were lower than users on D and Pt and higher on Ego Strength. Low Ego Strength in addicted samples is a common finding in recent investigations (Brown & Fayek, 1993; Johnson et al., 1992).

In studies comparing alcoholics with groups addicted to other drugs, some studies have found greater indications of psychopathology in subjects addicted to alcohol and cocaine (Brown & Fayek, 1993) or cocaine or marijuana alone (Greene, Adyanthaya, Morse, & Davis, 1993) than in those addicted to alcohol, whereas others have not found significant differences (e.g., Johnson et al., 1992, Walfish et al., 1990).

2.5. TPQ

Cloninger (1987a) has proposed that there are two types of alcoholism. Type II, the most common form, is characterized by high novelty seeking, low harm avoidance, and low reward dependence. Research on Cloninger's theory has recently been reviewed by Howard et al. (1997). In their review, the authors note that there have been some problems replicating the three-factor structure originally proposed by Cloninger. Cloninger himself has recently moved toward a seven-factor model (Cloninger, Svrakic, & Przybeck, 1993; Svrakic, Whitehead, Przybeck, & Cloninger, 1993). Howard et al. (1997) note that the most consistent finding stemming from Cloninger's theory is a confirmation of the relationship between high novelty seeking and substance abuse. High harm avoidance also seems to be linked with substance abuse.

2.6. Zuckerman Sensation-Seeking Scale

The relationship between sensation seeking and substance abuse is well documented (Zuckerman, 1987). Most recently Ball, Carroll, and Rounsaville (1994) have extended this research by examining some predictions from Cloninger's theory in relation to some expected associations with sensation seeking in a large sample of treatment-seeking and community cocaine abusers. In particular, they predicted that sensation seeking would be linked with Cloninger's Type II classification and thus would be associated with being male and having an earlier onset with a more severe and varied pattern of abuse and related psychosocial impairment. Sensation-seeking cocaine abusers were also expected to score higher on antisocial personality traits, conduct disorder, and family history of substance abuse. They also predicted that treatment outcome might be worse for addicts who scored higher on sensation seeking. Many of these hypotheses were confirmed in that high-sensation-seeking cocaine addicts had an earlier onset of problems with more varied and severe abuse of substances and more severe psychosocial impairment. A family history of conduct disorder, antisocial personality, and conduct disorder along with a lifetime history for these problems in the abusers themselves also occurred more frequently for high sensation seekers. Sensation seeking did not prove to be a very good predictor of drug use at follow-up but did contribute in predicting alcohol use.

2.7. Other Measures

Several recent studies have been completed comparing polysubstance abusers with other groups on a variety of measures. Amir (1994) compared polysubstance abusers in an Arabian inpatient sample with alcoholics, heroin addicts, and drug-free patients on the Lanyon Psychological Screening Inventory. Polysubstance users were the most extreme group and had alienation and discomfort scores that were significantly higher than the drug-free group. In another study of the kind described above, McCormick and Smith (1995) studied 3767 admissions to a VA substance abuse treatment program and examined the associations between polysubstance abuse with the Buss Durkee Hostility Inventory and NEO Hostility Scale. Polysubstance abuse was significantly associated with Buss Durkee Aggression ($r = .25$), Hostility ($r = .19$), and the NEO Hostility Scale ($r = .20$). Finally, Schinka, Curtiss, and Mulloy (1994) studied four drug-using groups, including alcohol abusers, cocaine abusers, alcohol and cocaine abusers, and polysubstance abusers, on the Personality Assessment Inventory. Discriminant analyses were conducted to identify discriminant functions that best separated the four groups. Three discriminant functions were identified. High paranoia, antisocial tendencies, and somatic concerns were associated with the polysubstance abusing group, and alcoholics scored lowest on these three discriminant functions. Taken together, these three studies indicate that more extreme personality scores on traits related to high P and N are common in polysubstance abusers.

2.8. Comorbidity Studies

Comorbidity studies provide another interesting source of evidence regarding the personality traits of drug addicts. Axis I comorbidity for schizophrenia spectrum disorders, for example, provides support for the high P traits of drug addicts. The high prevalence of neurotic spectrum disorders confirms the importance of high N in drug addiction. On the personality disorder side, the high prevalence of antisocial personality and borderline personality disorders also supports the high P, high N profiles of drug addicts. A brief review of this literature is provided below.

Results in general support very high prevalence for both Axis I and Axis II disorders in drug addicts. Clerici, Carta, and Cazzullo (1989), for example, found that in a sample of 226 heroin users tested in an Italian therapeutic community, 30% met Axis I diagnoses criteria, and 61% met Axis II criteria. In their sample, the most common form of Axis I diagnoses was for the Schizophrenic, Paranoid, Psychotic cluster that accounted for 21 of the 68 Axis I disorders. Halikas, Crosby, Pearson, Nugent, and Carlson (1994) examined the prevalence of psychiatric diagnoses in cocaine addicts and reported that 72.9% qualified for a lifetime prevalence of a psychiatric disorder. This rate was very comparable to results reported by Rounsaville and Anton (1991) with 73.5% and Carroll and Rounsaville (1992) with 73.0%. In these studies, the lifetime prevalence for any anxiety disorder ranged from 18.0% to 36.7%, and affective disorder ranged from 28% to 60.7%.

Regarding the ordering of the symptom occurrence, Halikas et al. (1994) asked subjects to report on the ordering of their symptoms and found that anxiety disorders preceded the onset of substance abuse, whereas depression followed the onset. These findings are consistent with results reported by others that showed that ex-addicts or addicts who are receiving methadone maintenance score lower on depression (Mintz, O'Brien, Woody, & Beck, 1979). Dorus and Senay (1980) also found results confirming this tendency in a longitudinal study. In their sample of substance abusers, 46% had high D scores on the Beck Scale and 29% on the Hamilton Scale when entering treatment. In an eight-month follow-up, these levels of depression were significantly reduced.

Recently there has been a burgeoning literature on the relationship between drug use and personality disorders. In particular, numerous studies examined have the relationships between drug use and either antisocial personality disorders or borderline personality disorders. Fortunately an extensive review of this literature has been conducted recently by Verheul et al. (1995). As one might expect, comorbidity rates vary greatly across studies depending on the samples and methods of assessment employed. Median rates given by Verhheul et al. (1995) provide a useful rough estimate of comorbidity patterns. The overall prevalence of personality disorders is estimated to be 44% in alcoholics, 70% for cocaine addicts, and 79% for opiate addicts. The prevalence of Antisocial personality disorder is estimated to be 18% for alcoholics, 24% for cocaine addicts, and 24% for opiate addicts. The prevalence of Borderline Personality Disorder is estimated to be 21% for alcoholics, 18% for cocaine addicts, and 7% for opiate addicts.

Personality disorders may even be more prevalent in polydrug users. DeJong, van den Brink, Harteveld, and van der Wielen (1993) reported that the prevalence of at least one personality disorder was 91% in their sample of polydrug users. O'Boyle (1993) examined the prevalence of Axis I and Axis II disorders in patients addicted to either one drug or more than one drug. Multiply addicted patients were more likely to have Axis I disorders such as depression, and Axis II disorders, such as borderline personality and antisocial personality, than patients addicted only to one drug.

2.9. Summary

In studies comparing addicts with the general population, results in general suggest that addicts score higher on P and related characteristics such as sensation seeking and low social conformity, and score higher on the prevalence of antisocial personality disorder. Addicts also score higher on neuroticism-related characteristics, but these results are not as strong. Addicts score higher on neuroticism scales, harm avoidance, and depression and affective disorders. Depression occurs after the onset of addiction problems and dissipates with treatment.

In comparing alcoholics with addicts, addicts are higher on a variety of measures of psychopathology, particularly P related traits. Alcoholics are not as paranoid, antisocial, or have as many somatic concerns. Addicts may also be more narcissistic. Polydrug users score highest on a variety of indicators of psychopathology and sensation seeking. They also score lower on Agreeableness and Conscientiousness, highest on paranoid, antisocial, and somatic concerns and more frequently suffer comorbidity for depression, antisocial personality disorders and borderline personality disorders.

3. Methodology

The methodology for this chapter involved combining the general population and clinical samples. To accomplish this objective, it was necessary to determine the variables that were comparable across the two samples and then form a combined data set including these variables. On the demographic side, the measures that were comparable across the two studies included: (1) gender, (2) race, (3) marital status, (4) employment status, (5) religious preference, (6) age, (7) income, and (8) education. Common alcohol measures across the two studies included a measure of daily alcohol consumption (ounces of ethanol/day), a measure of alcohol problems, and a measure of maximum consumption. The alcohol consumption measure was computed on the basis of the respondents' reported quantity and frequency of use of beer, wine, and liquor in the past year. The problems scale was based on a summation of subject responses to 15 items pertaining to alcohol problems. The maximum consumption variable was based on instances of heavy drinking (eight or more drinks per sitting) for liquor, including beer, wine, and distilled spirits. Brief MAST scores completed by the respondent for their mothers and fathers were also available. On the personality side, each study contained the same personality measures, including the EPQ, Trait Anxiety, Self Esteem, Ego-Strength, the Group Embedded Figures Test, and the Vando Reducer–Augmenter Scale.

The stages that were involved in the data analyses were as follows. First the general population sample was characterized as either nonalcoholic, alcoholic, or remitted alcoholic. Respondents were considered to be remitted alcoholics if they: (1) had a positive lifetime prevalence for alcohol abuse on any of the DSM-IIIR, MAST, or SADD; (2) had no recent drinking problems; (3) had no instances of eight or more drinks at a sitting in the past year; and (4) had not been drunk for more than one day in a row in the past year. For the clinical sample, respondents were classified as either alcoholic, alcohol and drug addicted, or drug addicted. This designation was based on the respondents" self-report regarding the nature of their addiction problem. The next step in the analyses involved comparing the six groups on their demographic characteristics, alcohol and drug consumption, and family history of abuse. To determine which demographic variables needed to be controlled in our comparisons of the groups on their personality characteristics, the next stage in the analyses involved computing the relationship between the demographic characteristics and personality. For these analyses, the ANOVA procedure was used on the nominal variables (gender, race, marital status, employment status, and religious preference), and correlations were computed for the continuous (age) and ordinal variables (income and education).

The final stage of the data analyses involved multivariate analyses to examine the association between the drug group classification and personality traits while controlling for demographic differences. For these analyses, the technique of Multiple Classification Analyses (Andrews, Morgan, & Sonquist, 1971) available in the SPSS program was employed. The Multiple Classification Analysis (MCA) program examines classification variables in a multiple regression type of analysis. The process of setting up dummy variables in each category for every variable in the analysis is completed by the MCA computer algorithm. Then the computer output provides a raw measure of association (Eta) between each independent variable and the dependent variable and measures associations (Betas) that indicate the unique contribution of each independent variable in predicting dependent variables after the effects of other independent variables and covariates have been removed. This computer algorithm, like multiple regression analysis, also provides a measure of the total amount of variance explained (R^2) in predicting the dependent variable. Because this program does not provide statistical comparisons of the adjusted means in the different groups, the SYSTAT ANCOVA program was employed to obtain the simple comparisons between the adjusted means (Tukey's Test).

4. Results

4.1. Demographic Comparisons

The demographic comparisons between our three general population and three treatment samples are provided in Table 7.3. These results show the strong demographic differences across groups that are common in this type of research and that need to be controlled. On gender, there is a higher percentage of males in all of the addict groups. For race, the pattern shows a higher percentage of blacks and natives in the addicted samples, whereas Asians are underrepresented. On marital status, divorce is much more common in the treatment samples. Unemployment is also more common in the treatment samples. With respect to religion, it is notable that alcoholics and addicts are more likely to report having no religion. On the age variable, the general population alcoholics and treatment samples of drug addicts and alcohol and drug addicts score lower. Income and education are lower in the treatment samples.

Table 7.3. Demographic comparisons by drug group

| | | General population (%) | | | Clinical sample (%) | | | | | | |
	n	Nonalcoholics	Remitted alcoholics	Alcoholics	Alcoholics	Drugs only	Alcohol and drugs	X^2	df	f	p
Gender								140.39			.000
Male	916	43.4	64.6	76.8	73.0	61.4	74.2				
Female	761	56.6	35.4	23.2	27.0	38.6	25.8				
Race								329.82	20		.000
White	1395	92.0	96.9	90.5	69.2	62.5	64.6				
Black	19	1.3	0.0	1.2	.4	6.3	0.0				
Asian	50	4.7	0.0	1.2	0.0	0.0	0.0				
Native	97	.7	1.5	6.5	22.5	16.7	24.1				
Other	50	1.4	1.5	.6	7.9	14.6	11.4				
Marital Status								289.45	15		.000
Single	401	16.5	6.2	43.5	32.7	33.9	52.2				
Married or equivalent	1045	75.3	78.5	45.8	39.0	41.1	19.6				
Widowed	41	2.0	4.6	3.0	3.7	1.8	2.2				
Divorced	187	6.3	10.8	7.7	24.5	23.2	26.1				
Employment Status								322.05	30		.000
Work full time	905	57.3	56.9	63.7	45.7	36.8	33.7				
Work part time	187	13.4	9.2	6.5	5.6	12.3	12.0				
Unemployed	176	3.9	9.2	7.7	25.5	24.6	38.0				
Student	82	5.2	0.0	11.9	.7	1.8	6.5				
Homemaker	145	10.6	12.3	1.8	6.4	8.8	3.3				
Retired	112	7.9	6.2	4.2	6.7	1.8	1.1				
Other	66	1.7	6.2	4.2	9.4	14.0	5.4				

Table 7.3. (cont'd)

		General population (%)			Clinical sample (%)						
	n	Nonalcoholics	Remitted alcoholics	Alcoholics	Alcoholics	Drugs only	Alcohol and drugs	X^2	df	f	p
Religious Preference								102.78	20		.000
Catholic	479	29.3	28.8	28.1	26.2	26.3	31.2				
Protestant	620	42.8	35.4	34.1	27.3	24.6	19.4				
Jewish	36	3.1	1.5	.6	.4	0.0	1.1				
Other	225	11.7	12.3	8.4	18.8	26.3	20.4				
None	304	13.1	18.5	28.7	27.3	22.8	28.0				
Mean Values											
Age	1672	42.77	43.66	34.86	40.12	34.49	32.28		5,1666	25.31	.000
Net worth	1531	3.83	3.69	3.50	2.84	2.24	2.18		5,1525	42.15	.000
Years of education	1673	13.33	13.31	12.77	11.89	11.71	11.36		5,1667	19.64	.000

4.1.1. Demographics and Personality

To determine which of the above demographic differences needed to be controlled in our analyses, the relationships between demographic characteristics
and personality were examined. Anova procedures were used for nominal variables such as gender (see Table 7.4), and correlations were computed for ordinal

Table 7.4. Mean Scores for Personality and Demographics for the General Population and Clinical Samples

	Male	Female	F	White	Black	Asian	Native	Other	F
		Gender				Race			
Extraversion									
EPQ-E	14.06	13.65	2.80	13.85	14.43	13.09	14.44	13.77	.72
Stimulus reducing									
VANDO Scale	25.66	19.80	186.25[a]	22.51	24.96	20.73	26.25	26.00	6.23[a]
Psychoticism/									
Social conformity									
EPQ-P	5.58	4.32	51.04[a]	4.52	6.12	4.89	8.38	6.73	34.50[a]
EPQ-L	8.29	10.03	61.37[a]	9.05	11.56	12.93	8.38	9.25	10.80[a]
Neuroticism									
Ego strength	43.70	41.68	31.97[a]	43.76	40.31	42.19	36.60	39.46	29.74[a]
EPQ-N	11.64	12.35	5.78[b]	11.47	11.19	10.01	15.70	13.85	14.40[a]
Self-esteem	31.59	31.95	2.03	32.18	32.45	31.69	29.52	30.05	8.25[a]
Trait anxiety	38.35	38.15	.17	37.27	38.57	38.30	44.33	42.24	14.42[a]
GEFT	8.42	7.11	26.00[a]	8.00	5.16	7.50	8.21	7.12	1.83

[a] $= p < .001.$
[b] $= p < .05.$

	Single	Married or equivalent	Widowed	Divorced	F
		Marital status			
Extraversion					
EPQ-E	15.00	13.52	12.96	13.55	9.63[a]
Stimulus reducing					
VANDO Scale	28.67	20.86	17.22	23.83	87.38[a]
Psychoticism /					
Social conformity					
EPQ-P	6.77	4.08	4.45	6.40	71.83[a]
EPQ-L	7.69	9.76	9.47	8.16	23.32[a]
Neuroticism					
Ego strength	41.80	43.79	41.09	40.05	19.14[a]
EPQ-N	13.50	10.84	13.37	14.34	32.77[a]
Self-esteem	30.88	32.41	31.79	30.23	15.72[a]
Trait anxiety	41.51	36.19	38.45	42.14	41.13[a]
GEFT	8.81	7.81	5.27	6.52	11.96[a]

[a] $= p < .001.$

Table 7.4. (cont'd)

	Work full time	Work part time	Un-employed	Student full time	Home-maker	Retired	Other	F
			Current employment status					
Extraversion								
EPQ-E	14.02	13.59	14.09	15.46	12.74	13.31	13.73	3.23[a]
Stimulus reducing								
VANDO Scale	23.82	20.52	26.77	30.03	17.73	15.72	24.49	40.79[b]
Psychoticism / Social conformity								
EPQ-P	4.62	4.72	7.89	6.26	4.01	3.29	6.67	34.20[b]
EPQ-L	8.94	9.88	7.11	7.39	10.85	11.21	8.55	16.83[b]
Neuroticism								
Ego strength	44.49	41.98	37.98	43.44	41.16	42.76	38.49	29.22[b]
EPQ-N	11.04	11.79	15.85	12.75	12.14	10.74	14.80	20.60[b]
Self-esteem	32.53	31.87	28.22	2.32	31.42	32.09	29.89	20.86[a]
Trait anxiety	36.83	37.53	45.52	39.62	37.65	35.87	43.06	24.33[a]
GEFT	8.38	7.58	7.84	10.57	6.36	4.80	6.62	14.67[b]

[a] $p < .01$.
[b] $p < .001$.

	Catholic	Protestant	Jewish	Other	None	F
		Religious Preference				
Extraversion						
EPQ-E	14.60	13.48	15.60	13.49	13.57	5.43[a]
Stimulus reducing						
VANDO Scale	23.23	20.72	22.34	23.91	26.64	23.21[a]
Psychoticism / Social conformity						
EPQ-P	5.24	3.82	3.97	5.93	6.41	35.58[a]
EPQ-L	9.71	9.40	8.97	8.76	7.73	10.09[a]
Neuroticism						
Ego strength	42.31	43.37	45.84	41.05	43.57	7.26[a]
EPQ-N	12.01	11.31	11.54	12.66	12.62	3.51[b]
Self-esteem	32.02	32.10	33.73	30.86	31.25	4.89[a]
Trait anxiety	38.17	36.87	37.28	40.37	39.35	6.49[a]
GEFT	6.90	7.78	7.76	7.91	9.49	11.70[a]

[a] $p < .001$.
[b] $p < .01$.

and continuous variables (see Table 7.5). These results in general show fairly strong relationships between demographic characteristics and personality, particularly for age and gender. On the gender dimension, males score higher on Stimulus reducing, higher on Psychoticism, and lower on social conformity. Males also score higher on Ego Strength and lower on Neuroticism than females. Males score higher on the GEFT, reflecting lower field dependence than females. On the

Table 7.5. Correlations Between Personality and Demographics for Combined General Population and Clinical Samples

	Age	Net worth	Years ed.
Extraversion			
EPQ-E	−.21[a]	.06[c]	.03
Stimulus reducing			
VANDO Scale	−.57[a]	−.06[c]	.01
Psychoticism /			
Social conformity			
EPQ-P	−.33[a]	−.30[a]	−.19[a]
EPQ-L	.28[a]	.03	−.07[b]
Neuroticism			
Ego strength	.06[b]	.37[a]	.35[a]
EPQ-N	−.19[a]	−.25[a]	−.20[a]
Self–esteem	.08[a]	.26[a]	.23[a]
Trait anxiety	−.18[a]	−.30[a]	−.20[a]
GEFT	−.30[a]	.13[a]	.35[a]

[a] = $p < .001$.
[b] = $p < .01$.
[c] = $p < .05$.

age variable, lower Extraversion, Stimulus Reducing, and Psychoticism are associated with being older. Older respondents score higher on the Lie Scale, Ego Strength, and Self-Esteem and lower on Neuroticism and Trait Anxiety. Older respondents performed worse on the GEFT. It is difficult to know how much the relationship between other demographic characteristics and personality may simply reflect underlying differences in age and gender without conducting multivariate analyses. To be safe, we conducted our multivariate analyses comparing clinical groups on personality and family history of alcohol abuse with all of these demographic characteristics included.

4.1.2. Alcohol Measures

In Table 7.6, the ANOVA results comparing general population and clinical groups on measures of alcohol consumption and problems are provided. Simple comparisons using Duncan's multiple range test revealed that the two clinical groups addicted to alcohol and alcohol and drugs had the highest scores ($p < .05$). The general population nonalcoholics and remitted alcoholics had the lowest scores ($p < .05$). The drug addicted group in the clinical sample and general population alcoholic group had scores that were significantly higher than the non-addicted samples and significantly lower than the two clinical groups addicted to alcohol ($p < .05$).

Table 7.6. Alcohol Consumption Patterns by Drug Group

	General population			Clinical sample				
	Nonalcoholics	Remitted alcoholics	Alcoholics	Alcoholics	Drugs only	Alcohol and Drugs	F	df
	μ	μ	μ	μ	μ	μ		
Average daily alcohol consumption	.40	.15	1.63	6.39	2.46	6.96	188.06[a]	5, 1657
Problems	.14	.00	1.59	2.52	.82	3.00	128.02[a]	5, 1671
> 8 drinks in a sitting in the last year	.21	.00	.88	.65	.54	.79	260.93[a]	5, 1528
Drug Abuse Screening Test (DAST)				3.85	16.32	13.73	168.02[a]	2, 398

[a] $= p < .001$

4.1.3. Drug Abuse

In Table 7.6 the means on the Drug Abuse Screening Test are provided for the three clinical samples. These analyses support the group classifications. The alcoholic group had the lowest score, and the drugs only group had the highest score (Note: All three groups differed significantly from the other group at the p < .05 level on Duncan's Multiple Range Test).

4.1.4. Family History of Alcohol Abuse

The means on fathers' alcohol abuse in the six groups adjusted for demographic factors are presented in Table 7.7. The results show significant group differences on both mothers' alcohol abuse and fathers' alcohol abuse. On the fathers' MAST, simple comparisons within these adjusted means show that the general population nonalcoholics differ significantly from the treatment sample of alcoholics (Tukey's test, p < .01), the treatment sample addicted to alcohol and drugs (Tukey's test, p < .01), and the remitted alcoholics (Tukey's test, p < .001). These results show an important relationship between fathers' alcoholism and problems of severe alcohol and drug abuse but not less severe alcohol abuse evident in the general population sample. A similar pattern emerges on the mothers' MAST. The general population nonalcoholics differ significantly from the treatment alcoholics (Tukey's test, p < .01) and treatment alcohol and drug addicted sample (Tukey's test, p < .05).

4.1.5. Personality

4.1.5a. Group Comparisons. Mean scores on the personality scales after demographic adjustments are presented in Table 7.8. These results show significant group differences on all of the personality scales, except the Group Embedded Figures Test. When the simple comparisons are considered, the pattern of results for group differences is similar on all of the Neuroticism-related scales. Higher Neuroticism and Trait Anxiety and lower Ego Strength and Self-Esteem are evident in groups that are currently addicted and especially in treatment samples. Simple comparisons using Tukey's test showed that all of the treatment samples scored higher on Trait Anxiety and Neuroticism and lower on Ego Strength and Self-Esteem than the nonalcoholic sample (p < .001 in all cases). Not much evidence of differences in Neuroticism occurred within the treatment samples. The results of analyses comparing the general population alcoholics and nonalcoholics were mixed. The general population alcoholics scored higher on Eysenck's Neuroticism Scale (Tukey's test, p < .001) and lower on Ego Strength than nonalcoholics (Tukey's test, p < .05) but did not differ in their Trait Anxiety or Self-Esteem scores. Also of interest is the finding that although remitted alco-

Table 7.7. Reports on Family History of Alcohol Abuse in General Population and Clinical Samples[a]

| | General population | | | Clinical sample | | | | |
	Nonalcoholics	Remitted alcoholics	Alcoholics	Alcoholics	Drugs only	Alcohol and Drugs	F	B
	μ	μ	μ	μ	μ	μ		
Fathers' MAST	1.59	3.46	2.31	2.67	1.90	3.23	7.34[b]	.18
Mothers' MAST	.42	.80	.71	.97	1.16	1.00	4.37[b]	.15

[a] Mean scores are adjusted for demographic factors and covariates.
[b] = $p < .001$

Table 7.8. Personality Comparisons for General Population and Clinical Samples[a]

| | General population | | | Clinical sample | | | | |
	Nonalcoholics	Remitted alcoholics	Alcoholics	Alcoholics	Drugs only	Alcohol and drugs	F	B
Extraversion								
EPQ-E	13.69	15.14	15.16	13.11	12.29	13.81	4.89[b]	.13
Stimulus reducing								
VANDO Scale	22.24	23.41	24.13	23.08	24.16	25.73	4.04[b]	.10
Psychoticism / Social conformity								
EPQ-P	4.15	4.78	5.95	5.78	7.85	7.39	22.78[b]	.29
EPQ-L	9.81	8.66	8.96	7.67	6.22	6.10	14.19[b]	.25
Neuroticism								
Ego strength	45.10	44.09	43.34	39.05	37.25	38.34	37.70[b]	.37
EPQ-N	9.88	11.01	11.86	16.30	16.81	17.00	49.15[b]	.45
Self-esteem	33.27	31.91	32.41	28.73	27.75	28.50	33.13[b]	.38
Trait anxiety	34.90	35.92	37.07	45.31	48.48	45.88	51.59[b]	.45
GEFT	8.08	7.85	7.85	7.89	9.03	8.85	.836	.05

[a]Mean scores are adjusted for demographic factors and covariates

[b] $= p < .001$

holics differ significantly from the clinical addiction samples on all four of the Neuroticism-related scales (Tukey's test, minimum $p < .001$), they do not differ significantly on these traits from either alcoholics or nonalcoholics in the general population. Taken as a whole, these results show that Neuroticism is a very important component of the clinical alcoholic profile and is also evident in general population alcoholics but to a much lesser degree.

On the Extraversion Scale, simple comparisons show that most groups do not differ on this dimension. General population alcoholics are more extraverted than clinical alcoholics (Tukey's test, $p < .01$), clinical drug addicts (Tukey's test, $p < .05$), and general population nonalcoholics (Tukey's test, $p < .05$). Perhaps general population alcoholics contain more of what Cloninger would characterize as Type II alcoholics whereas clinical samples contain more Type I alcoholics.

On the Vando Scale which has a strong correlation with sensation seeking (Barnes, 1985b), it was anticipated that the multiple drug group would score highest. This in fact occurred, and the multiple drug group differed most from the general population (Tukey's test, $p < .01$), but many of the simple comparisons with other groups are not significant.

Results on the P and Lie Scales follow a fairly orderly progression. There were higher P and lower Lie Scale scores in the most extreme groups (i.e., the two drug addicted groups) and lower P and higher Lie Scale scores in the nonalcoholic sample. Simple comparisons for the P scale showed that all currently addicted groups differed significantly from the non-alcoholic group in having higher P Scale scores (Tukey's test, minimum $p < .01$). Remitted alcoholics had scores that are between the clinical and normal groups. Simple comparisons showed that remitted alcoholics did not differ in their P scale scores from general population or clinical sample alcoholics nor did they differ from nonalcoholics when demographics were controlled. On the Lie Scale, a similar pattern emerged, and most of the addicted groups scored lower on social conformity than the nonalcoholic group (Tukey's test, $p < .001$), except the general population alcoholics who did not differ from nonalcoholics on their Lie Scale scores. Again, remitted alcoholics had intermediate scores that did not differ significantly from general population alcoholics, clinical alcoholics, or general population nonalcoholics.

On the Group Embedded Figures Test, there were no significant differences among groups when demographic characteristics were considered. These results are surprising in view of the consistent results in the literature that support an association between this dimension and alcohol abuse (Barnes, 1983).

4.1.5b. Correlations with the DAST within the Clinical Sample. In the clinical study, another strategy for examining the association between personality and drug use was available. In the clinical sample, respondents completed the DAST (Skinner, 1982). High scores on this test reflect heavy drug use and more negative consequences resulting from use. Correlations between the Personality Scale score

**Table 7.9. Correlations Between
Personality and DAST Scale Scores
for the Combined Clinical Sample**

	DAST r
Extraversion	
EPQ-E	.08
Stimulus reducing	
VANDO Scale	.32[a]
Psychoticism /	
Social conformity	
EPQ-P	.48[a]
EPQ-L	-.37[a]
Neuroticism	
Ego-strength	−.29[a]
EPQ-N	.28[a]
Self-esteem	−.23[a]
Trait anxiety	.30[a]
GEFT	.11[b]

[a] = $p < .001$.
[a] = $p < .05$.

and DAST Scale scores in the clinical sample were computed. These results presented in Table 7.9 show that Extraversion is unrelated to the severity of drug abuse. High scores on the Vando Scale are associated with higher DAST scores. These results are consistent with previous findings in a prison sample (Kohn, Barnes, & Hoffman, 1979) showing that higher scores on the Vando measure are associated with more frequent use of illicit drugs. High P and low L Scale scores are associated with higher DAST scores. Higher scores on Neuroticism-related characteristics are also associated with higher DAST scores. These results are consistent with results of earlier studies discussed in the literature review at the beginning of this chapter indicating that drug abuse commonly occurs with higher scores on P and N and related traits. Higher scores on the GEFT were moderately correlated with higher DAST scores, suggesting that more field independence is associated with more severe drug abuse. These last results could be explained by demographic differences such as age and or gender.

5. Summary and Conclusions

When clinical samples of alcohol and drug addicts are compared with normals, numerous demographic differences exist. These demographics are generally correlated with personality traits and need to be controlled when group comparisons are planned. Group differences in alcohol consumption and problems and on the DAST within the clinical sample supported the group designations employed in this study. The results from the analyses of Family History of Alcohol abuse support the importance of this factor for people who have addictions severe enough to warrant treatment. The parental alcohol effect on offspring is more general than specific, as indicated by the relationship between parental alcohol abuse and offspring drug abuse problems. Results involving the parental drug abuse data in this study should be interpreted cautiously because the data were not gathered from the parents themselves but were based on offspring reports.

The first objective in this project was to compare alcoholics in the treatment sample with the general population while controlling for demographics. We expected that alcoholics would score higher on Neuroticism, Psychoticism, and Field Dependence. The results in general supported these predictions, except that field dependence was not related to alcohol abuse diagnoses when demographic variables were controlled. The results are also fairly consistent with the results found in our general population longitudinal survey described in Chapter 5. In that study, Neuroticism and related traits, Psychoticism, and Stimulus Reducing were all correlated with alcohol use and abuse, whereas Extraversion and Field Dependence were less important. In the clinical sample, Neuroticism is more strongly associated with alcohol abuse than in our general population study. This confirms that Neuroticism and related traits are more important features of the Clinical Alcoholic Personality than the Prealcoholic Personality.

The second objective in this study was to compare alcoholics in treatment with alcoholics in the general population. As anticipated, alcoholics in the treatment sample generally had more severe drinking problems, family history of abuse, and personality traits. Alcoholics in the treatment sample were higher on Neuroticism and Psychoticism in particular, whereas alcoholics in the general population tended to be lower on these characteristics and more extraverted than alcoholics in treatment. These results support the importance of gathering data from both types of samples when conducting research on the relationship between personality and alcohol abuse.

The third objective in this chapter was to compare current alcoholics with former alcoholics. As expected, the remitted alcoholics did not differ much from the general population in their scores on Neuroticism and related characteristics. These results are consistent with prior research studies suggesting that scores on Neuroticism-related characteristics decline following treatment (Brown et al., 1991; Sher and Trull, 1994).

On scales such as the Vando Scale, the P Scale and the Lie Scale that were expected to be more strongly associated with the prealcoholic personality, it was anticipated that remitted alcoholics might more closely resemble clinical samples. Results were not very conclusive with regard to these traits. Although remitted alcoholics did not differ in these traits from clinical addict groups, they also scored close to the general population nonalcoholics on these traits. It was anticipated that because these characteristics were more closely linked with prealcoholic traits, some residual higher scores should be evident following remission of the addiction problem. One possible explanation for these findings is that people who give up their addiction may be more like nonaddicts to begin with than people who do not give up their addiction (see Eysenck, 1980). Research in the smoking area for example (Patton, Barnes, & Murray, 1993) has shown that ex-smokers tend to be more like nonsmokers in their personality traits than other current smokers.

The fourth objective in this study was to compare the personality characteristics of drug addicts with the general population with demographic characteristics controlled. These results were consistent with expectations in that the drug addicted samples were characterized by higher P, N, and reducing–augmenting scores. This is consistent with the research literature showing higher P, N, and sensation seeking in drug addicts described earlier in this chapter. Correlations carried out within the treatment sample also supported the association between these personality traits and drug addiction. High scores on the DAST were associated with higher Vando scores, high P, and high scores on Neuroticism and related characteristics. Low Lie Scale scores possibly reflecting lower social conformity were also found in the drug addicted groups and correlated with DAST scores. Groups addicted to drugs also scored higher on the family history of alcohol abuse than nonalcoholic persons in the general population.

The final objective in this chapter was to compare alcoholics and drug addicted or alcohol and drug addicted groups on their personality traits. All groups were expected to be higher on P, N, and stimulus reducing/sensation seeking than the general population, and drug addicts were expected to score higher on the Vando Scale and the P Scale. Results were consistent with these expectations. The drug addicted groups had the highest score on the P scale and the lowest score on the L Scale. The alcohol and drug addicted group had the highest Vando Scale score as well.

8

Personality and Treatment Outcome

Research on alcoholism treatment has failed to adequately define dimensional personality characteristics that relate to the pretreatment patterns of alcohol consumption in clinical alcoholics and to treatment outcome. Although some of this failure to isolate relevant predictors is likely to be related to heterogeneity in clinical alcoholic populations (e.g., neurotic versus antisocial alcoholic types; see Cloninger, 1983, 1987a), to the unreliability of certain measures (particularly outcome measures), and to inadequate control of demographic and other confounding variables (e.g., age, gender, and socioeconomic status), much of it is likely to be related to the lack of an adequate conceptual framework from which to organize, integrate, and interpret results. To address these issues, this chapter involves an attempt to replicate the structure of the WHDS general population model within the clinical sample and to test the capability of the models to predict the severity of the initial level of alcohol use in the clinical sample of alcoholics and the treatment outcome at six months.

The overall goal of this chapter is to explore the relationships between broad-based personality dimensions, consumption patterns prior to treatment, and the outcome of alcoholism treatment using currently available methodological advances based on the Structural Equation Modeling (SEM) technique (Bentler, 1995; Bentler & Wu, 1995; Bollen, 1989; Ullman, 1996). Focusing on a sample of problem drinkers from the Alcoholism Foundation of Manitoba, (AFM), the specific objectives of this study are as follows:

1. Objectives

To organize the various personality measures used in the study into a cohesive factorial structure of major personality dimensions using Structural

Equation Modelling (SEM) techniques and to relate this structure to that found in the WHDS general population sample.

To use SEM to evaluate the relationship, if any, between the major dimensions of personality found in the AFM sample and measures of alcohol consumption patterns and problems due to alcohol prior to treatment, while controlling for the effects of relevant demographic and other intervening variables.

To evaluate the relationship, if any, between pretreatment personality factors and treatment outcome six months after treatment.

2. A Review of the Outcome Research to Date

As previously mentioned, clinical research relating personality characteristics to alcoholism treatment outcome is very sparse and has yielded largely inconsistent findings. Interpretation of the existing clinical studies is difficult because they are so few and also because the different studies use varying methodologies, focus on different treatment populations, and use different measures for treatment effectiveness. Despite these difficulties, however, the literature does suggest that certain personality characteristics might be linked to treatment outcome in clinical settings.

One of the earliest studies relating personality to treatment outcome was that of Conley (1981). This study of 228 male alcoholics who participated in a 12-month follow-up after treatment at the Hazeldon Foundation treatment center in 1975 attempted to classify the subjects into alcoholic subgroups by virtue of their MMPI profiles and then relate each group to treatment outcome. The MMPI profiles led the investigators to classify their subjects into groups that represented neurotic, classic alcoholic, psychopathic, and psychotic alcoholics.

The four alcoholic types showed differences in treatment outcome assessed 12 months after completion of treatment. The neurotics reported feeling less angry and resentful at follow-up than other groups but reported less improvement in most other areas and a lower level of psychological well-being than other groups. The psychopathic group reported the highest rates of abstinence and reported improvement in social relationships, self-image, ability to handle problems, and reduction of anxiety. The psychotic group, on the other hand, reported high rates of both hospitalization and arrest during the follow-up period.

Another study of the same vintage (Zivich, 1981) used dimensional trait measures of personality (i.e., the Personality Research Form and the Sixteen Personality Factor Questionnaire) instead of a clinical tool such as the MMPI or DSM, but classified subjects into clinical categories to gauge treatment effectiveness. Using a sample of 102 men from Chicago's Alcoholic Treatment Center, and the techniques of factor analysis and cluster analysis, Zivich (1981) ascertained eight alcoholic subtypes. These were (1) aggressive, (2) obsessive-compulsive, (3) impulsive, (4) schizoid, (5) passive-dependent, (6) obsessive-dependent, (7) a mixed category, and (8) a category of no types. This was, in part, a replication of five alcoholic subtypes previously found by Nerviano (1976); the latter three types were not in Nerviano's (1976) findings.

On the basis of these subtypes, Zivich (1981) grouped his subjects into two prognostic categories because there were not sufficient numbers to allow statistical testing between each subtype. In the good prognosis group were alcoholics of the no-type, obsessive-compulsive, passive-dependent, and obsessive-dependent subtypes. In the poor prognosis group were alcoholics of the aggressive, impulsive, schizoid, and mixed subtypes. In accordance with the main hypotheses put forth in the study, alcoholics of subtypes included in the poor prognosis group did not do as well in treatment in terms of social adjustment and drinking behavior as good prognosis alcoholics did. One notable exception, however, was in relation to the impulsive subtypes; members in this subgroup were given a poor prognosis yet had high scores on treatment outcome. The author of this study states that a selection factor might have influenced the relationship, and more severely impulsive alcoholics dropped out of the study before follow-up was completed. The unexpected finding that impulsive subtypes did better at outcome was replicated in a subsequent study (Thurstin, 1988).

Other more recent studies of the relationship between personality factors and alcoholism treatment outcome have focused on DSM Axis II (i.e., developmental/personality) disorders. The usual strategy is to classify alcohol-dependent individuals in terms of comorbidity with Axis II disorders and then to explore the relationships between comorbid diagnoses and treatment outcome. In the handful of studies that have been done in this manner during the last decade, borderline personality, antisocial personality, and dependent personality have been looked at.

Nace, Saxon, and Shore (1986) conducted a one-year follow-up on 74 alcoholic inpatients consecutively admitted to a psychiatric hospital. Using the Diagnostic Interview for Borderlines (DIB, Gunderson, 1978), 13 (17.6%) of the patients were classified as having borderline personality disorder. This disorder is characterized as "a serious disturbance in personality functioning characterized by impulsivity, unpredictability, unstable and intense interpersonal relationships, intolerance for being alone, inappropriate anger, feelings of emptiness or boredom, and often disturbances in identity (American Psychiatric Association, 1980). The results of this study showed that borderlines did not differ from nonborderlines in terms of their post treatment alcohol use. They also did not differ significantly in terms of health, safety, or leisure, or in terms of their involvement in aftercare treatment. These results are consistent with those from another study (Poldrugo & Forti, 1988), where no relationship was found between borderline personality disorder and treatment outcome.

In addition to looking at borderline personality disorder, Poldrugo and Forti

(1988) also looked at antisocial and dependent personality types. In this study of 404 alcoholics admitted to the Psychiatric Clinic of the University of Trieste, Italy, the authors found that only dependent personality types showed significant improvement over all other groups. Other alcoholic personality types had comparable or even negative outcomes when compared to alcoholics who did not meet diagnostic criteria for any of the personality disorders explored in the study.

Another study of 266 alcoholics who had received extensive psychiatric assessment during their treatment (Rounsaville, Dolinski, Babor, & Meyer, 1987) revealed a relationship between antisocial personality and outcome. In this study, both men and women who were diagnosed as having antisocial personality disorder showed poorer outcome than those classified into other groups. A recategorization of groups based on primary psychiatric diagnosis (as determined by age of onset) yielded the same results—those who had antisocial personalities tended to drink more intensely at follow-up.

These results, however, were not replicated in several subsequent studies. In a study involving 141 alcohol dependent men, Cacciola, Alterman, Rutherford, and Snider (1995), found that those with antisocial personality diagnoses benefited from treatment and drank comparably to those without such diagnoses in a follow-up seven months following treatment. In a study involving 141 alcohol abusers, Longabaugh et al. (1994) found that those who had antisocial personalities averaged more abstinent days at an 18-month follow-up compared to those without such diagnoses.

A study by Powell et al. (1992), however, also failed to confirm the findings of Rounsaville et al. (1987). Measuring one-year follow-up outcomes for 360 males admitted to an inpatient alcoholism treatment program, the authors found that although subtyping alcoholics by comorbid psychiatric diagnosis was a good postdictor of clinical history, it was not a good predictor of drinking outcome. They also noted that psychiatric syndromes that co-occur with alcoholism function best as markers of current distress and predictors of later emotional suffering than as predictors for treatment outcome. The authors of the study offered several reasons why their results differed from those of Rounsaville et al. (1987), including the fact that the groups from the other study were not "pure" independent groups but had some overlap between categories. This resulted from the particular method that Rounsaville and his colleagues (1987) used to create groups for comparison.

A recent study (Nurnberg, Rifkin, & Doddi, 1993) suggests that the incidence of multiple comorbid diagnoses among alcoholic populations is, in fact, quite high. In their study of fifty alcoholics in an outpatient program, it was found that there were 84 diagnoses of personality disorder among the 32 patients who were diagnosed as having Axis II disorders comorbid with their alcoholism. This averages 2.6 personality disorders per patient, and multiple diagnoses occurred in 20 (62%) of them. The overlap was extensive, and multiple diagnoses were not limited to any one of the three Axis II diagnostic clusters defined by DSM.

Overall, the Nurnberg et al. study (1993) found that personality disorders were related to poorer outcome. The study was not, however, able to link specific personality disorders to specific outcomes. Although this lack of predictiveness is likely to be in part due to the small sample size, it is also likely that the heterogeneity within the various personality disorder diagnostic categories contributed to the nonspecificity of the findings.

3. Reasearch Propositions

As mentioned in the introduction, the overall goal of this chapter is to explore the relationships between broad-based personality dimensions, consumption patterns prior to treatment, and alcoholism treatment outcome. Unfortunately, the clinical outcome research to date offers little to draw from in terms of consistent results from which specific hypotheses for this study could be formulated. But fortunately, the results of the WHDS general population study (described in Chapter 5) can be used as a more systematic guide (because the WHDS identifies personality predictors of alcoholism that are associated with both problem severity and progression of symptoms in the general population, it is reasonable to conclude that these same predictors might function in a clinical sample). So, rather than relying on the inconsistencies of the existing clinical outcome research, the hypotheses for this study are formulated on the basis of the findings of the WHDS general population sample. In consideration of this, the following interrelationships between variables are hypothesized (see also Figure 8.1):

1. Using SEM, the various personality measures used in the study will be organizable into a cohesive factorial structure similar to that found in the WHDS general population model with variables loading on factors similar to Psychoticism, Extraversion, Neuroticism, and Stimulus Reducing.
2. Within a structural context similar to that of the WHDS general population model, personality factors similar to Stimulus Reducing and Psychoticism will be related to a factor comprised of indicators of alcohol use and alcohol problems prior to treatment.
3. Within a structural context similar to that of the WHDS general population model, personality factors similar to Stimulus Reducing and Psychoticism will be related to treatment outcome six months after treatment, either directly or indirectly. Individuals higher in these two factors will tend to drink more and experience more problems due to alcohol.

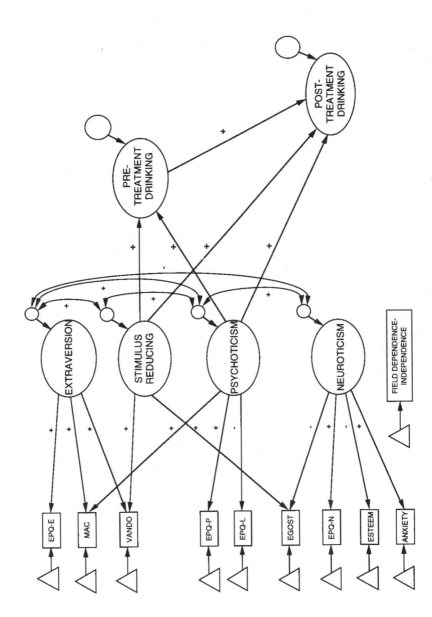

Figure 8.1. Hypothesized relationships between personality factors and outcome factors.

4. Sample Selection and Description

Subjects participating in this study (n = 363) were drawn from a larger sample of individuals (n = 420) who participated in either residential (inpatient) or community-based (outpatient) treatment at the Addiction Foundation of Manitoba in 1992, as described in Chapter 6. Individuals were excluded from the present study because they reported a history of abusing other drugs but not alcohol (n = 57). In the SEM portion of the analyses, a further 10 cases were removed because they failed to report their alcohol consumption prior to treatment. Consequently, the sample size for the structural models was reduced to 353.

The mean age of the clinical alcoholics was approximately 38 years (SD=11.0), and 74% were male. The sample was predominantly white (68%). The only racial group that was a significantly sized portion of the sample was people of first nation origin (23%); 9% classified themselves as "other." A majority of the sample (66%) was single (i.e., 38% never married, 25% divorced or separated, and 3% widowed), and the rest (34%) was married or equivalent. A total of 52% was either working (full or part time) or attending school (full or part time), 6% was homemakers, 5% was retired, 8% involved in "other" activities, and 29% was unemployed. On average, reported income was approximately $26,500 per year (SD = 17,600), and years of education was approximately 12 (SD = 2.8). A total of 59% was involved in the inpatient programs.

In terms of family history of alcohol abuse, the mean levels for the percentages of siblings, in-laws, and grandparents who were considered alcoholic were 36% (SD = 38.6), 37% (SD = 35.6), and 11% (SD = 20.1), respectively. The mean levels for mothers' and fathers' 13-item MAST scores (as reported by the respondents) were 1.5 (SD = 2.6) and 3.4 (SD = 4.0), respectively. Overall, the alcoholics in the clinical sample reported drinking an average of 6.5 ounces of absolute alcohol each day (SD = 6.6), had mean heavy drinking scores of 13.4 (SD = 17.5), and reported an average of 2.7 alcohol-related problems (SD = 2.1). These variables were constructed as described in Chapter 6. Table 8.1 lists basic descriptive statistics for all of the personality measures of the clinical alcoholic sample.

Out of the 353 selected for the study, 260 reported problems with alcohol alone, and 93 reported problems with other drugs, as well as with alcohol. Those in residential treatment (n = 208) differed from those in community-based treatment (n = 145) in that they were more likely to be males, more likely to be of native racial ancestry, and less likely to have been employed at the time of entry into treatment. They were also more likely to have consumed larger amounts of alcohol, drank heavier, and had more problems as a result of their alcohol use prior to entering treatment. Of the individuals meeting the criteria for inclusion in the study, 71% (n = 252) was reinterviewed at follow-up six months later.

Table 8.1. Descriptive Statistics of Personality Measures for AFM Sample Before Data Imputation[a]

	Mean	Items	Range	SD	Skew	Kurtosis
EPQ-E	13.50	23	2–23	5.12	−.92	−.28
MAC	25.70	54	15–37	4.61	−.64	−.07
VANDO	26.41	54	6–47	8.70	−.69	−.10
EPQ-P	7.55	34	0–25	4.15	.74	.79
EPQ-L	7.01	21	0–18	4.20	−.44	.44
EGOST	37.68	67	19–56	7.64	−.38	−.15
EPQ-N	16.65	24	1–24	5.29	−.18	−.71
Esteem	28.14	10	10–40	4.97	.41	.15
Anxiety	46.30	20	21–74	9.59	−.15	.13
GEFT	7.62	25	0–18	5.21	−1.11	.22

[a]The meaning of each variable is described fully in the measures section of Chapter 6.

5. Data Analyses

As in the WHDS general population model, data analyses proceeded in several stages. Initial analyses of the treatment data involved a series of univariate statistical tests. Subsequent analyses involved the use of SEM to develop a model of the latent factor structure underlying the covariance matrix of measured variables in the treatment data.

5.1. Initial Analyses

First, chi-square tests were conducted to check for possible differences in categorical demographic variables across residential and community treatment contexts. In a similar fashion, t-tests were conducted on demographic variables with continuous distributions, such as age. Differences detected by using these tests would indicate a need to account for these demographic variables in the overall structural models. Chi-square and t-test statistics were also calculated with respect to loss of respondents through attrition between pre-and posttreatment assessment.

Means and standard deviations of all drinking measures were calculated both pre- and posttreatment. Abstinence rates, incidence of heavy drinking, and incidence of resulting problems at the six-month follow-up period were also calculated for all of residential, community, and combined treatment groups. Chi-square procedures were used to determine statistically significant differences in these variables between residential and community treatment groups.

5.2. Analyses Using SEM

As discussed previously, SEM techniques were used in this project to develop models of the relationships between broad-based personality dimensions and alcohol consumption patterns. The structural models used for this study were facilitated by using the EQS program developed by Peter Bentler and his associates (Bentler, 1995; Bentler & Wu, 1995). To build and evaluate the models, maximum likelihood estimation (Bentler, 1995) was used, along with the Comparative Fit Index (CFI; Bentler, 1995). Although other goodness of fit indices, such as chi square/degrees-of-freedom ratios, and p values are available to guide the model building process, model building decisions were based mainly on the CFI because of the relatively small sample size. Using the CFI as a guide, a fit index of more than .90 is generally considered indicative of an acceptable model. This cutoff was chosen as a general rule of thumb because the alternative is to risk model overfitting (Aiken, Stein, & Bentler, 1994).

To use the EQS program, a data set with no missing data points had to be created. Numerical values for missing entries in the data set that contained all of the alcoholics ($n = 363$) were imputed using techniques described by Bentler (1995). Specifically, values for missing data were computed as either the mean value for the variable, the mean value for the variable by group, or as a predicted value estimated by a regression of a given variable on other variables that are significantly correlated with it and consistent with respect to theoretical considerations. These methods were considered appropriate because the proportion of missing data was quite small and because the assumption of multivariate normality that underlies current advanced missing data treatments (e.g., Arbuckle, 1996; Jamshidian & Bentler, in press) is unrealistic for these data. Alternative methods such as pairwise-present computations (e.g., Marsh, 1998) or computing an EM-based covariance matrix (e.g., Graham & Hofer, 1993) are not sufficient here because the raw data are needed for the robust statistics that we use. A distribution-free approach that permits missing data (Yuan & Bentler, 1996) is not available in public computer programs. Schafer (1997) and Duncan, Duncan, and Li (1998) discuss some other alternatives, such as multiple imputation, that we did not consider useful improvements in our situation. Once all appropriate data imputations were completed, the 10 cases which still contained missing data on alcohol consumption measures were removed from the final sample to be used for structural modeling.

The general strategy used in creating the structural model was to test the final model from the WHDS sample as closely as possible to see if the fit remained adequate when put to the AFM data. Because a reduced variable set was used for the AFM study, it was not possible to test the exact same model across the two different samples. For example, although the WHDS study contained multiple measures for both alcohol consumption and alcohol problem variables, the AFM study contained only two alcohol consumption variables and one alcohol problem variable. Therefore, it was not possible to re-create the same latent factor structure for the dependent variables used in the WHDS study. Another difference was that one of the socioeconomic indicator variables in the WHDS, job classification index, was not computed for the AFM data. Consequentially, a different variable reflecting employment status at the time of entering treatment was used instead. It was felt that this afforded as close an approximation as possible to the job classification variable used in the WHDS socioeconomic status factor.

To facilitate development of the structural models in the AFM sample, correlations between all the continuous demographic, personality, and drinking variables were calculated for the entire pretreatment sample. Noted differences in the simple bivariate correlations between this correlation matrix and the matrix for the same variables in the WHDS data were used as an aid in making decisions about adding and deleting of paths to both the measurement and structural models.

To assess the overall stability of the AFM model, three structural models were developed. The first structural model reflected an attempt to approximate, as closely as possible, the measurement and structural paths found in the WHDS general population model, as they related to pretreatment drinking in the AFM sample. During the construction of this model, confirmatory factor analytic (CFA) models for the three major sets of measured variables (background variables, personality variables, and drinking variables) were developed. CFA models contain latent constructs that represent factors underlying measured variables and correlations between such latent constructs. In the case of the background variables, the CFA model also contained correlations between distinctive measured variables (i.e., age and gender) and the latent constructs in that set. By definition, none of the CFA models contained structural paths between any of the latent constructs used in the models. It should be noted that, although all of the data used in this stage of modeling were collected at the same time, a decision was made to create a path structure with historical and demographic factors that predict personality factors which, in turn, predict the pretreatment drinking factor. The multilevel structure created in this stage was also used for the other models that were subsequently developed, and posttreatment drinking formed a fourth level in the final outcome model.

The second structural model of the AFM data was designed to test the relative stability of the AFM pretreatment model between those who were interviewed at follow-up and those who were not. To facilitate this, a two-sample technique was utilized. The goal of the two-sample model was to test if the pretreatment structural model could stand up statistically when divided into groups that represented the effects of attrition (i.e., alcoholics who completed follow-up interviews versus those who did not). The rationale for including this stage in the modeling process was that if the overall structure of the initial model held up, then it would give some weight to the argument that any differential outcome effects predicted by the final structural (i.e., posttreatment) model could be similar for respondents who were lost from the study due to attrition.

The third structural model of the AFM data was designed to reflect relationships between pretreatment factors and treatment outcome. This model contained all significant paths from the independent variables and the factors in the pretreatment model to the posttreatment drinking factor that underlies the measured treatment outcome variables. This model was formed by taking the initial structural model and then adding paths from these constructs to the posttreatment drinking factor. Paths were also allowed to form from pretreatment factors and variables directly to any of the three measured variables making up the posttreatment drinking factor.

6. Results

6.1. Initial Analyses

The alcoholics who were reinterviewed at follow-up were more likely to be older, to have been married (or equivalent) at the time of initial interview, to have a higher average annual income, and to have been working in the months prior to treatment. Those included in the follow-up were also less likely to be of native ancestry and reported lower percentages of in-laws who were alcoholic. Differences in most personality measures (but not on Ego Strength, GEFT, and Eysenck's Lie scale) and in alcohol-related problems at Wave I, but not average ethanol consumption or heavy drinking, were also noted. Those not reinterviewed were typically more extreme in personality measures that are usually typically associated with alcoholism (e.g., MAC higher by .25 standard deviations, VANDO higher by .30 standard deviations, and EPQ-P higher by .25 standard deviations) and reported having more alcohol-related problems in the months immediately preceding their participation in treatment (number or problems higher by .50 standard deviations). Interestingly, those not reinterviewed were lower in two Neuroticism-related variables (EPQ-N lower by .32 standard deviations and TRAIT lower by .27 standard deviations). No differences were found in terms of gender, abuse of other substances prior to intake, or in terms of participation in residential versus community treatment. Those in the residential settings, however, were more likely to have participated in follow-up aftercare services that were offered as an optional adjunct to treatment.

Significant reductions in mean levels were noted for all measured drinking variables between pre- and posttreatment assessments (see Table 8.2). In the six

Table 8.2. Mean Levels on Drinking Variables both Pre- and Posttreatment[a]

		Residential		Community		Total Sample	
		Pre-	Post-	Pre-	Post-	Pre-	Post-
ETHANOL	Mean	7.3	0.7	4.7	0.3	6.2	0.5
	(SD)	(6.4)	(2.0)	(5.8)	(0.8)	(6.3)	(1.6)
HEAVDRK	Mean	17.5	2.4	6.2	0.9	12.8	1.8
	(SD)	(19.4)	(7.6)	(10.1)	(3.6)	(17.1)	(6.3)
PROBS	Mean	2.8	1.2	1.9	0.6	2.4	1.0
	(SD)	(1.8)	(1.9)	(1.4)	(1.4)	(1.7)	(1.7)

[a]All mean differences are significant ($p < .001$).

months after treatment, the AFM alcoholics had reduced their average ethanol consumption to levels that were comparable to those of the nonalcoholics in the WHDS general population sample. Episodes of heavy drinking and problems resulting from alcohol, however, were more comparable to those of the general population alcoholics. Even when means for residential and community treatment groups were calculated separately, the trend of reduced levels of drinking and related problems during follow-up was stable.

Overall, 52.4% of the alcoholics who were treated reported that they had achieved and maintained abstinence throughout the entire six-month follow-up period. Only 28.2% of those treated reported at least one instance of heavy drinking in the six months posttreatment, and 33.7% reported experiencing at least one alcohol-related problem during the same period. This compares with 71.6% and 86.1% who had reported one or more instances of heavy drinking and alcohol-related problems prior to initial intake, respectively. The amount of improvement noted here is similar to that noted by Emrick (1975) in his assessment of the effectiveness of treatment to produce improvements in drinking behavior over a six-month follow-up period. When viewed from the perspective of residential versus community treatment, there were no differences in abstinence rates or instances of heavy drinking, but those who had been in residential treatment had a higher incidence of reporting at least one or more alcohol-related problem during the follow-up period. This is consistent with other studies that reported no substantial differences in outcome between inpatient and outpatient treatment (e.g., Miller & Hester, 1986).

6.2. SEM Analyses

6.2.1. Accounting for Missing Data

As previously described in the methods section, imputed values for missing data were calculated using the mean value for the variable in question, mean values by group, or regression. Whenever regression was used as a method for imputing data, the predictor variables used were both empirically and theoretically related (e.g., socioeconomic items used as predictors for other socioeconomic variables and neuroticism items used as predictors for other neuroticism items). Table 8.3 contains descriptive statistics for all of the personality variables used in the structural model after data imputation. Because the imputation methods used keep the means intact but reduce variability in the variables, it is critical to evaluate whether the score ranges of the variables have been reduced substantially. If this were to occur, biased estimates of parameter estimate variability would be obtained. Tables 8.1 and 8.3 are reassuring in this regard because the standard deviations (SDs) of the variables are virtually identical before and after imputation. Indeed, the skew and kurtosis of the variables also remain intact. These stabilities are due to the small amount of missing data.

6.2.2. Measurement Models

As previously described in the methods section, confirmatory factor analytic (CFA) models were created for all hypothesized latent variable structures. Within the demographic variables set (which included socioeconomic status and family history of alcoholism), CFA produced a model of the demographic variables with a fit index of $X^2(19; n = 353) = 33.53$, CFI $= .98$, $p = .31$. For the personality data set, CFA produced a four-factor measurement model that was similar in most respects to the hypothesized factorial structure found in the WHDS general population sample. The fit of the four factor measurement model for the AFM personality data was $X^2(30; n = 353) = 94.13$, CFI $= .95$, $p < .001$ (see Figure 8.2 for factor loadings for the AFM data).

Although similar in most respects, the latent structure of the four-factor per-

Table 8.3. Descriptive Statistics of Personality Measures for AFM Sample after Data Imputation[a]

	Mean	Items	Range	SD	Skew	Kurtosis
EPQ-E	13.53	23	2–23	5.09	−.29	−.90
MAC	25.70	54	15–37	4.55	−.07	−.57
VANDO	26.40	54	6–47	8.53	−.09	.62
EPQ-P	7.56	34	0–25	4.13	.78	.77
EPQ-L	7.00	21	0–18	4.17	.45	−.41
EGOST	37.63	67	19–56	7.56	−.14	−.34
EPQ-N	16.63	24	1–24	5.26	−.70	−.17
Esteem	28.15	10	10–40	4.87	.15	.56
Anxiety	46.35	20	21–74	9.48	.13	−.10
GEFT	7.62	25	0–18	5.20	.22	−1.11

[a]The meaning of each variable is described fully in the measures section of Chapter 6.

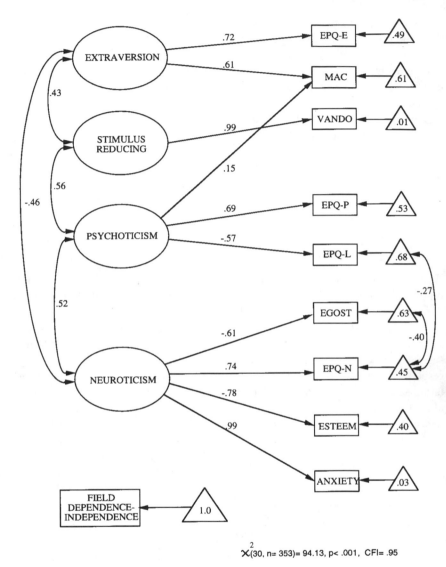

$$\chi^2_{(30, n= 353)}= 94.13, p< .001, CFI= .95$$

Figure 8.2. Four-factor CFA model for the AFM clinical alcoholics.

sonality CFA model for the AFM data differed somewhat from the personality structure found in the WHDS general population model. First, while there was a relatively minor path from Extraversion to VANDO in the WHDS model, there was no such path in the AFM model. Second, although there was a path in the WHDS model from Stimulus Reducing to EGOST, there was no such path in the AFM model. All other factor loadings from the WHDS personality structure were also significant in the AFM model. However, a correlation existed between the Extraversion and Psychoticism latent factors in the WHDS data but not in the AFM data. It should also be noted that the Stimulus Reducing factor in this model is essentially synonymous with the VANDO Scale because this factor did not have significant multiple indicators. As a consequence of the differences among the various factor loadings for measured variables on the personality factors and corresponding correlations between these factors, interpretation of these latent factors should be approached with some caution.

In the AFM data, there were also two sets of correlated errors between personality items, which were not present in the WHDS personality structure. These correlated error paths, both negative, were between EGOST and EPQ-N and between EPQ-N and EPQ-L. The negative correlation between the residuals in EPQ-N and EPQ-L imply that the model-reproduced negative correlation between these variables ($-.57 \times .52 \times .74 = -.22$) is insufficiently small to reproduce the observed negative correlation between these variables. Similarly, the negative correlation between EGOST and EPQ-N implies that the model-based correlation ($-.61 \times .74 = -.45$) is not as large as that found in the data. Thus, these pairs of variables are more similar than expected under the factor model alone. According to Eysenck and Eysenck (1976), a relatively high negative correlation between Neuroticism and the Lie Scale would tend to indicate a greater propensity toward dissimulation in an effort to be viewed in a favorable light. Because the Eysencks' research on this relationship was done mainly on samples of college students and therefore has questionable generalizability to populations that are substantially less socially conforming than average, the importance of this observed correlation in assessing the overall validity of the AFM data collected for this study is uncertain at best. One possible interpretation of this correlation, however, is that many of the alcoholics in the study were "in denial" regarding the severity of their drinking problem.

The CFA model for the drinking variables was handled in a manner slightly different from the other CFA models. Because there were only three measured variables for each of the two time periods (i.e., for pre- and posttreatment), CFA models could not be generated separately. The reasons for the inability of EQS to generate models for individual factors with three or less related variables is related to the degrees of freedom necessary to estimate a model. In a CFA model with only one factor and three measured variables, for example, there are six parameters to estimate and six data elements. The result is zero degrees of freedom, and hence the model cannot be tested. This is a model that shows a perfect fit every time, regardless of any underlying relationship between the measured variables! For a CFA model with one factor and two measured variables, the situation is even worse. There are four parameters to estimate, yet only three data points, resulting in a model that is underidentified and can not be estimated.

The strategy used to overcome this barrier was to estimate a CFA model simultaneously for pre- and posttreatment drinking. Of course, doing this allowed inclusion of only the 252 reinterviewed cases in the CFA model for drinking, instead of the 353 cases in the original pretreatment sample. It also meant, given a reasonable fit index, committing to a model that hypothesized a single drinking factor for each of the two periods. This was not perceived as detrimental to the overall goal of the study because the estimated paths in the structural models to be developed could form directly to any measured variable, if necessary, even if that variable were already predicted by another latent factor. The resulting model showed an acceptable fit, $X^2(8; n = 252) = 30.93$, CFI = .95, $p < .001$, but univariate tests of kurtosis showed a marked departure from normality of two of the outcome drinking variables (heavy drinking and ethanol consumption). Consequently, the model was reevaluated using robust statistics. The Satorra–Bentler Scaled chi-square statistic, which compensates for the nonnormality of the distribution, was 20.75, $p = .008$. Factor loadings of the drinking variables on their respective factors ranged from moderate to high, and only one variable (problems in the months prior to intake, .38) weighed in at less than .50. All were significantly different from zero, based on robust standard errors.

6.2.3. Structural Models

To create the structural model of personality and drinking prior to treatment, a path model containing three levels of factors was developed. To accomplish this, several modifications had to be made to the CFA models. These modifications included the addition of disturbance terms so that the factors in the second and third levels could be predicted as dependent variables. The disturbances were allowed to correlate in the same fashion as were the factors in the measurement model. An additional modification was that factor loading paths were allowed to be altered in magnitude, as well as added or dropped in accordance with the Lagrange and Wald tests for adding/dropping parameters. On the first level, factors that were hypothesized as background characteristics (i.e., SES and family history of alcoholism) were allowed to correlate with each other as per the measurement model. Age and gender were also allowed to correlate with the first-level factors. As a whole, this first-level factor/variable structure can be viewed as the context within which the personality structure in the model was studied. This is consistent with the strategy used in developing of the WHDS general population model.

Once this basic structure was set up, the pretreatment model was formed in several stages. First, approximations of all of the major structural paths from major variables and factors to higher level variables and factors that were present in the WHDS general population model were added as structural paths to the AFM pretreatment model. Then, all of these paths that were indicated as nonsignificant by the Wald test were removed from the model. In the third stage, other paths that were statistically significant by the Lagrange test and consistent with theoretical considerations were added to the model until the model reached a CFI of .90 or more. Finally, other paths that became nonsignificant through this process were deleted from the model. As a result, the three-level pretreatment model ended up fitting the covariance structure reasonably well but not well enough for the heightened risk of model overfitting ($X^2(209; n = 353) = 446.74$, CFI = .90, $p < .001$).

Then the pretreatment model was used in a test for comparative fit between the group of alcoholics who participated in the follow-up versus those who did not. To facilitate this, a two-sample technique was utilized (Bentler, 1995). In the first of two runs using this technique, cross group constraints were imposed so that all factor loadings, factor variances and covariances, and factor regression coefficients were equal between the reinterviewed and not reinterviewed groups. Covariances and regression paths relating to the independent background variables were also constrained to be equal across groups. Factor residual variances (i.e., disturbances) and dependent variable unique variances (i.e., error terms) were not constrained to be equal between groups. This is consistent with a strategy for testing constraints between groups that is outlined in the EQS Structural Equations Program Manual (Bentler, 1995). Then, in a second run, all cross group constraints were released, so that the previously constrained paths could form freely within each group. Then the X^2 values and fit indexes of the resulting models were compared.

The constrained model resulted in a CFI of .89, $X^2(454; n = 101) = 712.11$, $p < .001$. In the unconstrained model, a CFI of .89, $X^2(418; n = 101) = 666.23$, $p < .001$ was realized. The difference in fit between these two models, $X^2(36; n = 101) = 45.88$, did not reach statistical significance at conventional levels. Consequently, a conclusion that there was no structural difference between those who were and those who were not reinterviewed is not unreasonable. It should be noted that differences between the means of latent constructs and measured variables between the two groups were not tested in this evaluation. A test of this sort was seen as unnecessary because it was already apparent from the univariate tests that those not reinterviewed were of lower socioeconomic status, were more extreme in the severity of their drinking problems prior to treatment, and were more extreme in personality traits typically associated with more severe manifestations of the alcoholism syndrome.

The final stage of the modeling process involved adding a fourth level to the pretreatment model, so that the relationship between that structural model and treatment outcome could be determined for the 252 respondents who were included in the follow-up. The major pathways in the full structural equation model are shown in Figure 8.3. Figure 8.4 shows the factor loadings on demographic factors, and Figure 8.5 shows the loadings on personality factors. All of these factor loadings are those within the overall context of the model. Tables 8.4 and

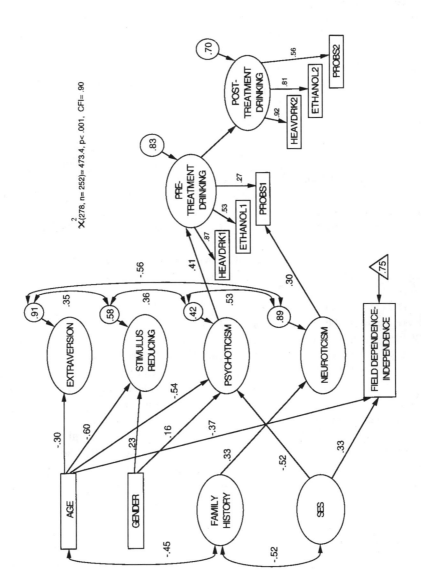

Figure 8.3. Major pathways in AFM posttreatment structural model.

8.5 contain the correlation matrix for major measured and latent variables and the paths not shown on any diagram, respectively. In all figures and tables, standardized parameter estimates are shown for ease of interpretation, even though all significance tests were based on the unstandardized solution. Factor disturbances and dependent variable error terms are also squared to ease interpretation.

From a practical perspective, placing the background factor/variable structure in a level of the model logically prior to the personality structure allowed the model to test for paths between these factors/variables and drinking behavior that were not mediated through personality. In the structural model, paths extending

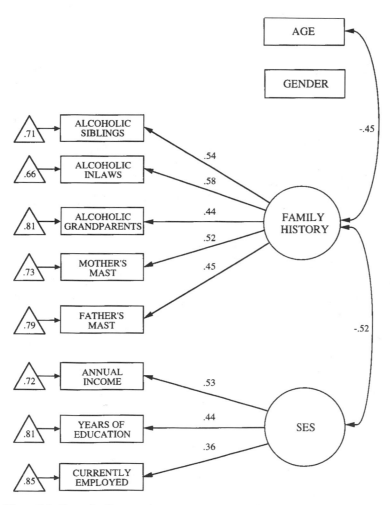

Figure 8.4. Factor loadings on demographic factors in the AFM posttreatment model.

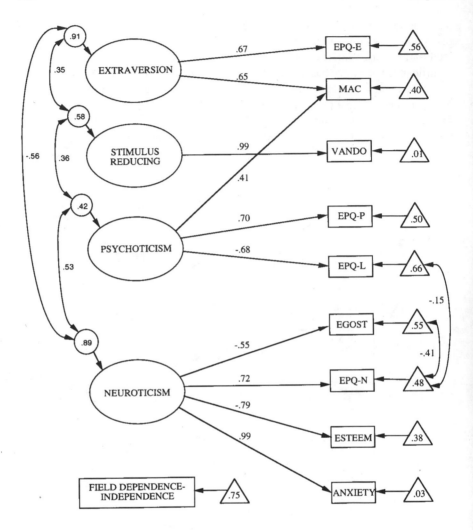

Figure 8.5. Factor loadings on personality factors in the AFM posttreatment model.

from these first-level factors/variables directly to the drinking factor (at either pre- or posttreatment) could be viewed as not being mediated through personality. On the other hand, paths extending from these factors/variables to any personality factor that has a path extending to one of the drinking factors can be viewed as being mediated through personality. The EQS program allows adding of both direct and indirect paths to a model, so that direct and mediated effects can be looked at simultaneously. In the final model, there were no direct paths

Table 8.4. Correlation Matrix of Major Measured and Latent Variables in AFM Posttreatment Model[a]

	Age	Gend.	GEFT	Fam. hist.	SES	Extra.	St. Red.	Psyc.	Neur.	Pre Drnk.	Post Drnk.
Age											
Gend.	.00										
GEFT	−.37	.00									
Fam. Hist.	−.45	.00	−.01								
SES	.00	.00	.33	−.52							
Extra.	−.30	.00	.11	.13	.00						
Stim. Red.	−.60	.23	.22	.27	.00	.43					
Psyc.	−.54	.16	.03	.51	−.52	.16	.54				
Neur.	−.15	.00	−.01	.33	−.17	−.46	.09	.49			
Pre Drnk.	−.22	.07	.01	.21	−.21	.07	.22	.41	.20		
Post Drnk.	−.12	.04	.01	.11	-.12	.04	.12	.22	.11	.55	

[a]Age=age of respondent; Gend.=gender; GEFT=Group Embedded Figures Test, a measure of field dependence; Fam. Hist.=family history of alcoholism; SES=socioeconomic status (based on education, income, and employment); Extra.=extraversion; St. Red.=stimulus reducing; Psyc.=psychoticism; Neur.=neuroticism; Pre-Drnk.=pretreatment drinking; Post-Drnk.=posttreatment drinking.

from any of the background factors or variables to either pre- or posttreatment drinking factors or variables.

The personality structure from the confirmatory model remained essentially the same within the context of the four-level structural model. All correlation paths between disturbances remained in the same direction and of the same order as the correlations between the factors within the personality measurement model. Factor loadings, although similar, changed somewhat when viewed from within the context of the structural model. One notable example was the MAC loading on the Psychoticism factor, which increased to resemble more closely its factor loading in the WHDS general population structural model.

For the most part, structural paths from the level one factors and major measured variables to level two personality factors were similar to those from the WHDS general personality model. There were some notable differences, however, First, in the AFM model, there was no path from gender to GEFT and no path from SES to Neuroticism. Second, although Family History of Alcoholism

Table 8.5. Paths Not Shown on Any Diagram in the AFM Posttreatment Model

	MAC	EPQ-L	EGOST
Age	.35		
Gender	.24		
SES		−.32	.30

predicted both Psychoticism and Neuroticism in the WHDS data, it predicted only Neuroticism in the AFM data. During the construction of the AFM models, it was noted that there was a path initially from Family History to both Psychoticism and Neuroticism but that the path to Psychoticism became nonsignificant as other structural paths were added to the model in the final stages. In the light of the apparent instability of this part of the model, caution should be exercised in interpreting the meaning of structural paths from Family History to either of these two factors. A caveat is also necessary due to the relatively high amount of missing data within the measured variables that make up the Family History latent construct.

Differences also existed in terms of which measured personality variables were predicted by background factors and variables. Whereas being female in the WHDS sample was associated with higher scores on EPQ-N, this association did not exist in the AFM data. Conversely, being male was associated with higher scores on MAC for the AFM data, but no association existed in the WHDS. Other associations between background variables/factors and measured personality variables, however, remained similar for both the WHDS and the AFM. Specifically, for both the WHDS and the AFM, being older was associated with higher MAC scores, and higher SES was associated with higher EGOST but lower EPQ-L scores. Overall, in the AFM data, the background structure accounted for 9% of the variance in Extraversion, 42% of the variance in Stimulus Reducing, 58% of the variance in Psychoticism, and 11% of the variance in Neuroticism.

As far as structural paths to level three and level four factors are concerned, there was one significant path from the Psychoticism latent personality construct that explained 17% of the variance in Pretreatment Drinking. Although there were no other paths from any other personality factor to Pretreatment Drinking, there was a direct path from Neuroticism to the variable that measured reported alcohol-related problems in the months prior to treatment. This means that reported problems were related to Neuroticism, whereas the other two measured variables loading on the Pretreatment Drinking factor were not. It should be noted that, in the final model, the pretreatment alcohol problems measured variable had a substantially lower weighting on the Pretreatment Drinking than the other two pretreatment measured variables. This could lead to an interpretation that the Pretreatment Drinking factor was more a measure of consumption patterns than of alcohol-related problems.

For the Posttreatment Drinking factor, Pretreatment Drinking was the only predictor and explained 30% of the variance. No other personality or background factors and/or variables showed a direct effect on the Posttreatment Drinking factor or on the three measured outcome variables loading on that factor. A decomposition of effects to test for indirect parametric effects indicated that an indirect effect of Psychoticism on Posttreatment Drinking through Pretreatment Drinking was statistically significant and had a standardized regression coefficient for the indirect effect of .20 ($p < .001$).

7. Discussion

7.1. Personality Structure of the AFM Sample

The first research hypothesis was that the various personality measures used in the AFM study would be organizable into a factorial structure similar to that found in the WHDS general population model, and variables loading on factors would be similar to Psychoticism, Extraversion, Neuroticism, and Stimulus Reducing. Except for a few minor differences, the latent personality structure developed for the data from the AFM sample closely resembled that of the WHDS general population sample. In both cases, a four-factor solution was possible. In both cases, the loadings on the four factors were more or less the same. Then, it may be concluded that the first hypothesis proposed was largely supported by the results of the study.

· In complicated structural models that incorporated latent variables, however, interpretation of the meaning of latent factors is often difficult. Theoretically, a latent factor in SEM represents an underlying construct that is directly unmeasurable (i.e., one whose existence can be inferred only through the correlations of measured variables that are indicative of that factor). When the measured variables loading on a given factor are developed theoretically as different measures of the same underlying construct (or when only one variable loads on a given factor), choosing a label for that factor can be relatively straightforward. However, when underlying factors are constructs related to a variety of variables that are disparate in their origins, interpretation becomes more difficult and, consequently, labeling more arbitrary. Finding an appropriate naming convention is further frustrated when the latent factors in question are structurally different between different samples used to test a hypothesized factorial structure.

In the four-factor solution from the AFM data, for example, the factor labeled Stimulus Reducing underlies only one measured variable, VANDO. Because VANDO is a measure of stimulus reducing–augmenting, the choice to call the latent factor Stimulus Reducing is unambiguous. This contrasts with the same factor in the WHDS data which was called Stimulus Reducing, even though it also weighed moderately on the measured variable EGOST. Interpretation of the Extraversion factor between the WHDS and the AFM data poses the same problem. In addition to EPQ-E and MAC, in the WHDS model the Extraversion factor is related to the measured variable VANDO. In the AFM model, it is not related to VANDO. Fortunately, interpretation of the remaining two factors, Psychoticism and Neuroticism, is less difficult, because each has the same measured variables weighing on them in both the WHDS and the AFM models.

The differences in personality structure between the WHDS general population and the AFM models are mainly due to differences in the covarying relationships between the measured personality variables in the WHDS and the AFM samples. Table 8.6 shows the Pearson correlation coefficients between the personality variables for both the WHDS and the AFM samples. It is possible that processes related to the development, progression, and/or continuation of alcoholism are responsible for the differences noted in personality structure between the general population sample and the alcoholics who sought treatment at the AFM. It is also possible that processes associated with detoxification from alcohol acted to alter the accurate measurement of personality traits in the AFM sample, even though efforts were made to minimize this possibility by interviewing respondents after the acute detoxification period had ended. This, of course, would contribute to error beyond that caused by measurement error inherent in the personality tests and/or type I error.

7.2. Pretreatment Structural Model

The second research hypothesis was that Stimulus Reducing and Psychoticism would be related to the Pretreatment Drinking Factor. This hypothesis was only partially confirmed in the structural model of pretreatment personality and drinking because only Psychoticism was a predictor of Pretreatment Drinking. Psychoticism accounted for 17% of the total variance in this factor.

This result indicates that different processes are evident in the clinical alcoholics compared to drinkers in the general population. Although the WHDS model suggests that two processes lead to problems with alcohol, the AFM clearly suggests only one. Several explanations for this apparent disparity are both reasonable and consistent with the findings of other studies. For example, it is possible that many general population drinkers who consume more alcohol solely because

Table 8.6. Correlations Between Personality Measures for WHDS Population Sample and AFM Clinical Sample

	EPQ-E	MAC	VANDO	EPQ-P	EPQ-L	EGOST	EPQ-N	EST.	TRAIT	GEFT
EPQ-E		.41	.44	.11	−.11	.12	−.11	.23	−.20	ns
MAC	.44		.26	.13	ns	ns	ns	.09	−.09	−.10
VANDO	.34	.34		.35	−.25	.23	ns	.09	ns	.21
EPQ-P	ns	.17	.41		−.21	−.17	.14	−.18	.25	ns
EPQ-L	−.04	−.15	−.30	−.38		−.09	−.20	.11	−.14	−.28
EGOST	.16	ns	ns	−.29	.19		−.57	.44	−.58	.29
EPQ-N	−.16	ns	ns	.28	−.38	−.66		−.47	.72	−.08
Esteem	.30	.23	ns	−.27	.25	.47	−.56		−.67	.12
Trait	−.27	−.21	ns	.30	−.31	−.59	.73	−.76		−.11
GEFT	ns	ns	.19	ns	−.22	ns	ns	ns	ns	

[a]Correlations in the upper right portion of table are from WHDS general population sample; correlations in lower left portion are from the AFM clinical sample; ns - nonsignificant.

they are stimulus reducers either develop less alcohol-related problems or can resolve their drinking problems without seeking formal treatment. Consequently, many drinkers who exhibit this pathway to alcohol problems would not be included in the AFM sample. This explanation is consistent with findings from other studies that document the high incidence of resolving problem drinking without formal treatment for a majority of people who have drinking problems (Sobell, 1994; Vaillant, 1983).

Alternatively, processes related to the development and maintenance of alcohol-related problems might contribute to the relative importance of Psychoticism over Stimulus Reducing in predicting pretreatment drinking in a clinical sample such as the AFM. Regardless of why the AFM alcoholics drank heavily in the first place (e.g., sensation seeking as a result of stimulus-reducing tendencies), they might be continuing in a pathological pattern of alcohol consumption mainly because of personality traits related to psychoticism. This may be especially true for drinkers who initially are relatively low in ego strength. In this sense, alcoholism might have taken on "a life of it's own" for these drinkers in a fashion similar to that described by Vaillant (1983). Of course, a combination of these two explanations or even other explanatory processes may be responsible for the observed differences in the relationship between personality dimensions and drinking found in these two diverse samples.

It is interesting to note that a personality structure that was not hypothesized as having a relationship to pretreatment drinking did, in fact, have such a relationship. Although the Neuroticism factor was not structurally related to the Pretreatment Drinking factor as a whole, it was related to the measured variable of alcohol-related problems prior to treatment. From this type of data, however, it is impossible to determine whether those who were more neurotic actually experienced more alcohol-related problems or just reported more of them because of heightened sensitivity to the turmoil in their life experiences. Regardless, this finding provides some support for the original Barnes (1983) model where neuroticism plays a distinct role in the continuation of alcoholic drinking patterns.

7.3. Posttreatment Structural Model

The third research hypothesis was that Stimulus Reducing and Psychoticism would be either directly or indirectly related to the Posttreatment Drinking factor that measured alcohol consumption and related problems in the six months after completing treatment. Although there were no measurable direct or indirect effects from Stimulus Reducing on Posttreatment Drinking, there was a measurable indirect effect from Psychoticism that was mediated through Pretreatment Drinking. This finding indicates that Psychoticism influences posttreatment drinking patterns primarily through pretreatment drinking patterns. This is a pathway that one would expect to find in a clinical sample such as this. A direct effect, which would indicate a relationship between Psychoticism and change in drinking patterns (i.e., progression in alcoholism), is less likely to be expected in clinical samples where patterns of alcohol consumption are already firmly established.

Although there was no direct effect of personality on posttreatment drinking behavior, there are a variety of other reasons why an existing direct personality effect might not have been detected. First of all, although the personality structures of those lost through attrition was similar to those who were reinterviewed, those not reinterviewed tended to be more extreme in alcoholism-related personality traits and had more problems due to alcohol in the months prior to seeking treatment. Because these respondents were likely to have been at a higher risk of relapse in the six months after treatment, it is possible that their inclusion in the follow-up portion of the study might have led to a different finding. Second, because there were only three measured variables on each of the drinking factors and no separate factors for alcohol consumption versus alcohol problems, the sensitivity of the follow-up measures might have been compromised. Finally, due to the relatively strong treatment effects, low variability in the outcome measures (resulting in highly skewed distributions for posttreatment measured variables) might have compromised the ability of the EQS program to detect a significant covariance relationship between personality and Posttreatment Drinking. Although the maximum likelihood estimation method with robust statistics available in the EQS program can compensate for marked divergence from multivariate normality, a nonparametric technique becomes more appropriate when divergence is so extreme as to reduce distributions to a state more categorical than normal.

Table 8.7 contains a univariate example from the AFM data that illustrates how nonnormality of distributions can effect estimates of association between variables. At pretreatment, when the distributions of the drinking variables were relatively normal, estimates of linear association between EPQ-P and pretreatment drinking variables using the Pearson correlation statistic are all significant. Using the same statistic at posttreatment, the EPQ-P variable does not correlate significantly with any of the outcome variables. Assessing the same strengths of association using Kendall's tau statistic, however, produces a statistically significant result for all three of the posttreatment drinking measures. Kendall's tau is a special nonparametric measure of association for ordinal variables.

Regardless of the methodological issues described above, it appears that the bivariate correlations between the Psychoticism measured variables and alcohol consumption pattern variables were generally lower posttreatment. This suggests that processes involved in the time between pre-and posttreatment either may have altered the relationship between Psychoticism and drinking patterns or acted to change relative scores on this personality factor for a substantial number of individuals between pre- and posttreatment assessment. If the former is true, then the relationship between personality and drinking patterns might have been disrupted, at least in the short term, by the treatment. If the latter is true, then pretreatment personality scores might not correlate well with posttreatment drinking measures, even though posttreatment personality scores may correlate well with posttreatment drinking. Unfortunately, because only pretreatment personality scores were gathered during data collection, a test of this hypothesis was not possible.

A conclusion that there may be short term fluctuations in either the connection between personality and drinking behavior or between pretreatment personality and posttreatment personality is not incompatible with the results of previous studies that attempted to relate various psychiatric personality disorders to treatment outcome. For example, some studies found groups which one would expect to be higher in Psychoticism (i.e., the psychopathic group, Conley, 1981; and the group of impulsive types, Zivich, 1981) that actually did better than some other groups in treatment outcome. Other studies found that groups with antisocial personality (e.g., Poldrugo & Forti, 1988; Rounsaville et al., 1987) and groups with personality disorders (Nurnberg et al., 1993) fared worse at outcome. Still other studies concluded either that there were no differences between those with borderline personality and those without it (Nace et al., 1986) or that comorbid psychiatric diagnosis, although a good postdictor of low functioning prior to treatment, was not a reliable predictor of treatment outcome. One would expect that those with antisocial personality, personality disorder, borderline personality, and/ or comorbid psychiatric diagnosis would tend to score higher on the Psychoticism dimension.

These findings of variability in treatment outcome for those one would expect to be higher in Psychoticism emphasizes that, at least in the short term, there is not a clearly observable direct relationship between this personality characteristic and treatment outcome. Apparently, looking at personality from the perspective of continuous dimensions, as opposed to clinical diagnostic categories, did little to improve the ability of the personality structure, as defined, to predict short term treatment outcome, when pretreatment drinking was taken into consideration.

8. Implications

Several implications stem from the results of this study. First of all, measured personality variables for the alcoholics in the AFM clinical alcoholic sample form into a cohesive dimensional personality structure, similar in most ways to the personality structure contained in the WHDS general population model. Second, only one dimension in this personality structure, psychoticism, has demonstrated a direct relationship to pretreatment alcohol consumption patterns within this sample. This suggests a different association between personality and alcohol abuse than the dual association suggested by the WHDS general population model. Where there may be two structural paths in the general population leading to alcohol dependency, in clinical populations, one of these paths may no longer be relevant. Third, at least in the short term, one major dimension of personality structure, as defined in this study, does not have a direct impact on treatment outcome. It does, however, have an indirect effect on treatment outcome through pretreatment functioning drinking patterns.

Although on the surface, the finding of only an indirect relationship between a major pretreatment personality dimension (Psychoticism) and posttreatment drinking patterns could be interpreted as a failure to confirm one of the main hypotheses in the study, this "nonfinding" is not too surprising in a clinical sample because in a sample such as this, alcohol consumption patterns are likely to be already well established and/or to have reached a high level of severity prior to treatment. In samples where alcohol consumption patterns are less well established and/or not as severe, such as in the WHDS general population sample, one would expect to find a direct effect because progression of the alcoholism syndrome is more likely to occur. Of course, it is possible that, given a longer follow-up period, a direct effect of Psychoticism on subsequent drinking patterns (i.e., progression of alcoholism) could be evidenced even within the clinical sample. The question "does Psychoticism predict long-term posttreatment drinking patterns above and beyond initial pretreatment drinking patterns?" was not addressed in this study but should be the subject of further investigation. Despite the fact that an absence of a direct effect did not come as a surprise, it still may be important as a heuristic device. In addition to pointing toward possible methodological limitations inherent in this study, it challenges researchers to study personality-related processes that are outside the scope of this investigation.

IV

SUBGROUPS OF ALCOHOLICS

9

Types of Alcoholics in the General Population and Clinical Samples

Research on personality and the different types of alcoholics has usually been done only on clinical samples. This leads to a problem in that one is never sure whether the distribution of the different types of personality profiles has more to do with the particular treatment setting chosen than the actual distribution of these profiles in the general population. In this chapter we examine the types of alcoholics that occur in the general population and clinical samples of alcoholics when the personality scores in the samples are subjected to cluster analytic procedures. The primary objectives in this chapter are as follows:

1. To cluster analyze the personality scores of a group of general population alcoholics to determine the optimum number and nature of the personality types in this sample;
2. To compare the derived clusters on their demographic characteristics, drinking history, and personality scores;
3. To cluster analyze the personality scores of a group of clinical alcoholics to determine the optimum number and nature of personality types in this sample.
4. To compare the derived clusters in the clinical sample on their demographic characteristics, drinking history, and personality scores.
5. To compare the distributions of the derived personality clusters in the general population and clinical samples.

There are two different kinds of research in the field of subtyping alcoholics. One kind of research draws on a theoretical perspective, whereas the other is more empirically driven and relies on cluster analyses of samples of alcoholics using a variety of personality tests such as the MMPI.

1. Theoretical Perspectives

1.1. Cloninger

One of the more frequently cited perspectives on the subtypes of alcoholism is the perspective advanced by Cloninger (1987a). Cloninger (1987a) hypothesized that there are two different kinds of alcoholism. Type I alcoholism is characterized by later onset and by lower association with antisocial behavior. It is more common in females and is hypothesized as less strongly linked with a family history of alcohol abuse. The personality traits hypothesized as associated with Type I alcoholism include lower novelty seeking, higher reward dependence, and higher harm avoidance. Type II alcoholics, it is hypothesized, have an earlier onset of the disorder. A stronger association with antisocial behavior, male gender, and a family history of alcohol abuse is also hypothesized for Type II alcoholics. Personality traits associated with Type II alcoholism, it is hypothesized, include higher novelty seeking, lower harm avoidance, and lower reward dependence. Type II alcoholism is also hypothesized as the more prevalent form of the disorder.

In a recent review of the literature pertaining to Cloninger's theory, Howard et al. (1997) concluded that (1) there were some problems in replicating the factor structure of the Cloninger test; (2) the Cloninger novelty-seeking dimension was strongly predictive of alcohol and drug abuse, but that relationships with the other dimensions were less conclusive; (3) the link between Type II alcoholism and family history of abuse was not strongly supported; and (4) there were some questions about the hypothesized link between gender and Type II alcoholism.

From the standpoint of the current investigation, the most critical issue regarding Cloninger's theory is whether or not the hypothesized classification with respect to personality traits is supportable. The study that is most relevant to this issue is the investigation by von Knorring et al. (1987). In that investigation, male alcoholics were classified as either Type I or Type II based on the age of onset and presence or absence of social complications. Type II alcoholics have an earlier onset with more complications. When comparisons were conducted on the Karolinska Personality Scales, the results indicated that Type II alcoholics are characterized by more somatic anxiety and verbal aggression, lower scores on socialization and inhibition of aggression, and higher scores on the impulsive sensation-seeking psychopathy factor. Von Knorring et al. (1987) concluded that it was important to keep alcoholism associated with antisocial behavior separate from other forms of alcoholism. A recent investigation by Hallman, von Knorring, and Oreland (1996) compared Type I and Type II alcoholics and found that Type II alcoholics had lower platelet MAO and a higher prevalence for antisocial and borderline personality types. This pattern of results is consistent with Cloninger's (1987a) theory.

1.2. MacAndrew

As noted in the introductory chapter, MacAndrew (1979) has also hypothesized that there are two different kinds of alcoholics and that the 85% of the alcoholics identified by the MacAndrew Scale are considered primary substance abusers. These individuals are high on Neuroticism and Extraversion. MacAndrew (1979) hypothesized that the second group of alcoholics would also be high on Neuroticism but lower on Extraversion. The MacAndrew classification system differs somewhat from Cloninger's hypothesized system in that MacAndrew predicts that both groups would be high on Neuroticism. It should be noted that the MacAndrew classification system is based on results from clinical samples where the scale was developed. Results in the von Knorring et al. (1987) study described above, in which clinical samples of alcoholics were employed, were consistent with the MacAndrew perspective in that both of the alcoholic subtypes scored high on scales measuring anxiety. In younger samples however, alcohol and substance abuse are sometimes found in conjunction with lower neuroticism or harm avoidance (e.g., Massey, Walfish, & Krone, 1992; Pulkkinen & Pitkanen, 1994), perhaps confirming the Cloninger classification system for people at the prealcoholic age level.

1.3. Babor

In reviewing the literature on alcoholic subtypes, Babor et al. (1992) concluded that there is strong evidence for at least two types of alcoholism. Babor et al. (1992) describe one type of alcoholism (Type B) that is characterized by earlier onset, more rapid development or course, symptoms that are more severe, greater psychological vulnerability, and poorer treatment prognosis. The second type of alcoholism (Type A) is characterized by the opposite pattern, including later onset, less rapid development, less severe symptoms, less vulnerability psychologically, and better treatment prognosis. Research by Babor et al. (1992) found support for their distinctions in that Type B alcoholism was associated with earlier onset and more childhood risk factors, including a family history of alcoholism, than Type A alcoholism. Type B alcoholism was accompanied by more current psychopathology, more severe dependence on alcohol and other drugs, more life stress, and poorer prognosis than Type A alcoholism.

1.4. Zucker

In reviewing the literature on typologies of alcoholics, Zucker, Fitzgerald, and Moses (1995) concluded that the literature supports the idea that there are at least two forms of alcoholism. One form of alcoholism is characterized by antisocial traits that are somewhat stable over the life course, and the second form of alcoholism is not associated with stable antisocial traits and is also perhaps associated with less psychopathology in general. Research by Zucker's group (Ichiyama, Zucker, Fitzgerald, & Bingham, 1996; Zucker, Ellis, Bingham, Fitzgerald, & Sanford,1996) identified some of the characteristics associated with antisocial alcoholism, including earlier onset, more psychopathology, poorer social functioning, denser family history, more problems in social relationships, and more self-neglect.

1.5. Blackson

Research at the Centre of Education and Drug Abuse Research (CEDAR) has focused on the importance of childhood temperament in the etiology of alcoholism. Recently, Blackson (1994) conducted research suggesting that the concept of difficult versus easy temperament might form a useful categorization system for subtyping individuals at risk of developing alcoholism. In this research, cluster analyses were conducted on samples of fathers (including alcoholics and nonalcoholics) and sons on the Revised Dimensions of Temperament Survey. The results suggested that both fathers and sons could be separated into two groups that differ on the basis of temperament difficulty. The difficult temperament group was characterized by high activity level, social withdrawal, rigidity, poor quality of mood, poor task orientation, and dysthrythmicity. The difficult temperament group of sons was also characterized by high-risk family environments and a number of other high-risk attributes associated with the development of alcohol abuse, including higher aggressivity and unconventionality, more peer delinquency, and lower cognitive performance.

2. Empirically Oriented Studies

Reviewing the empirical studies that have employed cluster analyses on samples of alcoholics using standard personality batteries is problematic for a number of reasons. Some of the problems plaguing this literature include (1) total reliance on unrepresentative samples of alcoholics, (2) the use of personality tests such as the MMPI which contain a lot of overlapping scales, (3) the use of differing cluster analytic procedures from one study to the next, (4) the lack of any compelling statistical or theoretical arguments for identifying the number of clusters to be chosen, and (5) sample sizes that are often too small to provide reliable cluster solutions. Despite these numerous problems, some consistent findings have been reported.

2.1. MMPI

The MMPI is the most frequently used personality measure for describing alcoholics. Graham and Strenger (1988) reviewed the data on hospitalized alcoholics and suggested that six subtypes can be reliably distinguished:

1. a psychopathology-depression type, with no other abnormal scores
2. a profile with depression and some schizoid features and high psychopathy
3. a psychopathy with secondary depression or mania
4. a psychopathy-mania profile
5. a profile with high hypochondriasis, depression, and hysteria with secondary psychopathy (similar to the neurotic personality disorder type described previously)
6. a profile with a high score on the faking bad validity scale

A small study by Sheppard, Smith, and Rosenbaum (1988) identified three clusters similar to the first three Graham and Strenger (1988) clusters. These were identified from a sample tested on admission. However, at discharge the only unique feature was an elevated psychopathology scale score. Using the MMPI, Dush and Keen (1995) looked at subtypes of alcoholics before and after treatment. They identified four clusters that roughly correspond to sensation-seeking, neurotic-introvert, and psychotic and neurotic types. However, the typology did not endure after treatment. Once again, a high psychopathology scale score was the only enduring feature of the clusters.

These studies point to another important limitation of clinical studies on subtypes of alcoholics. When alcoholics go for treatment, they may be experiencing a variety of different symptom patterns as they undergo withdrawal. Individuals may respond to the stress of withdrawal in different ways and with different symptom patterns, but these symptom patterns may not reflect the underlying personality of that individual. This makes it important to conduct cluster analytic studies of untreated samples of alcoholics preferably in the general population.

2.2. MCMI

Several cluster analytic studies have been conducted on alcoholic samples with the MCMI. This research has been nicely summarized by Matano, Locke, and

Schwartz (1994). In summarizing six studies including their own, Matano et al. (1994) found that the negativistic-passive-aggressive cluster occurred most frequently and accounted for 24% of the cases, on average across the six studies. The next most common cluster was a low psychopathology compulsive-conforming cluster (18%), followed closely by a narcissistic-antisocial-histrionic cluster (17%). Other clusters were somewhat more complex in patterning and less common in occurrence. Here again, it is likely that the profile patterns could be simplified considerably if the sample were tested following treatment. It would also simplify matters greatly if nonoverlapping measures of personality psychopathology were used. A personality scale that followed either a three-factor or five-factor format to measure personality disorder psychopathology with no use of overlapping items would certainly help to clear up a lot of the confusion in cluster analysis and alcoholism research.

2.3. Personality Assessment Inventory

Schinka (1995) used the Personality Assessment Inventory developed by Morey (1991) to examine alcoholic subtypes in a sample of 301 inpatients in a short-term treatment program. Seven clusters were identified and labeled as (1) depressed, (2) dysphoric, (3) antisocial, (4) personality disorder, (5) normal, (6) somatic concerns, and (7) distressed. The sample in this study included a large number of homeless (25%) and unemployed persons (70%), suggesting that this group may have a higher level of dysfunction and additional social problems that might be exacerbated by their drinking. The wide range of symptom patterns presented in this group might have been enhanced by their social circumstances and withdrawal symptoms in the short-term therapy program. It is likely that the number of clusters derived would have dropped a lot following treatment. At least three of the clusters that were derived have fairly minimal psychopathology and would be likely to collapse into one group following treatment, including the normal group, the somatic concerns group, and the dysphoric group.

3. Summary

Research conducted on various theoretical perspectives linked with subtypes of alcoholics is fairly consistent in showing that there are two major subtypes of alcoholics. The first type is an antisocial or personality psychopathology group, and the second type is less antisocial/distressed. Empirical studies of clinical samples show a broader range of clusters. The antisocial/severe psychopathology group occurs frequently, but a range of neurotic spectrum clusters also occur. The number and range of the neurotic personality clusters is dramatically reduced when samples are tested at follow-up after treatment.

4. Subtypes of Alcoholics in the General Population

4.1. Method

4.1.1. Sample

Of the 1257 participants in the WHDS, 192 were classified as alcoholics on the basis of a DIS-based diagnosis, which is based on the DSM III-R classification. This is a measure of lifetime alcohol abuse or dependence. A statistical comparison of the alcoholics with the rest of the general population sample shows that the alcoholics are younger ($F(1,1250) = 35.9$, $p < .001$), tend to be less educated ($F(1,1255) = 3.61$, $p = .058$), have slightly lower incomes ($F1,1151) = 5.9$, $p < .02$), are more likely to be male ($X^2_{(1)} = 59.2$, $p < .001$), and are more likely to have alcoholic fathers ($X^2_{(3)} = 26.9$, $p < .001$).

4.1.2. Measures

4.1.2a. Personality. The personality measures used to derive the clusters were the Eysenck EPQR scales (Eysenck et al., 1985), the Vando Reducer–Augmenter Scale (Barnes, 1985b; Vando, 1969), the MMPI Barron Ego Strength (Barron, 1953) and the MacAndrew Scale (MacAndrew, 1965), the Rosenberg Self-Esteem Scale (Rosenberg, 1965), and the Group Embedded Figures Test (Witkin et al., 1971). These measures are described in Chapter 4.

4.1.2b. Demographics. Demographic characteristics that were used to compare clusters included age, income, occupational status, and education.

4.1.2c. Alcohol Measures. The alcohol measures that were used in the cluster comparisons included the average number of ounces of alcohol consumed per day, the number of alcohol problems reported, the number of DSM III-R symptoms reported, the score on the brief MAST, and the score on the SADD. These measures are described in Chapter 4.

4.1.2d. Family Background of Alcohol Abuse. Variables that were used in the analyses for this chapter included the reported number of family members that were alcoholic, the father's and mother's short MAST, as completed by the respondent, and estimates regarding the percentage of siblings, aunts and uncles, and grandparents who were alcoholic. These measures are also described in Chapter 4.

4.1.3. Data Analysis

A cluster analysis was performed to determine whether the general population alcoholics could be grouped on the basis of their personalities. The definition of the term "clusters" is vague, and the terms "internal cohesion" and "external isolation" are often used to reflect properties of clusters (Everitt, 1993). There is no general agreement on the use of a unique statistical criterion to determine the number of clusters, as well as cluster membership. For example, Blashfield and Aldenderfer (1988) note that there are over 300 types of cluster analytic methods. Strack and Lorr (1994) provide an overview. There are at least 30 criteria for identifying the optimum number of clusters (e.g., Milligan & Cooper, 1985), but none of these criteria has gained widespread acceptance. In the alcoholic personality literature reviewed in this chapter, most of the articles have not used statistical criteria for selecting the optimum number of clusters. In this analysis, Ward's (1963) hierarchical method for cluster formation was used. This is a form of variance method that seeks to minimize information loss by using an error sums of squares criterion. With this procedure, the means for all variables are calculated for each cluster, and the squared Euclidean distance to the cluster mean is calculated and summed across cases. The clusters that merge at each step have the smallest increase in the sum of square within-cluster distances. The computer output provided includes a dendrogram, which illustrates clusters and coefficient values at each step of the clustering procedure. Although the Euclidean distance calculation is scale-dependent (i.e., it depends on the unit of measurement of the variables), this problem can be circumvented by standardizing the measures before analysis, as is done in this study. Data from the 192 general population alcoholics were cluster analyzed with the SPSS program (Norusis, 1993).

The criteria used for selecting the optimum number of clusters was based on two considerations. First, the prior theory reviewed in this chapter provides a strong basis for looking at the two-cluster solution. Prior reserch in clinical samples also suggests that the solutions based on four and five clusters capitalize on transient withdrawal symptoms in clinical samples and may not be stable solutions. Second, the suitability of the two-cluster solution was ascertained by examining the dendrogram and agglomeration schedule. The optimum cluster solution occurs at the point where clusters cease forming from relatively similar patterns and begin agglomerating significantly different patterns (Sheckter & Scott, 1998).

4.2. Results

In Table 9.1 the results show that the two clusters are clearly delineated along the personality dimensions employed in this study. On the Extraversion dimension, the groups differ significantly on the Eysenck Scale, but not on the MacAndrew Alcoholism Scale. The groups do not differ significantly on the Vando Reducer–Augmenter Scale. On the Neuroticism dimension, the groups differ significantly on all of the scales in the direction of higher neuroticism in the smaller cluster. On the P/antisocial dimension, the clusters also differ significantly and have higher P

**Table 9.1. Means of the Two General Population
Clusters of Alcoholics on Personality Measures[a]**

	Cluster	
	1 $n = 134$	2 $n = 55$
Extraversion		
Extraversion	16.1	14.5[b]
MAC	22.9	24.1
Stimulus reducing		
Vando	27.1	26.1
Neuroticism		
EPQ-N	8.5	17.5[c]
Ego strength	48.3	37.3[c]
Self-esteem	34.2	28.9[c]
Trait anxiety	31.7	45.8[c]
P/Antisocial		
EPQ-P	4.4	7.1[c]
EPQ-L	8.7	7.2[b]
Field Dependence (GEFT)	10.3	6.1[c]

[a]Based of n tests.
[b] $= p < .05$.
[c] $= p < .001$.

and lower social conformity in the smaller cluster. The smaller cluster is also significantly more field-dependent.

Analysis of variance was also used to compare the groups on potentially relevant demographic measures and alcohol-related measures. The means of the two clusters on alcohol measures and demographic characteristics are shown in Table 9.2. One important demographic difference that emerged is that the small cluster is less educated ($F(1,1187) = 7.9$, $p < .01$). Another important difference is that females are more likely to be in the small cluster than males. Forty percent of the female alcoholics are in the small cluster, and 25% of the male alcoholics fall into that group ($X^2_{(1)} = 3.88$, $p < .05$). The small cluster has signs of greater difficulty with alcohol. They have higher symptom levels ($F(1,187) = 14.2$, $p < .001$), more alcohol-related problems ($F(1,187) = 8.6$, $p < .01$), and greater alcohol dependence ($F(1,187) = 6.2$, $p < .01$). However, they do not drink more ($F(1,187 = 3.2$, ns) and are not more likely to have gone for treatment during their lives ($F(1,187) = 3.6$, ns). In terms of a family history of alcoholism, the only notable difference between the clusters is that the small cluster is more likely to have alcoholic fathers ($F(1,187) = 4.3$, $p < .05$).

In this study, two clusters of general population alcoholics were identified. About 70% of the alcoholics were included in the larger cluster. This cluster was much less neurotic (low Neuroticism and Trait Anxiety, high Self-Esteem and

Table 9.2. Means of the Two General Population Clusters of Alcoholics on Demographics and Alcohol Measures

	Cluster 1 $n = 134$	Cluster 2 $n = 55$
Demographic measures		
Age	35.5	35.0
Income	37,500	34,900
Occupational status	8.9	10.2
Education	13.4	12.1[a]
Alcohol measures		
Alcoholism symptoms	4.7	6.0[a]
Daily consumption	1.1	1.8
Alcohol problems	2.0	3.5[a]
SMAST	4.1	6.5
SADD	3.8	6.0[a]
Family background of alcoholism		
Percent of family alcoholic	33.6	52.4
Father's SMAST	22.1	3.4[b]
Mother's SMAST	0.62	0.9
Alcoholic siblings (%)	16.9	22.7
Alcoholic aunts/uncles (%)	17.6	21.0
Alcoholic grandparents (%)	9.3	8.5

[a] $p < .01$.
[b] $p < .05$.

Ego Strength) than the small cluster. They were also much less antisocial, more socially conforming (i.e., low Lie Scale score), more field-independent, and were more extraverted on the Eysenck scale than the small cluster. These are characteristics associated with greater psychological health. This cluster also had fewer alcohol-related social problems and was less alcohol-dependent than the smaller cluster. The prognosis for this group would be much better than for the other 30% of the general population alcoholics. The smaller group has greater personality problems and also more alcohol-related social problems. The group was much higher than the large group on all of the facets of neuroticism (high EPQ-N, high Trait Anxiety, low Ego Strength and low Self-Esteem). The group has high levels of impulsivity and antisocial characteristics (high P) and is more nonconforming (low L). It also has a higher incidence of paternal alcoholism.

The smaller cluster characterized by lower extraversion, more neuroticism and psychoticism, and poorer cognitive performance fits the difficult temperament, high-risk group described by Blackson (1994). Results are also fairly consistent with the Babor et al. (1992) and Zucker et al. (1995) classification systems. Babor et al. (1992) hypothesized that there would be a subgroup of alcoholics characterized by greater psychopathology, and Zucker (1995) hypothesized that there would be a group of alcoholics characterized by antisocial characteristics and perhaps more psychological distress. The results do not, however, support the Cloninger (1987a) or MacAndrew (1979) proposed classification systems.

If the Cloninger (1987a) system were accurate, one would expect to see differences on the Vando Reducer-Augmenter dimension and perhaps the MacAndrew Scale as well, supporting a low sensation-seeking or Type I group of alcoholics. Results here do not support a low sensation-seeking form of alcoholism. In the MacAndrew system, one would expect to see a high MAC group that accounts for 80–85% of the cases and a low MAC group that accounts for the smaller group of cases. Nothing like that emerged here.

5. Subtypes of Alcoholics in the Clinical Sample

5.1. Method

5.1.1. Sample

The sample for the analyses presented in this section includes all of the patients in our clinical sample (described in Chapter 6) who were addicted to either alcohol or alcohol in combination with other drugs. This resulted in a treatment sample of 327 alcoholics.

5.1.2. Measures

5.1.2a. Personality. The personality measures included in the analyses presented here were the same personality measures employed in our general population analyses described in the first part of this chapter.

5.1.2b. Demographic Characteristics. The demographic characteristics examined in this study included age, gender, education, ethnicity (native versus nonnative), and employment status (working versus nonworking).

5.1.2c. Alcohol and Substance Use. The alcohol measures examined here included the age at first drink, the estimated number of ounces of ethanol consumed per day based on quantity and frequency reports of consumption, and the estimated maximum number of drinks consumed per day. The drug use measures examined here included the scores on the DAST and their answers regarding whether or not they were receiving treatment only for alcohol use or for alcohol and drug use problems. These measures are described in more detail in Chapter 6.

5.1.2d. Family History of Alcohol Abuse. The questions used for these analyses are the same as those used in the general population study.

5.1.3. Data Analysis

Cluster analysis of the treatment alcoholics ($n = 327$) was undertaken using Ward's (1963) hierarchical agglomerative method on standardized data (to reduce problems associated with different scale variabilities). Criteria for selecting the optimum number of clusters were the same as those used for study number 1 (i.e., parsimony and examination of the dendogram and agglomeration schedule).

5.2. Results

Once again a two-cluster solution was selected on the basis of visual examination of the dendrogram and emphasis on theoretical parsimony. Table 9.3 shows the means of the personality measures for each cluster and includes an F ratio to test the statistical significance of the difference.

    The personality characteristics have been arranged according to the factor structure that has been identified in previous chapters. The EPQ-E and MacAndrew Scales are measures of extraversion, the Vando Reducer–Augmenter Scale is a measure of stimulus reducing–augmenting, the EPQ-N, Ego Strength, Self-Esteem and, Trait Anxiety measures indicate neuroticism, and the EPQ-P and EPQ-

Table 9.3. Means of the Two Clinical Clusters of Alcoholics on Personality Measures

	Cluster 1 ($n = 171$)	Cluster 2 ($n = 156$)
Extraversion		
EPQ-E	12.8	14.4[b]
MAC	25.5	25.7
Stimulus reducing		
Vando	27.2	25.4
Neuroticism		
EPQ-N	20.2	12.6[c]
Ego strength	33.0	43.0[c]
Self-esteem	25.4	31.3
Trait anxiety	52.8	38.8[c]
Antisocial		
EPQ-P	9.0	6.0[c]
EPQ-L	5.5	8.4[c]
Field dependence	8.3	7.5

[a]Based on f tests.
[b] $= p < .01$.
[c] $= p < .001$.

L Scales measure antisocial characteristics. The GEFT remains a separate construct measuring field dependence.

There is no appreciable difference on extraversion, and only the EPQ-E shows a statistical effect, such that the first cluster is more introverted. This lack of difference is consistent with the general population sample, where there was no difference between clusters on the MAC and the Vando. However, the first cluster was more extraverted in that sample. Furthermore, if we look at the actual value (see Table 9.1) in both samples, the second cluster has almost the identical value. Thus the difference is not just a relative difference between the samples, but a real difference.

In terms of neuroticism-related characteristics, there are strong significant differences on all four measures. Cluster one has higher EPQ-N and Trait Anxiety and lower Self-Esteem and Ego-Strength scores. The magnitude of the differences is quite striking, and all statistical comparisons are significant beyond $p <$ .001. This is certainly a more neurotic group than the members of cluster 2. When we look back to the comparison of the two clusters in the general population sample, the alcoholic sample cluster 1 is more like the general population sample cluster 2.

In addition to differences in neuroticism-related characteristics, there are also differences in antisocial characteristics. Cluster 1 has a much higher EPQ-P Scale score, and a much lower EPQ-L Scale score, possibly reflecting lower social conformity.

There were no differences between the two clusters in field dependence (8.3 vs 7.5), which is in contrast to the general population sample, where the first cluster was more field-independent (10.3 vs 6.1).

Next, the two alcoholic clusters were compared for drinking characteristics. Significant differences are shown on Table 9.4. The first cluster began drinking at

Table 9.4. Means of the Two Clinical Clusters of Alcoholics on Drinking and Drug Use Measures

	Cluster membership		F	p
	Cluster 1 $n = 171$ (52.3%)	Cluster 2 $n = 156$ (47.7%)		
Drinking variables				
Age at first drink	12.9	14.6	20.2	<.001
DAST	8.8	4.1	36.4	<.001
Average daily consumption	7.7	5.4	9.7	<.01
Maximum number of drinks in a day	30.9	26.8	4.1	<.05
Addiction classification				
Alcohol only	117	127		<.01
Alcohol and other drugs	54	29	7.3 (chi-square)	

a younger age and has a higher daily consumption of alcohol in the past year. They also had a higher maximum number of drinks consumed in a day and a higher level of drug abuse. Consistent with the latter finding, they are also more likely to report a preference for other drugs in addition to alcohol.

The next set of comparisons examines the families of these alcoholics and compares the level of alcoholism in the two clusters. The clusters clearly differ on family history of alcoholism (Table 9.5). The first cluster had more parents, grand-parents, and siblings with alcoholism, perhaps suggesting a stronger genetic component to their alcoholism, compared with the second cluster. In addition, both mother's and father's MAST scores were significantly higher, again suggesting a stronger familial link with alcoholism in this cluster than in the second cluster.

In terms of demographic characteristics (see Table 9.6), the first cluster (which comprised about 53% of the total sample), was less educated, had lower annual family income, and was less likely to be working. These characteristics may also be related to the fact that the first cluster was also more likely to include women and had a higher percentage of Aboriginal Canadians than the second cluster.

The results of the cluster analyses in the clinical sample confirm that there are two main types of alcoholism. In the clinical sample, the group that we have characterized as the difficult temperament or the antisocial/distressed group comprises a much higher percentage of the sample (about 53%). This is not surprising as one would anticipate a lot more personality disturbance in a clinical sample. The pattern of results obtained again agrees pretty well with the theoretical positions put forward by Babor et al. (1992), Blackson (1994), and Zucker et al. (1995). There is a form of alcoholism that is characterized by higher Neuroticism, higher Psychoticism, more severity and diversity in symptoms of alcohol and drug abuse, and a stronger family loading for alcohol abuse. Once again, the results did not support the Cloninger (1987a) or MacAndrew (1979) predictions.

The presence of a group of alcoholics who are characterized by high N and high P and greater severity of problems is consistent with the literature reviewed earlier in which a strong association between alcoholism and personality disorders was discussed (see Verheul et al., 1995). The findings here that this group

Table 9.5. Means of the Two Clinical Clusters of Alcoholics on Family History of Alcoholism Indicators

	Cluster membership		F	p
	Cluster 1	Cluster 2		
Percent of alcoholic grandparents	13.9	7.2	8.4	<.01
Percent of alcoholic siblings	44.7	25.9	18.6	<.001
Percent of alcoholic aunts and uncles	42.9	30.7	7.9	<.01
Mother's MAST	2.0	1.0	11.5	.001
Father's MAST	4.5	2.3	26.8	.001

Table 9.6. Demographic Characteristics of the Two Clinical
Clusters of Alcoholics

		Cluster 1	Cluster 2	F or chi-square	p
Age		35.0	40.2	22.6	<.001
Gender					
	Female	60	30		
	Male	111	126	10.3	<.001
Education (in years)				5.7	<.05
Native	No	129	132		
	Yes	42	24	4.3	<.05
Working?	Yes	90	97		
	No	68	43	4.8	<.05

can contain over 50% of the cases in a clinical sample suggests that comorbid personality disorders may be very common in alcoholics and are important to consider in planning appropriate interventions.

6. Summary and Conclusions

The first objective in this chapter was to cluster analyze the personality scores of a group of general population alcoholics to determine the optimum number of and the nature of the personality types in this sample. The results supported a two-cluster solution that provided groups of alcoholics who were clearly delineated by the personality traits measured.

The second objective in this chapter was to compare the derived clusters in the general population on their personality, drinking history, and demographic characteristics. The largest group of alcoholics in the general population sample was characterized by higher Extraversion, lower Neuroticism, lower Psychoticism, and greater Field Independence. The smaller cluster which comprised about 29% of the alcoholic sample was characterized by more severe alcohol problems and by a higher reported frequency for paternal alcohol problems. The derived personality clusters were consistent with the profiles described by Blackson (1994), Babor et al. (1992), and Zucker et al. (1995) in describing their personality typology systems and less consistent with the typology systems described by MacAndrew (1979) and Cloninger (1987a).

The third objective in this chapter was to cluster analyze the personality scores of clinical alcoholics to identify the optimum number and nature of personality types characterizing this sample. Again the results showed that a two-cluster solution provided clusters that were distinct in their personality profiles.

This time the cluster that had more deviant personality traits accounted for a higher percentage of the alcoholics (53%).

The fourth objective in this chapter was to compare the derived clusters on personality traits, alcohol and substance use patterns, and demographic traits. In these analyses the results again strongly confirmed the differentiation of the two clusters. Again a difficult temperament cluster emerged that was characterized by high P and high N. This group also showed a stronger pattern of addiction reflected by their higher scores on alcohol and substance abuse indicators. The difficult temperament group also had a higher loading for a family history of alcohol abuse, as assessed by a variety of indicators. As with the cluster analytic solution in the general population sample, the results here were considered consistent with the theorizing of Blackson (1994), Babor et al. (1992), and Zucker et al. (1995).

The final objective was to compare the distribution and characteristics of the personality clusters derived in the general population and clinical samples. Results showed that fairly similar cluster solutions were obtained in the two samples. A high P and high N or difficult temperament cluster emerged in both samples but accounted for a much higher percentage of cases in the clinical sample. Overall, the results suggest that stimulus reducing/sensation seeking measured by the Vando Scale is common in both forms of alcoholism uncovered in both general population and clinical samples. Personality traits associated with personality disorders (e.g., high N and high P) occur in a smaller percentage of alcoholics in the general population than in the clinical sample. It is interesting to note that the difficult temperament group in the clinical sample was more strongly differentiated on the basis of family density for alcohol abuse than in the general population sample. These results suggest that family history may have a particularly strong influence in the development of a severe form of alcohol abuse that is associated with a difficult temperament pattern. Although it is possible that genetics could account for this pattern of results, environment may also play a role. As noted in the research described by Blackson (1994) and Zucker et al. (1995), in particular, dysfunctional family environments may frequently occur in conjunction with severe forms of alcohol abuse involving personality disorder types of psychopathology.

V

THE PREALCOHOLIC
PERSONALITY

10

The Prealcoholic Personality
in the General Population
and Clinical Samples

Although the MacAndrew Alcoholism Scale (MacAndrew, 1965) has frequently been used as a measure of the prealcoholic or addiction-prone personality, MacAndrew himself argued that his test was not specifically developed for this purpose and that tests work best when they are designed for the specific purpose at hand. MacAndrew (1979) suggested that a test developed for the intended purpose of early identification and possibly based on a broader item pool than the MMPI would have potential for identifying the addiction-prone individual. A scale of this type would be designed to measure what has been called elsewhere (Barnes, 1979,1983) the "prealcoholic personality" rather than the "alcoholic personality." In this chapter, initial scale construction efforts at developing a measure of the "prealcoholic personality" are described. The specific objectives in this chapter are described below.

1. Objectives

1. To develop a personality test to measure the prealcoholic personality.
2. To examine the reliability and validity of the test in the general population.
3. To examine the ability of the Prealcoholic Personality (PAP) test to predict changes in alcohol consumption and abuse over time in the general population, and compare the ability of the PAP to prospectively predict

changes in alcohol consumption and abuse with the ability of two other measures of this type, the MAC Scale and EPQ-A, to predict the same criteria.

4. To examine the PAP scores, reliability, and validity in a clinical sample, and determine the utility of the test to discriminate clinical alcoholics from nonalcoholics and drug addicts. To compare the capability of the PAP in discriminating groups with the capability of the MAC Scale and the EPQ-A.

5. To examine the personality correlates of the PAP in a clinical sample.

6. To examine the utility of the PAP in predicting treatment outcome for alcohol and drug addicts, and compare this utility with the utility of the EPQ-A and MAC Scales.

2. The MAC and EPQ-A Scales

The WHDS data set contains two addiction scales that will be utilized in the analyses presented in this chapter. The MacAndrew Alcoholism Scale (MacAndrew, 1965) was originally developed to discriminate alcoholics from other psychiatric patients. The MAC scale was included in the current investigation because it has been widely used in the addiction area and has been shown to prospectively predict the risk of developing alcoholism (Hoffman, Loper, & Kammeier, 1974) even though it was not developed specifically for this purpose.

The EPQ-A is a 32-item scale developed from the EPQ by Gossop & Eysenck (1980). The criterion used to select items was the ability of the items to discriminate addicts from normals.

In a separate publication based on the Winnipeg Health and Drinking Survey, we compared the reliability and validity of the MAC Scale and EPQ-A in our sample (Patton, Barnes, & Murray, 1994). The reliability for both of these scales was quite low (alpha = .64 for the EPQ-A and alpha = .57 for the MAC). Both measures were generally significantly correlated with drinking measures, and the correlations were somewhat higher for the MacAndrew Scale. Analyses comparing the correlations of the MAC scale and EPQ-A with other personality measures showed that the MAC scale had its highest correlations with Extraversion (r = .41), Stimulus Reducing (r = .27), and Psychoticism (r = .18) whereas the EPQ-A had its highest correlations with Neuroticism (.84) and Trait Anxiety (.64). The EPQ-A also picks up on the Psychoticism/low Social Conformity component of the addictive personality (e.g., r = .29 with P and r = −.51 with the Lie Scale). This pattern of correlation suggests that the MacAndrew Scale is more strongly associated with "prealcoholic personality traits" and the EPQ-A with "clinical alcoholic," or in this case "clinical addict" traits.

3. Test Construction

To develop a measure of the prealcoholic personality, the ideal research design would be to test subjects using a broad range of personality items before the onset of drinking, follow these subjects over a number of years, and determine the set of personality items that best predicted the development of alcoholism. Because this design is not very feasible, given the large number of years that it takes to develop alcoholism, particularly in late onset alcoholics, another strategy was employed in the current investigation. To determine personality items that would be more likely to reflect the underlying vulnerability to alcoholism, we decided to select personality items that were linked with both a family loading for alcoholism and a current diagnosis of alcoholism. It is recognized that a high correlation between a personality item and a family history of alcoholism could reflect either genetic transmission of a personality characteristic or the contribution of the alcoholic family environment to the development of personality. In either case, these characteristics are likely to be present before the development of alcoholism in the offspring.

In our general population sample ($n = 1257$), respondents were asked about their parents' drinking. Two hundred and three respondents reported that either their father or their mother was an alcoholic according to the Short Michigan Alcoholism Screening test cutoff (a score of more than 5). These 203 are labeled Family History positive (FH+). The remaining 1054 are labeled Family History negative (FH–). The FH+ and FH– (no alcoholism in either parent) were compared on all 299 items of our personality test battery. The personality questionnaire battery included the revised version of the Eysenck Personality Questionnaire (EPQ-R, Eysenck, Eysenck, & Barrett, 1985); two research scales from the MMPI, Ego Strength (Barron, 1953) and the MacAndrew Alcoholism Scale (MAC; MacAndrew, 1965); the Vando Reducer–Augmenter scale (VANDO; Barnes, 1985b; Vando, 1969); the trait subscale of the State-Trait anxiety inventory, (TRAIT; Spielberger, Gorsuch, and Lushene, 1970); and the Rosenberg (1965) Self-Esteem Inventory. Sixty-three items discriminated between the two groups at the $p < .001$ level of statistical significance.

As noted in the methodology chapter, general population respondents were also asked about their own level of drinking. The measures included an index of the quantity and frequency of beer, wine, and hard liquor intake during the past 30 days. From this measure, we were able to derive a measure of the number of ounces of alcohol per day. Cahalan and Room (1974) also presented a measure of problems associated with the use of alcohol, and this index is included. Other measures included both short versions of the Michigan Alcoholism Screening Test (Selzer, Vinokur, & Van Rooijen, 1975; Pokorny et al., 1972). These indices are widely used in the alcohol area and provide a lifetime measure of alcoholism based on sociological theories (e.g., Room, 1972). The Diagnostic Interview Schedule (DIS; Robins et al., 1989), a protocol for measuring DSM III-R criteria for alcohol abuse and dependence, was used to obtain an alcoholism diagnosis in the general population sample. Both the general population and the clinical samples completed the MAST with reference to their parents' drinking to obtain a measure of parental alcoholism.

One hundred and ninety-two respondents in the community survey were classified as alcoholic, according to the DIS. Twenty-three of the family history positive items discriminated between these 192 alcoholics and the 1053 nonalcoholics at the $p < .001$ level. Most of these 23 items had correlations greater than .20 with the total number of symptoms of alcoholism. Item characteristics of the scale for the full sample ($n = 1257$) were examined. The 23 items selected and their item-total correlations are presented on Table 10.1. All of the item-total correlations are greater than .20. A sum score was obtained, and the scale was called the Prealcoholic Personality Measure (PAP).

The scale has satisfactory reliability (Cronbach's alpha = .76 in the full sample). Cronbach's alpha was also calculated with alcoholics eliminated from the sample (alpha = .75) and showed that there is no effect of including alcoholics. The test–retest reliability in the general population sample was even more impressive when computed over the two-year period of the study ($r = .82$, $n = 988$).

The frequency distributions for the PAP scores in the full general population sample are presented in Table 10.2. Decimals indicate prorating of scores if individual items were missed. If more than 20% of the items were missing, then the subject was deleted from the analysis. The data from 12 subjects were lost using this criteria. The mean total score on the PAP is 6.41 (SD = 3.87).

As noted above, our basic test construction strategy involved selecting personality-relevant items from a half-dozen scales that significantly discriminated groups on the basis of family history, as well as own level of drinking. As a result, the content of items that might be found to discriminate could be quite varied and, in the sense of factor analysis, might be multidimensional rather than unidimensional. In other words, this strategy is quite distinct from a strategy writing items to assess a narrow and homogenous personality dimension which of necessity should be unidimensional. Nonetheless, because the items are intended to measure a single predisposition toward alcoholism, we hoped that the resulting items would be positively intercorrelated, reflecting a positive manifold, and contain a large general factor. In fact such a factor should exist, given the positive item-total correlations reported in Table 10.1.

In a combined sample of 1603 respondents, we found that all 23 items were indeed positively correlated with each other. Of the 253 correlations, only three were negative, and trivially so (–.00, –.02, and –.04). To evaluate how dominant a large factor might be, we used MicroFACT (Waller, 1995) to compute analyses

Table 10.1. PAP Item Analysis[a]

Item	Original scale	Item total correlation
1. Do you give money to charities? (R)	EPQ-P	.31
2. Would you take drugs which may have strange or dangerous effects?	EPQ-P	.31
3. Do you often feel "fed up"?	EPQ-N	.32
4. Have you often gone against your parents' wishes?	EPQ-P	.33
5. Have people said that you sometimes act rashly?	EPQ-E	.28
6. Do you go to church almost every week? (R)	MMPI-EGOST	.22
7. Have you had very strange or peculiar experiences?	MMPI-EGOST	.41
8. Do you have strange or peculiar thoughts?	MMPI-EGOST	.43
9. Have you had blank spells in which your activities were interrupted and you did not know what was going on around you?	MMPI-EGOST	.26
10. Have you lived the right kind of life?(R)	MMPI-MAC	.29
11. Have your parents often objected to the kind of people you went around with?	MMPI-MAC	.33
12. Did you play hooky from school quite often as a youngster?	MMPI-MAC	.38
13. Did you ever feel that strangers were looking at you critically?	MMPI-MAC	.30
14. Have you ever been in trouble with the law?	MMPI-MAC	.20
15. Are you unable to keep your mind on one thing?	MMPI-MAC	.27
16. Do you prefer (a)endurance sports (b)games with rests	VANDO	.22
17. Do you prefer (a) sports cars (b) passenger cars	VANDO	.34
18. Do you prefer (a) loud music (b) quiet music	VANDO	.46
19. Do you prefer (a) electric music (b) unamplified music	VANDO	.36
20. Do you prefer (a) rock music (b) ballads	VANDO	.40
21. Would you prefer to be (a) stuntman (b) propman?	VANDO	.35
22. Are you a steady person? (R)	TRAIT	.28
23. Do you wish you could have more respect for yourself?	ESTEEM	.24

[a] EGOST = Barron's Ego-Strength scale; EPQ-E = Eysenck's Extraversion scale; EPQ-N = Eysenck's Neuroticism scale; EPQ-P = Eysenck's Psychoticism scale; ESTEEM = Rosenberg's Self-Esteem scale; MAC = MacAndrew scale; TRAIT = Spielberger's Trait Anxiety scale; VANDO = Vando's Reducer-Augmenter scale; items 16–21 score of a = 1, b = 0; items 22 and 23 were reduced to two-point scales by combining two low points and two high points to create a 0, 1 two-point scale; items marked by an (R) add one point to the PAP scale score if answered in the negative; for all other items, an affirmative response adds one point to the PAP scale score.

based on tetrachoric correlations. Although the assumption of underlying normality of distributions that is required for these correlations to be good estimates of the true relationships among continuous counterparts to our binary items may be questionable, tetrachorics are known to be less sensitive to item difficulty factors than standard Pearson correlations. The largest eigenvalue of the correlation matrix accounted for 35% of the variance in the items. The next largest eigenvalue accounted for only 11% of the variance, and those remaining trailed off. Similar results were obtained from analysis that removed two contentwise ques-

Table 10.2. Frequency Distribution of PAP Scores in the General Population ($n = 1245$)

PREALC	Frequency	Percent	Cumulative frequency	Cumulative percent
0	30	2.4	30	2.4
1	62	5.0	92	7.4
1.045	4	0.3	96	7.7
1.095	3	0.2	99	8.0
2	93	7.5	192	15.4
2.09	2	0.2	194	15.6
2.19	1	0.1	195	15.7
2.3	1	0.1	196	15.7
2.421	1	0.1	197	15.8
3	120	9.6	317	25.5
3.136	6	0.5	323	25.9
4	129	10.4	452	36.3
4.182	4	0.3	456	36.6
5	127	10.2	583	46.8
5.227	3	0.2	586	47.1
5.476	1	0.1	587	47.1
5.75	2	0.2	589	47.3
6	117	9.4	706	56.7
6.273	3	0.2	709	56.9
6.571	3	0.2	712	57.2
6.9	1	0.1	713	57.3
7	99	8.0	812	65.2
7.318	3	0.2	815	65.5
7.667	1	0.1	816	65.5
8	87	7.0	903	72.5
8.364	6	0.5	909	73.0
8.762	3	0.2	912	73.3
9	71	5.7	983	79.0
9.2	1	0.1	984	79.0
9.409	8	0.6	992	79.7
9.684	1	0.1	993	79.8
10	62	5.0	1055	84.7
10.454	3	0.2	1058	85.0
11	39	3.1	1097	88.1
11.5	1	0.1	1098	88.2
12	36	2.9	1134	91.1
12.545	1	0.1	1135	91.2
13	40	3.2	1175	94.4
13.591	1	0.1	1176	94.5
14	19	1.5	1195	96.0
14.636	2	0.2	1197	96.1
14.95	1	0.1	1198	96.2
15	10	0.8	1208	97.0
16	15	1.2	1223	98.2
17	10	0.8	1233	99.0
17.524	1	0.1	1234	99.1
18	5	0.4	1239	99.5
19	5	0.4	1244	99.9
21	1	0.1	1245	100.0

tionable items (blank spells, drug taking). Loadings on the first unrotated principal factor ranged from .47 to .65, substantial enough for our purposes. We consider these results consistent with the idea of a positive manifold of prealcoholic item content.

4. General Population Results

4.1. PAP Scores and Demographic Characteristics

The next step in the analysis of the PAP is to examine the correlation of the scale score with demographic measures, personality, smoking and drinking. The associations with demographics are presented in Table 10.3. There is a gender difference, and males score higher than females on the PAP ($F(1,1244) = 57.31$, $p < 0.001$). A significant marital status effect was also found, and single people scored much higher than the other groups ($F(4,1240) = 61.01$, $p < 0.001$). This is probably a function of the strong association between age and marital status ($r = -51$, $p < .001$). The correlations with education and income were quite low ($r = -.09$ and $r = -.14$, $p < .001$), although statistically significant with this large a sample. Age has a strong correlation with the PAP for older respondents who scored lower. The PAP is comprised of a number of traits that decline with age, including psychoticism, neuroticism, and stimulus reducing/sensation seeking. The PAP may be tapping primarily into what Cloninger calls Type II alcoholism which is also age related (i.e., more common in younger people).

Table 10.3. Association of the PAP with Demographic Characteristics

	n	Mean	SD
Variable			
Gender			
Males	607	7.26	4.06
Females	638	5.60	3.69
	F (1,1244) = 57.31, P < 0.0001		
Marital Status			
Single	244	9.58	4.23
Married	863	5.53	3.41
Widowed	27	4.96	4.39
Divorced	84	6.97	3.80
Separated	27	5.82	3.06
	F(4,1240) = 61.01, P < 0.0001		
Correlations with continuous measures			
	r		
Years of education	-0.09[a]		
Family income	-0.14[a]		
Age	-0.51[a]		

[a]Signficant level p < .01.

Then, PAP scores were examined for their association with drinking in the family of origin. Respondents were asked to compete the short MAST for both their mothers and their fathers and to indicate how many brothers, sisters, biological aunts and uncles, and grandparents had alcohol problems. The results of the correlational analyses that examined associations between the PAP and the family history of drinking problems are presented in Table 10.4. For comparison, correlation coefficients are also reported for the EPQ-A and MAC. The PAP correlated with mother's MAST ($r = .18$, $p < .001$) and father's MAST ($r = .26$, $p < .001$), the percentage of siblings ($r = .14$, $p < .001$) and first degree relatives ($r = .21$, $p < .001$) with alcoholism problems, and the proportion of grandparent's who were alcoholic ($r = .19$, $p < .001$). These correlations confirm the association between PAP scores and family loading for alcoholism. Significant associations between family history variables and the two other addiction personality scales were also found, and these correlations had a somewhat lower magnitude.

It is not surprising that the PAP has a higher correlation with the family loading of alcohol abuse, given that this was one of the criteria used to select PAP items. Past research with the MAC scale has found inconsistent results for the association between the MAC and the family history of alcohol abuse. Saunders and Schuckit (1981) found a positive association whereas Sher and McGrady (1984) did not find a significant correlation with the MAC Scale overall but did find significant associations with certain subscales of the MAC. Our results are consistent with previous studies showing a fairly weak effect in the larger sample. The size of the sample used in the current study allowed sufficient statistical power for results to be detected as significant.

4.2. PAP Scores and Personality

Next, we examined the association of the PAP with other personality measures in the general population sample. Care must be taken with the interpretation of these

Table 10.4. Alcohol Personality Measures and Family History of Alcohol Abuse

	PAP	EPQ-A	MAC
	r	r	r
Father's MAST	.26[a]	.18[a]	.13[a]
Mother's MAST	.18[a]	.12[a]	.10[a]
Grandparent alcoholism	.19[a]	.14[a]	.05
Sibling alcoholism	.14[a]	.10[a]	.09[a]
Aunt/Uncle alcoholism	.21[a]	.13[a]	.13[a]

[a]Significance level $p < .001$.

Table 10.5. Correlations Between the PAP and Personality Measures in the General Population

	Common items	Pearson r (full sample)	Pearson r (alcoholics eliminated)
Psychoticism	3	.55[a]	.49[a]
Extraversion	1	.26[a]	.24[a]
Neuroticism	1	.42[a]	.41[a]
Lie scale	0	−.33[a]	−.31[a]
Reducer–augmenter	6	.65[a]	.64[a]
Trait anxiety	1	.39[a]	.39[a]
Self-esteem	1	−.26[a]	−.25[a]
MMPI ego strength	4	−.23[a]	−.21[a]
MMPI MacAndrew	6	.29[a]	.23[a]
EPQ-A	0	.51[a]	.48[a]
Field dependence	0	.05	.05

$^a = p < .001.$

correlations because there is some item overlap. The strength of the correlations and the number of common items is shown in Table 10.5. Again, eliminating alcoholics from the sample did not change the strength nor the statistical significance of the observed associations.

The correlations with all of the personality measures, except the Group Embedded Figures Test, the measure of field dependence, were statistically significant. There were high positive correlations with Psychoticism ($r = .55$, $p < .001$) and Reducing–Augmenting ($r = .64$, $p < .001$) suggesting that the prealcoholic personality is high in P and high in stimulus reducing/sensation seeking, which is consistent with theory and prior observations discussed in the introductory chapters of this book. High scores were also moderately associated with characteristics associated with Neuroticism, including the EPQ Neuroticism Scale ($r = .42$, $p < .001$), Trait Anxiety ($r = .39$, $p < .001$), low Self-Esteem ($r = −.26$, $p < .001$), and low Ego Strength ($r = −.23$, $p < .001$). A moderate correlation with the MAC Scale ($r = .29$, $p < .001$), suggests both similarity and difference in terms of construct overlap. Last, the negative correlation with the EPQ Lie Scale ($r = −.33$, $p < .001$) suggests a possible link between a lower need for social conformity and the prealcoholic personality. Comparison of the correlations between the full sample and the sample with the alcoholics removed shows that there is little effect from including the alcoholics in the sample. The strength of the correlations is about the same across all measures.

4.3. PAP Scores and Drinking

The general population survey is a two-wave survey with a two-year interval
between testings. All personality measures and drinking measures were administered at both waves. The PAP was constructed on information gathered at the first
wave. Thus it is possible to examine both cross sectional and longitudinal correlations with the various indices of addiction, specifically, smoking and drinking.
This will provide a demonstration of both criterion and discriminant validity. The
correlations with drinking at Wave 1 are all statistically significant and in the
expected direction (see Table 10.6). The strengths of the correlations are moderate,
and higher correlations occur with the more severe indices of heavy or problem
drinking. For example, the correlations with the number of times of drinking
more than eight drinks ($r = .39$, $p < .001$), the sum of alcohol-related problems ($r =
.38$, $p < .001$), and alcohol dependency (SADD $r = .41$, $p < .001$ and DSM $r = .53$)
are higher than the correlation with the measure of alcohol consumption ($r = .23$,
$p < .001$). For comparison, the correlations between the drinking measures and the
EPQ-A and the MacAndrew Scale are also provided in Table 10.6. These correlations
follow a pattern similar to those observed with the PAP but are lower in magnitude.

   To determine whether the patterns of correlation between the PAP and alco-

**Table 10.6. Correlation of the PAP, MAC, and EPQ-A with Drinking and Smoking
at Time 1 and at Time 2 in the General Population**

	PAP cross-sectional	PAP longitudinal	MAC cross-sectional	MAC longitudinal	EPQ-A cross-sectional	EPQ-A longitudinal
	r	r	r	r	r	r
Drinking						
Oz. of alcohol per day	$.23^a$	$.18^a$	$.17^a$	$.14^a$	$.10^a$	$.01$
Drinking more than 8 drinks	$.39^a$	$.39^a$	$.22^a$	$.18^a$	$.12^a$	$.09^b$
Alcohol dependency (SADD)	$.41^a$	$.42^a$	$.20^a$	$.18^a$	$.29^a$	$.28^a$
MAST (10 item)	$.27^a$	$.27^a$	$.22^a$	$.19^a$	$.19^a$	$.15^a$
MAST (13 item)	$.36^a$	$.24$	$.25^a$	$.16^a$	$.27^a$	$.07^c$
Sum of problems	$.38^a$	$.35^a$	$.23^a$	$.08^a$	$.26^a$	$.18^a$
DSM Symptoms	$.53^a$	$.47^a$	$.29^a$	$.23^a$	$.33^a$	$.22^a$
Smoking						
Average amount smoked	$.09$	$.08$				

$^a p < .001.$
$^b p < .01$
$^c p < .05.$

hol use and smoking varied by age and or gender group, separate correlations were computed by age and gender groups (see Table 10.7). These results were generally consistent across age and gender groups, except that the PAP was not strongly correlated with measures of the volume of alcohol consumed in the oldest group. There are a couple of possible reasons for this lower correlation. In older males there are quite a few previous heavy drinkers who are now abstaining. In the older female sample, there are a lot of lifelong abstainers, likely due to the stronger social disapproval of female drinking in this age cohort.

The ultimate test of any measure of the prealcoholic personality is whether or not the measure can predict changes in drinking status over time. Individuals who are higher on the prealcoholic dimension should be at a higher risk of increasing their drinking and developing more problems as time goes by. To test this prediction, we ran a series of regression analyses using the PAP at Time 1, along with demographic control variables and the Time 1 score on the alcohol measure predicted as independent variables, and the Time 2 alcohol measure as the dependent variable. Thus Time 1 alcohol consumption was included in the regression predicting consumption at Time 2, Time 1 problems in the analyses predicting Time 2 problems, etc. Simple regression analyses were computed, and the results are reported in Table 10.8. These analyses provide a very stringent test of the ability of the PAP to predict alcohol use and abuse. The two-year period between waves is also fairly short to allow changes in drinking behavior to occur. The results in Table 10.8 show that the PAP predicts DSM III alcohol abuse symptoms even when Time 1 alcohol abuse symptoms and demographic control variables are included in the analyses. Alcohol Dependence symptoms at Time 2 are also predicted by the PAP even when Time 1 alcohol dependence symptoms and demographic characteristics are controlled. Because the PAP did not predict either alcohol consumption or problems we ran these analyses separately in three

Table 10.7. Correlations of the PAP with Drinking across Age and Gender Categories (General Population Sample)

	Young (18–35)		Middle (36–49)		Older (50–64)	
	Men	Women	Men	Women	Men	Women
Max	.22[a]	.27[b]	.35[b]	.32[b]	.00	.22[a]
SADD	.40[b]	.31[b]	.39[b]	.32[b]	.16[c]	.40[b]
Mast 10	.29[b]	.22[b]	.35[b]	.23[b]	.34[b]	.33
Mast 13	.36[b]	.29[b]	.45[b]	.30[b]	.41[b]	.40[b]
Problems	.46[b]	.30[b]	.39[b]	.29[b]	.34[b]	.08
Ethanol	.21[a]	.13[c]	.33[b]	.21[a]	−.02	.04
DSM	.47[b]	.41[b]	.51[b]	.45[b]	.39[b]	.47[b]

[a] = $p < .01$.
[b] = $p < .001$.
[c] = $p < .05$.

Table 10.8. Multiple Regression Analyses Predicting Time 2 Alcohol Measures in the General Population[a]

Wave 1 predictors	Oz./day	Wave 2 alcohol measures Problems	DSM	Depend.
Prealc	.06	.06	.17[b]	.20[b]
Oz./day	.46[b]			
Problems		.44[b]		
DSM symptoms			.51[b]	
Dependence				.50[b]
Age	.07	.02	−.02	−.01
Education	.02	−.06	−.04	−.07[d]
Income	.06	−.03	−.02	−.01
Married/other	−.09[c]	−.03	−.03	.00
Gender	.10[b]	.05[d]	.04	.01
Unemployed/other	−.03	.04	−.03	−.04
R^2	.28	.25	.41	.39

[a]Not married = 0, married = 1, Gender, Female = 0, Male = 1: employed/other = 0, Unemployed =1.
[a] = $p < .001$.
[b] = $p < .01$.
[d] = $p < .05$.

different age groups (18–34, 35–49, and 50–65). In these analyses, it was noteworthy that the PAP predicted alcohol consumption in the youngest age group. Evidently the PAP predicts the earlier symptoms of alcoholism (i.e., consumption) in younger samples and the later symptoms of alcoholism in older samples. The PAP was not a good predictor of increasing problems in any of the age groups.

To compare the effectiveness of a measure of the prealcoholic personality as a predictor of the development of symptoms of alcoholism with other addiction personality scales not designed for this purpose, we ran the same regressions as above for the MacAndrew and EPQ-A Scales. As expected, the MacAndrew Scale did not prospectively predict the development of alcoholism symptoms. The EPQ-A had a significant but modest association with the development of problems (Beta = .07, $p < .05$) and alcohol dependence symptoms (Beta = .13, $p < .01$).

5. Clinical Sample Results

5.1. Cross-Validation in a Clinical Sample

Although the PAP Scale was intended to be a measure of the prealcoholic personality rather than the clinical alcoholic personality, the availability of a clinical sample allows us to compare scores on this measure in a clinical sample with alcoholics and control subjects in the general population. As noted in Chapter 6, the Alcoholism Foundation of Manitoba's (AFM) clinical sample was comprised of 421 individuals of whom 270 were judged to be addicted to alcohol, 93 to a combination of drugs and alcohol, and 57 to drugs alone. Before conducting our group comparisons, the reliability of the PAP in the clinical sample was examined. Results showed that the scale had satisfactory reliability in the clinical sample (Cronbach's alpha = .82).

5.1.1. Correlational Analyses

Correlations between the PAP Scale and validity criteria in the combined clinical sample are provided in Table 10.9. In the original scale development project, the PAP was significantly correlated with a family history of alcohol abuse and the respondent's own alcohol use and abuse. The clinical sample results confirm these associations. High PAP Scale scores are significantly associated with the Mother's MAST and Father's MAST completed by the respondents. The PAP is also significantly correlated with alcohol consumption and abuse measured by heavy drinking and problems. Correlations with smoking and coffee consumption are also significant. Also of interest are findings showing that the PAP is correlated negatively with the reported age at which the person began smoking and drinking. High personality vulnerability for alcoholism measured by the PAP is associated with the earlier onset of drinking and smoking.

To compare the means of the clinical and general population samples, demographic characteristics associated with personality and the clinical group status had to be controlled. MCA analyses compared the clinical groups on the prealcoholic personality test while controlling for demographic factors and covariates, as done in Chapter 7. The results of these analyses are presented in Tables 10.10 and 10.11. In the ANOVA table, the results show that the drug group

Table 10.9. Correlations Between the PAP and Validity Criteria in the Clinical Sample

	PAP
Father's MAST	.32[a]
Mother's MAST	.25[a]
Alcohol consumption (oz./day)	.16[a]
Alcohol problems	.31[a]
Heavy drinking (# of times 8 or more at a sitting)	.29[a]
Cigarettes (#/day)	−.07
Coffee consumption (cups/day)	.12[b]
Age Began Smoking	−.23[a]
Age Began Drinking	−.40[a]

[a] $p < .05$.
[b] $p < .001$.

Table 10.10. MCA Analysis of Variance Table

Source of variation	DF	Mean square	F
Main Effects			
Drug group	5	845.18	81.91[a]
Gender	1	480.24	46.54[a]
Race	4	42.60	4.13[b]
Marital status	3	44.63	4.33[b]
Current employment	6	18.14	1.76
Religious preference	4	45.51	4.41[b]
Covariates			
Age	1	7441.45	371.96[a]
Net worth	1	1550.56	721.18[a]
Years of education	1	778.17	150.27[a]
Explained	26	824.64	79.92[a]
Residual	1427	10.32	
Total	1453	24.89	
Covariate	ßeta		
Age	−.18		
Net worth	−.72		
Years of education	−.27		

[a] $p < .001$.
[b] $p < .01$.

factor was a significant predictor of the prealcoholic personality test scores. Several demographic variables, including age, net worth, education, gender, race, marital status, and religious preference were also significant predictors of the PAP Scale scores. The adjusted PAP Scale means by drug group and demographic factors are displayed in Table 10.11. Within the clinical sample, alcoholics who also use drugs scored highest, drug users scored next highest, and alcoholics scored lowest. On the adjusted PAP means, all three groups scored significantly higher than the general population (Tukey test, $p < .001$). Statistical comparisons within the clinical samples showed that alcoholics differed significantly from those addicted only to both alcohol and drugs (Tukey test, P<.001), but not quite from those addicted to drugs ($p < .06$). The drugs and drugs and alcohol groups did not differ significantly.

These results were a little surprising to us at first and a little disconcerting. The PAP was developed exclusively on the basis of item correlations with alcohol abuse criteria, and yet the drug using group scored higher than the clinical sample of alcoholics. At first glance, this does not provide very good evidence of discriminant validity. Now, it is recognized in the addictions field that different forms of substance misuse tend to co-occur and that common mechanisms underlie addiction to both alcohol and drugs (for a review see Miller, Guttman, & Chawla, 1997). Common genetic factors are particularly important in predicting substance misuse that interferes with normal functioning. Although common genetic fac-

Table 10.11. MCA Adjusted PAP Means by Groups

	n	Unadjusted		Adjusted for factors and covariates	
	n	PAP mean	ETA	PAP mean	Beta
Drug group			.64		.43
Clinical alcohol only	207	12.08		10.97	
Clinical drugs only	40	14.49		12.55	
Clinical both	69	15.62		12.94	
Gen. pop. no alcohol	918	5.67		6.41	
Gen.pop.alcohol	158	10.23		8.81	
Gen.pop. remission	62	7.61		8.20	
Gender					
Female	647	6.53	.24	7.12	.14
Male	807	8.95		8.48	
Race			.33		.07
White	1272	7.41		7.83	
Black	17	10.18		9.52	
Asian	46	6.03		7.62	
Native	76	13.99		8.91	
Other	43	11.68		6.85	
Marital Status			.44		.08
Single	331	11.41		8.40	
Married or equivalent	931	6.31		7.63	
Widowed	35	6.55		7.22	
Divorced	157	9.96		8.36	
Employment Status			.39		.06
Work full time	819	7.62		7.89	
Work part time	160	6.59		7.44	
Unemployed	142	12.55		8.57	
Student	70	10.21		7.68	
Homemaker	118	5.86		7.43	
Retired	92	4.71		8.15	
Other	53	10.00		7.80	
Religious Preference			.28		.08
Catholic	410	7.77		7.69	
Protestant	548	6.52		7.59	
Jewish	34	6.12		8.65	
Other	184	8.88		7.96	
None	278	10.24		8.54	

tors are important, they do not account for all of the genetic variance in heavy substance use (Swan, Carmelli, & Cardon, 1996).

One of the underlying genetic mechanisms that might account for the comorbidity in alcohol and drug misuse is the D2 dopamine receptor gene (Noble, 1996). In the research by Uhl, Persico, and Smith (1992) for example, an association was found between the D2 receptor gene, or so-called alcohol gene and substance abuse. Noble et al. (1993) also found that a higher concentration for this receptor gene is associated with cocaine dependence. Research on other alcoholism scales such as the MacAndrew Scale (Burke and Marcus, 1977) has also found an association between alcoholism scale scores and addiction. It is likely that the test we have developed should more appropriately be considered a measure of the "addiction-prone personality" rather than the "prealcoholic personality."

One of the interesting findings in our group comparisons was that our general population sample of remitted alcoholics did not differ significantly from our general population alcoholics in their PAP scores. This result is as anticipated if the scale is actually measuring prealcoholic traits as opposed to conditions that arise from the alcohol abuse and are likely to return to normal following cessation of alcohol abuse.

To determine whether the pattern of results observed with the PAP would also occur when group comparisons were made with the MAC and the EPQ-A, we ran a similar set of group comparative analyses with these measures. The unadjusted and adjusted means for the six groups on the three tests are provided in Table 10.12. The EPQ-A performs well in discriminating the clinical groups, and the ordering of the groups is similar to the PAP test. The MacAndrew test also shows a similar pattern of results with a somewhat weaker separation of the groups. These results are consistent with expectations, given the way these measures were developed. The EPQ-A was designed to separate clinical groups of addicts from normals, the PAP was designed to measure the prealcoholic personality, and the MAC test was designed to discriminate alcoholics from psychiatric patients.

Within the clinical sample, another method for examining the association between addictive personality scales and drug abuse was available. Correlations between the three addictive personality scales and the DAST measure of drug abuse were computed. Results showed that all three measures correlated significantly with the DAST ($r = .54, p < .001$ for the PAP; $r = .22, p < .001$ for the MAC; and $r = .43, p < .001$ for the EPQ-A). The results are consistent with these in the group comparative analyses described above. The PAP and the EPQ-A test have strong associations with drug abuse, and the MAC has the weakest association.

5.2. PAP Personality Correlates in the Clinical Sample

Correlations between the PAP and personality scales included in the clinical study are shown in Table 10.13. In the clinical sample, the general pattern of correlations between the PAP and personality is the same as in the general population, but there are also some interesting differences. The PAP is associated with higher Psychoticism, Stimulus Reducing or sensation seeking as measured by the Vando Scale, lower Ego Strength and Self-Esteem, and more Neoroticism and Trait Anxi-

Table 10.12. Personality Indicators of Addiction in General Population and Clinical Samples

| | General population | | | Clinical sample | | | | |
	Non-alcoholics	Remitted alcoholics	Alcoholics	Alcoholics	Drugs only	Alcohol and drugs	F	B
Prealcoholic Personality								
Mean	5.67	7.61	10.23	12.08	14.49	15.62	81.91[a]	.43
Adjusted mean[a]	6.41	8.20	8.81	10.97	12.55	12.94		
MacAndrew Scale								
Mean	21.33	22.61	23.36	25.00	25.21	27.35	18.91[a]	.28
Adjusted mean[a]	21.75	22.59	22.91	24.08	24.34	26.11		
Eysenck Addiction Scale								
Mean	6.66	8.52	9.15	14.43	17.03	16.33	109.42[a]	.58
Adjusted mean[a]	6.86	8.72	8.78	14.14	16.55	15.51		

[a] Adjusted means are adjusted for demographics including gender, race, marital status, employment status, and religious preference as factors and age, net worth, and education as covariates.
[b] significance level $p < .001$.

Table 10.13. Correlations Between
the PAP and Personality Measures in
the Clinical Sample

	Pearson r
Psychoticism	.68[a]
Extraversion	.11[b]
Neuroticism	.52[a]
Lie scale	−.55[a]
Reducer–augmenter	.58[a]
Trait anxiety	.47[a]
Self-esteem	−.40[a]
MMPI ego strength	−.44[a]
MMPI MacAndrew	.31[a]
EPQ-A	.63[a]
Field dependence	.15[c]

[a] $p < .001$.
[b] $p < .05$.
[c] $p < .01$.

ety. In the clinical sample, the correlation with stimulus reducing is slightly lower than in the general population, whereas the correlations with anxiety and ego-strength related measures are somewhat higher. It is hard to say whether this different pattern of correlations reflects differences in the sampling procedures used in obtaining the two samples or perhaps shifts in the personality traits of the alcoholic sample toward more "clinical alcoholic" traits, as the course of alcoholism has progressed.

5.3. PAP Scores and Treatment Outcome

In the clinical sample, a six-month follow-up was undertaken by telephone, and more than 80% of the respondents were reinterviewed. At follow-up, subjects were asked questions regarding alcohol consumption, problems due to drinking, legal drug use, and illegal drug use. In a series of simple regression analyses, the PAP along with several demographic characteristics was used to predict alcohol and drug use behaviors in the groups addicted to either alcohol or drugs at the time of initial treatment. The results (see Table 10.14) showed that the Prealcoholic Personality Test predicted alcohol consumption and problems in the alcohol addicted group at follow-up. Other findings in the alcohol addicted group were that (1) older alcoholics drank more and had more problems at follow up; and (2) women had more drinking problems than men at follow-up and were more likely

Table 10.14. The PAP and Treatment Outcome Criteria for AFM Clients Addicted to Alcohol (n = 232)

Predictor	Alcohol Use		Drug Use	
	Oz. per day ß	Problems ß	Legal ß	Illegal ß
PAP	.29[a]	.28[a]	.21[c]	.28[a]
Education	−.02	−.02	−.06	.01
Income	−.04	.01	.04	−.05
Married	−.06	−.12	.07	.02
Unemployed	−.05	−.03	.00	.01
Age	.22[b]	.16[c]	.13	−.03
Gender	.01	−.15[c]	−.21[b]	.06
R^2	.07	.09	.07	.10

[a] $p < .001$.
[b] $p < .01$.
[c] $p < .05$.

to use prescription drugs than men. Parallel sets of analyses predicting treatment outcome in the alcoholic group were run using the EPQ-A and the MacAndrew Scale as personality predictors in separate analyses. Results were fairly comparable, and the EPQ-A contributed significantly in predicting the four treatment outcome criteria. But all of the beta weights were somewhat lower. The MacAndrew Scale predicted two of the outcome criteria (oz./day and illegal drug use), but again at a somewhat lower magnitude of prediction.

The PAP also predicted alcohol problems and illegal drug use at follow-up in the drug addicted sample (see Table 10.15). Other findings in the drug addicted sample were that (1) married people had fewer alcohol problems than unmarried people and (2) female addicts were more likely to use prescription drugs. In the parallel analyses using the EPQ-A and MacAndrew tests in this sample, the EPQ-A contributed significantly in predicting alcoholic problems (Beta = .27, $p < .05$) and legal drug use (Beta = .24, $p < .01$), but the MacAndrew test did not predict any treatment outcome criteria in this sample.

The results of our longitudinal analyses in the clinical sample show that the Prealcoholic Personality Test is a significant predictor of more alcohol and drug use and problems during follow-up. These results suggest that clients who have these characteristics may have a more difficult time overcoming their addiction. It is unlikely that these findings can be explained by some artifact because we controlled for a number of potential demographic, confounding influences. The PAP performs somewhat better than other measures of personality and addiction in predicting treatment outcome, particularly for alcoholics.

Table 10.15. The PAP and Treatment Outcome Criteria for AFM Clients Addicted to Drugs (n = 83)

Predictor	Alcohol Use		Drug Use	
	Oz. per day β	Problem β	Legal β	Illegal β
PAP	.11	.34[a]	.14	.28[b]
Education	−.18	.02	−.07	.22
Income	.18	.06	.15	−.03
Married	−.20	−.25[b]	.04	.10
Unemployed	−.13	−.03	.00	−.07
Age	.14	.07	−.06	−.15
Gender	.08	−.09	−.40[c]	−.13
R^2	.13	.17	.17	.11

[a] $p < .001$.
[b] $p < .01$.
[c] $p < .05$.

6. Summary and Conclusions

The first objective in this chapter was to develop a measure of the "Prealcoholic Personality." Criteria that were used to select items were an association with a family history of alcohol abuse and a current DSM-III R diagnosis of alcohol abuse. A total of 23 items met this criteria and were selected for further analyses.

The second objective in this chapter was to examine the reliability and validity of the Prealcoholic Personality (PAP) test. The 23-item scale had satisfactory internal consistency and high stability over time, as indicated by a test–retest correlation of .82 during a six-month period. Ample evidence was available for the validity of the new scale. Correlations with demographics were generally as anticipated and followed a pattern similar to the prevalence of alcohol abuse with higher scores in males and younger respondents. Correlations with a variety of measures of family history of alcohol abuse were also significant. Correlations with personality measures were also consistent with results in the alcoholic personality literature described in Chapters 1 and 2. High scores on the PAP were associated with higher psychoticism, stimulus reducing, higher neuroticism and anxiety, and lower ego strength and self-esteem.

The third and perhaps most critical objective in this chapter was to examine the ability of the PAP to predict changes in alcohol abuse patterns over time. If the PAP is in fact a measure of the "prealcoholic personality," it should predict the development of these symptoms. It is also important to show whether a test designed specifically for predicting the risk of alcoholism can in fact do this better than measures not designed specifically for this purpose. Longitudinal analyses confirmed the prospective utility of the PAP in predicting the development of addictive symptoms, even when the levels of symptoms at Time 1 were controlled in the analyses. The PAP also performed better than the MacAndrew Scale or the EPQ-Addiction Scale in predicting the development of addictive symptoms. These results provide strong support for the validity of the PAP and support the initial contention by MacAndrew (1979) that scales perform best when they are developed with a specific purpose in mind.

The EPQ-Addiction Scale performs quite well in discriminating clinical groups because this is the criterion that was used for developing the scale. The PAP and EPQ-A Scales may be fairly complementary measures that could be used together where the PAP measures the prealcoholic personality and the EPQ-A the clinical addict personality. Although the MacAndrew Scale did not perform as well as the two other scales in either prospectively predicting development of addiction or separating alcoholics and addicts from normals, it should be remembered that the scale was developed to separate alcoholics from other psychiatric patients. In a study designed to compare the PAP, EPQ-A, and MAC Scales in discriminating alcoholics from other psychiatric patients, the MAC Scale might in fact perform the best.

The next objective in this chapter was to test the reliability and validity of the PAP in a clinical sample. The internal consistency for the PAP was satisfactory in the clinical sample (alpha = .82). Some evidence for the validity of the scale in the clinical sample was also obtained in that clinical alcoholics scored much higher on the scale than the general population. The fact that remitted alcoholics continued to have a score on this test that was not any lower than alcoholics in the general population also supported the idea that this scale is measuring a stable "prealcoholic" component of the alcoholic personality. A surprising result occurred in the clinical group comparisons in that drug addicted cases scored higher than alcoholics on the PAP. Similar findings were found on other measures such as the MacAndrew and EPQ-A suggesting that there may be an underlying vulnerability to addiction in general rather than a specific underlying vulnerability to alcohol abuse. Correlations between the PAP and the Drug Abuse Screening Test supported the interpretation of the PAP as a measure of vulnerability to addiction rather than a specific vulnerability to alcohol abuse.

The final objective in this chapter was to determine whether the PAP would be useful in predicting treatment outcome in our clinical sample. PAP scores were used along with demographic control variables as predictors of treatment outcome at a six-month follow-up interview for alcoholics and drug addicts. The results showed that the PAP predicted alcohol consumption and problems for alcohol addicted clients at follow-up and drug use at follow-up for drug addicted clients. The PAP also performed better in this function than the MacAndrew Scale. The EPQ-A also proved somewhat useful in predicting treatment outcome.

Taken as a whole, the data presented in this chapter provide very strong evidence that the PAP measures an underlying personality vulnerability to alcohol and drug abuse. This vulnerability prospectively predicts the development of symptoms in the general population and problems following treatment for alcohol and drug abuse. Because the Prealcoholic Personality test is also strongly associated with drug abuse, we have chosen to relabel the scale as the "Addiction-Prone Personality" test and this is the name that will be applied to this measure in the following sections of this book.

11

The Development
of the Prealcoholic/Addiction
Prone Personality

It is interesting that although there are a lot of articles on the "alcoholic personality," there is not a lot of research on the development of prealcoholic or addiction-prone personality traits. In other words, what are the environmental conditions that lead to the development of personality traits that predispose a person to become addicted to alcohol and/or drugs? In reviewing the family socialization and alcoholic personality literature, we did not find any articles in fact that looked at conditions in the environment, such as parenting, for example, and the development of traits such as those measured by the MacAndrew Alcoholism Scale. There is, however, a fair amount of literature on family socialization influences on personality development in general and a similar amount of literature in the areas of family socialization and the development of substance misuse and delinquent behavior. Before reviewing this literature, some discussion is required of the methodological difficulties involved in studying family socialization influences on personality development.

One of the most widely held beliefs in the fields of developmental psychology, social psychology, family sociology, and family studies is that parents have strong influences on the development of their children. Faith in this belief is buttressed primarily by cross-sectional studies demonstrating an association between parenting style and child outcomes. In particular, research by Baumrind (1967, 1971) and a host of others (e.g., Lamborn, Mounts, Steinberg, & Dornbusch, 1991) has tended to show that youngsters raised in "authoritative" homes score better on a variety of developmental outcomes including achievement, social development, self-esteem, and mental health (Maccoby and Martin, 1983). Although

Baumrind (1967, 1971) categorized parenting styles into three main types, including (1) authoritative, (2) authoritarian, and (3) permissive, it is now recognized that it is preferable to employ a two-dimensional categorization system of parenting in which the two dimensions consist of a parental warmth and acceptance dimension, and the other dimension is an index of parental control or strictness (e.g., Lamborn et al., 1991).

Recent developments in the field of behavioral genetics have brought the interpretation of the results of the traditional child rearing practices and personality development research into serious question (for recent reviews on this topic see Reiss, 1995; Rowe, 1994). Reiss (1995), for example, noted that because genetic associations have been found between both family process variables and many of the developmental outcomes examined in the family socialization literature, this contamination needs to be controlled in family research designs. In particular, it is noteworthy that one of the strongest family correlates of developmental outcomes, maternal care, has been shown to have a strong genetic component (Pérusse, Neale, Heath, & Eaves, 1994). Research from both twin studies and adoption studies reviewed by Rowe (1994) have consistently demonstrated (1) negligible between family variance for personality traits, and (2) consistently low correlations in the personality characteristics of children raised in adoptive homes between siblings and between adoptive children and their parents. These findings are generally interpreted as inconsistent with a strong family socialization influence on personality development.

The new perspective on the limited influence of family socialization on developmental outcomes proposed by behavioral geneticists has not gone unchallenged. In particular, articles by Wachs (1983) and Hoffman (1991) have been critical of the conclusions reached by behavioral geneticists. One of the major arguments against the interpretations made by the behavioral geneticists is that their conclusions regarding the minimal influence produced by between family factors rests on a set of questionable assumptions and does not measure the effects of intrafamily factors directly. Most behavioral genetic studies have not included measures of the family environment that would be approved by developmentalists.

In addition to the problems associated with controlling the confounding influences of genetic factors, the personality development literature has been criticized for relying on retrospective offspring reports of parenting (Halverson, 1988). Retrospective reports are liable to be inaccurate for several reasons, including forgetting, selective recall, and current values that affect recall. Only been a limited number of studies have attempted to examine the reliability of retrospective recall by correlating retrospective accounts of parenting with reports of parenting made earlier. In one of these studies, Finkel and McGue (1993) concluded that retrospective accounts were only moderately reliable. The highest correlations were .43 for cohesiveness and .45 for punishment. It should be noted, however, as pointed out by McCrae and Costa (1988), that it is important to separate random error variance from selective recall or forgetting. Some of the parenting measures used by Finkel and McGue (1993) were rather unreliable, and if the corrections for this unreliability are made, the test–retest correlations go as high as .88 for punishment. This is hardly a "modest" correlation for data gathered 25 years apart. Although retrospective data are not perfect, they certainly may have some utility, particularly when perspectives are gathered from more than one family member.

1. Family Socialization Influences on Personality Development

In Chapter 10, the personality correlates of the addiction-prone personality were examined. Traits associated with vulnerability to abuse alcohol and other drugs include high psychoticism, high neuroticism and related characteristics such as low ego-strength, high extraversion and sensation seeking, and low social conformity. These characteristics together share some similarity with what others have called a "difficult temperament."

In the cross-sectional research relating the two main parenting dimensions to personality and psychiatric symptoms, results have been fairly consistent in showing that dysthymic personality traits and neurotic spectrum disorders are associated with parenting that is low in care and high in restrictiveness (see McCrae & Costa, 1988; Parker, 1979; Whitbeck et al., 1992). On the Five-Factor Inventory, for example, McCrae and Costa (1991) reported that strong parental love was associated with low neuroticism. In the Parker (Parker, 1979; Parker, Tupling, & Brown, 1979) research as well, parenting that was characterized as high on control and low on affection was associated with depressed affect, whether the parenting ratings were done by the persons themselves or by their parents. McCrae and Costa (1988) also reported that parenting that was high in loving, as reported by respondents, was associated with higher extraversion, openness, agreeableness, and conscientiousness. In general, acting out kinds of behavior and personality traits are commonly found in association with parenting that is lacking in warmth and inconsistent with respect to discipline (e.g., Quinton & Rutter, 1984). This latter association was confirmed in longitudinal research by McCord (1979) who reported that stronger maternal affection and supervision during childhood was associated with lower rates of criminal activity during adulthood. Similar findings have been observed in the research on difficult temperament. Blackson (1994) reported that family dysfunction and maladaptive parenting were associated with difficult temperament in offspring. In a longitudinal study on the continuity of difficult temperament in adolescence, Tubman and Windle (1995) found that lower levels of family support are associated with a continuous difficult temperament.

The family environment is also an important factor in the development of personality disorders. In a 33-year longitudinal study on the offspring of male alcoholics, Drake and Vaillant (1988) found that poor relationships with one's mother in childhood were associated with personality disorders in adulthood.

At least two studies have been conducted to date where family socialization influences on personality development have been studied directly while controlling for possible genetic confounds. Bouchard and McGue (1990) examined the associations between the family environment and personality in an adopted twin sample. Family environment was assessed by the Family Environment Scale (Moos & Moos, 1986), and personality was assessed by the California Psychological Inventory (Gough, 1969). The results indicated that there were several significant associations between the respondents' perceptions of their family environment and personality. Extraversion was significantly correlated with the encouragement of individual growth. Emotional stability was correlated significantly with cohesion. Consensuality was significantly correlated with all three of the family environment factors, and high consensuality was found in association with perceived parenting that was high on cohesion, positive constraint, and encouragement of individual growth. In the Cadoret adoption research (Cadoret, Yates, Troughton, Woodworth, & Stewart, 1995), the psychiatric histories of the adoptive parents were studied in relation to the development of antisocial personality disorders in offspring. Results showed that there was a positive association between having a disturbed adoptive parent and the development of antisocial personality traits.

2. Family Socialization Influences on the Development of Substance Misuse

The view that parents are the primary socialization agent is consistent with a number of classic theories about the family. Parsons (1955) characterized the basic function of the family as the socialization of children. This included the creation of personality by internalizing of the cultural system that maintains the social order and role awareness. A lack of proper socialization may result in a failure to internalize the dominant cultural values of society, including the need for achievement and the development of problem behaviors such as alcohol and drug abuse. The development of problem drinking has also been explained from the perspective of family socialization by Jessor (Jessor & Jessor, 1977; Jessor, 1987) as learned behavior shaped by culture and personal experience. Within the larger context of problem behavioral theory, Jessor (1987) suggests that three systems of psychosocial influence can act as "instigations" or as "controls" against problem behaviors such as adolescent drinking and drug use. The three systems are personality, behavior, and perceived environment, which operate in a dynamic relationship with factors conducive to problem behavior, and factors that constrain it (Sadava, 1987). The theory takes into account social structure, demography, and aspects of parental and peer socialization.

Another theory that posits an important role for parenting influences on the development of adolescent problem behaviors is the theory developed by Patterson and colleagues (Patterson, DeBaryshe, & Ramsey, 1989). In their developmental model of antisocial behavior, they hypothesize that antisocial parents will be at a significant risk for ineffective disciplinary practices which in turn will predict conduct disorders in offspring. Conduct disorders will then lead to academic failure and peer rejection. After these experiences, the adolescent is likely to begin associating more with deviant peer groups and to develop more chronic delinquent behavior. Research suggests that the Patterson model can be applied to a wide range of adolescent problem behaviors, including substance misuse (Dishion, Duncan, Eddy, Fagot, & Fetrow, 1994; Duncan & Duncan, 1996).

Zucker (1976, 1979) has also developed a conceptual framework to organize and explain the various determinants of adolescent drinking within a developmental context. This approach includes three classes of influence or levels of variables: (1) sociocultural and community influences, (2) group influences, and (3) intraindividual influences. Parental influence is categorized, along with peer relationships and other intimate family relationships, under group influences. The effect of both sociocultural and group influences on drinking behavior is indirect and operates only through intraindividual factors (cognitive structure, personality, and genetic influences). Using data from both adolescents and their parents, Zucker and Barron (1973) found that heavy-drinking boys had parents who drank more than others, were more antisocial, and used isolation as a punishment. The boys also perceive their fathers as emotionally cold, a point that we will return to shortly. Both Zucker and Jessor suggest that multidimensional approaches to understanding initiation and maintenance of drinking are necessary, and Zucker (1979) has been especially active in looking at the interaction of genetic and environmental factors in the development of alcohol abuse.

The major family theories have been incorporated into a model of adolescent drinking developed by Grace Barnes and associates at the Institute for Research on Alcoholism (Barnes, 1977; Barnes, 1990; Barnes, Farrell, & Cairns, 1986; Barnes, Farrell, & Windle, 1987; Barnes & Welte, 1986; Barnes & Welte, 1988; Barnes & Windle, 1987). The substantial body of literature from this group has focused on the impact on the family on the development of drinking in adolescence, using primarily the social learning approach. According to the theory, teenagers are socialized into drinking by modeling their parents, and there is abundant evidence that adult drinking patterns are correlated with adolescent drinking patterns (e.g., Barnes et al., 1986; Barnes & Welte, 1990; Zucker, 1976).

More recently, Grace Barnes examined the role of parenting practices on the development of adolescent drinking (in addition to other problem behaviors).

Consistent with Jessor, parental support and control are thought to be useful predictors of drinking (Barnes & Farrell, 1992). Support is defined as behavior that
indicates to the children that they are valued, accepted, and loved. Control is
defined as behavior intended to direct the child's behavior in a manner that is
acceptable to the parents. This includes coercive control (hitting and grounding),
inductive control, and rules for behavior and monitoring. Increased coercive control is associated with more problem behaviors, including increased levels of problem drinking. High levels of support are associated with the lowest levels of drinking, drug use, deviance, and school misconduct. Generally speaking, relationship
factors such as family adaptability and cohesion are better predictors of drug and
alcohol use in adolescence than structural factors (family size and birth order).
Barnes (1990) has provided a broad conceptual framework for examining findings relating family factors to the development of drinking in adolescents. The
model incorporates Parson's socialization view, the parent–child interaction literature, Jessor's problem behavior theory, and Zucker's developmental framework.

It is also possible that not all of the association between parental practices
and offspring scores on personality and problem behaviors is produced by parental practices that cause offspring outcomes. Ralph Tarter and colleagues (Tarter,
Blackson, Martin, Loeber, & Moss, 1993) have hypothesized that children of
alcoholics have more difficult temperaments and that this difficult temperament
produces more coercive and less effective parenting which in turn leads to more
internalizing and externalizing problems. In their research on the sons of alcoholics
and nonalcoholics (aged 10–12), the results confirmed that the sons of alcoholics had
more difficult temperaments, received less effective parenting and demonstrated more
internalizing and externalizing behavior problems (Tarter et al., 1993). The design of this study did not allow determining the causal direction of this effect.

The association between low parental care and substance abuse and other
problem behaviors is now well supported by numerous cross-sectional and several longitudinal studies. The relationship between low parental care and higher
tobacco use was recently reported by Melby, Conger, Conger, and Lorenz (1993),
and low maternal care was found associated with more substance abuse in a recent study conducted by Cooper, Pierce, and Tidwell (1995). The relationship
between aspects of the family environment and alcohol and substance misuse has
been supported in several recent longitudinal investigations. Two of these investigations involved long time frames. McCord (1988) found support for an association between family environments in childhood and adult alcoholism. In particular, early environments characterized by fathers' alcoholism, mothers' esteem
for the father, and low parental control were associated with the development of
alcoholism some twenty years later. Shedler and Block (1990) found an association between mothers' parenting at age three and adult substance misuse. Mothers of frequent users were characterized as cold, unresponsive, underprotective,
and providing little encouragement.

Several recent longitudinal investigations covering shorter periods of time have also reported significant associations between family environmental characteristics and adolescent drug use and delinquency. In the UCLA longitudinal research program, aspects of the family environment have been examined alongside other psychosocial predictors in prospectively predicting sustance use. The results of this research have been reported in a series of articles. Using data obtained independently from 557 mothers and their sons or daughters when the children were in grades 7–9, and following the adolescents three years later, Newcomb and Bentler (1988a) found that mother drug use and family disruption (not having both parents in the home) affected the adolescents' socially deviant attitudes, as well as drug use. In turn, these mediating adolescent variables affected subsequent socially deviant attitudes, as well as drug use (use of cigarettes, alcohol, marijuana, and hard drugs). Family disruption also affected the offsprings' emotional distress and thought organization. Newcomb and Rickards (1995) further reported that for both women and men, parent drug-use problems predicted poor family support, and family support was strongly associated with good adult intimate relationships.

Family influences are typically part of a larger social nexus within which the family members operate. An important part of this social nexus is the construct of "social support" which has been considered relevant in the social psychological literature to the health of individuals (e.g., Newcomb, 1990). A high quality of social support received as well as given by an individual within the family is indicative of good interpersonal relationships within the family that often transfers well to social relationships outside the family. In their study of 654 individuals across eight years from early adolescence to young adulthood, Newcomb and Bentler (1988b) assessed the perceived quality of relationships of the adolescent with their parents, their family, as well as adults in general and peers, and found that these variables formed a strong factor of social support. Controlling for social conformity and general drug use, they found that every young adult problem area (such as psychosomatic complaints, emotional distress, work problems, and health problems) was reduced by the presence of stronger social support during adolescence. Following the same sample for another four years into adulthood, Newcomb, Scheier, and Bentler (1993) found that the effects of social support were somewhat reduced over this longer 12-year time span and that early adolescent emotional distress (self-derogation, depression, lack of self-acceptance), which correlated −.6 with social support, had the larger impact on various adult mental health outcomes. Because there seems to be a strong genetic component to affective illness (e.g., McGue & Bouchard, 1998), this result may reflect the growing influence of genetic determinants of mental health over the longer time span.

In their study of concurrent and predictive risk factors for drug use among 994 adolescent 10th–12th graders, Newcomb, Maddahian, & Bentler (1986) found that a scale composed of ten different risk factors was reliably associated with several types of alcohol and drug use. They also reported that the risk factors significantly predicted increased drug use across a one-year period, controlling for inital levels of use. The risk factors included many that typically predict alcohol abuse: poor academic achievement, low religious commitment, early alcohol use, poor self-esteem, psychopathology (depression), poor relationships with parents, deviance, sensation seeking, and exposure to peer and adult models of drug use. In this study, poor relationships with parents, as assessed by a four-item scale, was thus only one of several contributors to increased risk of substance use. Newcomb and Felix-Ortiz (1992) expanded this risk factor conception to incorporate protective factors as well and found that vulnerability measured by both protective and risk factors and their interaction was highly associated with drug use in adolescence, moderately associated with certain types of drug use in young adulthood, and strongly associated with heightened drug problems in adulthood.

In an important recent longitudinal investigation, Cohen, Richardson, and LaBree (1994) examined the family environmental precursors of the onset of drinking and tobacco use in a large sample of sixth and seventh graders. Results confirmed that the family environment had an important effect on the onset of smoking and drinking. In families where children reported better communication and more time spent with parents, there were lower onset rates for alcohol and tobacco use.

Terry Duncan and colleagues have been conducting a series of longitudinal investigations examining the association between various aspects of the family environment and the development of alcohol and drug use. In one of these investigations, a sample of youths aged 11–14 was followed during a four-year period, and latent growth curve methodology was used to predict initial levels of alcohol use and change in use for each cohort. The major predictors examined included family cohesiveness and peer influences. Results showed that family cohesiveness predicted initial use, particularly for older adolescents. Changes in family cohesion was not as predictive of changes in alcohol use as changes in peer encouragement, but family cohesion did have a significant lagged effect (i.e., initial levels of family cohesion predicted alcohol use later on). In another longitudinal investigation involving adolescent smokers and nonsmokers, Duncan, Duncan, Biglan, and Ary (1998) used a latent growth modeling approach to examine the associations between family and peer controls and the development of substance use. Higher substance abuse was found in families where there was more parent-child conflict and less monitoring. Moreover, increasing levels of parent–child conflict was associated with faster acceleration in substance use.

In another recent longitudinal investigation involving adolescent samples, Bates and Labouvie (1995) reported that low parental control was associated with high-risk developmental trajectories of use intensity and problems. Dobkin, Tremblay, and Sacchitelle (1997) have been conducting longitudinal research on factors associated with the development of early onset substance abuse. Their analyses showed that boys' disruptive behavior and mothers' lack of nurturance were two important factors predicting early onset substance abuse.

Only one study conducted to date has examined the association between family environmental characteristics, such as parenting, and alcohol use in adoptive families. McGue, Sharma, and Benson (1996) examined the relationship between various aspects of the family environment and alcohol use and problems in biological and adoptive children living in the same families. Their study found that the relationship between family environment predictors and offspring alcohol use patterns was stronger in biological than in adoptive children. In particular, alcohol use and abuse was greater in biological children when the family was less cohesive, less democratic, less religious, and when the parents drank more. Weaker relationships were observed in adoptive children, with no significant effect of parental drinking on offspring drinking. These results are consistent with claims made by behavioral geneticists such as Reiss (1995) and Rowe (1994) that the family environment effects on offspring outcomes have been overestimated.

In the current investigation, we anticipated that strong parental care would be associated with lower scores for the addiction-prone personality. This prediction is based on the consistent relationship observed in the literature between addiction-prone personality traits and substance abuse, on the one hand, and low parental care, on the other. Based on social learning theory, it was also anticipated that there would be an association between parental addiction-prone personality traits and similar characteristics in their offspring. Although numerous studies have shown associations between parent personality and psychopathology and offspring personality, these studies are difficult to interpret because of the confounding of genetic and social influences. Children of alcoholics, for example, have scored higher on measures of difficult temperament (e.g., Tarter et al., 1993). High novelty seeking mothers are more likely to have sons who are higher on alcohol and drug use (Gabel et al., 1997). Children of alcoholics generally display more childhood psychopathology than nonalcoholics and are particularly susceptible to externalizing problems (for a review, see West & Prinz, 1987). None of the literature actually proves that any of the effects occur as a result of social influences rather than genetic transmission. The current investigation will investigate the association between the addiction-prone personality trait in parents and offspring in both biological and adoptive families. If there is any true socializing influence of parental personality on the development of offspring personality, the association between parental addiction-prone personality traits and offspring scores should hold up in both biological and adoptive samples.

3. Objectives

The major objectives in this chapter are as follows:

1. To employ the data gathered from the Vancouver Family Survey to examine the reliability and validity of the Addiction-Prone Personality Scale in adults and youths from biological and adoptive families.
2. To examine the reliability and validity of a reduced 21-item scale that eliminates a couple of items in the original PAP containing content directly related to alcohol and drug involvement. Norms in alcoholic and nonalcoholic groups will also be computed.
3. To examine the associations between the Addiction-Prone Personality and the five-factor personality scales.
4. To examine the associations between various facets of the home environment and Addiction-Prone Personality scores in youths from biological and adoptive families. The inclusion of a group of adoptive families will enable us to control for the contamination of genetic influences on personality development. In addition, the project endeavors to investigate and control for subject perception biases by gathering data from several family members and using statistical techniques such as structural equation modeling that are designed to reduce the contributions of measurement error. The main aspects of the family environment that were considered important for investigation in the current project include (1) family demographics, (2) personality characteristics of the rearing parents, (3) family cohesion and adaptability, and (4) parenting.

4. Methodology

4.1. Design

The data for this project are taken from the Vancouver Family Survey. The primary objective in the Vancouver Family Survey is to examine the associations between the family environment and the risk for substance use and misuse. The design for the Vancouver Family Survey proposed to collect data from a large representative sample of intact families with children in the 15–24 age range living at home in the greater Vancouver area. The age range for this study is comparable to the age range employed (16–22) in the Minnesota adoption study (Scarr, Webber, Weinberg, & Wittig, 1981) and is fairly ideal for acquiring retrospective accounts of child rearing experiences over the course of the child's development.

4.2. Procedure and Subjects

In the original design for the Vancouver Family Survey, we proposed to screen more than 100,000 families to identify a sample of intact families with children in the 15–24 age range living at home. We were also hoping that this process would identify a sufficient number of adoptive families, preferably with the children adopted before the age of two, to allow us to recruit 450 biological and 150 adoptive families. The sample for the original wave of data collection was identified through a directory of telephone listings in the Greater Vancouver area. After the first set of screening interviews was conducted (19,253 contacts), it became evident that the percentage of intact adoptive families with children in the appropriate age range was very low in the original sample and particularly low on the west side of the Greater Vancouver area. Therefore, the screening process for the remainder of the study was concentrated on the east side.

In the end, this process yielded a large ($n = 5120$) sample of biological families eligible for participation, but only 177 adoptive families. Less than 10% of the contacts refused to answer the original screening interview after at least five calls were made. Then, biological families were selected at random for recruitment into the study, along with all of the adoptive families that had been identified. Then, the selected families were sent a letter explaining the purpose of the study in general terms including the mention of a $50.00 fee per family for participation. Then, families were contacted by telephone, and an attempt was made to arrange a visit to each family to administer questionnaires to both parents and the youngest child in the 15–24 age range. Families were included only if all three family members were willing to participate. The average time for individuals to complete the questionnaires was approximately one hour. This procedure yielded data from a sample of 477 biological families and 75 adoptive families (family participation rate of 53%). After it became apparent that the screening process was very costly for identifying adoptive families, the recruitment strategy was expanded to include recruitment through newspaper advertisements and referrals. This process produced an additional sample of 57 adoptive families. In the process of data cleaning, three randomly selected adoptive families, one nonrandomly selected adoptive family, and one biological family were dropped for not meeting study inclusion criteria. This produced a final sample of 601 families.

4.3. Measures

4.3.1. Demographics

In addition to age and gender, each respondent was asked a number of demographic questions. Demographic questions that were selected as important in the current investigation as control variables included primarily measures of socioeconomic status (income, education, and occupational status) as reported by both the mother and father.

4.3.2. Personality

Each family member completed a personality battery that consisted of the NEO Five-Factor Inventory, Form S, and the 23-item Addiction-Prone Personality Test described in Chapter 10. The NEO Five-Factor Inventory, Form S (FFI; Costa and McCrae, 1991), was used to measure the personality dimensions of Neuroticism, Extraversion, Openness, Agreeableness, and Conscientiousness.

The Prealcoholic or Addiction-Prone Personality was assessed by administering the 23-item test described in Chapter 10. In the Vancouver Family Survey, all of the items were adapted to the same format (a yes versus no response format). A copy of the test administered in the Vancouver Family Survey is provided in Appendix A. In the Vancouver Family Survey, we also tried removing two of the items whose content was most directly related to substance misuse, including item 11 which refers to blank spells and item 20 regarding whether the person would take drugs having dangerous effects. From now on in this book, the 23-item version of the test will be referred to as the Addiction-Prone Personality-23 (APP-23) and the 21-item version of the test as the Addiction-Prone Personality-21 (APP-21). The Cronbach's alphas for the two different versions of the test are summarized in Table 11.1. The measures of internal consistency do not vary much between the original and shortened version of the test. As noted earlier, internal consistency is not the best measure of reliability for a test that is multifactorial.

4.3.3. Family Environment

Perceptions of the family environment were assessed by two different instruments for measuring family systems and parenting. The family system was assessed by asking each family member to complete the Faces II instrument developed by Olson (Olson & Tiesel, 1991). Faces II contains two scales designed to measure adaptability and cohesion. Test–retest reliabilities for these scales over a 4-week period are very good ($r = .83$ for cohesion and $r = .80$ for reliability, Olson & Tiesel, 1991). Initially, Olson (1986) proposed a circumplex model suggesting that families with extreme scores on adaptability and cohesion would show poorer

Table 11.1. Reliabilities of the 23-Item and 21-Item Addiction-Prone Personality (APP) Scales in Four Samples[a]

	Mothers	Fathers	Sons	Daughters
	a	a	a	a
APP-23	.64	.68	.67	.73
APP-21	.63	.66	.66	.72

[a] Biological and adoptive families are combined for these analyses.

adjustment. Recent research with the Faces measure (Farrell & Barnes, 1993) suggests, however, that cohesion has a linear relationship to positive outcomes. Higher adaptability also predicts more positive outcomes, particularly for girls (Farrell & Barnes, 1993). Cronbach alpha reliabilities for the Faces II in the current sample were .86 for cohesion and .74 for adaptability in the adult sample and .87 for cohesion and .80 for adaptability in the youth sample.

Parenting was assessed by having each family member fill out the Parker (Parker, Tupling, & Brown, 1979) Parental Bonding Instrument (PBI). This instrument contains 13 items that measure parental overprotection and 12 items that assess parental care. High care is defined by affection, emotional warmth, empathy, and closeness. High overprotection has been defined as control, intrusion, excessive contact, and prevention of independent behavior. The test–retest reliability of the care and overprotection scales are quite high over a three-week interval ($r = .74$ and $r = .69$, respectively). Validity data on these scales are fairly extensive showing high correlations between self-reports and interviewer ratings, particularly for care, and high correlations for siblings raised in the same families. In this study, our youth sample filled out the instrument twice, once for each parent, and parents were asked to report on their own parenting over the first 15 years of the child's life. Reliabilities (Cronbach's alpha) in the adult sample were .78 for Care and .75 for Overprotection. In the youth sample, reliabilities were also high at .90 for Mother Care and .91 for Father Care, and .86 for Mother Overprotection and .91 for Father Overprotection.

4.4. Data Analyses

The first stage in the data analyses involved preparing a demographic summary of the sample characteristics and comparing the demographic characteristics of the biological and adoptive samples using chi-squared and t statistics, as appropriate. The next stage of the data analyses involved computing reliabilities, means, and standard deviations for the personality and family environmental measures.

Correlations were also computed between the parent addiction-prone personality (APP) scores and offspring personality scores in both the biological and adoptive samples. Midparent personality scores were also computed and correlated with offspring scores. Midparent scores have been used in prior adoption studies and are slightly better predictors of offspring personality than individual parent personality scores (e.g., Scarr et al., 1981).

In the next stage of the analyses, correlations between family environmental variables, including both youth and parent perceptions, and youths' APP scale scores were examined in biological and adoptive samples. The final stage of the data analyses involved computing structural equation models predicting offspring prealcoholic personality traits in the biological and adoptive samples. For these analyses, the EQS program (Bentler, 1995) was employed. To use the EQS program for structural equation modeling, a data set with no missing data points had to be created. Numerical values for missing entries in the data set were imputed using techniques described by Bentler (1995). Specifically, values for missing data were computed as either the mean value for the variable, the mean value for the variable by group, or as a predicted value estimated by a regression of a given variable on other variables which are significantly correlated with it and consistent with respect to theoretical considerations.

A decision was made to build separate models for youths' and for parents' perceptions of the family environment. This decision was based on the findings that youths' perceptions were quite different from those of their parents and they that also were much more strongly correlated with the youths' personality than parent perception (see Table 11.7). Research by Tein, Roosa, & Michaels (1994) suggests that these differences may be due to systematic reporting biases and that parent and child reports should not be aggregated. The overall strategy employed was to build initial models on the combined biological and adoptive samples and then to test for statistically significant differences between biological and adoptive samples via constrained and nonconstrained nested two-sample models.

For each of the two combined (i.e., biological and adoptive) models constructed in the analyses, a measurement model of family environment was first developed in accordance with theoretical and empirical considerations. Within these measurement models, factors were allowed to correlate with each other. Although correlated errors were not routinely added between all the theoretically related variables in the models, paths of this type were added to the models if their contribution to the X^2 statistic was large relative to further measurement paths. Both the LaGrange and Wald tests of statistical significance were used as aids in the decision making process. Once the measurement models were complete (i.e., the comparative fit index was at least .90 and no more major paths or correlated errors were added), disturbance terms were created, so that the family environmental factors could be predicted as dependent factors in the models.

In the next step of the analyses, the Addiction-Prone Personality variables were added to the models as both independent and dependent variables. In both models, the parents' midpoint score on the APP-21 scale was added as an independent variable. Youths' APP-21 scale scores were added as dependent variables in both models. Because all personality scores were via self-report, the same variables were used in both the youths' and the parents' perception models. A variable representing age and a latent factor representing familial SES were also added to the models as independent variables/factors and allowed to correlate with each other and also with the personality independent variable (i.e., parental APP-21 midpoint).

In the next stage of the model building process, hypothesized paths from the family environmental factors to the youths' APP-21 scale variable were added to the models and tested for statistical significance using the Wald test. Paths from the parent midpoint APP-21 variable to the corresponding youth APP-21 variable were also added. Only paths that were deemed nonsignificant using the Wald test were removed from the models. Once all nonsignificant paths were removed from the models, paths from the age variable and the SES factor to the dependent variable were added. Because the addition of these paths was relatively minor and did not alter the strength of the paths from family environment and parents' personality to youths' personality, they were removed from both final combined models. Variables initially included in the structural equation models are summarized in Figure 11.1.

5. Results and Discussion

5.1. Demographic Characteristics

Demographic characteristics in the biological and adoptive families are summarized in Table 11.2. These results show that biological families differ from adoptive families in several respects, and that adoptive parents and their children are somewhat older. Adoptive families also score higher on a couple of the measures of socioeconomic status.

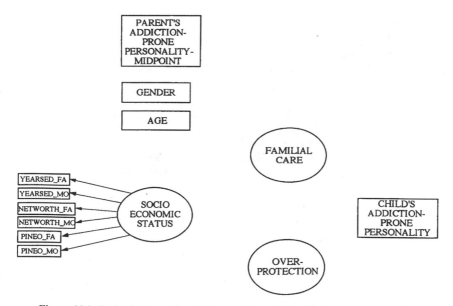

Figure 11.1. Initial factors and variables used to predict addiction-prone personality.

Table 11.2. Comparison of Means for Demographic Variables Between Biological and Adoptive Families

	Biological families (mean)	Adoptive families (mean)	F	df	Sig.
Mother's					
Age	45.90	49.63	61.60	(1, 598)	.0000
Education	13.76	14.52	12.29	(1, 595)	.0005
Income	6.38	6.61	1.29	(1, 569)	.2561
Father's					
Age	48.33	51.55	39.04	(1, 593)	.0000
Education	14.11	14.46	1.59	(1, 598)	.2072
Income	6.51	6.80	2.14	(1, 586)	.1437
Child's					
Age	17.66	18.59	13.66	(1, 599)	.0002

5.2. The APP-21 and Five-Factor Personality Traits

Correlations between APP-21 Scale scores and Five-Factor Personality Scale scores for the four major demographic groups in the Vancouver Family Survey are presented in Table 11.3. The pattern of correlations is consistent across the four groups and shows that the APP is associated with higher Neuroticism and lower Agreeableness and Conscientiousness. These results are consistent with correlations reported in the previous chapter showing that high APP-23 scores are associated with high Psychoticism and high Neuroticism and are also consistent with prior research relating the five-factor model to alcohol abuse (Martin & Sher, 1994) in which alcohol abuse was associated with high Neuroticism and low Agreeableness and low Conscientiousness.

Table 11.3. Correlations Between the Addiction-Prone Personality Scale (APP-21) and the Five-Factor Personality Scale Within Gender and Age Groups[a]

	Mother's APP-21	Father's APP-21	Son's APP-21	Daughter's APP-21
Neuroticism	.42[b]	.38[b]	.40[b]	.37[b]
Extraversion	−.01	−.06	−.08	−.06
Openness	.05	.06	−.02	.11
Agreeableness	−.27[b]	−.30[b]	−.42[b]	−.47[b]
Conscientiousness	−.19[b]	−.17[b]	−.33[b]	−.34[b]

[a]Biological and adoptive families are combined for these analyses.
[a] $= p < .001$.

5.3. The APP and Substance Abuse

The Vancouver Family Survey provides an excellent sample for validating the ability of the 23-item APP test and the 21-item APP test to predict substance abuse in general population samples of youths from both biological and adoptive families and their parents. This sample provides an excellent opportunity to test the ability of these measures to predict a variety of substance use and abuse indicators across different age and gender cohorts. The results of these correlations are presented in Table 11.4. Correlations reported in these tables are between each person's personality scores and their own reports of substance use. The results in Table 11.4 generally support the ability of the APP-23 and APP -21 scales to predict a variety of alcohol and drug use indicators across age and gender cohorts. In general, the correlations with the APP-23 and APP-21 scales and substance abuse indicators are similar. This suggests that dropping the two items whose content is more directly related to substance abuse would not affect the predictive ability of the scale much. In the younger cohorts, the measures are strongly correlated with most of the substance use indicators. It is interesting that the correlations are just as strong if not stronger in the female sample than in the male sample in the offspring age group. In the adult sample, the personality measures correlate more strongly with substance use and alcohol problems than with consumption itself. Many of the adults with a prior history of problems may have learned strategies for moderating their drinking.

The Vancouver Family Survey also contains a couple of measures of alcohol addiction including the CAGE and the MAST. Using a cut point of 2 on the CAGE as a crude measure of alcohol addiction, we classified all mothers, fathers, sons, and daughters as either alcoholic or nonalcoholic. Then, the scores of each alcoholic and nonalcoholic subsample on the APP-21 and APP-23 were compared in our combined biological and adoptive samples. Means on the 23-item APP and the 21-item APP test are shown in Table 11.5 for alcoholics and nonalcoholics in the four demographic biological groups (including mothers, fathers, daughters, and sons). As also shown in Table 11.5, the alcoholic and nonalcoholic groups all differ significantly in their 23-item APP and 21-item APP scale scores. The 21-item test does not lose much of its ability to separate groups by eliminating the two items with alcohol-related content.

5.4. Parent and Offspring Personality Correlations

Correlations between the parent APP-21 scale scores and offspring personality scores are presented in Table 11.6. The results in the biological sample are pretty much as expected, and a somewhat higher correlation occurs between the parent midpoint APP-21 scale score and offspring APP-21 scale scores. In the adoptive

Table 11.4. Correlations Between Addiction-Prone Personality (21) Items and APP (23) Items with All Substance Use Scales in Biological and Adoptive Families

SUBSTANCE USE	Fathers	Mothers	Sons	Daughters
Smoking average 1				
APP-21	.26[b]	.15[b]	.24[b]	.25[b]
APP-23	.26[b]	.15[b]	.26[b]	.27[b]
Smoking average 2				
APP-21	.26[b]	.14[b]	.24[b]	.26[b]
APP-23	.26[b]	.14[b]	.25[b]	.29[b]
Get drunk				
APP-21	.15[b]	.05[b]	.18[c]	.37[b]
APP-23	.14[b]	.05[b]	.21[b]	.40[b]
Ethanol average 1				
APP-21	.08	.05	.18[c]	.37[b]
APP-23	.08	.04	.20[b]	.40[b]
Ethanol average 2				
APP-21	.09[d]	.01	.20[b]	.32[b]
APP-23	.08[d]	.01	.22[b]	.34[b]
Heavy drinking				
APP-21	−.01	.09[d]	.11	.32[b]
APP-23	−.01	.09[d]	.14[d]	.34[b]
MAST				
APP-21	.24[b]	.15[b]	.15[c]	.21[b]
APP-23	.25[b]	.15[b]	.17[c]	.24[b]
CAGE				
APP-21	.28[b]	.20[b]	.21[b]	.25[b]
APP-23	.29[b]	.20[b]	.22[b]	.25[b]
Harm ever				
APP-21	.29[b]	.22[b]	.31[b]	.37[b]
APP-23	.31[b]	.22[b]	.34[b]	.39[b]
Harm Recent				
APP-21	.10[d]	.15[b]	.17[c]	.16[b]
APP-23	.10[d]	.15[b]	.20[b]	.18[b]
Marijuana				
APP-21	.25[b]	.13[c]	.34[b]	.48[b]
APP-23	.25[b]	.13[c]	.39[b]	.53[b]
Other drugs				
APP-21	.06	−.04	.27[b]	.40[b]
APP-23	.07	−.04	.30[b]	.44[b]
Medications				
APP-21	.16[b]	.13[c]	.18[c]	.01
APP-23	.18[b]	.13[c]	.20[b]	.01

[a]Biological and adoptive families are combined for these analyses.
[b] $p < .001$.
[c] $p < .01$.
[d] $p < .05$.

Table 11.5. Mean Scores Using One-Way Anova on APP-21 and APP-23 Measures for Parents and Children by CAGE Indices of Alcohol Use

CAGE indicator group	n	APP-21	F	APP-23	F
Fathers					
Alcoholic	131	6.81	25.00[a]	7.03	28.55[a]
Nonalcoholic	448	5.29		5.37	
Mothers					
Alcoholic	69	5.84	19.97[a]	5.96	20.31[a]
Nonalcoholic	493	4.30		4.37	
Sons					
Alcoholic	49	12.47	10.25[b]	13.30	13.51[a]
Nonalcoholic	247	10.85		11.27	
Daughters					
Alcoholic	33	11.11	8.73[b]	11.78	9.37[b]
Nonalcoholic	257	9.14		9.55	

[a] p < .001.
[b] p < .01.

sample, however, the correlation with the mothers' APP-21 scale score is higher than the midpoint correlation, suggesting perhaps a stronger environmental influence of the mothers' APP-21 scale score in the adoptive sample. The closeness of the magnitude of the correlations between midpoint scores of the biological parents and those of their offspring and adoptive parents' midpoint scores and those of their offspring is not consistent with a strong genetic influence for this characteristic. On the Five-Factor Inventory data in our sample, for example, we have found that the median correlation was .07 in our adoptive sample and .19 in our biological sample (Barnes, Patton, Anderson, & Perkins, 1996). This is a more typical pattern of results that is more consistent with a pattern of genetic influence on personality.

Table 11.6. APP-21 Correlations Between Parents and Children in Biological and Adoptive Families

	Biological sample Youth's APP-21	Adoptive Sample Youth's APP-21
Mother's APP-21 scale	.17[a]	.26[b]
Father's APP-21 scale	.19[a]	.11
Midpoint APP-21 scale	.22[a]	.24[b]

[a] p < .001.
[b] p < .001

5.5. Family Environment and APP-21 Scale Scores

Correlations between the perceptions of the family environment expressed by various family members and APP-21 scale scores for offspring are presented in Table 11.7. Results in general are consistent across various reporters. For cohesion and adaptability, in particular, the results are consistent and higher family cohesion and adaptability are associated with lower APP-21 scale scores in offspring. On the related variables measuring parental care, the results also seem to suggest that stronger parental care is associated with lower APP-21 scale scores. As might be expected, correlations are somewhat higher when youth perceptions of the family environment are correlated with their own reports on personality. The magnitude of the correlations between the family environment and APP-21 scale scores does not drop off appreciably in the adoptive sample, as might be expected, if there were a strong genetic confound accounting for these associations. This hypothesis will be tested more empirically in the following section.

Table 11.7. Correlations Between Family Environment Perceptions and APP-21 Scale Scores in Biological and Adoptive Samples

	Biological sample youth APP-21 ($N = 473$)	Adoptive sample youth APP-21 ($n = 128$)
Parent perceptions		
Fathers' perceptions		
Cohesion	−.19[a]	−.31[a]
Adaptability	−.10[b]	−.22[b]
Care	−.13[c]	−.00
Overprotection	.09	−.10
Mothers' perceptions		
Cohesion	−.23[a]	−.32[a]
Adaptability	−.15[a]	−.21
Care	−.08	−.26[c]
Overprotection	.03	.16
Youth perceptions		
Cohesion	−.40[a]	−.48[a]
Adaptability	−.35[a]	−.36[a]
Father care	−.31[a]	−.26[a]
Father overprotection	.24[a]	.15
Mother care	−.36[a]	−.40[a]
Mother overprotection	.28[a]	.26[a]

[a] $p < .001$.
[b] $p < .05$.
[c] $p < .01$.

5.6. Structural Equation Models

The next stage in the data analyses involved building structural equation models to predict APP-21 scale scores in the youth sample. The first step in the model development process involved building an overall model to fit the data in the combined biological and adoptive samples. The next stage in the data analyses involved placing constraints on the measurement and structural paths to require that these paths be the same in the biological and adoptive samples. Results confirmed that there were no significant decrements in the fit of the models in either the youths' perceptions or parents' perception models when their measurement and structural paths were constrained to be equal. The results for the final fully constrained youths' perception model are summarized in Figure 11.2. The results for the fully constrained parents' perception model are summarized in Figure 11.3. The variable characteristics for all variables used in these models are summarized in Table 11.9.

In the final youths' perception model (Figure 11.2), the model fit the data very well with a high CFI of .97. There were three significant predictors of the youths' Addiction-Prone Personality Scale scores. The strongest predictor of the youths' APP-21 scale scores was the Familial Care Factor. This factor is comprised of maternal and paternal care and family cohesion and adaptability as perceived by the youths. The youths' gender also contributed significantly in predicting APP scale scores. Males had higher scores than females. Parent personality also played an important role. Higher parent APP-21 Scale scores, as measured by the parental midpoint on this measure, were a significant predictor of the youths' APP-21 Scale scores.

The parents' perception model (see Figure 11.3) results also fit the data very well (CFI = .94). The results are reassuring in that a very similar pattern of prediction emerges when the parent perceptions of the family environment are used to predict the youths' personality, as when the youths' perceptions are employed. Again, familial care is predictive of the youths' APP-21 scale scores but at a somewhat lower magnitude of prediction than when the youths' perceptions are employed. The parent APP-21 midpoint and gender again predict in a very similar fashion. The one notable difference in the parents' perception model is an indirect effect of the parental personality on the youths' personality acting through the effect of the parent personality on the family environment. When the parent perceptions of the home environment are employed, the results suggest that a home environment that has parents with higher scores on the APP-21 can be characterized as somewhat less caring.

In the results described above, data are consistent in showing that the environmental influence on the APP-21 Scale scores in offspring are consistent in both biological and adoptive families. High Familial Care is protective against the development of addiction-prone personality characteristics in both biological

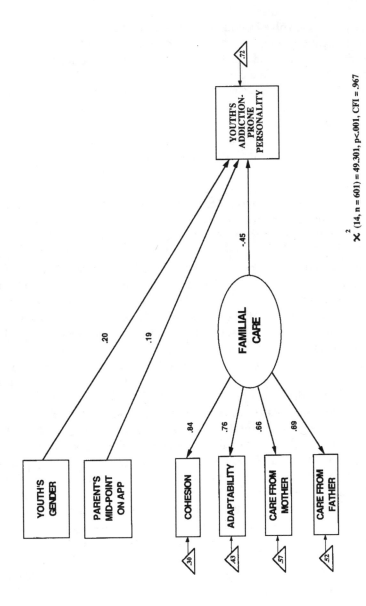

χ^2 (14, n = 601) = 49.301, p<.001, CFI = .967

Figure 11.2. Youths' perception model of addiction-prone personality.

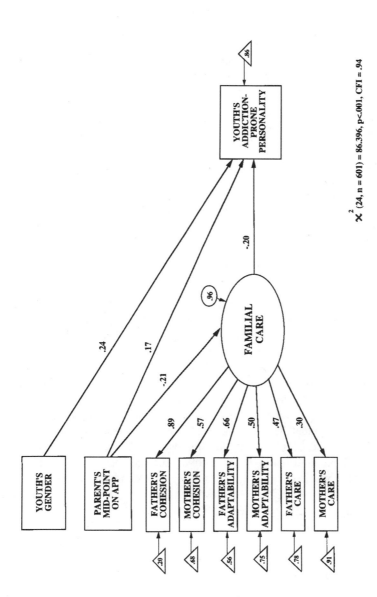

Figure 11.3. Parents' perception model of addiction

χ^2 (24, n = 601) = 86.396, p<.001, CFI = .94

Table 11.8. Characteristics of Variables Used in the Structural Models in the Development of APP-21 (after Data Imputation)

	Mean	# of items	Range	SD	Skew	Kurtosis
Youths' age	17.85	1	13–25	2.56	.76	−.30
Youths' gender	.50	1	0–1	.50	−.01	−2.00
Fathers' perspective						
Cohesion	4.72	16	1–8	1.56	−.22	−.48
Adaptability	5.13	16	1–8	1.41	−.63	−.25
Care	27.80	12	11–36	5.19	−.53	−.22
Mothers' perspective						
Cohesion	4.92	16	1–8	1.58	−.16	−.55
Adaptability	5.20	16	1–8	1.42	−.66	−.26
Care	31.04	12	16–36	4.26	−.86	.16
Youths' perspective						
Cohesion	3.82	16	1–8	1.67	.34	−.77
Adaptability	4.17	16	1–8	1.78	−.06	−1.16
Maternal care	27.97	12	6–36	6.66	−.94	.31
Paternal care	24.43	12	0–36	7.47	−.62	−.01
Parents' midpoint APP	5.01			2.32	.55	.33
Youths' APP-21	10.26			3.56	.05	−.18

and adoptive families. Data are also consistent in this investigation in showing that parental addiction-prone personality traits are associated with similar traits in their offspring. Although these results are not surprising, what is surprising is that these effects are of the same order of magnitude in biological and adoptive samples. Although our study is not designed to test specifically for genetic effects, these results are not consistent with a strong genetic pattern of inheritance for this trait. In the biological sample, the pathway between the parents' personality and offspring personaltiy can include both biological and socializing influence components. In the adoptive sample, this pathway includes only a socializing influence component. The finding that these pathways are similar in strength in our biological and adoptive samples suggests that there is not a very strong genetic component contributing to the pathway between parental APP scores and offspring APP scores in our biological sample. As it stands, these results suggest that the parent personality affects the development of this trait in offspring either directly, perhaps through processes such as modeling, or indirectly through the influence that this characteristic has on shaping the family environment.

6. Summary and Conclusions

The first objective in this chapter was to employ the data from the Vancouver Family Survey to examine the reliability and validity of the Addiction-Prone Personality Scale in a new general population sample. Results showed that, although the APP-23 Scale had modest internal consistency in this study, excellent results were found in support of the validity of the scale. The APP-23 was a strong predictor of alcohol and drug abuse problems in different age and gender cohorts. In particular, strong evidence showed that respondents who were classified as alcoholic on the CAGE screening test scored higher than nonalcoholics in all of our age and gender cohorts.

The second objective in this study was to examine the reliability and validity of a shortened version of the APP that removed two items whose content was directly related to substance misuse. Results showed that removing the two items from the APP did not reduce the reliability of the scale or change the correlations with validity criteria to any extent. The APP-21 Scale was highly correlated with substance abuse variables across age and gender cohorts, and alcoholics on the CAGE test scored higher than nonalcoholics on this measure in all of our age and gender cohorts.

The third objective in this chapter was to examine the associations between the APP-21 scale and the Five-Factor Personality scales. Correlational anlayses revealed a consistent pattern of results across age and gender cohorts, and higher APP-21 scale scores were found in association with higher Neuroticism and lower Agreeableness and Conscientiousness. These results were consistent with both our earlier research on the APP and research by Martin and Sher (1994) on the Five-Factor Scales and alcohol abuse.

The final objective in this chapter was to look at the family environment and the development of the Addiction-Prone Personality in biological and adoptive families. Prior research on the development of personality traits and the development of alcohol abuse has generally not controlled for the confounding influence of genetics. The current investigation also had several other strengths in that the data were gathered from a large general population sample of families and the family environment reports were based on more than one source. Results in this chapter showed that more caring and cohesive family environments were associated with lower scores on the Addiction-Prone Personality in both biological and adoptive families. Although these results were somewhat stronger when based on youth reports rather than parent reports, the results were nevertheless consistent.

Parent APP personality traits were also associated with these traits in their offspring in both biological and adoptive families. An interesting pattern emerged here in the correlational analyses suggesting that the mother's APP may have a stronger effect in adoptive families and the father's APP a stronger effect in biological families.

In the structural equation modeling analyses, strong support was found for the generalizability of the models across biological and adoptive families. These results are consistent with earlier studies in the personality area and in the addictions field showing that the development of difficult temperament and addictive behaviors is associated with home environments that are less caring. In particular the results are consistent with the theorizing by Grace Barnes that parental social-ization influences personality development which in turn affects the risk of ad-diction-prone behaviors. Although these results are not consistent with claims by behavioral geneticists that the family environment has a very limited influence on personality development, it is still possible that these claims could be correct. Our results could be explained by children having Addiction-Prone Personality traits alienating their parents and receiving less supportive parenting as a result. Longitudinal research in an adoptive sample would be required to test this possi-bility. It is also possible that the Addiction-Prone Personality may fall more into the realm of what some investigators, such as Cloninger et al. (1994), might call character rather than temperament. This aspect of personality may in fact be more liable to environmental influence than traits such as extraversion and neuroticism which may be under stronger genetic control. In fact, our own analyses based on the Vancouver data (Barnes et al., 1996) suggest that other personality traits as-sessed by the Five-Factor Inventory are not as strongly associated with aspects of the family environment.

Appendix

SELF-CHARACTERIZATION

Part I
The next questions are about things you do or prefer. Please place a tick mark (✓) in the most appropriate box (□).

		Yes	No
O1.	Have you had very strange or peculiar experiences?	01 □	02 □
O2.	Have you often gone against your parent's wishes?	01 □	02 □
O3.	Are you a steady person?	01 □	02 □
O4.	Do you wish you could have more respect for yourself?	01 □	02 □
O5.	Have you ever been in trouble with the law?	01 □	02 □
O6.	Do you prefer rock music over ballads?	01 □	02 □
O7.	Have your parents often objected to the kind of people you went around with?	01 □	02 □
O8.	Have you lived the right kind of life?	01 □	02 □
O9.	Have people said that you sometimes act too rashly?	01 □	02 □
O10.	Do you prefer loud music over quiet music?	01 □	02 □
O11.	Have you had blank spells in which your activities were interrupted and you did not know what was going on around you?	01 □	02 □
O12.	Are you unable to keep your mind on one thing?	01 □	02 □
O13.	Do you go to church almost every week?	01 □	02 □
O14.	Do you prefer sports cars over passenger cars?	01 □	02 □
O15.	Do you often feel "fed up"?	01 □	02 □
O16.	Do you have strange or peculiar thoughts?	01 □	02 □
O17.	Would you prefer to be a stunt-man/woman over a prop-man/woman?	01 □	02 □
O18.	Do you prefer endurance sports over games with rests?	01 □	02 □
O19.	Did you ever feel that strangers were looking at you critically?	01 □	02 □
O20.	Would you take drugs which may have strange or dangerous effects?	01 □	02 □
O21.	Did you play hooky from school quite often as a youngster?	01 □	02 □
O22.	Do you prefer electric music over unamplified music?	01 □	02 □
O23.	Do you give money to charities?	01 □	02 □

VI

CONCLUSIONS

12

Integration and Conclusions

In the current investigation, we have endeavored to study the role of personality factors in the development of alcohol abuse and other forms of substance misuse. Three main research strategies have been employed in this investigation. The first research strategy employed was to conduct a general population longitudinal study (called the Winnipeg Health and Drinking Survey or WHDS) of the relationship between personality and alcohol abuse. In this investigation, a large age and sex stratified sample from Winnipeg, Manitoba, was employed to examine the longitudinal patterns of association between latent personality factors and alcohol consumption and abuse patterns. This study was unique in many respects in the addiction field. An attempt was made to gather data on a large representative sample of adults aged 18–65 followed over a two-year period. The epidemiological approach employed here allowed us to obtain general population estimates on the patterns of alcohol consumption and prevalence of alcohol abuse measured by a variety of indicators. The personality measures used in this investigation were fairly extensive and included measures such as the Group Embedded Figures Test that are not usually administered in general population samples. The age and sex stratified sample allowed examining of the stability of the predictive patterns between personality and alcohol use and abuse across these different age and gender categories. The use of multiple measures of most personality constructs and the alcohol use and abuse dependent variables allowed employing of a powerful new data analytic strategy, structural equation modeling (Bentler, 1995), to test the longitudinal pattern of associations between personality and alcohol use and abuse.

The second research strategy employed in this investigation was to recruit a clinical sample of alcoholics and drug addicts to supplement the data gathered in the Winnipeg Health and Drinking Survey. This strategy follows in the tradition established by Brown and Harris (1978) for investigating risk factors associated with abnormal behavior. Clinical samples represent extreme cases of the disorder being investigated that may not always be accessible in general population surveys. Our research confirmed that the clinical sample was much more pathological in terms of its alcohol abuse patterns than alcoholics in the general population. The addition of a clinical sample allowed us to determine which personality factors were effective in predicting alcohol use and abuse in the general population and in discriminating clinical alcoholics from normals. Although numerous studies are available comparing clinical samples of alcoholics with normals, these studies have rarely incorporated general population control samples and have seldom screened out alcoholics or former alcoholics in their control samples. The addition of a six-month follow-up in our clinical sample also allowed us to examine the association between personality and treatment outcome.

The third research strategy involved in this program of research has been to conduct a general population family survey to examine the association between aspects of the family environment and the development of the addiction-prone personality. This study is the first investigation of this kind. The research design for this study was very strong in that data were gathered from families selected from the general population. Extensive data on family socializing patterns and influences were gathered from three family members, including both parents and one offspring in the 14–24 age group. The design for this study also included a sample of adoptive families. Initially the design for this study provided for recruitment of adoptive families on the same basis as biological families (i.e., general population screening). When this design proved impractical, a volunteer sample of adoptive families was added to the design. The addition of this nonrandom component to the design did not adversely affect the results in any way.

Two other unique components of the current investigation are worth noting. Recent research has suggested that there may be at least two major types of alcoholism which Cloninger (1987a) calls Type I and Type II alcoholism. Cluster analyses were conducted on both our general population and clinical samples of alcoholics to test this theory. The method used in doing this component of the research is another fairly unique aspect in the current investigation because no prior studies on the subtypes of alcoholics have looked at subtypes of alcoholics in the general population and in a clinical sample. Finally, the current investigation attempted to develop a measure of the prealcoholic personality. MacAndrew (1979) suggested that a test designed with this specific purpose in mind might be more effective in predicting the risk of the development of alcoholism. The availability of a general population longitudinal sample allowed us to develop a subset of personality items that were designed specifically to predict the development of alcoholism. The availability of a clinical sample allowed us to conduct further reliability and validity analyses on this measure. The availability of a second general population sample from the Vancouver Family Survey allowed us another opportunity to examine the reliability and validity of our measure and to test for possible developmental antecedents.

1. Prevalence Patterns

The lifetime prevalence for alcohol abuse in the Winnipeg sample was 23.3% for men and 7.6% for women. The prevalence pattern is similar to results reported in other surveys employing similar data collection procedures. Logistic regression analyses procedures were employed to determine the relative contribution of demographic characteristics in predicting alcohol consumption and abuse patterns. In the multivariate analyses predicting alcohol abuse, results showed that the highest abuse rates occurred among the male population, the young English speakers, and unmarried respondents. These results are consistent with findings reported in previous surveys on the epidemiology of alcohol abuse (e.g., Bland et al., 1988) and are also consistent with the patterns for predicting alcohol and drug related deaths in the province of Manitoba (Trott et al., 1981). In a study of the demographic factors associated with alcohol and drug associated deaths as determined by analyses of coroner reports, Trott et al. (1981) reported higher scores for alcohol and drug involvement in the deaths of males, the unmarried, and younger persons and lower rates of involvement for foreign-born persons.

2. Personality and Alcohol Abuse

In the correlational analyses, results were for the most part consistent with expectation. Alcohol use and abuse was generally higher for respondents who scored higher on Psychoticism, Stimulus Reducing, Neuroticism, and related characteristics such as Anxiety. Of particular interest in the correlational analyses were the relatively weak correlations observed between field dependence as measured by the Group Embedded Figures Test and all of the measures of alcohol consumption and abuse. The WHDS is the first major investigation that examined this association in the general population.

In the structural equation modeling analyses, the personality structure that emerged was not entirely consistent with the hypothetical personality structure model. In particular Ego Strength did not emerge as its own factor, but loaded on Neuroticism. The Neuroticism and Psychoticism dimensions emerged as anticipated. On the Extraversion factor, it was decided to allow a separate factor to emerge for Stimulus Reducing–Augmenting rather than allowing this dimension to load on the Extraversion factor. This solution seemed to fit the data best and separated out the component of extraversion that is most directly linked with alcohol abuse. The sociability facet of extraversion is not linked with alcohol abuse, whereas the impulsivity/sensation-seeking component is. Although the personality structure selected in this study is fairly complex due to the multifactorial nature of some of the measures employed such as the MacAndrew Scale and Ego-Strength Scale, this personality structure proved stable across time and across age and gender groups. A fairly similar personality structure also emerged in the clinical sample, providing further evidence for the generalizability of this structure.

Several possible structural models for the alcohol consumption measures were considered in the WHDS study, including a single-factor model and a two-factor (use/abuse) model. The model that worked best was a two-factor model with some overlapping loadings. Once again this structural model proved stable across gender groups and time but was somewhat less stable across age groups.

The longitudinal analyses employing personality measures showed that the personality traits assessed in this study were extremely stable across time (i.e., test–retest median correlation = 0.78). These results are consistent with previous adult life span studies showing high correlations for personality traits assessed across time (McCrae & Costa, 1984).

In the structural equation modeling analyses, the data supported a dual process or two-pathway model of alcohol addiction. In the first wave of the data, alcohol use was predicted by a Stimulus-Reducing factor and Problems were predicted by the Psychoticism dimension. The Stimulus-Reducing factor is comprised of high scores on the Vando Reducer Scale and high scores on Ego Strength. Stimulus reducers on the Vando (1969) Scale are higher on sensation seeking (Barnes, 1985b; Dragutinovich, 1986). If you examine the items on the Vando Scale, you see that many of the items involve choices between items that are high versus low in stimulus intensity (e.g., preference for rock music over ballads). People who are less sensitive to pain (i.e. reducers) more commonly select items reflecting preference for higher stimulus intensity. Zuckerman (1994) has noted that the content of his sensation-seeking scale and the Vando R-A Scale are similar and that the scales are nearly equivalent in what they measure. The positive loading for the Ego-Strength Scale on the Stimulus-Reducing Factor suggests that people with stronger egos are more able to tolerate strong sensations. This is consistent with ego theory (e.g., Bellak et al., 1973) which says that a strong ego is expected to be better able to regulate stimulation. Presumably, a strong ego is better able to contain energy within the system rather than discharging the energy or becoming overwhelmed.

The longitudinal structural equation models suggested that a dual process model is required to explain the relationship between personality and the development of alcohol abuse. In the dual process model, the first pathway to alcohol abuse starts with stimulus reducing, which could also be characterized as healthy sensation seeking or pleasure seeking leading to alcohol consumption which in turn leads to heavier consumption and eventually to problems. This pathway to alcohol abuse is linked with gender and in part accounts for the gender difference in alcohol use and abuse. Males score higher on the stimulus-reducing factor which accounts in part for their heavier consumption and higher scores on alcohol abuse measures. The finding that this pathway is stronger in our youngest sample suggests that this pathway may be particularly important in the earliest stages of the development of alcohol abuse problems and is likely to begin before the earliest age examined in this study. Longitudinal studies by Cloninger et al. (1988) and others (Bates et al, 1986; Bates & Labouvie, 1995; Masse & Tremblay, 1997; Newcomb & McGee, 1991; Teichman et al., 1989) have generally supported the relationship between novelty seeking or sensation seeking and the development of substance use. Zuckerman (1994) has noted that sensation seeking is very important in initiating of substance use but probably less important in the maintaining of use after tolerance and dependence has developed.

The second pathway to alcohol abuse is a more direct pathway that leads straight from the Psychoticism dimension to Alcohol Abuse. The Psychoticism latent variable is comprised of higher Eysenck P scores, lower social conformity (i.e., lower Lie Scale scores), and higher MacAndrew Scale scores. This dimension is probably linked with higher impulsivity and lower self-regulation. Individuals who are high on the Psychoticism factor are more prone to develop alcohol problems, and the pattern of results in the longitudinal analyses are consistent with a causal prediction for Psychoticism on Alcohol Abuse. In other words, the P dimension predicts Time 2 Alcohol Abuse, even when Time 1 Alcohol Abuse is controlled, suggesting that the P dimension predicts changes in alcohol abuse patterns.

Results that show a strong pattern of association between the Psychoticism dimension and alcohol abuse and a pattern that is consistent with a causal direction going from Psychoticism to Alcohol Abuse are consistent with the results of previous longitudinal research described in this book. Numerous longitudinal studies have shown a link between P related characteristics such as impulsivity (Hagnell et al., 1986, Jones, 1968; Loper et al., 1973), undercontrolled temperament (Caspi et al., 1997), antisocial characteristics (Robins et al., 1962; Rydelius, 1981), low agreeableness (Gotham et al., 1997), psychosis proneness (Kwapil, 1996), nonconformity (Kammeier et al., 1973), hyperactivity (af Klinteberg et al., 1993), proneness to school and behavioral problems (Dobkin et al., 1995; Drake & Vallaint, 1988), and alcohol abuse.

In our longitudinal analyses predicting alcohol use and abuse, a family history of alcohol abuse was related to alcohol abuse both directly and indirectly. One major pathway from family history to abuse went through the Psychoticism dimension. Not all of the influence of the family history of abuse on alcohol abuse was mediated through Psychoticism, because a direct pathway was evident from family history of abuse to alcohol abuse. The design of this study does not allow us to determine whether the pathways from a family history of abuse to alcohol abuse are genetic or environmental. In families where alcohol abuse is common, high P characteristics may be prevalent, and these traits may be passed on to offspring via genetic transmission (Eysenck, 1978). High P characteristics and alcohol abuse may also disrupt the family environment and produce less caring and effective parenting, which in turn can predict the development of addiction-prone personality characteristics, as noted in Chapter 11. The direct influence of a family history of alcohol abuse on alcohol abuse could also be caused by direct genetic influence or by an environmental effect such as modeling.

In the structural equation models predicting alcohol use and abuse, the models held up well across gender. Much of the gender effect on alcohol use and abuse was mediated through personality. Males scored higher on Stimulus Reducing and on Psychoticism, placing them at higher risk of heavier alcohol consumption and abuse.

In the structural equation modeling predicting alcohol use and abuse, the results that did not occur in the analyses are as interesting as some of the results that did occur. In particular, it is interesting to note that neither the Field Dependence dimension nor the Anxiety latent factor made any independent contribution to the development of alcohol abuse.

3. Personality and Alcohol and Drug Abuse in the Clinical Study

In the clinical component of this investigation, the clinical sample of alcoholics, drug addicts, and combined alcohol and drug addicts was compared with alcoholics, nonalcoholics, and remitted alcoholics in the general population. Personality traits were also used to predict the level of alcohol use and abuse at admission to treatment and treatment outcome. In the comparisons between the various groups, it was evident that the treatment sample scored much higher on neuroticism and related characteristics than the nontreatment sample of alcoholics. Neuroticism is an important factor in clinical samples of alcoholics and other addicts. It is not possible from the design of our clinical study to know certainly whether the higher neuroticism evident in the clinical sample occurred following the development of addiction problems or prior to the development of addiction problems. It is possible that the higher neuroticism evident in our clinical sample could be associated with more severe levels of alcohol abuse and that the general population study missed out in testing the more severe cases. It is also possible that less distressed cases of alcohol abuse (lower N) will find less intensive forms of therapy for their disorder and not show up as often in the clinical sample.

On the other hand, it seems very likely that at least some of the distress or high N evident in our clinical sample is due to the distress arising from their condition. The clinical study did not assess personality following treatment to determine whether or not symptoms of neuroticism would decline following treatment. However, several other studies that have shown declines in neuroticism and related characteristics following treatment (e.g., Schuckit, Irwin, & Brown, 1990). The remitted alcoholics in our sample had scores that were closer to the general population norms for neuroticism and related characteristics than those of the clinical alcoholics and addicts. Longitudinal research by Kammeier et al. (1973) also suggests that clinical samples of alcoholics were no more neurotic that their college freshman classmates when both groups were assessed in college with the MMPI.

In the structural equation models examining the relationship between personality and pre- and posttreatment alcohol use, a personality structure emerged similar to that observed in the general population sample. One of the personality factors linked with alcohol abuse in the general population, Psychoticism, also emerged in the clinical sample. The Stimulus-Reducing/sensation-seeking factor did not prove significant in the clinical sample. This supports Zuckerman's (1994) contention that sensation seeking and related traits are more important in the earlier stages of the development of the addiction problem. The fact that the Neuroticism latent factor predicted the problems dependent variable may argue for some role for Neuroticism in exacerbating the development of alcohol problems in the later stages of the disorder. Perhaps high N contributes to the distress experienced by drinkers as they start to experience more severe problems from their drinking. More drinking to reduce this tension and more consequent problems may result then. The tension-reducing explanation for alcohol abuse may be more tenable for explaining alcohol problems as people approach the stage of their disorder leading up to treatment. This might explain why so much attention has been given to this factor in the clinical literature.

In our structural equation models predicting treatment outcome, personality factors did not contribute directly in predicting treatment outcome, but the psychoticism dimension did predict outcome indirectly through an association with the initial level of severity of alcohol abuse. As noted earlier, the control for prior levels of alcohol abuse included in these analyses made it unlikely that direct paths between personality and drinking would emerge at follow-up.

4. Alcoholic Subtypes

The results of the cluster analyses showed that two major clusters of alcoholics occurred in the general population and clinical samples of alcoholics. One of these clusters in each case was characterized by more extreme scores on scales indicative of high N and high P. This cluster accounted for 29% of the alcoholics in the general population and 53% of the clinical sample. The difficult temperament group was also characterized in each case by more severe dependence on alcohol and drugs and a stronger family loading for alcohol abuse, particularly in the clinical sample. These results were judged consistent with theorizing by Babor et al. (1992), Blackson (1994), and Zucker et al. (1995) regarding the two major types of alcoholism. Each of these theories describes a high N, high P type of severe alcohol abuse.

5. The Addiction-Prone Personality

One of the major objectives in our research has been to develop a measure of the prealcoholic, as opposed to the clinical alcoholic personality. By selecting a set of personality items that was associated with both a family history of alcohol abuse and current alcohol abuse, we were hoping to develop a test that would be useful as a predictor of one's vulnerability to developing alcoholism. Results suggest that our efforts to develop a measure of the prealcoholic personality were quite successful. The 23-item scale that we developed had satisfactory reliability and validity and most importantly was useful in predicting the development of alcohol abuse problems in our longitudinal analyses. The prealcoholic personality test combines elements of the two latent personality factors, Stimulus Reducing and Psychoticism that were important in predicting alcohol use and abuse in our general population sample.

Cross-validation of the prealcoholic personality test in our clinical sample showed that the test was reliable and valid in our clinical sample and was also useful in discriminating alcoholics from nonalcoholics. A surprise occurred here in that the prealcoholic measure was as strongly if not more strongly linked with the risk of other addiction problems as when the risk of developing alcohol abuse. Therefore, the decision was made to change the name of the test to the Addiction-Prone Personality or APP Test. Scores on the APP test were successfully used to predict treatment outcome for both alcohol and drug addicts, confirming the importance of this measure as a test of the underlying vulnerability to addiction.

5.1. Development of the Addiction-Prone Personality

The final research strategy employed in our investigation was to conduct a family socialization study and examine the linkages between aspects of the family environment and the occurrence of addiction-prone personality traits in biological and adoptive families. Analyses in Chapter 11 confirmed the validity of the APP as a measure of vulnerability to alcohol and drug abuse. A 21-item version of the APP was also developed that eliminated two items that were deemed to be closely linked with substance abuse itself rather than underlying personality vulnerability. Structural equation modeling analyses were successful in identifying two environmental pathways to the occurrence of APP traits that were applicable in both biological and adoptive families. Higher scorers on the APP personality were found in families that were characterized by their lower level of parental care and higher score on parental APP characteristics. These analyses were judged important in that they suggested that the APP does not measure a temperament that is largely determined by genetics but measures personality or character traits that are at least partly under environmental control.

6. Integration with Other Theoretical Perspectives

In the next section, we discuss a number of theoretical perspectives in the addiction field that are leading to a coalescence of ideas around the nature of personality vulnerability to addiction. The theoretical perspectives that we consider include those of notable psychologists, psychiatrists, and addictions researchers, including Freud, Eysenck, Tarter, Zuckerman, Cloninger, Sher, Blum, and Zucker.

6.1. Freud

Freud actually did not have very much to say himself with respect to alcohol abuse. There are very few references to the issue in the collected works, and most of the references do not speak directly to the issue of the factors involved in causing alcohol abuse. With respect to the broader issue, however, of what drives peoples' behavior, Freud (1955, p. 76) stressed that it was seeking after pleasure and avoiding pain. For the developing infant, the sensation of pleasure is paired initially with gratification of an oral nature followed by anal and genital gratification. According to Freud (1955, p. 188), the satisfaction derived from alcohol is akin to erotic satisfaction. Freud (1955, p. 272) also speculated that masturbation was the "primary addiction" and that other forms of addiction arose as a substitute or replacement for these activities.

Following Freud, other psychoanalytic writers such as Fenichel (1945) focused on the importance of oral gratification in addiction rather than on the importance of addiction in meeting the human need for pleasure and alleviation of pain. More recently Khantzian (1985) attempted to develop a self-medication theory that took into account the psychic needs of different type of substance abusers. Addicts in general suffer from painful psychic states, and according to Khantzian (1985), the specific drug chosen is selected to modulate these needs. For example, narcotic addicts, it is hypothesized, prefer drugs that dampen rage and aggression, whereas cocaine addicts prefer drugs that dampen distress from depression, hypomania, and hyperactivity. Although our clinical study was not designed to specifically address the personality characteristics of persons addicted to individual drugs, there were a lot more similarities than differences in our analyses comparing alcoholics and drug addicts. Addicts, in general, are high on stimulus reducing, reflecting higher sensation-seeking or reward-seeking needs. These results are consistent with Freud's original contention that addiction operates in service of the pleasure principle.

6.2. Eysenck

In Eysenck's theory (Eysenck & Eysenck, 1985), there are three main personality dimensions including Psychoticism, Neuroticism, and Extraversion. In general, Eysenck (Eysenck & Eysenck, 1976) hypothesized that deviant behavior would occur when the person was not as susceptible to conditioning (high P, high N, and high Extraversion) and when the environment did not provide optimum learning conditions. In the case of addiction, then, one would expect to find the highest number of alcoholics and addicts among persons who were high P, high N, and high E growing up in unfavorable environments. More recently, Eysenck (1997) hypothesized a resource model of addiction whereby drug using habits are acquired because they serve a useful function for the individual. Eysenck (1997) noted that alcohol and drug addiction are frequently found in association with high P and to some extent with high N. Eysenck (1997) hypothesized that the relationship between the P dimension and dopamine functioning, as reported by Gray, Pickering, and Gray (1994), probably plays an important role in this relationship. Eysenck (1997) hypothesized that drugs are likely to produce a stronger reinforcing effect for individuals who are high on the P dimension because of the differences in the way their dopamine systems function. The results in our longitudinal analyses and clinical comparisons showed that high scores on the P dimension are associated with alcohol and drug addiction. The Addiction-Prone Personality Test is also highly correlated with the Psychoticism dimension, suggesting that the APP test may also be associated with dopamine functioning.

6.3. Zuckerman

Zuckerman (1994) noted that in the original optimum level of arousal theory, higher levels of depressant drugs were not anticipated for sensation seekers. In the most recent formulation of his theory, Zuckerman (1994) notes that sensation seekers are at a higher risk of all types of substance abuse, including alcohol abuse. In general, the data are consistent with the recent formulation of the theory, and Zuckerman (1994) notes that sensation seeking may be particularly important in the earlier stages of developing of the addiction problem. Zuckerman (1994) also noted that the Vando (1969) Reducer–Augmenter Scale is practically identical in content to his measure and essentially measures the same construct. Therefore, the results in our general population study are consistent with Zuckerman's (1994) theory in that high scores on the Vando Reducer–Augmenter Scale (i.e., sensation seeking) are highly predictive of alcohol consumption patterns, particularly in younger samples. Zuckerman (1994) also hypothesized that anxiety would not be an important factor in predicting alcohol use in our younger samples, and this hypothesis was also supported.

6.4. Tarter

Ralph Tarter (Tarter et al., 1985) has hypothesized that temperament in childhood would be an important factor in predicting the development of alcohol abuse in adulthood. In particular, Tarter et al. (1985) hypothesized that high activity levels, low attention span persistence, and high emotionality and low soothability would be predictive of the development of alcohol abuse in adulthood. In recent research looking at temperament and substance abuse, Tarter, Laird, Kabene, Bukstein, and Kaminer (1990) reported that activity level was particularly important in predicting adolescent substance abuse. Two longitudinal investigations have confirmed the importance of the constellation of temperament traits associated with "difficult temperament" as predictive of the development of substance abuse. Lerner and Vicary (1984) investigated the association between the possession of difficult temperament characteristics (i.e., slow adaptability, withdrawal responses, negative mood, high intensity of reactions, biological irregularity) in childhood and the use of tobacco, marijuana, and alcohol in early adulthood. Results confirmed the association between difficult temperament in childhood and adult substance abuse. In another more recent longitudinal investigation, Tubman and Windle (1995) examined the association between continuous difficult temperament and substance abuse. The results showed an association between continuous difficult temperament and higher levels of cigarette and alcohol use.

In our own research, the APP test measures traits that could also be characterized as difficult temperament. The APP test is highly correlated with high P and high N. The APP test, like the difficult temperament cluster, also proves to be an important predictor of the development of alcohol abuse problems.

6.5. Cloninger

Cloninger has hypothesized that there are two different types of alcoholism, Type I alcoholism and Type II alcoholism. The first type of alcoholism is characterized by later onset, a weaker family history of abuse, and by personality traits that include high reward dependence, low novelty seeking and high harm avoidance. The second type of alcoholism, Type II, it is hypothesized, is the most prevalent form of the disorder, is more common in men, has a stronger association with a family history of abuse, and has an earlier onset and association with other problem indicators, including aggression. The personality traits associated with Type II alcoholism include high novelty seeking, low harm avoidance, and low reward dependence.

It is difficult to make direct comparisons between our results and Cloninger's (1987a) theory because our latent personality variables do not line up exactly with Cloninger's system. Harm avoidance, for example, in the Cloninger system combines aspects of both neuroticism and introversion. Some evidence is available in our data to support Cloninger's theory. Cloninger predicts that novelty seeking is predictive of alcohol abuse in early onset alcohol abuse. The strong association between our stimulus-reducing/sensation-seeking factor and alcohol use in our youngest age strata (18–34) supported this hypothesis.

In our analyses examining the different types of alcoholics in the clinical and general population samples reported in Chapter 9, we did not find a pattern of results consistent with Cloninger's (1987a) theory.

6.6. Blum

Blum et al. (1990) reported that the A1 allele of the dopamine receptor gene occurred with a much higher frequency in the DNA of brain samples taken from alcoholics following autopsy than in a comparison sample. This particular receptor was chosen because of the important role of the dopaminergic system in alcohol-related behaviors. Blum et al. (1990) cautioned that their results would have to be replicated because of failures in the past to replicate molecular genetic findings linking particular loci of inheritance with neuropsychiatric disorders. In a recent review of the research in this area, Gelertner, Goldman, and Risch (1993) concluded that the body of data collected to date did not support an association between the A1 Allele of D2 and alcoholism. However, Gelertner et al., (1993) did not employ scientifically approved meta-analytic procedures to combine the results of different studies. In our own reanalysis of this data, using standard meta-analytic procedures, as advocated by Rosenthal (1984), we found that the overall pattern of results supported an association between the A1 D2 Allele and alcoholism ($p < .001$, overall). The magnitude of this effect was $r = .15$ when all studies were combined, and somewhat stronger ($r = .23$) when studies not screening alcoholics from their control groups were excluded. The relationship between the A1 allele of D2 and the severity of alcohol abuse was also significant overall ($p < .004$, $r = .21$). Recent research has shown that the A1 D2 allele is also associated with drug abuse (Noble et al., 1993) and cigarette smoking (Noble et al., 1994).

In their book on the addictive brain, Blum and Payne (1991) described the processes by which a person might become an alcoholic. For people with an underlying vulnerability to alcohol abuse, which includes fewer dopamine receptors, one might expect a more rapid course of development for the disorder. The first use of the drug will be a very powerful reinforcing experience leading to frequent and excessive use. Initially, the use of alcohol or other drugs might compensate for the underlying deficiency, but as time goes on, the dopamine system will be compromised even further, and the person will have to use more or stronger drugs to try and overcome their discomfort. Following treatment, this group of individuals will still have their initial underlying vulnerability or disease that they will have to deal with in some fashion (Miller & Blum, 1996). For other people who do not have the underlying vulnerability, the process of addiction will be somewhat different and will follow a different course. As people without the underlying vulnerability are exposed to opportunities to use alcohol or drugs and use these substances regularly, they will develop addiction to these substances. This addiction may develop more slowly and perhaps be less severe. Following treatment for their addiction, these individuals might be expected to lead relatively normal lives and perhaps resume moderate consumption of alcohol patterns.

In a recent book, Miller and Blum (1996) described the linkage between Attention Deficit Hyperactivity Disorder (ADHD) and the A1of D2 allele. They have now labeled the disorder or disease associated with this condition as "reward deficiency syndrome." The finding that ADHD is associated with the alcohol gene is consistent with the results of research conducted by Tarter (Tarter et al., 1977) and others in showing a relationship between hyperactivity, minimal brain dysfunction, and alcohol abuse.

The results in our research are consistent with the findings of Blum et al. (1990) and the theorizing by Blum and colleagues (Blum & Payne, 1991; Miller and Blum, 1996). In our longitudinal research in the general population, Stimulus Reducing or sensation seeking, as measured by the Vando (1969) Scale, is associated with heavier alcohol consumption patterns leading to alcohol abuse and, this pattern was strongest in the youngest sample. In our comparisons of clinical and general population samples, scores on traits associated with sensation seeking such as higher Vando (1969) Scale scores and Higher Eysenck P scale scores were higher in substance abusing populations. The results of our research on the development of a measure of the "Addiction-Prone Personality" are particularly interesting with respect to the theorizing by Blum (Blum & Payne, 1991). The questionnaire items comprising the Addiction-Prone Personality test include items that reflect a preference for high intensity stimulation and suggest higher impulsivity and lower self-regulation. High scores on the Addiction-Prone Personality were associated with a family history of alcohol abuse in several samples. The Addiction-Prone Personality test also predicted alcohol abuse prospectively. Individuals who scored high on the Addiction-Prone Personality test also had a poorer prognosis for recovery following treatment. Given this pattern of results, we are confident that scores on the APP test will eventually be associated with the A1 of D2 allele pattern.

6.7. Sher

In reviewing the relationship between personality and disinhibitory psychopathology, Sher and Trull (1994) describe a deviance proneness model that fits well with the results of our research. According to this model, a combination of difficult temperament (i.e., high impulsivity and disinhibition) and poor parental socialization may make a person more vulnerable to engaging in unsocialized behavior. This in turn is posited to lead to school problems and more associations with deviant peers. These hypotheses sound very similar to the results found in the Vancouver Family Survey where parental socialization practices were associated with the development of an addiction-prone personality. In the research by Sher et al. (1991), a behavioral undercontrol factor contributed to predicting of the development of alcohol abuse problems. This latent variable was comprised of measures suggesting that it was similar to a combination of our Stimulus Reducing and Psychoticism latent factors. The behavioral undercontrol factor is no doubt very similar to our Addiction-Prone Personality measure which is a combination of items taken from traits similar to those included in the Sher et al. (1991) behavioral undercontrol factor.

6.8. Watson

In a recent article titled "Behavioral disinhibition versus constraint: A dispositional perspective," Watson and Clark (1993) describe the development of a scale designed to measure disinhibition. This measure correlates with the Eysenck Psychoticism dimension (Watson & Clark, 1993), and measures something akin to what is being measured by our Psychoticism latent factor. Watson and Clark (1993) found that this measure is correlated with alcohol and drug use and is also predictive of abuse of these substances and consequent problems. Watson and Clark (1993) noted that disinhibited individuals perceived that the risks associated with substance abuse are lower. The model of disinhibitory psychopathology developed by Watson and Clark (1993) is stated as follows:

> The disinhibitor possesses both a strong nervous system that protects the individual from the pain of negative stimuli, and also a sensitive reward system that enhances the pleasure of positive stimuli. (p. 524)

This description fits very well with our results and the interpretation of our data. Two factors are involved in the development of addiction. One of these factors is a positive attraction to the use of drugs, perhaps facilitated by the reward deficiency syndrome described by Miller and Blum (1996). The second factor is the lack of an inhibition or respect for the possible negative consequences of alcohol and drug misuse. This lack of inhibition may be related to a lower sensitivity to pain evident in stimulus reducers, as measured by the Vando (1969) Scale, or to impulsivity or a lack of self-regulation, as measured by our Psychoticism latent factor. The Addiction-Prone Personality test combines these two factors to provide a powerful predictor of the risk of developing alcohol and drug misuse problems.

6.9. Zucker

Zucker (Zucker et al., 1995) has hypothesized that there are two different types of alcoholic. One type is associated with antisocial behavior and also associated with less effective rearing conditions in the home environment. This position is similar to the position advanced by Sher (Sher & Trull, 1994) and is also consistent with the data found in our research. We found evidence for two forms of alcoholism in both our general population and clinical samples. One of these forms of alcoholism was associated with the high P and high N characteristic of the antisocial personality. Our results on the development of the addiction-prone personality are also consistent with the Zucker (Zucker et al., 1995) theory in that we found strong confirmation that the family environment is associated with the development of the addiction-prone personality even when the confounding influences of genetic factors were controlled in our design.

6.10. UCLA Longitudinal Research Program

The UCLA program of longitudinal research has incorporated a different set of individual difference variables than those used in the current research and has focused more on the prediction of alcohol and drug use in general rather than on alcohol abuse. Nevertheless, there are some strong parallels in the pattern of results reported in the UCLA research and our Canadian research program. In the UCLA research, sensation seeking in adolescents' it was found, predicted a wide variety of adult drinking-problem consequences, including driving while intoxicated (Stacy, Newcomb, & Bentler, 1993). Stacy, Newcomb, and Bentler (1991b) noted, however, that the stability of the sensation-seeking factor was not that high (.39) across the nine-year period from adolescence to young adulthood and that the components of sensation seeking (e.g., experience seeking, thrill and adventure seeking, disinhibition, and boredom) had different patterns of predictors in males and females.

In the UCLA research and in the Jessor (Jessor et al., 1991) longitudinal research as well for that matter, one of the important contributing factors has been tolerance of deviance (Jessor et al., 1991) and general law abidance (Huba & Bentler, 1984; Guy, Smith, & Bentler, 1994; McGee & Newcomb, 1992). For example, McGee and Newcomb (1992) studied latent constructs of drug use, academic orientation, social conformity, criminal behavior, and sexual involvement over four periods at four-year intervals in a community sample and reported that a second-order construct of general deviance was consistent with a general problem behavioral syndrome. More specifically, deviant attitudes and behaviors also have been found to be a major contributor to problem substance use among adolescents (e.g., Ellickson & Hays, 1991; Huba & Bentler, 1983). Such attitudes and behaviors probably reflect genetic influences and lack of effective socialization, as well as peer influences and all of which contribute to further deviance and substance use and thus problem behavior. As an example of this line of research, in their longitudinal study of adolescent development and drug use, Huba and Bentler (1984) studied the effects of law abidance, positive self-concept, friends' poor school performance, and peer culture involvement on subsequent alcohol and drug use and deviant behavior. Controlling for the other constructs, law abidance, conservatism, and religious commitment formed a strong factor of law abidance that proved to be a strong predictor of less alcohol use and deviance across four years of adolescence. Similarly, in a longitudinal study of adolescents in the Boston suburban area, Guy, Smith, and Bentler (1994) followed 657 participants across twelve years (from 1969 to 1981), assessing several socialization variables during the initial periods and a variety of substance use behaviors and potentially negative consequences of substance use at follow-up. Higher levels of self-reported obedience and law abidance during early adolescence predicted less drug use two to four years later and, in turn, less drug use in young adulthood. Not surprisingly, adolescent obedience and law abidance also predicted more ethical and conventional behavior in young adulthood.

In our own longitudinal investigation of alcohol abuse (reported in Chapter 5), a strong pattern of association was found between our Psychoticism latent factor and alcohol abuse. Low social conformity measured by the Eysenck Lie Scale is a component of our P latent factor. Thus, these findings are consistent with the findings in the Jessor (Jessor et al., 1991) and UCLA longitudinal research.

The developmental perspective of Newcomb & Bentler (1988) is also consistent with our findings on the addiction-prone personality. Newcomb and Bentler (1988) described a theory of precocious development as a precursor, correlate, and consequence of alcohol and drug use. In this perspective, substance users tend to bypass, circumvent, or shorten the typical maturational process of school, work, and marriage and engage in adult behaviors and roles before they have amassed sufficient maturity to handle them well. An assumption of their theory is that such precocious development may be influenced by biological factors such as early maturity and personality factors such as the inability to delay gratification and sensation seeking. All of these influences lead to initiation of adult-like behaviors such as smoking and drinking that are then reinforced by peers for their seeming adult-like behavior. But these influences also generate a pseudomaturity that foreshortens critical developmental time during which important skills typically are being learned. For example, pseudomature persons may drink to excess before they have generated enough social skills or cognitive control to avoid its various negative consequences. Newcomb (1996) studied a sample of teenagers across a 16-year period and found that pseudomaturity, reflected in a general construct and specific scales, was significantly associated with numerous aspects of later adult role functioning. A general lifestyle of pseudomaturity led to overall negative consequences. The characteristics of the pseudomature individual, including early maturation, sensation seeking, and inability to delay gratification, are in concordance with the traits associated with the addiction-prone personality described in Chapters 10 and 11.

6.11. Integrative Models

Personality comprises only one of the factors involved in predicting alcohol and drug misuse. A number of investigators such as Sher (Sher & Trull, 1994), Zucker (Zucker et al., 1995), Jessor (1987), and Grace Barnes (Barnes, 1990) have begun to develop models that integrate personality and other factors that have been shown to be important in predicting the risk of alcohol and drug misuse. The term that has been commonly used to describe an overarching framework that could be developed in the addiction field is the "biopsychosocial perspective." In our own research, we have begun to develop models to try and integrate the role of personality with the role played by other factors in explaining the risk of alcohol and drug use and problems. These models generally take two possible forms. Personality may be considered as either a mediating influence in the development of addiction or as a moderating influence. An example of a mediated model that was recently proposed and examined (Barnes, Patton, & Marshall, 1998) in the Vancouver Family Survey is presented in Figure 12.1. The results of our analyses supported the mediating role of the Addiction-Prone Personality placed between the Family Environment on the one side of the model and problem behaviors on the other side. Personality variables may also have a moderating influence on the development of alcohol and drug use. Some possible moderating influences that we are currently examining include the possible moderating influence of the Addiction-Prone Personality on the effects of Family Stress on the occurrence of

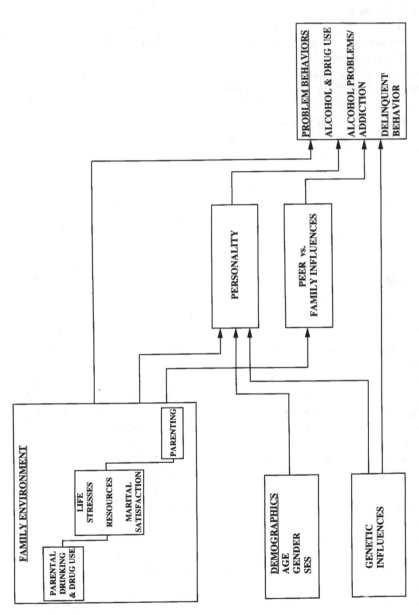

Figure 12.1. Hypothetical model: family environment and problem behaviors.

alcohol and drug misuse (Barnes & Parker, in progress). Preliminary analyses suggest that strong Family Stress in combination with high APP traits in offspring produce more alcohol and drug misuse. Another possible moderated model might involve looking at the interaction between strong parental care and the APP. Perhaps low amounts of care in combination with an addiction-prone personality places a person at greater risk of alcohol and drug misuse.

7. Policy and Program Design Implications

If personality is related to alcohol abuse, then what are the policy implications of these findings? Personality tends to be very stable, particularly in adulthood (McCrae & Costa, 1985a). This is not surprising in view of fact that major personality dimensions are rooted in biological processes (Zuckerman, 1989) and that recent findings have even identified a particular genetic structure associated with sensation seeking (Ebstein et al., 1996). It seems unlikely then that personality characteristics can be easily changed to reduce the risk of alcohol abuse once a person reaches adulthood. This reality has led the critics of personality research to argue that this limits the utility of personality research. If personality cannot be changed, then what is the point of knowing that it causes alcohol abuse or anything else for that matter? As personality researchers, we believe that no behavior can be adequately understood without examining the behavior in relation to individual differences. We also believe that understanding the fundamental causes of any problem behavior is the only way to design effective interventions, whether these be primary prevention, secondary prevention, or tertiary care of the disorder. Thus, the results of our research have important implications in all of these areas. Some of the implications/program design issues that we have been able to deduce thus far from this research are listed below.

1. Results in the Vancouver Family Survey reported in Chapter 11 suggest that the family environment may play an important role in developing of the addiction-prone personality. Homes that are characterized by low parental care and parents with high APP traits produce higher APP scores in offspring. These results suggest that environmental interventions, such as parenting programs, might be one avenue for reducing the levels of high-risk traits in offspring. Programs such as the Kids and Drugs Parenting Program which was implemented in Manitoba, Canada, was effective in changing parents' behavior in the direction of being less coercive and more caring (Barnes & Greenwood, 1985). The home environment is only one of the environments where children spend their time. Perhaps we can alter other environments where children spend their time, including schools, foster care, and juvenile justice systems, to make these

environments more caring as well, and thus reduce the vulnerability of youths to alternative sources of rewards readily available through substance misuse.

2. In the tertiary care of alcohol abuse, proper attention to the personality antecedents of alcohol abuse should be incorporated into the intake assessments. In particular, treatment protocols may be quite different for clients with high impulsivity, along with their alcohol abuse, than for clients who have arrived at their addiction primarily through reward seeking, but not poor impulse control. New forms of treatment should be developed based on the underlying personality traits of the client. It is apparent that many people who give up their alcohol addiction simply replace it with another addiction that satisfies their reward needs (e.g., caffeine, smoking). For those whose alcohol addiction is primarily associated with reward seeking, treatments designed to meet these needs without drugs (e.g., exercise, acupuncture, meditation) might be the most effective. Others, whose problems with alcohol are more associated with poor impulse control and social nonconformity, might respond better to treatment approaches that take these personality characteristics into account.

3. Public policies need to reflect a better understanding of the alcohol abuse process. For example, our research shows that reward-seeking behavior constitutes one of the major pathways to alcohol abuse. It seems likely that the producers of alcoholic beverages have already known this for years through their own research, using focus groups, etc. After completing this research we have become aware of the very insidious nature of the lifestyle ads that capitalize on the association between the use of their product and sensation-seeking behaviors. These ads are very powerful in that they target the young, a group that is most susceptible to this type of approach. It is likely that these ads are very effective and reinforce the classical conditioning of two very rewarding activities for young sensation seekers. It is interesting that the distilled spirits producers have been actively campaigning against the lifestyle ads for beer producers because they have been losing market share. It is also evident in our research and in research by others that, although the overall consumption of alcohol has been declining in society, there is a very high rate of alcohol consumption and abuse among the young. In addition to eliminating the lifestyle ads, public policy makers should also be concerned with the number of activities available today where sensation seeking occurs in conjunction with alcohol consumption. The more activities that we offer young people that combine these two activities, the greater the potential for producing addiction to alcohol.

4. Primary prevention should be modified to include a stronger focus on the importance of reward seeking in alcohol abuse, and greater attention

should be paid to alternative ways of obtaining brain center reward stimulation.

5. Individuals who have high psychoticism/antisocial personality and who have problems with impulse control may be particularly vulnerable to problems associated with alcohol. Primary prevention programs need to be designed to reach people with low impulse control and low social conformity. Family based programming may be a suitable alternative here because these problems run in families. In particular, parents with children who are difficult to manage (e.g., attention deficit disorder and hyperactivity) may need more support in raising their children.

6. Impulsive and undersocialized individuals will always be a risk to themselves and society, but these risks can be minimized by healthy public policy. For example, strong sanctions against drinking and driving along with better enforcement has reduced the incidence of this behavior. The high P individuals, in particular, could be protected from themselves by strong sanctions against drunken behavior in society. Strong policies supporting server control in bars, for example, might help prevent alcohol abuse and some of the negative consequences.

7. In the medical view of alcohol abuse, individuals with underlying vulnerabilities are perceived as having a disorder that needs to be fixed. From the perspective of an individual difference, all human differences are expressions of natural variation that can have either positive or negative social consequences. Although the term Psychoticism has a very negative connotation, many of the most creative members of society, including artists, musicians, poets, etc., would probably score high on this dimension (Eysenck, 1995). The social form that a particular underlying vulnerability produces is very much influenced by society. If a people have addiction-prone personalities and are raised in the Mormon culture, for example, they may never try alcohol and never be affected by this disorder. In the future we would like to extend our research to be able to identify the healthy means of adjustment that are being achieved by individuals with addiction-prone personalities. Even if in the future we are able to link scores on our Addiction-Prone Personality Scale with a person's underlying genetic structure, this would not indicate that alcohol abuse is biologically predetermined for these individuals. Although biology may indeed be destiny, it is only destiny in a very general way. Particular destiny is ultimately shaped through the dynamic interplay between social influences and individual actions.

References

Abrams, D. B., & Niaura, R.,S. (1987). Social learning theory. In H. T. Blane & K. E. Leonard (Eds.), *Psychological theories of drinking and alcoholism.* New York: Guilford.

Abrams, D. B., & Wilson, G. T. (1979). Effects of alcohol on social anxiety in women: Cognitive versus physiological processes. *Journal of Abnormal Psychology, 88,* 161–173.

af Klinteberg, B., Andersson, T., Magnusson, D., & Stattin, H. (1993). Hyperactive behavior in childhood as related to subsequent alcohol problems and violent offending: A longitudinal study of male subjects. *Personality and Individual Differences, 15(4),* 381–388.

Aiken, L. S., Stein, J. A., & Bentler, P. M. (1994). Structural equation analyses of clinical subpopulation differences and comparative treatment outcomes: Characterizing the daily lives of drug addicts. *Journal of Consulting and Clinical Psychology, 62,* 488–499.

Allen, J. P. (1991). Personality correlates of the MacAndrew Alcoholism Scale: A review of the literature. *Psychology of Addictive Behaviors, 5(2),* 59–65.

Allen, L. R. (1969). Self-esteem of male alcoholics. *Psychological Record, 19,* 381–389.

American Psychiatric Association (1980). *Diagnostic and statistical manual of mental disorders,* 3rd ed. Washington, DC: American Psychiatric Association.

Amir, T. (1994). Personality study of alcohol, heroin, and polydrug abusers in an Arabian gulf population. *Psychological Reports, 74,* 515–520.

Anderson, R. E., Barnes, G. E., Patton, D., & Perkins, T. M. (1999). Personality in the development of substance abuse. In I. Mervielde, I. Deary, F. De Fruyt, & F. Ostendorf (Eds.), *Personality Psychology in Europe, Vol. 7.* Tilburg: Tilburg University Press.

Andrew, M., & Cronin, C. (1997). Two measures of sensation seeking as predictors of alcohol use among high school males. *Personality and Individual Differences, 22(3),* 393–401.

Andrews, F. M., Morgan, J. N., & Sonquist, J. A. (1971). *Multiple classification analysis: A report on a computer program for multiple regression using categorical predictors.* Ann Arbor, MI: University of Michigan, Survey Research Center.

Andrucci, G. L., Archer, R. P., Pancoast, D. L., & Gordon, R. A. (1989). The relationship of MMPI and sensation seeking scales to adolescent drug use. *Journal of Personality Assessment, 53,* 253–266.

Arbuckle, J. L. (1996). Full information estimation in the presence of incomplete data. In G. A. Marcoulides & R. E. Schumacker (Eds.), *Advanced structural equation modeling: Issues and techniques* (pp. 243–277). Mahwah, NJ: Erlbaum.

Arnett, J. (1994). Sensation seeking: A new conceptualization and a new scale. *Personality and Individual Differences, 16*(2), 289–296.

Austin, J. T., & Calderon, R. F. (1996). Theoretical and technical contributions to structural equation modeling: An updated annotated bibliography. *Structural Equation Modeling, 3*, 105–175.

Babor, T. F. (1990). Epidemiology, advocacy and ideology in alcohol studies. *Journal of Studies on Alcohol, 51*, 293–295.

Babor, T. F., Hoffmann, M., DelBoca, F. K., Hesselbrock, V., Meyer, R. E., Dolinsky, Z. S. & Rounsaville, B. (1992). Types of alcoholics, I: Evidence for an empirically derived typology based on indicators of vulnerability and severity. *Archives of General Psychiatry, 49*, 599–608.

Bailey, W., Hustmyer, F., & Kristofferson, A. (1961). Alcoholism, brain damage and perceptual dependence. *Quarterly Journal of Studies on Alcohol, 22*, 387–393.

Ball, S. A., Carroll, K. M., & Rounsaville, B. J. (1994). Sensation seeking, substance abuse, and psychopathology in treatment-seeking and community cocaine abusers. *Journal of Consulting and Clinical Psychology, 62*(5), 1053–1057.

Ballard, R. G. (1959). The interaction between marital conflict and alcoholism as seen through MMPI's of marriage partners. *American Journal of Orthopsychiatry, 29*, 528–546.

Baraga, D. J. (1977). Self-concept in children of alcoholics. *Dissertation Abstracts International, 39*, 368-B

Barnes, G. E. (1976). Individual differences in perceptual reactance: A review of the stimulus intensity modulation individual differences dimension. *Canadian Psychological Review, 17*, 29–52.

Barnes, G. E. (1979). The alcoholic personality: A reanalysis of the literature. *Journal of Studies on Alcohol, 40*(7), 571–634.

Barnes, G. E. (1980). Characteristics of the clinical alcoholic personality. *Journal of Studies on Alcohol, 41*, 894–910.

Barnes, G. E. (1983). Clinical and prealcoholic personality characteristics. In B. Kissin & H. Begleiter (Eds.), *The pathogenesis of alcoholism: Psychosocial factors* (pp. 113–195). Brooklyn: Plenum Publishing.

Barnes, G. E. (1985a). Stimulus intensity modulation and alcoholism. In J. J. Sanchez-Sosa (Ed.), *Health and clinical psychology* (pp.223–236). Amsterdam: Elsevier Science.

Barnes, G. E. (1985b). The Vando R-A scale as a measure of stimulus reducing-augmenting. In J. Strelau, F. Farley, & A. Gale (Eds.), *The biological bases of personality and behavior: Theories, measurement techniques, and development* (pp. 117–180). Washington, DC: Hemisphere.

Barnes, G. E., & Greenwood, L. (1985). *Kids and drugs: A pilot evaluation study.* Report prepared for the Alcoholism Foundation of Manitoba.

Barnes, G. E., Greenwood, L., & Sommer, R. (1990). Personality and alcohol use in college students. Unpublished research.

Barnes, G. E., Patton, D., & Sharp, D. The D2 receptor gene and alcoholism: A meta-analysis. (unpublished manuscript).

Barnes, G. E., Patton, D., Anderson, R. A., & Perkins, T. (1996). Family environments and personality development. Presented at the 8th European Conference on Personality, Ghent, Belgium.

Barnes, G. E., Patton, D., & Marshall, S. K. (1998). *Family environments and substance abuse.* Ottawa, ON: Health Canada/NHRDP Project No. 6610-2073-102.

Barnes, G. M. (1977). The development of adolescent drinking behavior: An evaluative review of the impact of the socialization process within the family. *Adolescence, 12*, 571–591.

Barnes, G. M. (1990). Impact of the family on adolescent drinking patterns. In R. L. Collins, K. E. Leonard & J. S. Searles (Eds.), *Alcohol and the family: Research and clinical perspectives* (pp. 137–161). New York: Guilford.

Barnes, G. M., & Farrell, M. P. (1992). Parental support and control as predictors of adolescent drinking, delinquency and related problem behaviors. *Journal of Marriage and the Family, 54*, 763–776.

Barnes, G. M., Farrell, M. P., & Cairns, A. L. (1986). Parental socialization factors and adolescent drinking behaviors. *Journal of Marriage and the Family, 48*, 27–36.

Barnes, G. M., Farrell, M. P., & Windle, M. (1987). Parent-adolescent interactions in the development of alcohol abuse and other deviant behaviors. *Family Perspectives, 21*(4), 321–335.

Barnes, G. M., & Welte, J. W. (1986) Patterns and predictors of alcohol use among 7–12th grade students in New York State. *Journal of Studies on Alcohol, 47*, 53–62.

Barnes, G. M., & Welte, J. W. (1988). Predictors of driving while intoxicated among teenagers. *Journal of Drug Issues, 18*, 367–384.

Barnes, G. M., & Welte, J. W. (1990). Prediction of adult's drinking patterns from the drinking of their parents. *Journal of Studies on Alcohol, 51*(6), 523–526.

Barnes, G. M., & Windle, M. (1987). Family factors in adolescent alcohol and drug abuse. *Pediatrician—International Journal of Child and Adolescent Health, 14*, 13–18.

Barrett, P., & Eysenck, S. B. G. (1984). The assessment of personality factors across 25 countries. *Personality & Individual Differences, 5*, 615–632.

Barron, F. (1953). An ego strength scale which predicts response to psychotherapy. *Journal of Consulting Psychology, 17*, 327–333

Bates, M. E., & Labouvie, E. W. (1995). Personality-environment constellations and alcohol use: A process-oriented study of intraindividual change during adolescence. *Psychology of Addictive Behaviors, 9*(1), 23–35.

Bates, M. E., Labouvie, E. W., & White, H. R. (1986). The effect of sensation seeking needs on alcohol and marijuana use in adolescence. *Bulletin of the Society of Psychologists in Addictive Behaviors, 5*(1), 29–36.

Baumrind, D. (1967). Child care practices anteceding three patterns of pre-school behavior. *Genetic Psychology Monographs, 75*, 43 -88.

Baumrind, D. (1971). Current patterns of parental authority. *Developmental Psychology Monographs, 4*(1, Pt. 2).

Beckman, L. J. (1975). Women alcoholics: A review of social and psychological studies. *Journal of Studies on Alcohol, 36*(7), 797–824.

Beckman, L. J. (1978). Self-esteem of women alcoholics. *Journal of Studies on Alcohol, 39*, 491–498.

Beckman, L. J., & Bardsley, P. E. (1981). The perceived determinants and consequences of alcohol consumption among young women heavy drinkers. *International Journal of Addiction, 16*, 75–88.

Bedi, A. R., & Halikas, J. A. (1985). Alcoholism and affective disorders. *Alcoholism, 9*, 133–134.

Belfer, M. L., Shader, R. I., Carroll, M., & Harmatz, J. S. (1971). Alcoholism in women. *Archives of General Psychiatry, 25*, 540–544.

Bellak, L., Hurvich, M., & Gediman, H. K. (1973). *Ego functions in schizophrenics, neurotics, and normals: A systematic study of conceptual, diagnostic and therapeutic aspects.* New York: Wiley.

Benjamin, J., Li, L., Patterson, C., Greenberg, B. D., Murphy, D. L., & Hamer, D. H. (1996). Population and familial association between the D4 dopamine receptor gene and measures of novelty seeking. *Nature Genetics, 12*, 81–84.

Bennett, L. A., Wolin, S. J., & Reiss, D. (1988). Cognitive, behavioral, and emotional problems among school-age children of alcoholic parents. *American Journal of Psychiatry, 145*(2), 185–190.

Benson, C. S., & Heller, K. (1987). Factors in the current adjustment of young adult daughters of alcoholic and problem drinking fathers. *Journal of Abnormal Psychology, 96*(4), 305–312.

Bentler, P. M. (1990). Comparative fit indexes in structural models. *Psychological Bulletin, 107*(2), 238–246.

Bentler, P. M. (1992). Etiologies and consequences of adolescent drug use: Implications for prevention. *Journal of Addictive Diseases, 11*, 47–61.

Bentler, P. M. (1995). *EQS structural equations program manual.* Encino, CA: Multivariate Software.

Bentler, P. M. & Dudgeon, P. (1996). Covariance structural analysis: Statistical practice, theory, and directions. *Annual Review of Psychology, 47*, 563–592.

Bentler, P. M., & Wu, E. J. C. (1995). *EQS for Windows user's guide.* Los Angeles: BMDP Statistical Software.

Berg, N. L. (1971). Effects of alcohol intoxication on self-concept. *Quarterly Journal of Studies on Alcohol, 32*, 442–453.

Bergman, H., Holm, L., & Agren, G. (1981). Neuropsychological impairment and a test of the predisposition hypothesis with regard to field dependence in alcoholics. *Journal of Studies on Alcohol, 42*(1), 15–23.

Berman, S. M., & Noble, E. P. (1995). Reduced visuospatial performance in children with the D2 dopamine receptor A1 allele. *Behavior Genetics, 25*(1), 45–58.

Berkowitz, A., & Perkins, H. W. (1988). Personality characteristics of children of alcoholics. *Journal of Consulting and Clinical Psychology, 56*(2), 206–209.

Bibb, J. L., & Chambless, P. L. (1986). Alcohol use and abuse among diagnosed agoraphobics. *Behavior Research and Therapy, 24*, 49–58.

Blackson, T. C. (1994). Temperament: A salient correlate of risk factors for alcohol and drug abuse. *Drug and Alcohol Dependence, 36*, 205–214.

Bland, R. C., Orn, H., & Newman, S. C. (1988). Lifetime prevalence of psychiatric disorders in Edmonton. *Acta Psychiatrica Scandinavica, 77*(suppl 338), 24–32.

Blashfield, R. K., & Aldenderfer, M. S. (1988). The methods and problems of cluster analysis. In J. R. Nesselroade & R. B. Cattell (Eds.), *Handbook of multivariate experimental psychology,* 2nd ed. (pp. 447–473). New York: Plenum Publishing.

Block, J. (1971). *Lives through time.* Berkeley, CA: Bancroft.

Blowin, A., Bornstein, R., & Trites, R. (1978). Teenage alcohol use among hyperactive children: A five year follow-up study. *Journal of Pediatric Psychology, 3*, 188–194.

Blum, K., Noble, E. P., Sheridan, P. J., Montgomery, A., Ritchie, T., Jagadeeswaran, P., Nogami, H., Briggs, A. H., & Cohn, J. B. (1990). Allelic association of human dopamine D2 receptor gene in alcoholism. *Journal of the American Medical Association, 263*(15), 2055–2060.

Blum, K., & Payne, J.E . (1991). *Alcohol and the addictive brain: New hope for alcoholics from biogenic research.* Toronto, Canada: Maxwell Macmillan.

Bollen, K. A. (1989). *Structural equations with latent variables.* New York: Wiley.

Bouchard, T. J., Jr., & McGue, M. (1990). Genetic and rearing environmental influences on adult personality: An analysis of adopted twins reared apart. *Journal of Personality, 58*(1), 263–291.

Bowen, R. C., Cipywnyk, D., D'Arcy, C., & Keegan, D. (1984). Alcoholism, anxiety disorders, and agoraphobia. *Alcoholism: Clinical and Experimental Research, 8*(1), 48–50.

Brennan, A. F., Walfish, S., & Aubuchon, P. (1986). Alcohol use and abuse in college students. I. A review of individual and personality correlates. *The International Journal of the Addictions, 21*(4&5), 449–474.

Brook, J. S., & Cohen, P. (1992). A developmental perspective on drug use and delinquency. In J. McCord (Ed.), *Facts, frameworks and forecasts: Advances in criminological theory* (Vol.3, pp. 137–156). New Brunswick, NJ: Transaction Publishers.

Brook, J. S., Whiteman, M. M., & Finch, S. (1992). Childhood aggression, adolescent delinquency, and drug use: A longitudinal study. *Journal of Genetic Psychology, 153*, 369–383.

Brown, G. W., & Harris, T. (1978). *Social origins of depression: A study of psychiatric disorder in women*. New York: Free Press.

Brown, H. P. (1992). Substance abuse and the disorders of the self: Examining the relationship. *Alcoholism Treatment Quarterly, 9*(2), 1–27.

Brown, R. A., & Cutter, H. S. G. (1977). Alcohol, customary-drinking behavior and pain. *Journal of Abnormal Psychology, 86*, 179–188.

Brown, S. A., Irwin, M., & Schuckit, M. A. (1991). Changes in anxiety among abstinent male alcoholics. *Journal of Studies on Alcohol, 52*(1), 55–61.

Brown, S. A., & Munson, E. (1987). Extroversion, anxiety and the perceived effects of alcohol. *Journal of Studies on Alcohol, 48*(3), 272–276.

Brown, T. G., & Fayek, A. (1993). Comparison of demographic characteristics and MMPI scores from alcohol and poly-drug alcohol and cocaine abusers. *Alcoholism Treatment Quarterly, 10*(1/2), 123–135.

Browne, M. W., & Arminger, G. (1995). Specification and estimation of mean and covariance models. In G. Arminger & M. E. Sobel (Eds.), *Handbook of statistical modeling for the social and behavioral sciences* (pp. 185–249). New York: Plenum Publishing.

Buchsbaum, M. S., & Ludwig, A. M. (1980). Effects of sensory input and alcohol administration on visual evoked potentials in normal subjects and alcoholics. In H. Begleiter (Ed.), *Biological effects of alcohol*. Proceedings of the International Symposium on Biological Research in Alcoholism, Zurich, Switzerland. New York: Plenum Publishing.

Bulik, C. M., Sullivan, P. F., McKee, M., Weltzin, T. E., & Kaye, W. H. (1994). Characteristics of bulimic women with and without alcohol abuse. *American Journal of Drug and Alcohol Abuse, 20*(2), 273–283.

Burke, H. (1983). "Markers" for the MacAndrew and the Cavior Heroin Addiction MMPI scales. *Journal of Studies on Alcohol, 44*, 558–563.

Buss, A. H., & Plomin, R. (1984). *Temperament: Early developing personality traits*. Hillsdale, NJ: Erlbaum.

Byrne, B. M. (1994). *Structural equation modeling with EQS and EQS/Windows*. Thousand Oaks, CA: Sage.

Cacciola, J. S., Alterman, A. I., Rutherford, M. J., & Snider, E. C. (1995). Treatment response of antisocial substance abusers. *Journal of Nervous and Mental Disease, 183*, 166–171.

Cadoret, R., & Winokur, G. (1972). Depression in alcoholism. *Annals of the New York Academy of Science, 233*, 34–39.

Cadoret, R. J., Yates, W. R., Troughton, E., Woodworth, G., & Stewart, M. A. (1995). Genetic-environmental interaction in the genesis of aggressivity and conduct disorders. *Archives of General Psychiatry, 52*, 916–924.

Cahalan, D., & Cisin, L.,H. (1968). American drinking practices: Summary of the findings from a national probability sample. I: Extent of drinking by population subgroups. *Quarterly Journal of Studies on Alcohol, 29*, 130–151.

Cahalan, D., & Room, R. (1974) *Problem drinking among American men*. New Haven: College & University Press.

Calaycay, P. R., & Altman, H. A. (1985). A study of personality characteristics of outpatient alcoholics. *Journal of Alcohol and Drug Education, 31*(1), 8–15.

Calsyn, D. A., Roszell, D. K., Walter, R. D., & O'Leary, M. R. (1983). Exploration of the relationship between frequency of illness, attrition from alcohol treatment, neuropsychological status and field dependence. *Drug and Alcohol Dependence, 12*(4), 363–369.

Cameron, O. G., Liepman, M. R., Curtis, G. C., & Thyer, B. A. (1987). Ethanol retards desensitisation of simple phobias in non-alcoholics. *British Journal of Psychiatry, 150*, 845–849.

Campbell, B. K., & Stark, M. J. (1990). Psychopathology and personality characteristics in different forms of substance abuse. *The International Journal of the Addictions, 25*(12), 1467–1474.

Cantwell, D. P. (1972). Psychiatric illness in the families of hyperactive children. *Archives of General Psychiatry, 27*, 414–417.

Cappell, H., & Greeley, J. (1987). Alcohol and tension reduction: An update on research and theory. In H. T. Blane & K. E. Leonard (Eds.), *Psychological theories of drinking and alcoholism* (pp. 15–54). Buffalo, NY: Guilford.

Carrol, K. M., & Rounsaville, B. J. (1991). Contrast of treament seeking and untreated cocaine abusers. *Archives of General Psychiatry, 49*(6), 464–471.

Caspi, A., Harrington, H., Moffitt, T. E., Begg, D., Dickson, N., Langley, J., & Silva, P. A. (1997). Personality differences predict health-risk behaviors in young adulthood: Evidence from a longitudinal study. *Journal of Personality and Social Psychology, 73*(5), 1052–1063.

Caspi, A., & Silva, P. A. (1995). Temperamental qualities at age three predict personality traits in young adulthood: Longitudinal evidence from a birth cohort. *Child Development, 66*, 486–498.

Cattell, R. B., Eber, H. W., & Tatsuoka, M. M. (1970). *Handbook for the Sixteen Personality Factor Questionnaire (16 PF).* Champaign, IL: Institute for Personality and Ability Testing.

Charlampous, K. D., Ford, B. K., & Skinner, T. J. (1976). Self-esteem in alcoholics and nonalcoholics. *Quarterly Journal of Studies on Alcohol, 37*, 990–994.

Chassin, L., Presson, C. C., Bensenberg, M., Corty, E., Olshavsky, R. W., & Sherman, S. J. (1981). Predicting adolescents' intentions to smoke cigarettes. *Journal of Health and Social Behavior, 22*, 445–455.

Chess, S. B., Neuringer, C., & Goldstein, G. (1971). Arousal and field dependency in alcoholics. *Journal of General Psychology, 85*, 93–102.

Chinnian, R. R., Taylor, L. R., Subaie, A. A., Sugumar, A., & Jumaih, A. A. (1994). A controlled study of personality patterns in alcohol and heroin abusers in Saudi Arabia. *Journal of Psychoactive Drugs, 26*(1), 85–88.

Churchill, J. C., Broida, J. P., & Nicholson, N. L. (1990). Locus of control and self-esteem of adult children of alcoholics. *Journal of Studies on Alcohol, 51*(4), 373–376.

Ciarrocchi, J. W., Kirschner, N. M., & Fallik, F. (1991). Personality dimensions of male pathological gamblers, alcoholics, and dually addicted gamblers. *Journal of Gambling Studies, 7*(2), 133–141.

Ciotola, P. V., & Peterson, J. F. (1976). Personality characteristics of alcoholics and drug addicts in a merged treatment program. *Journal of Studies on Alcohol, 37*(9), 1229–1235.

Clair, D., & Genest, M. (1987). Variables associated with the adjustment of offspring of alcoholic fathers. *Journal of Studies in Alcohol, 48*, 345–355.

Clerici, M., Carta, I., & Cazzullo, C. L. (1989). Substance abuse and psychopathology: A diagnostic screening of Italian narcotic addicts. *Social Psychiatry and Psychiatric Epidemiology, 24*, 219–226.

Cloninger, C. R. (1983). Genetic and environmental factors in the development of alcoholism. *Journal of Psychiatric Treatment and Evaluation, 5*, 487–496.

Cloninger, C. R. (1986). A unified biosocial theory of personality and its role in the development of anxiety states. *Psychiatric Development, 4*, 167–226.

Cloninger, C. R. (1987a). Neurogenetic adaptive mechanisms in alcoholism. *Science, 236*, 410–416.

Cloninger, C. R. (1987b). Tridimensional Personality Questionnaire (Version 4). Unpublished manuscript.

Cloninger, C. R., Bohman, M., & Sigvardsson, S. (1981). Inheritance of alcohol abuse: Cross-fostering analysis of adopted men. *Archives of General Psychiatry, 38*, 861–868.

Cloninger, C. R., Przybeck, T. R., Svrakic, D. M., & Wetzel, R. D. (1994). *The Temperament and Character Inventory (TCI): A guide to its development and use.* St. Louis, MO: Center for Psychobiology of Personality, Washington University.

Cloninger, C. R., Sigvardsson, S., & Bohman, M. (1988). Childhood personality predicts alcohol abuse in young adults. *Alcoholism: Clinical and Experimental Research, 12,* 494–505.

Cloninger, C. R., Sigvardsson, S., Przybeck, T. R., & Svrakic, D.,M. (1995). *European Archives of Psychiatry and Clinical Neuroscience, 245,* 239–244.

Cloninger, C. R., Sigvardsson, S., von Knorring, A. L., & Bohman, M. (1988). The Swedish studies of the adopted children of alcoholics: A reply to Littrell. *Journal of Studies on Alcohol, 49*(6), 500–509.

Cloninger, C. R., & Svrakic, D. M. (1994). Differentiating normal and deviant personality by the seven factor personality model. In S. Strack & M. Lorr (Eds.), *Differentiating normal and abnormal personality.* New York: Springer.

Cloninger, C. R., Svrakic, D. M., & Przybeck, T. R. (1993). A psychobiological model of temperament and character. *Archives of General Psychiatry, 50,* 975–990.

Coger, R. W., Dymond, A. M., Serafetinides, E. A., Lowenstam, I., & Pearson, D. (1976). Alcoholism: Averaged visual evoked response amplitude-intensity slope and symmetry in withdrawal. *Biological Psychiatry, 11,* 435–443.

Cohen, D. A., Richardson, J., & LaBree, L. (1994). Parenting behaviors and the onset of smoking and alcohol use: A longitudinal study. *Pediatrics, 94*(3), 368–375.

Comings, D. E., Ferry, L., Bradshaw-Robinson, S., Burchette, R., Chiu, C., & Muhleman, D. (1996). The dopamine D2 receptor (DRD2) gene: A genetic risk factor in smoking. *Pharmacogenetics, 6,* 73–79.

Conger, J. J. (1956). Alcoholism - Theory, problem and challenge: Reinforcement theory and the dynamics of alcoholism. *Quarterly Journal of Studies on Alcohol, 17,* 296–305.

Conley, J. J. (1981). An MMPI typology of male alcoholics: Admission, discharge, and outcome comparisons. *Journal of Personality Assessment, 45,* 33–39.

Cooney, N. L., Kadden, R. M., & Litt, M. D. (1990). A comparison of methods for assessing sociopathy in male and female alcoholics. *Journal of Studies on Alcohol, 51*(1), 42–48.

Cooper, M. L., Pierce, R. S., & Tidwell, M. O. (1995). Parental drinking problems and adolescent offspring substance use: Moderating effects of demographic and familial factors. *Psychology of Addictive Behaviors, 9*(1), 36–52.

Costa, P. T., Jr., & McCrae, R. R. (1991). Facet scales for agreeableness and conscientiousness: A revision of the NEO personality inventory. *Personality and Individual Differences, 12,* 887–898.

Costa, P. T., & McCrae, R. R. (1992). *Revised NEO Personality Inventory (NEO PI-R) and NEO Five-Factor Inventory (NEO-FFI): professional manual.* Odessa, FL: Psychological Assessment Resources.

Costa, P. T., McCrae, R. R., & Arenberg, D. (1980). Enduring dispositions in adult males. *Journal of Personality and Social Psychology, 38,* 793–800.

Cox, B. J., Norton, R. G., Swinson, R. P., & Endler, N. S. (1990). Substance abuse and panic-related anxiety: A critical review. *Behavior Research and Therapy, 28,* 385–393.

Craig, R. J. (1979). Personality characteristics of heroin addicts: A review of the empirical literature with critique II. *International Journal of Addictions, 14,* 607–626.

Craig, R. J., Vernis, J. S., & Wexler, S. (1985). Personality characteristics of drug addicts and alcoholics on the Millon Clinical Multiaxial Inventory. *Journal of Personality Assessment, 49,* 156–160.

Curran, P. S., West, S. G., & Finch, J. F. (1996). The robustness of test statistics to nonnormality and specification error in confirmatory factor analysis. *Psychological Methods, 1,* 16–29.

Darkes, J., Greenbaum, P. E., & Goldman, M. S. (1998). Sensation seeking—disinhibition and alcohol use: Exploring issues of criterion contamination. *Psychological Assessment, 10*(1), 71–76.

Davis, C., Cowles, M., & Kohn, P. (1982). Strength of the nervous system and augmenting-reducing: Paradox lost. *Personality and Individual Differences, 4*(5), 491–498.

Davis, C., Cowles, M., & Kohn, P. (1984). Behavioral and physiological aspects of the augment-ing-reducing dimension. *Personality and Individual Differences*, 5(6), 683–691.

Delatte, J. G., & Delatte, G. M. (1984). Young and old alcoholics: Some personality differences. *Journal of Clinical Psychology*, 40(2), 613–616.

DeJong, C. A. J., van den Brink, W., Harteveld, F. M., & van der Wielen, E. G. M. (1993). Person-ality disorders in alcoholics and drug addicts. *Comprehensive Psychiatry*, 34(2), 87–94.

De Obaldia, R., & Parsons, O. (1984). Reliability studies on the primary-secondary alcoholism classification questionnaire and the HK/MBD childhood symptoms checklist. *Journal of Clini-cal Psychology*, 40, 1257–1263.

De Obaldia, R., Parsons, O., & Yohman, R. (1983). Minimal brain dysfunction symptoms claimed by primary and secondary alcoholics: Relation to cognitive functioning. *International Jour-nal of Neuroscience*, 20, 173–182.

De Palma, N., & Clayton, H. D. (1958). Scores of alcoholics on the Sixteen Personality Factor questionnaire. *Journal of Clinical Psychology*, 14, 390–392.

Digman, J. M., & Inouye, J. (1986). Further specification of the five robust factors of personality. *Journal of Personality and Social Psychology*, 50, 116–123.

Dishion, T. J., Duncan, T. E., Eddy, M., Fagot, B., & Fetrow, R. (1994). The world of parent and peers: Coercive exchanges and children's social adaptation. *Social Development*, 3, 255–268.

Dobkin, P. L., Tremblay, R. E., Masse, L. C., & Vitaro, F. (1995). Individual and peer characteris-tics in predicting boys' early onset of substance abuse: A seven-year longitudinal study. *Child Development*, 66, 1198–1214.

Dobkin, P. L., Tremblay, R. E., & Sacchitelle, C. (1997). Predicting boys' early-onset substance abuse from father's alcoholism, son's disruptiveness and mother's parenting behavior. *Journal of Consulting and Clinical Psychology*, 65(1), 86–92.

Donovan, D. M., & Jessor, R. (1985). Structure of problem behavior in adolescence and young adulthood. *Journal of Consulting and Clinical Psychology*, 53, 241–249.

Donovan, D. M., Jessor, R., & Costa, F. M. (1988). Syndrome of problem behavior in adolescence: A replication. *Journal of Consulting and Clinical Psychology*, 56(5), 762–765.

Donovan, D. M., & Marlatt, G. A. (1982). Personality subtypes among driving-while-intoxicated offenders: Relationship to drinking behavior and driving risk. *Journal of Consulting and Clini-cal Psychology*, 50, 241–249.

Dorus, W., & Senay, E. C. (1980). Depression, demographic dimensions, and drug abuse. *Ameri-can Journal of Psychiatry*, 137, 699–704.

Dragutinovich, S. (1986). Stimulus intensity reducers: Are they sensation seekers, extraverts or strong nervous types? *Personality and Individual Differences*, 8(5), 693–704.

Drake, R. E., & Vaillant, G. E. (1988). Predicting alcoholism and personality disorder in a 33-year longitudinal study of children of alcoholics. *British Journal of Addiction*, 83, 799–807.

Duncan, S. C., & Duncan, T. E. (1996). A multivariate latent growth curve analysis of adolescent substance use. *Structural Equation Modeling*, 3, 323–347.

Duncan, S. C., Duncan, T. E., Biglan, A., & Ary, D. (1998). Contributions of the social context to the development of adolescent substance use: A multivariate latent growth modeling approach. *Drug and Alcohol Dependence*, 50, 57–71.

Duncan, T. E., Duncan, S. C., & Hops, H. (1994). The effects of family cohesiveness and peer encouragement on the development of adolescent alcohol use: A cohort-sequential approach to the analysis of longitudinal data. *Journal of Studies on Alcohol*, 55(5), 588–599.

Duncan, T. E., Duncan, S. C., & Li, F. (1998). A comparison of model- and multiple imputation-based approaches to longitudinal analyses with partial missingness. *Structural Equation Mod-eling*, 5(1), 1–21.

Dunn, G., Everitt, B., & Pickles, A. (1993). *Modeling covariances and latent variables using EQS*. London: Chapman & Hall.

References

Dush, D. M., & Keen, J. (1995). Changes in cluster analysis subtypes among alcoholic personalities after treatment. *Evaluation and the Health Professions, 18*(2), 152–165.

Earlywine, M., & Finn, P. R. (1991). Sensation seeking explains the relation between behavioral disinhibition and alcohol consumption. *Addictive Behaviors, 16*(3–4), 123–128.

Earlywine, M., Finn, P. R., & Martin, C. S. (1990). Personality and risk for alcohol consumption: A latent variable analysis. *Addictive Behaviors, 15*, 183–187.

Earleywine, M., Finn, P. R., Peterson, J. B., & Pihl, R. O. (1992). Factor structure and correlates of the Tridimensional Personality Questionnaire. *Journal of Studies on Alcohol, 53*(3), 233–238.

Ebstein, R. P., & Belmaker, R. H. (1997). Saga of an adventure gene: Novelty seeking, substance abuse and the dopamine D4 receptor (D4DR) exon III repeat polymorphism. *Molecular Psychiatry, 2*, 381–384.

Ebstein, R. P., Levine, J., Geller, V., Auerbach, J., Gritsenko, I., & Belmaker, R. H. (1998). Dopamine D4 receptor and serotonin transporter promoter in the determination of neonatal temperament. *Molecular Psychiatry, 3*, 238–246.

Ebstein, R. P., Novick, O., Umansky, R., Priel, B., Osher, Y., Blaine, D., Bennett, E. R., Nemanov, L., Katz, M., & Belmaker, R. H. (1996). Dopamine D4 receptor (D4DR) exon III polymorphism associated with the human personality trait of novelty seeking. *Nature Genetics, 12*(1), 78.

Eddy, C. C. (1979). The effects of alcohol on anxiety in problem- and nonproblem-drinking women. *Alcoholism: Clinical and Experimental Research, 3*, 107–114.

Edwards, G. (1986). The alcohol dependence syndrome: A concept as stimulus to inquiry. *British Journal of Addiction, 81*, 171–183.

Edwards, G., & Gross, M. M. (1976). Alcohol dependence: Provisional description of a clinical syndrome. *British Medical Journal, 1*, 1058–1061.

Edwards, G., Hensman, C., Hawker, A., & Williamson, V. (1966). Who goes to Alcoholics Anonymous? *The Lancet, 2*, 382–384.

Eliany, M., Giesbrecht, N., Wellman, B., & Wortley, S. (1989). Alcohol and other drug use by Canadians: A National Alcohol and Other Drugs Survey technical report. Ottawa, ON: Health Promotion Studies Unit, Health and Welfare Canada, 1992, Supply and Services Canada Cat. No. H39-251/1992E.

Ellickson, P. L., & Hays, R. D. (1991). Antecedents of drinking among young adolescents with different alcohol use histories. *Journal of Studies on Alcohol, 52*, 398–408.

Elwood, R. W. (1993). The clinical utility of the MMPI-2 in diagnosing unipolar depression among male alcoholics. *Journal of Personality Assessment, 60*(3), 511–521.

Emrick, C. D. (1975). A review of psychologically oriented treatment of alcoholism II: The relative effectiveness of different treatment approaches and the effectivenss of treatment versus no treatment. *Journal of Studies on Alcohol, 36*, 88–108.

Epstein, S. (1979). The stability of behavior I: On predicting most of the people much of the time. *Journal of Personality and Social Psychology, 37*, 1097–1126.

Erwin, J. E., & Hunter, J.,J. (1984). Prediction of attrition in alcoholic aftercare by scores on the Embedded Figures Test and two Piagetian tasks. *Journal of Consulting and Clinical Psychology, 52*(3), 354–358.

Everitt, B. S. (1993). *Cluster analysis*. Toronto, ON: Wiley.

Eysenck, H. J. (1978). Psychopathy, personality & genetics. In R. D. Hare & D. Schalling (Eds.), *Psychopathic behavior: Approaches to research*. New York: Wiley.

Eysenck, H. J. (1980). *The causes and effects of smoking*. Beverly Hills, CA: Sage.

Eysenck, H. J. (1990). Genetic and environmental contributions to individual differences: The three major dimensions of personality. *Journal of Personality, 58*, 245–261.

Eysenck, H. J. (1991). Dimensions of personality: 16, 5 or 3? - Criteria for a taxonomic paradigm. *Personality and Individual Differences, 12*(8), 773–790.

ysenck, H. J. (1992). A reply to Costa and McCrae: P or A and C—The role of theory. *Personality and Individual Differences, 13*(8), 867–868.

Eysenck, H. J. (1995). *Genius: The natural history of creativity*. New York: Cambridge University Press.

Eysenck, H. J. (1997). Addiction, personality and motivation. *Human Psychopharmacology: Clinical and Experimental, 12*(Suppl 2), S79–S87.

Eysenck, H. J., & Eysenck, M. W. (1985). *Personality and individual differences: A natural science approach*. New York: Plenum Publishing.

Eysenck, H. J., & Eysenck, S. B. G. (1976). *Psychoticism as a dimension of personality*. London: Hodder & Stoughton.

Eysenck, S. B. G., Eysenck, H. J., & Barrett, P. (1985). A revised version of the psychoticism scale. *Personality and Individual Differences, 6*, 21–29.

Fals-Stewart, W., & Lucente, S. (1994). Effect of neurocognitive status and personality functioning on length of stay in residential substance abuse treatment: An integrative study. *Psychology of Addictive Behaviors, 8*(3), 179–190.

Farrell, M. P., & Barnes, G. M. (1993). Family systems and social support: A test of the effects of cohesion and adaptability on the functioning of parents and adolescents. *Journal of Marriage and the Family, 55 (Feb.)*, 119–132.

Fenichel, O. (1945). *The psychoanalytic theory of neurosis*. New York: Norton.

Finkel, D., & McGue, M. (1993). Twenty-five year follow-up of child-rearing practices: Reliability of retrospective data. *Personality and Individual Differences, 15*(2), 147–154.

Finn, P. R., Earleywine, M., & Pihl, R. O. (1992). Sensation seeking, stress reactivity, and alcohol dampening discriminate the density of a family history of alcoholism. *Alcoholism: Clinical and Experimental Research, 16*(3), 585–590.

Finn, P. R., & Pihl, R. O. (1987). Men at risk for alcoholism: The effect of alcohol on cardiovascular response to unavoidable shock. *Journal of Abnormal Psychology, 96*, 230–236.

Finn, P. R., & Pihl, R. O. (1988). A comparison between two different groups of alcoholics on cardiovascular reactivity and sensitivity to alcohol. *Alcoholism: Clinical and Experimental Research, 12*, 742–747.

Finn, P. R., Zeitouni, N. C., & Pihl, R. O. (1990). Effects of alcohol on psychophysiological hyperreactivity to nonaversive and aversive stimuli in men at risk for alcoholism. *Journal of Abnormal Psychology, 99*(1), 79–85.

Finney, J. C., Smith, D. F., Skeeters, D. E., & Auvenshire, C .D. (1971). MMPI alcoholism scales. Factor structure and content analysis. *Quarterly Journal of Studies on Alcohol, 32*, 1055–1060.

Frances, R., Timm, S., & Bucky, S. (1980). Studies of familial and nonfamilial alcoholism. I. Demographic studies. *Archives of General Psychiatry, 37*, 564–566.

Freud, S. (1955). *The standard edition of the complete psychological works of Sigmund Freud* (J. Strachey, Trans., Ed.). London: The Hogarth Press and The Institute of Psychoanalysis.

Fruhstorfer, H., & Soveri, P. (1968). Alcohol and auditory evoked responses in man. *Acta Physiologica Scandinavica, 74*, 26A–27A.

Fuller, G. B. (1966). *Research in alcoholism with the 16PF test*. Champaign, IL: Institute for Personality and Ability Testing, Inform. Bull. No.12.

Gabel, S., Stallings, M. C., Schmitz, S., Young, S. E., Crowley, T. J., & Fulker, D. W. (1997). Personality dimensions in mothers and sons: Relationship to adolescent substance misuse. *Personality and Individual Differences, 23*(1), 79–86.

Gelernter, J., Goldman, D., & Risch, N. (1993). The A 1 allele at the D2 Dopamine receptor gene and alcoholism. *Journal of the American Medical Association, 269*(13), 1673–1677.

Glantz, M., & Pickens, R. (Eds.) (1992). *Vulnerability to drug abuse*. Washington, DC: American Psychological Association.

References

Glenn, S. W., & Parsons, O. A. (1989). Alcohol abuse and familial alcoholism: Psychosocia͏ lates in men and women. *Journal of Studies on Alcohol, 50*(2), 116–127.

Glueck, S., & Glueck, E. (1950). *Unraveling juvenile delinquency.* New York: The Commonwea͏ Fund.

Glueck, S., & Glueck, E. (1968). *Delinquents and non-delinquents in perspective.* Cambridge, MA: Harvard University Press.

Goldstein, G., & Chotlos, J. W. (1965). Dependency and brain damage in alcoholics. *Perceptual Motor Skills, 21,* 135–150.

Golightly, C., & Reinehr, R. C. (1969). 16PF profiles of hospitalized alcoholic patient: Replication and extension. *Psychological Reports, 24,* 543–545.

Goodwin, D. W. (1985). Alcoholism and genetics. *Archives of General Psychiatry, 42,* 171–174.

Goodwin, D. W., Schulsinger, F., Hermansen, L., Guze, S. B., & Winokur, G. (1973). Alcohol problems in adoptees raised apart from their alcoholic biologic parents. *Archives of General Psychiatry, 28,* 238–243.

Goodwin, D. W., Schulsinger, F., Hermansen, L., Guze, S. B., & Winokur, G. (1975). Alcoholism and the hyperactive child syndrome. *Journal of Nervous and Mental Disease, 160*(5), 349–353.

Gossop, M., & Eysenck, S. (1980). A further investigation into the personality of drug addicts in treatment. *British Journal of Addiction, 75,* 305–311.

Gossop, M., & Eysenck, S. (1983). A comparison of the personality of drug addicts in treatment with that of a prison population. *Personality and Individual Differences, 4,* 207–209.

Gotham, H. J., Sher, K. J., & Wood, P. K. (1997). Predicting stability and change in frequency of intoxication from the college years to beyond: Individual-difference and role transition variables. *Journal of Abnormal Psychology, 104*(4), 619–629.

Gough, H. G. (1969). *Manual for the California Psychological Inventory.* Palo Alto, CA: Consulting Psychologists Press.

Gough, H. G. (1994). Theory, development, and interpretation of the California Psychological Inventory Socialization scale. *Psychological Reports, 75*(1, Pt2), 651–700.

Gough, H. G. (1987). *California Psychological Inventory administrator's guide.* Palo Alto, CA: Consulting Psychologists Press.

Graham, J. R. (1987). *The MMPI: A practical guide.* New York: Oxford University Press.

Graham, J. R., & Strenger, V. E. (1988). MMPI characteristics of alcoholics: A review. *Journal of Consulting and Clinical Psychology, 56*(2), 197–205.

Graham, J. W., & Hofer, S. M. (1993). *EMCOV reference manual.* Los Angeles, CA: University of Southern California Institute for Prevention Research.

Grant, B. F. (1997). Prevalence and correlates of alcohol use and DSM-IV alcohol dependence in the United States: Results of the National Longitudinal Alcohol Epidemiologic Survey. *Journal of Studies on Alcohol, 58,* 464–473.

Gray, N. S., Pickering, A. D., & Gray, J. A. (1994). Psychoticism and dopamine D2 binding in the basal ganglia using single photon emission tomography. *Personality and Individual Differences, 17*(3), 431–434.

Greene, R. L., Adyanthaya, A. E., Morse, R. M., & Davis, L. J. (1993). Personality variables in cocaine- and marijuana-dependent patients. *Journal of Personality Assessment, 61,* 224–230.

Grilo, C. M., Fehon, D. C., & Walker, M. (1996). A comparison of adolescent inpatients with and without substance abuse using the Millon Adolescent Clinical Inventory. *Journal of Youth and Adolescents, 25,* 379–388.

Gross, M. M., Begleiter, H., Tobin, M., & Kissin, B. (1966). Changes in auditory evoked response induced by alcohol. *Journal of Nervous and Mental Diseases, 143,* 152.

Gross, W. F. (1971). Self-concepts of alcoholics before and after treatment. *Journal of Clinical Psychology, 27,* 539–541.

W. F., & Alder, L. O. (1970). Aspects of alcoholic's self-concepts as measured by the Tennessee self-concept scale. *Psychological Reports, 27*, 431–434.

ve, W. M., Eckert, E. D., Heston, L., Bouchard, T. J., Segal, N., & Lykken, D. T. (1990). Heritability of substance abuse and antisocial behavior: A study of monozygotic twins reared apart. *Biological Psychiatry, 27*, 1293–1304.

Gunderson, J. G. (1978). Discriminating features of borderline patients. *American Journal of Psychiatry, 135*, 792–796.

Guy, S. M., Smith, G. M., & Bentler, P. M. (1994). The influence of adolescent substance use and socialization on deviant behavior in young adulthood. *Criminal Justice and Behavior, 21*, 236–255.

Haberman, P. W., & Baden, M. M. (1978). *Alcohol, other drugs and violent death*. New York: Oxford University Press.

Hagnell, O., Lanke, J., Rorsman, B., & Ohman, R. (1986). Predictors of alcoholism in the Lundby study-II. Personality traits as risk factors for alcoholism. *European Archives of Psychiatry and Neurological Sciences, 235*, 192–196.

Halikas, J. A., Crosby, R. D., Pearson, V. L., Nugent, S. M., & Carlson, G. A. (1994). Psychiatric comorbiditiy in treatment-seeking cocaine abusers. *American Journal on Addictions, 3*(1), 25–35.

Hallman, J., von Knorring, L., Edman, G., & Oreland, L. (1991). Personality traits and platelet monoamine oxidase activity in alcoholic women. *Addictive Behaviors, 16*(6), 533–541.

Hallman, J., von Knorring, L., & Oreland, L. (1996). Personality disorders according to DSM-III-R and thrombocyte monoamine oxidase activity in type 1 and type 2 alcoholics. *Journal of Studies on Alcohol, 57*(2), 155–161.

Halverson, C.F., Jr. (1988). Remembering your parents: Reflections on the retrospective method. *Journal of Personality, 56(2)*, 435–449.

Harford, T. C., & Parker, D. A. (1994). Antisocial behavior, family history, and alcohol dependence symptoms. *Alcoholism: Clinical and Experimental Research, 18*(2), 265–268.

Harwood, M. K., & Leonard, K. E. (1989). Family history of alcoholism, youthful antisocial behavior and problem drinking among DWI offenders. *Journal of Studies on Alcohol, 50*(3), 210–216.

Hayes, R. W., Schwarzbach, H., Schmeier, G., & Stacher, G. (1975). Hospitalized chronic alcoholic patients without field-dependent performance in the rod-and-frame test. *Journal of Psychology, 99*, 19–52.

Hennecke, L. (1984). Stimulus augmenting and field dependence in children of alcoholic fathers. *Journal of Studies on Alcohol, 45*(6), 486–492.

Herd, D. (1994). Predicting drinking problems among black and white men: Results from a national survey. *Journal of Studies on Alcohol, 55*, 61–71.

Hesselbrock, M. N. (1991). Gender comparison of antisocial personality disorder and depression in alcoholism. *Journal of Substance Abuse, 3*(2), 205–219.

Hesselbrock, V. M., Hesselbrock M. N., & Stabenau, J. R. (1985). Subtyping of alcoholism in male patients by family history and antisocial personality. *Journal of Studies on Alcohol, 49*, 89–98.

Hesselbrock, V. M., Hesselbrock, M. N., & Workman-Daniels, K. L. (1986). Effect of major depression and antisocial personality on alcoholism: Course and motivational patterns. *Journal of Studies on Alcohol, 47*(3), 207–212.

Hewett, B., & Martin, W. (1980). Psychometric comparisons of sociopathic and psychophysiological behavior of alcoholics and drug abusers versus a low drug control population. *International Journal of the Addictions, 15*, 77–105.

Hilton, M. E. (1991). Regional diversity in U.S. drinking practices. In W. B. Clark & M. E. Hilton (Eds.), *Alcohol in America: Drinking practices and problems* (chapter 17). Albany, NY: State University of New York Press.

References

Hire, J. N. (1978). Anxiety and caffeine. *Psychological Reports, 42*(3, Pt 1), 833–834.

Hoffman, H., Loper, R. G., & Kammeier, M. L. (1974). Identifying future alcoholics with MI alcoholism scales. *Quarterly Journal of Studies on Alcohol, 35*, 490–498.

Hoffman, L. W. (1991). The influence of the family environment on personality: Accounting for sibling differences. *Psychological Bulletin, 110*(2), 187–203.

Holmes, D. S. (1967). Male-female differences in MMPI ego strength: An artifact. *Journal of Consulting Psychology, 31*(4), 408–410.

Hopper, J. L., White, V. M., Macaskill, G. T., Hill, D. J., & Clifford, C. A. (1992). Alcohol use, smoking habits and the junior Eysenck personality questionnaire in adolescent Australian twins. *Acta Genet Med Gemellol, 41*, 311–324.

Howard, M. O., Kivlahan, D., & Walker, R. D. (1997). Cloninger's tridimensional theory of personality and psychopathology: Applications to substance use disorders. *Journal of Studies on Alcohol, 58*(1), 48–66.

Hoyle, R. (Ed.) (1995). *Structural equation modeling: Concepts, issues, and applications*. Thousand Oaks, CA: Sage.

Hu, L., & Bentler, P. M. (1995). Evaluating model fit. In R. Hoyle (Ed.), *Structural equation modeling: Concepts, issues, and applications* (pp. 76–99). Thousand Oaks, CA: Sage.

Hu, L., & Bentler, P. M. (in press). Fit indexes in covariance structure modeling: Sensitivity to model misspecification. *Psychological Methods*.

Hu, L., Bentler, P. M., & Kano, Y. (1992). Can test statistics in covariance structure analysis be trusted? *Psychological Bulletin, 112*(2), 351–362.

Huba, G. J., & Bentler, P. M. (1983). Test of a drug use causal model using asymptotically distribution free methods. *Journal of Drug Education, 13*(1), 3–14.

Huba, G. J., & Bentler, P. M. (1984). Causal models of personality, peer culture characteristics, drug use and criminal behaviors over a five year span. In D. W. Goodwin, K. T. Van Dusen, & S. A. Mednick (Eds.), *Longitudinal research in alcoholism* (pp. 73–94). Boston, MA: Kluwer-Nijhoff.

Huesman, L. R., & Eron, L. D. (1992). Childhood aggression and adult criminality. In McCord, J. (Ed.), *Facts, frameworks and forecasts: Advances in criminological theory* (Vol. 3, 137–156). New Brunswick, NJ: Transaction Publishers.

Hur, Y-M., McGue, M., & Iacono, W. G. (1998). The structure of self-concept in female preadolescent twins: A behavioral genetic approach. *Journal of Personality and Social Psychology, 74*(4), 1069–1077.

Hurlburt, G., Gade, E., & Fuqua, D. (1984). Personality differences between AlcoholicsAnonymous members and nonmembers. *Journal of Studies on Alcohol, 48*(2), 170–171.

Ichiyama, M. A., Zucker, R. A., Fitzgerald, H. E., & Bingham, C. R. (1996). Articulating subtype differences in self and relational experience among alcoholic men using structural analysis of social behavior. *Journal of Consulting and Clinical Psychology, 64*(6), 1245–1254.

Jacobson, G. R., Pisani, V. D., & Berenbaum, H. L. (1970). Temporal stability of field dependence among hospitalized alcoholics. *Journal of Abnormal Psychology, 76*, 10–12.

Jaffe, L. T., & Archer, R. P. (1987). The prediction of drug use among college students from MMPI, MCMI, and Sensation Seeking scales. *Journal of Personality Assessment, 51*(2), 243–253.

James, M. F., Duthie, A. M., Duffy, B. L., McKeag, A. M., & Rice, C. P. (1978). Analgesic effect of ethyl alcohol. *British Journal of Anaethesiology, 50*, 129–141.

Jamshidian, M., & Bentler, P. M. (in press). ML estimation of mean and covariance structures with missing data using complete data routines. *Journal of Educational and Behavioral Statistics*.

Jang, K. L., Livesley, W. J., & Vernon, P. A. (1995). Alcohol and drug problems: A multivariate behavioural genetic analysis of co-morbidity. *Addiction, 90*, 1213–1221.

Jellinek, E. M. (1945). The problem of alcohol. In Yale Studies on Alcohol, *Alcohol, science and society* (pp. 153–178). Westport, CT: Greenwood Press.

R. (1987). Problem-behavior theory, psychosocial development, and adolescent problem drinking. *British Journal of Addiction, 82*(4), 331–342.

..or, R., Donovan, J. E., & Costa, F. M. (1991). *Beyond adolescence: Problem behavior and young adult development.* New York: Cambridge University Press.

Jessor, R., & Jessor, S. L. (1977). Problem behavior and psychosocial development: A longitudinal study of youth. New York: Academic Press.

Johnson, J. G., Bornstein, R. F., & Sherman, M. F. (1996). A modified scoring algorithm for the PDQ-R: Psychiatric symptomology and substance use in adolescents with personality disorders. *Educational and Psychological Measurement, 56*(1), 76–89.

Johnson, R. S., Tobin, J. W., & Cellucci, T. (1992). Personality characteristics of cocaine and alcohol abusers: More alike than different. *Addictive Behaviors, 17*(2), 159–166.

Johnson, S. D., Gibson, L., & Linden, R. (1978). Alcohol and rape in Winnipeg, 1966–1975. *Journal of Studies on Alcohol, 39*(11), 1887–1894.

Jones, B. M., & Parsons, O. A. (1972). Specific versus generalized deficits of abstracting ability in chronic alcoholics. *Archives of General Psychiatry, 26*, 380–384.

Jones, M. C. (1968). Personality correlates and antecendents of drinking patterns in adult males. *Journal of Consulting and Clinical Psychology, 32*, 2–12

Kadden, R. M., Litt, M. D., Donovan, D., & Cooney, N. L. (1996). Psychometric properties of the California Psychological Inventory Socialization scale in treatment seeking alcoholics. *Psychology of Addictive Behaviors, 10*(3), 131–146.

Kaij, L. (1960). *Alcoholism in twins.* Stockholm: Almqvist &Wiksell International.

Kammeier, M. L., Hoffman, H., & Loper, R. G. (1973). Personality characteristics of alcoholics as college freshmen and at time of treatment. *Quarterly Journal of Studies on Alcohol, 34*, 390–399.

Karp, S. A., Poster, D. C., & Goodman, A. (1963). Differentiation in alcoholic women. *Journal of Personality, 31*, 386–393.

Karp, S. A., Witkin, H. A., & Goodenough, D. R. (1965). Alcoholism and psychological differentiation: Effect of alcohol on field dependence. *Journal of Abnormal Psychology, 70*, 262–265.

Keehn, J. D. (1970). Neuroticism and extraversion: Chronic alcoholics' reports on effects of drinking. *Psychological Reports, 27*, 767–770.

Kellner, F. (1997). Alcohol. In P. MacNeil & I. Webster (Eds.), Canada's Alcohol and other Drugs Survey 1994: A discussion of the findings (chapter 2). Ottawa, ON: Office of Alcohol, Drugs and Dependency Issues, Health Canada. Public Works and Government Services Canada Cat: H39-338/1-1994E.

Kendler, K. S., Heath, A. C., Neale, M. C., Kessler, R. C., & Eaves, L. J. (1992). A population-based twin study of alcoholism in women. *Journal of the American Medical Association, 268*, 1877–1882.

Khantzian, E. J. (1985). The self-medication hypothesis of addictive disorders: Focus on heroin and cocaine dependence. *American Journal of Psychiatry, 142*(11), 1259–1264.

Killen, J. D., Hayward, C., Wilson, D. M., Haydel, K. F., Robinson, T. N., Taylor, C. B., Hammer, L. D., & Varady, A. (1996). Predicting onset of drinking in a community sample of adolscents: The role of expectancy and temperament. *Addictive Behaviors, 21*(4), 473–480.

Kilpatrick, D. G., McAlhany, D. A., McCurdy, R. L., Shaw, D. L., & Roitzsch, J. C. (1982). Aging, alcoholism, anxiety, and sensation seeking: An exploratory investigation. *Addictive Behaviors, 7*, 97–100.

Kilpatrick, D. G., Sutker, P. B., & Smith, A. D. (1976). Deviant drug and alcohol use: The role of anxiety, sensation seeking, and other personality variables. In M. Zuckerman & C. D. Spielberger (Eds.), *Emotions and anxiety: New concepts, methods, and applications.* Hillsdale, NJ: Lawrence Erlbaum Associates-John Wiley.

Knop, J., Teasdale, T. W., Schulsinger, F., & Goodwin, D. W. (1985). A prospective study of young

References

men at risk for alcoholism: School behavior and achievement. *Journal of Studies on Alcohol, 51*(2), 142–147.

Knowles, E. E., & Schroeder, D. A. (1990). Personality characteristics of sons of alcohol abusers. *Journal of Studies on Alcohol, 51*(2), 142–147.

Kohn, P. M., Barnes, G. E., & Hoffman, F. M. (1979). Drug use history and experience seeking among adult male correctional offenders. *Journal of Consulting and Clinical Psychology, 47*, 708–715.

Koopmans, J. R., & Boomsma, D. I. (1996). Familial resemblances in alcohol use: Genetic or cultural transmission? *Journal of Studies on Alcohol, 57*, 19–28.

Koopmans, J. R., van Doornen, L. J. P., & Boomsma, D. I. (1997). *Alcoholism: Clinical and Experimental Research, 21*(3), 537–546.

Kristofferson, M. W. (1968). Effect of alcohol on perceptual field dependence. *Journal of Abnormal Psychology, 73*, 387–391.

Kwapil, T. R. (1996). A longitudinal study of drug and alcohol use by psychosis-prone and impulsive-nonconforming individuals. *Journal of Abnormal Psychology, 105*(1), 114–123.

Labouvie, E. W. (1987). Relation of personality to adolescent alcohol and drug use: A coping perspective. *Drug and Alcohol Abuse in Children and Adolescence, 14*, 19–24.

Labouvie, E. W., & McGee, C. (1986). Relation of personality to alcohol and drug use in adolescence. *Journal of Consulting and Clinical Psychology, 54*(3), 289–293.

Lachar, D., Berman, W., Grisell, J. L. & Schooff, K. (1976). The MacAndrew scale as a general measure of substance abuse. *Journal of Studies on Alcohol, 37*, 1609–1615.

Lafferty, P., & Kahn, M. W. (1986). Field dependence or cognitive impairment in alcoholics. *International Journal of the Addictions, 21*(11), 1221–1232.

La Grange, L., Jones, T. D., Erb, L., & Reyes, E. (1995). Alcohol consumption: Biochemical and personality correlates in a college student population. *Addictive Behaviors, 20*(1), 93–103.

Lamborn, S. D., Mounts, N. S., Steinberg, L., & Dornbusch, S. M. (1991). Patterns of competence and adjustment among adolescents from authoritative, authoritarian, indulgent, and neglectful families. *Child Development, 62*, 1049–1065.

Lawford, B. R., Young, R. M., Rowell, J. A., Gibson, J. N., Feeney, G. F. X., Ritchie, T. L., Syndulko, K., & Noble, E. P. (1997). Association of the D2 dopamine receptor A1 allele with alcoholism: Medical severity of alcoholism and type of controls. *Biological Psychiatry, 41*, 386–393.

Leonard, K. E., & Blane, H. T. (1988). Alcohol expectancies and personality characteristics in young men. *Addictive Behaviors, 13*, 353–357.

Lerner, J. V., & Vicary, J. R. (1984). Difficult temperament and drug use: Analyses from the New York longitudinal study. *Journal of Drug Education, 14*(1), 1–7.

Levenson, R. W., Oyama, O. N., & Meek, P. S. (1987). Greater reinforcement from alcohol for those at risk: Parental risk, personality risk, and sex. *Journal of Abnormal Psychology, 96*(3), 242–253.

Lewis, C. E., Dustman, R. E., & Beck, E. C. (1970). The effects of alcohol on visual and somatosensory evoked responses. *Electroencephalography and Clinical Neurophysiology, 28*, 202–205.

Lewis, C. E., Rice, J., & Helzer, J. E. (1983). Diagnostic interactions: Alcoholism and antisocial personality. *Journal of Nervous and Mental Disease, 171*, 105–113.

Limson, R., Goldman, D., Roy, A., & Lamparski, D. (1991). Personality and cerebrospinal fluid monoamine metabolites in alcoholics and controls. *Archives of General Psychiatry, 48*(5), 437–441.

Liskow, B., Powell, B. J., Nickel, E. J., & Penick, E. (1991). Antisocial alcoholics: Are there clinically significant diagnostic subtypes? *Journal of Studies on Alcohol, 52*(1), 62–69.

Little, G. L., & Robinson, K. D. (1989). Relationship of DUI recidivism to moral reasoning, sensation seeking, and MacAndrew alcoholism scores. *Psychological Reports, 65*, 1171–1174.

ɔdhi, P. H., & Thakur, S. (1993). Personality of drug addicts: Eysenckian analysis. *Personality and Individual Differences, 15*(2), 121–128.

Longabaugh, R., Rubin, A., Malloy, P., Beattie, M., Clifford, P. R., & Noel, N. (1994). Drinking outcomes of alcohol abusers diagnosed as antisocial personality disorder. *Alcoholism: Clinical and Experimental Research, 18*(4), 778–785.

Loper, R. G., Kammeier, M. L., & Hoffmann, H. (1973). MMPI characteristics of college freshmen males who later become alcoholics. *Journal of Abnormal Psychology, 82,* 159–162.

Ludwig, A. M., Bendfeldt, F., Wikler, A., & Cain, R. B. (1978). Loss of control in alcoholics. *Archives of General Psychiatry, 35,* 370–373.

Ludwig, A. M., Cain, R. B., & Wikler, A. (1977). Stimulus intensity modulation and alcohol consumption. *Journal of Studies on Alcohol, 38,* 2049–2056.

Lukas, J. H. (1987). Visual evoked potential augmenting-reducing and personality: The vertex augmenter is a sensation seeker. *Personality and Individual Differences, 8*(3), 385–395.

Lundin, R. W., & Sawyer, C. R. (1965). The relationship between test anxiety, drinking patterns and scholastic achievement in a group of undergraduate college men. *Journal of General Psychology, 73,* 143–146.

Lundy, C. (1987). Sex-role conflict in female alcoholics: A critical review of the literature. *Alcoholism Treatment Quarterly, 4*(1), 69–78.

MacAndrew, C. (1965). The differentiation of male alcoholic outpatients from nonalcoholic psychiatric outpatients by means of the MMPI. *Quarterly Journal of Studies on Alcohol, 26,* 238–246.

MacAndrew, C. (1979). Evidence for the presence of two fundamentally different, age independent characterological types within unselected runs of male alcohol and drug abusers. *American Journal of Drug and Alcohol Abuse, 6,* 207–221.

MacAndrew, C. (1980). Male alcoholics, secondary psychopathy and Eysenck's theory of personality. *Personality and Individual Differences, 1,* 151–160.

MacAndrew, C. (1981). What the Mac scale tells us about men alcoholics: An interpretive review. *Journal of Studies on Alcohol, 42,* 604–625.

MacAndrew, C. (1983). Alcoholic personality or personalities: Scale and profile data from the MMPI. In W. M. Cox (Ed.), *Identifying and measuring alcoholic personality characteristics* (pp. 73–85). New Directions for Methodology of Social and Behavioral Sciences, no. 16. San Francisco: Jossey-Bass.

Macaskill, G. T., Hopper, J. L., White, V., & Hill, D. J. (1994). Genetic and environmental variation in Eysenck personality questionnaire scales measured on Australian adolescent twins. *Behavior Genetics, 24*(6), 481–491.

Maccoby, E., & Martin, J. (1983). Socialization in the context of the family: Parent-child interaction. In E. M. Hetherington (Ed.), P. H. Mussen (Series Ed.), *Handbook of child psychology: Vol. 4. socialization, personality, and social development* (pp. 1–101). New York: Wiley.

Malatesta, V. J., Sutker, P. B., & Treiber, F. A. (1981). Sensation seeking and chronic public drunkenness. *Journal of Consulting and Clinical Psychology, 49*(2), 292–294.

Marsh, D. T., Stile, S. A., Stoughton, N. L., & Trout-Landen, B. L. (1988). Psychopathology of opiate addiction: Comparative data from the MMPI and MCMI. *American Journal of Drug and Alcohol Abuse, 14*(1), 17–27.

Marsh, H. (1998). Pairwise deletion for missing data in structural equation models: Nonpositive definite matrices, parameter estimates, goodness of fit, and adjusted sample size. *Structural Equation Modeling, 5*(1), 22–36.

Martin, R. L., Cloninger, R. C., & Guze, S. B. (1982). Alcoholism and female criminality. *Journal of Clinical Psychiatry, 43*(10), 400–403.

Martin, E. D., & Sher, K. J. (1994). Family history of alcoholism, alcohol use disorders and the five-factor model of personality. *Journal of Studies on Alcohol, 55*(1), 81–90.

References

Martsh, C. T., & Miller, W. R. (1997). Extraversion predicts heavy drinking in college studen. *Personality and Individual Differences, 23*(1), 153–155.

Marvel, G. A., & Hartmann, B. R. (1986). An "economic" theory of addiction, hypomania, and sensation seeking. *International Journal of the Addictions, 21*(4&5), 495–508.

Masse, L. C., & Tremblay, R. E. (1997). Behavior of boys in kindergarten and the onset of substance use during adolescence. *Archives of Genetic Psychiatry, 54*, 62–68.

Massey, R. F., Walfish, S., & Krone, A. (1992). Cluster analysis of MMPI profiles of adolescents in treatment for substance abuse. *Journal of Adolescent Chemical Dependency, 2*(2), 23–33.

Matano, R. A., Locke, K. D., & Schwartz, K. (1994). MCMI personality subtypes for male and female alcoholics. *Journal of Personality Assessment, 63*(2), 250–264.

Mayer, J. E. (1988). The personality characteristics of adolescents who use and misuse alcohol. *Adolescence, 23*(90), 383–404.

Mayfield, D., McLeod, G., & Hall, P. (1974). The CAGE questionnaire: Validation of a new alcoholism screening instrument. *American Journal of Psychiatry, 13*(10), 1121–1123.

McCord, J. (1972). Etiological factors in alcoholism, family and personal characteristics. *Quarterly Journal of Studies on Alcohol, 33*, 477–486 or 1020–1027.

McCord, J. (1979). Some child-rearing antecedents of criminal behavior in adult men. *Journal of Personality and Social Psychology, 37*(9), 1477–1486.

McCord, J. (1988). Identifying developmental paradigms leading to alcoholism. *Journal of Studies on Alcoholism, 49*, 357–362.

McCormick, R. A., & Smith, M. (1995). Aggression and hostility in substance abusers: The relationship to abuse patterns, coping style, and relapse triggers. *Addictive Behaviors, 20*(5), 555–562.

McCrae, R. R., & Costa, P. T. (1984). *Emerging lives, enduring dispositions: Personality in adulthood.* Boston: Little, Brown.

McCrae, R. R., & Costa, P. T., Jr. (1985a). Comparison of EPI and psychoticism scales with measures of the five factor model of personality. *Personality and Individual Differences, 6*, 587–597.

McCrae, R. R., & Costa, P. T., Jr. (1985b). Openness to experience. In R. Hogan & W. H. Jones (Eds.), *Perspectives in personality* (Vol. 1, pp. 145–172). Greenwich, CT: JAI Press.

McCrae, R. R., & Costa, P. T., Jr. (1987). Validation of the five factor model of personality across instruments and observers. *Journal of Personality and Social Psychology, 52*, 81–90.

McCrae, R. R., & Costa, P. T., Jr. (1988). Recalled parent-child relations and adult personality. *Journal of Personality, 56*(2), 417–433.

McCrae, R. R., & Costa, P. T., Jr. (1989). The structure of interpersonal traits: Wiggins's circumplex and the five-factor model. *Journal of Personality and Social Psychology, 56*(4), 586–595.

McCrae, R. R., & Costa, P. T. (1991). The NEO Personality Inventory: Using the Five-Factor Model in counseling. *Journal of Counseling and Development, 69*(4), 367–372.

McGee, L., & Newcomb, M. D. (1992). General deviance syndrome: Expanded hierarchical evaluations at four ages from early adolescence to adulthood. *Journal of Consulting and Cliical Psychology, 60*, 766–776.

McGue, M., & Bouchard, T. J. (1998). Genetic and environmental influences on human behavioral differences. *Annual Review of Neuroscience, 21*, 1–24.

McGue, M., Sharma, A., & Benson, P. (1996). Parent and sibling influences on adolescent alcohol use and misuse: Evidence from a U.S. adoption cohort. *Journal of Studies on Alcohol, 57*(1), 8–18.

McMahon, R. C., & Davidson, R. S. (1986). An examination of depressed versus non-depressed alcoholics in inpatient treatment. *Journal of Clinical Psychology, 42*, 177–184.

Melby, J. N., Conger, R. O., Conger, K. J., & Lorenz, F. O. (1993). Effects of parental behavior on tobacco use by young male adolescents. *Journal of Marriage and the Family, 55*, 439–454.

ﾍdelson, W., Johnson, N., & Stewart, M. (1971). Hyperactive children as teenagers: A follow-up study. *Journal of Nervous and Mental Disease, 153*, 273–279.

Miller, D., & Blum, K. (1996). *Overload: Attention deficit disorder and the addictive brain.* Kansas City: Andrews and McMeel.

Miller, N. S., Guttman, J. C., & Chawla, S. (1997). Integration of generalized vulnerability to drug and alcohol addiction. *Journal of Addictive Diseases, 16*(4), 7–22.

Miller, P. M., Hersen, M, Eisler, R. M., & Hilsman, G. (1974). Effects of social stress on operant drinking of alcoholics and social drinkers. *Behavior Research and Therapy, 12*, 67–72.

Miller, W. R., & Hester, R. K. (1986). Matching problem drinkers with optimal treatments. In W. E. Miller & N. Heather (Eds.), *Treating addictive behaviors: Processes of change.* New York: Plenum Publishing.

Milligan, G. W., & Cooper, M. C. (1985). An examination of procedures for determining the number of clusters in a data set. *Psychometrika, 50*(2), 159–179.

Mintz, J., O'Brien, C. P., Woody, G., & Beck, A. T. (1979). Depression in treated narcotic addicts, ex-addicts, non-addicts and suicide attempters: Validation of a very brief depression scale. *American Journal of Drug and Alcohol Abuse, 6*, 385–396.

Moore, R. H. (1984). Construct validity of the MacAndrew scale: Secondary psychopathic and dysthymic-neurotic character orientations among adolescent male misdemeanor offenders. *Journal of Studies of Alcohol, 46*(2), 128–131.

Moos, R. H., & Billings, A. G. (1982). Children of alcoholics during the recovery process. *Addictive Behaviors, 7*, 155–163.

Moos, R. H., & Moos, B. S. (1986). *Manual: Family Environment Scale.* Palo Alto, CA: Consulting Psychologists Press.

Morey, L. C. (1991). *Personality assessment inventory.* Odessa, FL: Psychological Assessment Resources.

Morrison, J. R., & Stewart, M. A. (1971). A family study of the hyperactive child syndrome. *Biological Psychiatry, 3*, 189–195.

Mueller, R. O. (1996). *Basic principles of structural equation modeling.* New York: Springer Verlag.

Mullaney, J. A., & Trippett, C. J. (1979). Alcohol dependence and phobias: Clinical description and relevance. *British Journal of Psychiatry, 135*, 565–573.

Murray, R. M., Clifford, C. A., & Gurling, H. M. D. (1983). Twin and adoption studies: How good is the evidence for a genetic role? In M. Galanter (Ed.), *Recent developments in alcoholism,* (Vol. 1, pp. 25–48). New York: Plenum Publishing.

Murray, R. M., Gurling, H. M. D., Bernadt, M., Ewusi-Mensah, I., Saunders, J. D., & Clifford, C. A. (1984). Do personality and psychiatric disorders predispose to alcoholism? In G. Edwards & J. Littlejohn (Eds.), *Pharmacological treatments for alcoholism.* New York: Methuen.

Murray, R. P., Barnes, G. E., & Patton, D. (1994). The relative performance of diverse measures of alcohol abuse and dependence in a community sample. *Journal of Studies on Alcohol, 55*(1), 72–80.

Musgrave-Marquart, D., Bromley, S. P., & Dalley, M. B. (1997). Personality, academic attribution, and substance use as predictors of academic achievement in college students. *Journal of Social Behavior and Personality, 12*(2), 501–511.

Nace, E. P., Saxon, J. J., & Shore, N. (1986). Borderline personality disorder and alcoholism treatment: A one-year follow-up study. *Journal of Studies on Alcohol, 47*, 196–200.

Nathan, P. E. (1988). The addictive personality is the behavior of the addict. *Journal of Consulting and Clinical Psychology, 56*, 183–189.

Nerviano, V. J. (1976). Common personality patterns among alcoholic males: A multivariate study. *Journal of Consulting and Clinical Psychology, 44*, 104–110.

Nestadt, G., Romanoski, A. J., Samuels, J. F., Folstein, M. F., & McHugh, P. R. (1992). The relationship between personality and DSM-III Axis I disorders in the population: Results from an epidemiological survey. *The American Journal of Psychiatry, 149*, 1228–1233.

Newcomb, M. D. (1990). Social support and personal characteristics: A developmental and inter-actional perspective. *Journal of Social and Clinical Psychology, 9*, 54–68.

Newcomb, M. D. (1996). Pseudomaturity among adolescents: Construct validation, sex differences, and associations in adulthood. *Journal of Drug Issues, 26*, 477–504.

Newcomb, M. D., & Bentler, P. M. (1988a). The impact of family context, deviant attitudes, and emotional distress in adolescent drug use: Longitudinal latent-variable analyses of mothers and their children. *Journal of Research in Personality, 22*, 154–176.

Newcomb, M. D., & Bentler, P. M. (1988b). Impact of adolescent drug use and social support on problems of young adults: A longitudinal study. *Journal of Abnormal Psychology, 97*, 64–75.

Newcomb, M. D., & Bentler, P. M. (1988). *Consequences of adolescent drug use.* Newbury Park, CA: Sage.

Newcomb, M. D., & Felix-Ortiz, M. (1992). Multiple protective and risk factors for drug use and abuse: Cross-sectional and prospective findings. *Journal of Personality and Social Psychology, 63*, 280–296.

Newcomb, M. D., Maddahian, E., & Bentler, P. M. (1986). Risk factors for drug use among adolescents: Concurrent and longitudinal analyses. *American Journal of Public Health, 76*, 525–531.

Newcomb, M. D., & McGee, L. (1991). Influence of sensation seeking on general deviance and specific problem behaviors from adolescence to young adulthood. *Journal of Personality and Social Psychology, 61*(4), 614–628.

Newcomb, M. D., & Rickards, S. (1995). Parent drug-use problems and adult intimate relationships: Associations among community samples of young adult women and men. *Journal of Counselling Psychology, 42*, 141–154.

Newcomb, M. D., Scheier, L., & Bentler, P. M. (1993). Effects of adolescent drug use on adult mental health: A prospective study of a community sample. *Experimental and Clinical Psychopharmacology, 1*, 215–241.

Noble, E. P. (1996). The gene that rewards alcoholism. *Scientific American, March/April*, 52–61.

Noble, E. P., Blum, K., Khalsa, M. E., Ritchie, T., Montgomery, A., Wood, R. C., Fitch, R. J., Ozkaragoz, T., Sheridan, P. J., Anglin, M. D., Paredes, A., Treiman, L. J., & Sparkes, R. S. (1993). Allelic association of the D2 dopamine receptor gene with cocaine dependence. *Drug and Alcohol Dependence, 33*, 271–285.

Noble, E. P., Blum, K., Ritchie, T., Montgomery, A., & Sheridan, P. J. (1991). Allelic association of the D2 dopamine receptor gene with receptor binding characteristics in alcoholism. *Archives of General Psychiatry, 48*, 648–654.

Noble, E. P., Ozkaragoz, T. Z., Ritchie, T. L., Zhang, X., Belin, T. R., & Sparkes, R. S. (in press). D2 and D4 dopamine receptor polymorphisms and personality. *American Journal of Medical Genetics.*

Noble, E. P., St. Jeor, S. T., Ritchie, T., Syndulko, K., St. Jeor, S. C., Fitch, R. J., Brunner, R. L., & Sparkes, R. S. (1994). D2 dopamine receptor gene and cigarette smoking: A reward gene? *Medical Hypotheses, 42*, 257–260.

Noller, P., Law, H., & Comrey, A. L. (1987). Cattell, Comrey, and Eysenck personality factors compared: More evidence for the five robust factors? *Journal of Personality and Social Psychology, 53*, 755–782.

Norton, G. R., Malan, J., Cairns, S. L., Wozney, K. A., & Broughton, R. (1989). Factors influencing drinking behavior in alcoholic panickers and non-panickers. *Behavior, Research and Therapy, 27*, 167–171.

Norusis, M. J. (1993). *SPSS for Windows: Professional statistics. Release 6.0.* Chicago, IL: SPSS Inc.

Nurnberg, H. G., Rifkin, A., & Doddi, S. (1993). A systematic assessment of the comorbidity of DSM-III-R personality disorders in alcoholic outpatients. *Comprehensive Psychiatry, 34*, 447–454.

O'Boyle, M. (1993). Personality disorder and multiple substance dependence. *Journal of Personality Disorders, 7*(4), 342–347.

O'Connor, L. E., Berry, J. W., Morrison, A., & Brown, S. (1995). The drug-of-choice phenomenon: Psychological differences among drug users who preferred different drugs. *The International Journal of the Addictions, 30*(5), 541–555.

Ogden, M. E., Dundas, M., & Bhat, A. V. (1989). Personality differences among alcohol misusers in community treatment. *Personality and Individual Differences, 10*(2), 265–267.

O'Gorman, P. A. (1975). Self-concept, locus of control, and perception of father in adolescents from homes with and without severe drinking problems. Doctoral dissertation, Fordham University.

Olson, D. H. (1986). Circumplex model VII: Validation studies and FACES III. *Family Process, 25*, 337–351.

Olson, D. H., & Tiesel, J. (1991). *FACES II: Linear scoring and interpretation*. St. Paul, MN: University of Minnesota.

Orford, J., Waller, S., & Peto, J. (1974). Drinking behavior and attitudes and their correlates among university students in England. *Quarterly Journal of Studies on Alcohol, 35*, 1316–1374.

Parker, F. B. (1959). A comparison of the sex temperament of alcoholics and moderate drinkers. *American Sociological Review, 24*, 366–374.

Parker, F. B. (1969). Self-role strain and drinking disposition at a pre-alcoholic age level. *The Journal of Social Psychology, 78*, 55–61.

Parker, F. B. (1972). Sex-role adjustment in alcoholic women. *Quarterly Journal of Studies in Alcohol, 33*, 647–657.

Parker, F. B. (1975). Sex-role adjustment and drinking disposition of women college students. *Quarterly Journal of Studies on Alcohol, 36*, 1570–1573.

Parker, G. (1979). Parental characteristics in relation to depressive disorders. *British Journal of Psychiatry, 134*, 138–147.

Parker, G., Tupling, H., & Brown, L. B. (1979). A parental boding instrument. *British Journal of Medical Psychology, 52*, 1–10.

Parsons, T. (1955). Family structure and the socialization of the child. In T. Parsons & R. F. Bales, *Family, socialization and interaction processes* (pp. 35–131). New York: Free Press.

Patterson, G. R., DeBaryshe, B. D., & Ramsey, E. (1989). A developmental perspective on antisocial behavior. *American Psychologist, 44*(2), 329–335.

Patton, D., Barnes, G. E., & Murray, R. P. (1993). Personality characteristics of smokers and ex-smokers. *Personality and Individual Differences, 15*(6), 653–654.

Patton, D., Barnes, G. E., & Murray, R. P. (1994). *Types of alcoholics in the general population*. Presented at the 55th Annual Convention of the Canadian Psychological Association, Penticton, British Columbia.

Pedersen, W. (1991). Mental health, sensation seeking and drug use patterns: A longitudinal study. *British Journal of Addiction, 86*, 195–204.

Penick, E. C., Powell, B. J., Liskow, B. I., Jackson, J. O., & Nickel, E. J. (1988). The stability of coexisting psychiatric syndromes in alcoholic men after one year. *Journal of Studies on Alcohol, 49*(5), 395–404.

Penk, W. E., Charles, H. L., Patterson, E. T., Roberts, W. R., Dolan, M. P., & Brown, A. S. (1982). Chronological age differences in MMPI scores of male chronic alcoholics seeking treatment. *Journal of Consulting and Clinical Psychology, 50*, 322–324.

Pérusse, D., Neale, M. C., Heath, A. C., & Eaves, L. J. (1994). Human parental behavior: Evidence for genetic influence and potential implication for gene-culture transmission. *Behavior Genetics, 24*(4), 327–335.

Peterson, J. B., Weiner, D., Pihl, R. O., & Finn, P. R. (1991). The Tridimensional Personality Questionnaire and the inherited risk for alcoholism. *Addictive Behaviors, 16*(6), 549–554.

Petrie, A. (1967). *Individuality in pain and suffering.* Chicago: University of Chicago Press.

Pickens, R. W., Svikis, D. S., McGue, M., Lykken, D. T., Heston, L. L., & Clayton, P. J. (1991). Heterogeneity in the inheritance of alcoholism: A study of male and female twins. *Archives of General Psychiatry, 48,* 19–28.

Pihl, R. O., Peterson, J., & Finn, P. (1990). Inherited predisposition of alcoholism: Characteristics of sons of male alcoholics. *Journal of Abnormal Psychology, 99,* 291–301.

Pihl, R. O., & Spiers, P. (1978). Individual characteristics in the etiology of drug abuse. *Progress in Experimental Personality Research, 8,* 93–105.

Pisani, V. D., Jacobson, G. R., & Berenbaum, H. L. (1973). Field dependence and organic brain deficit in chronic alcoholics. *International Journal of the Addictions, 8,* 559–564.

Pokorny, A. D., Miller, B. A., & Kaplin, H. B. (1972). The brief MAST: A shortened version of the Michigan alcoholism screening test. *American Journal of Psychiatry, 129,* 342–345.

Poldrugo, F., & Forti, B. (1988). Personality disorders and alcoholism treatment outcome. *Drug and Alcohol Dependence, 21,* 171–176.

Powell, B. J., Penick, E. C., Nickel, E. J., Liskow, B. I., Riesenmy, K. D., Campion, S. L., & Brown, E. F. (1992). Outcomes of co-morbid alcoholic men: A 1-year follow-up. *Alcoholism: Clinical and Experimental Research, 16,* 131–138.

Powell, B. J., Penick, E. C., Othmer, E., Bingman, S. F., & Rice, A. S. (1982). Prevalence of additional psychiatric syndromes among male alcoholics. *Journal of Clinical Psychiatry, 43*(10), 404–407.

Prescott, C. A., Hewitt, J. K., Heath, A. C., Truett, K. R., Neale, M. C., & Eaves, L. J. (1994). Environmental and genetic influences on alcohol use in a volunteer sample of older twins. *Journal of Studies on Alcohol, 55,* 18–33.

Prescott, C. A., Neale, M. C., Corey, L. A., & Kendler, K. S. (1997). Predictors of problem drinking and alcohol dependence in a population-based sample of female twins. *Journal of Studies on Alcohol, 58*(2), 167–181.

Pulkkinen, L., & Pitkanen, T. (1994). A prospective study of the precursor to problem drinking in young adulthood. *Journal of Studies on Alcohol, 55*(5), 578–587.

Quinton, D., & Rutter, M. (1984). Parents with children in care: I. Current circumstances and parenting. *Journal of Child Psychology and Psychiatry, 25,* 211–229.

Quirk, S., McCormick, R., & Zegarra, J. (1996). Personality, coping styles and pattern of substance abuse. Presented at the 104th Annual Convention of the American Psychological Association, Toronto, Canada.

Quitkin, F. M., & Rabkin, J. G. (1982). Hidden psychiatric diagnosis in the alcoholic. In Soloman, J. (Ed.), *Alcoholism and clinical psychiatry.* New York: Plenum Publishing.

Raistick, D., Dunbar, G., & Davidson, R. (1983). Development of a questionnaire to measure alcohol dependence. *British Journal of Addiction, 78,* 89–95.

Rankin, H., Stockwell, T., & Hodgson, R. (1982). Personality and alcohol dependence. *Personality and Individual Differences, 3,* 145–151.

Rathus, S., Fox, J., & Ortins, J. (1980). The MacAndrew Scale as a measure of substance abuse and delinquency among adolescents. *Journal of Clinical Psychology, 36,* 579–583.

Ratliff, K. G., & Burkhart, B. R. (1984). Sex differences in motivations for and effects of drinking among college students. *Journal of Studies on Alcohol, 45,* 26–32.

Rearden, J. J., & Markwell, B. S. (1989). Self-concept and drinking problems of college students raised in alcohol-abused homes. *Addictive Behaviors, 14,* 225–227.

Regier, D. A., Farmer, M. E., Rae, D. S., Locke, B. Z., Keith, S. J., Judd, L. L., & Goodwin, F. K. (1990). Comorbidity of mental disorders with alcohol and other drug abuse. *Journal of the American Medical Association, 264,* 2511–2518.

Reich, J., & Chaudry, D. (1987). Personality of panic disorder alcohol abusers. *The Journal of Nervous and Mental Disease, 175*(4), 224–228.

Reiss, D. (1995). Genetic influence on family systems: Implications for development. *Journal of Marriage and the Family, 57*(Aug.), 543–560.

Rhodes, R. J., Carr, J. E., & Jurji, E. D. (1968). Interpersonal differentiation. *Perceptual and Motor Skills, 27*, 172–174.

Richman, J. A., & Flaherty, J. A. (1990). Alcohol-related problems of future physicians prior to medical training. *Journal of Studies of Alcohol, 51*(4), 296–300.

Robertson, E. D., Fournet, G. P., Zelhart, P. F., & Estes, R. E. (1987). Relationship of field dependence/independence to adaption-innovation in alcoholics. *Perceptual and Motor Skills, 65*, 771–776.

Robins, L. N. (1966). *Deviant children grow up: A sociological and psychiatric study of sociopathic personality.* Baltimore: Williams and Witkins.

Robins, L. N., Bates, W. M., & O'Neal, P. (1962). Adult drinking patterns of former problem children. In D. J. Pittman & D. R. Snyder (Eds.), *Society, culture and drinking patterns* (pp. 395–412). New York: Wiley

Robins, L. N., Helzer, J., Cottler, L., & Goldring, E. (1989). *NIMH Diagnostic Interview Schedule: Version III Revised (DIS-III-R).* St. Louis, MO: Washington University.

Robyak, J. E., Floyd, D. R., & Donham, G. W. (1982). *A comparison of the personality characteristics and patterns of alcohol abuse among continuous and binge alcoholics.* Unpublished manuscript, Bay Pines VA Medical Center.

Romanov, K., Kaprio, J., Rose, R. J., & Koskenvuo, M. (1991). Genetics of alcoholism: Effects of migration on concordance rates among male twins. *Alcohol and Alcoholism,* (Supplement #1), 137–140.

Room, R. (1972). Drinking patterns in large U.S. cities: A comparison of San Francisco and national samples. *Quarterly Journal of Studies on Alcohol, Supplement No. 6*, 28–57.

Rosenberg, C. M. (1969). Young alcoholics. *British Journal of Psychiatry, 115*, 181–188.

Rosenberg, M. (1965). *Society and the adolescent self-image.* Princeton: Princeton University Press.

Rosenthal, R. (1984). *Meta-analytic procedures for social research.* Beverly Hills, CA: Sage.

Rosenthal, T. L., Edwards, N. B., Ackerman, B. J., Knott, D. H., & Rosenthal, R. H. (1990). Substance abuse patterns reveal contrasting personal traits. *Journal of Substance Abuse, 2*, 255–263.

Ross, C. F. J. (1971). Comparison of hospital and prison alcoholics. *British Journal of Psychiatry, 118*, 75–78.

Ross, H. E., Glaser, F. B., & Germanson, T. (1988). The prevalence of psychiatric disorders in patients with alcohol and other drug problems. *Archives of General Psychiatry, 45*, 1023–1031.

Ross, H. E., Glaser, F. B., & Stiasny, S. (1988). Sex differences in the prevalence of psychiatric disorders in patients with alcohol and drug problems. *British Journal of Addiction, 83*, 1179–1192.

Ross, S. M. (1973). Fear, reinforcing activities and degree of alcoholism: A correlational analysis. *Quarterly Journal of Studies on Alcohol, 34*, 823–828.

Rounsaville, B. J., & Anton, S. F. (1991). Psychiatric diagnoses of treatment-seeking cocaine abusers. *Archives of General Psychiatry, 48*(1), 43–51.

Rounsaville, B. J., Dolinski, Z. S., Babor, T. F., & Meyer, R. E. (1987). Psychopathology as a predictor of treatment outcome in alcoholics. *Archives of General Psychiatry, 44*, 505–513.

Rowe, D. C. (1994). *The limits of family influence: Genes, experience and behavior.* New York: Guilford.

Rushton, J. P., Brainerd, C. J., & Pressley, M. (1983). Behavioral development and construct validity: The principle of aggregation. *Psychological Bulletin, 94*, 18–38.

Rydelius, P. A. (1981). Children of alcoholic fathers: A longitudinal prospective study (Sweden). In S. A. Mednick & A. F. Baert (Eds.), *Prospective longitudinal research: An empirical basis for the primary prevention of psychosocial disorders* (pp. 296–297). New York: Oxford University Press.

Rydelius, P. A. (1983a) Alcohol abusing teenage boys: Testing a hypothesis on the relationship between alcohol abuse and social background factors, criminality and personality in teenage boys. *Acta Psychiatrica Scandinavica, 68*, 368–380.

Rydelius, P. A. (1983b). Alcohol abusing teenage boys: Testing a hypothesis on alcohol abuse and personality factors using a personality inventory. *Acta Psychiatrica Scandinavica, 68*, 381–35.

Sadava, S. W. (1987). Psychosocial interactionism and substance abuse. *Drugs and Society, 2*(1), 1–30.

Salamy, A., & Williams, H. L. (1973). The effects of alcohol on sensory evoked and spontaneous cerebral potentials in man. *Electroencephalography and Clinical Neurophysiology, 35*, 3–11.

Sales, S. M. (1971). Need for stimulation as a factor in social behavior. *Journal of Personality and Social Behavior, 19*, 124–134.

Sandahl, C., Lindberg, S., & Bergman, H. (1987). The relation between drinking habits and neuroticism and weak ego among male and female alcoholic patients. *Acta Psychiatrica Scandinavica, 75*, 500–508.

Satorra, A., & Bentler, P. M. (1994). Corrections to test statistics and standard errors in covariance structure analysis. In A. von Eye & C. C. Clogg (Eds.), *Latent variables analysis: Applications for developmental research* (pp. 399–419). Thousand Oaks, CA: Sage.

Saunders, G. R., & Schuckit, M. A. (1981). MMPI scores in young men with alcoholic relatives and controls. *The Journal of Nervous and Mental Disease, 169*, 456–458.

Scarr, S., Webber, P. L., Weinberg, R. A., & Wittig, M. A. (1981). Personality resemblance among adolescents and their parents in biologically related and adoptive families. *Journal of Personality and Social Psychology, 40*(5), 885–898.

Schafer, J. L. (1997). *Analysis of incomplete multivariate data.* London: Chapman & Hall.

Scheier, L. M., Botvin, G. J., & Baker, E. (1997). Risk and protective factors as predictors of adolescent alcohol involvement and transitions in alcohol use: A prospective analysis. *Journal of Studies on Alcohol, 58*(6), 652–667.

Schiavi, R. C. (1990). Chronic alcoholism and male sexual dysfunction. *Journal of Sex and Marital Therapy, 16*(1), 23–33.

Schinka, J. A. (1995). PAI profiles in alcohol-dependent patients. *Journal of Personality Assessment, 65*(1), 35–51.

Schinka, J. A., Curtiss, G., & Mulloy, J. M. (1994). Personality variables and self-medication in substance abuse. *Journal of Personality Assessment, 63*(3), 413–422.

Schneier, F. R., Martin, L. Y., Liebowitz, M. R., Gorman, J. M., & Fyer, A. J. (1989). Alcohol abuse in social phobia. *Journal of Anxiety Disorders, 3*, 15–23.

Schumacker, R. E., & Lomax, R. G. (1996). *A beginner's guide to structural equation modeling.* Mahway, NJ: Erlbaum.

Schuckit, M. A. (1987). Biological vulnerability to alcoholism. *Journal of Consulting and Clinical Psychology, 55*, 301–309.

Schuckit, M. A., Engstrom, D., Alpert, R., & Duby, J. (1981). Differences in muscle tension response to ethanol in young men with and without family histories of alcoholism. *Journal of Studies on Alcohol, 42*, 918–924.

Schuckit, M. A., Hesselbrock, V. M., Tipp, J., Nurnberger, J. I., Anthenelli, R. M., & Crowe, R. R. (1995). The prevalence of major anxiety disorders in relatives of alcohol dependent men and women. *Journal of Studies on Alcohol, 56*, 309–317.

Schuckit, M. A., Irwin, M., & Brown, S. A. (1990). The history of anxiety symptoms among 171 primary alcoholics. *Journal of Studies on Alcohol, 51*(1), 34–41.

Schuckit, M. A., Irwin, M., & Mahler, H. I. M. (1990). Tridimensional personality questionnaire scores of sons of alcoholics and nonalcoholics. *American Journal of Psychiatry, 147*(4), 481–487.

Schucket, M. A., Klein, J., Twitchell, G., & Smith, T. L. (1994). Personality test scores as predictors of alcoholism almost a decade later. *American Journal of Psychiatry, 151*(7), 1038–1042.

Schuckit, M. A., & Penn, N. E (1985). Performance on the rod and frame test for men at elevated risk for alcoholism and controls: A pilot study. *American Journal of Drug and Alcohol Abuse, 11*, 113–118.

Schumacker, R. E., & Lomax, R. G. (1996). *A beginner's guide to structural equation modeling.* Mahwah, NJ: Erlbaum.

Schwartz, M. F., & Graham, J. R. (1979). Construct validity of the MacAndrew scale. *Journal of Consulting and Clinical Psychology, 47*, 1090–1095.

Scida, J., & Vannicelli, M. (1978). Sex-role conflict and women's drinking. *Journal of Studies on Alcohol, 40*, 28–44.

Selzer, M. L., Vinokur, A., & van Rooijen, L. (1975). A self-administered Short Michigan Alcoholism Screening Test (SMAST). *Journal of Studies on Alcohol, 36*, 117–126.

Shaw, D. M., MacSweeney, D. A., Johnson, A. L., & Merry, J. (1975). Personality characteristics of alcoholic and depressed patients. *British Journal of Psychiatry, 126*, 56–59.

Shaw, J. A., Donley, P., Morgan, D. W., & Robinson, J. A. (1975). Treatment of depression in alcoholics. *American Journal of Psychiatry, 132*, 641–644.

Sheckter, M. E., & Scott, D. A. (1998, June). Cluster analysis in alcoholic personality research: Time for a reassessment? Poster session presented at the Canadian Psychological Association Convention, Edmonton, AB, Canada.

Shedler, J., & Block, J. (1990). Adolescent drug use and psychological health. *American Psychologist, 45*, 612–630.

Sheppard, D., Smith, G. T., & Rosenbaum, G. (1988). Use of MMPI subtypes in predicting completion of a residential alcoholism treatment program. *Journal of Consulting and Clinical Psychology, 56*, 590–596.

Sher, K .J. (1987). Stress response dampening. In H. T. Blane & K. E. Leonard (Eds.), *Psychological theories of drinking and alcoholism* (pp. 227–271). New York: Guilford.

Sher, K. J., Bylund, D. B., Walitzer, K. S., Hartmann, J., & Ray-Prenger, C. (1994). Platelet Monoamine Oxidase (MAO) activity: Personality, substance use and the stress-response-dampening effect of alcohol. *Experimental and Clinical Psychopharmacology, 2*(1), 53–81.

Sher, K. J., & Levenson, R. W. (1982). Risk for alcoholism and individual differences in the stress-response-dampening effect of alcohol. *Journal of Abnormal Psychology, 91*(5), 350–367.

Sher, K. J., & McCrady, B. S. (1984). The MacAndrew alcoholism scale: Severity of alcohol abuse and parental alcoholism. *Addictive Behaviors, 9*, 99–102.

Sher, K. J., & Trull, T. J. (1994). Personality and disinhibitory psychopathology: Alcoholism and antisocial personality disorder. *Journal of Abnormal Psychology, 103*(1), 92–102.

Sher, K. J., & Walitzer, K. S. (1986). Individual differences in the stress-response-dampening effect of alcohol: A dose-response study. *Journal of Abnormal Psychology, 95*(2), 159–167.

Sher, K. L., Walitzer, K. S., Wood, P. K., & Brent, E. E. (1991). Characteristics of the children of alcoholics: Putative risk factors, substance use and abuse, and psychopathology. *Journal of Abnormal Psychology, 100*(4), 427–448.

Sigurdsson, J. F., & Gudjonsson, G. H. (1996). Psychological characteristics of juvenile alcohol and drug users. *Journal of Adolescence, 19*, 41–46.

Simon, T. R., Stacy, A. W., Sussman, S., & Dent, C. W. (1994). Sensation seeking and drug use among high risk Latino and Anglo adolescents. *Personality and Individual Differences, 17*(5), 665–672.

Simonsson, P., Berglund, M., Oreland, L., Moberg, A. L., & Alling, C. (1992). Serotonin-stimulated phosphoinositide hydrolysis in platelets from post-withdrawal alcoholics. *Alcohol and Alcoholism, 27*, 607–612.

Skinner, H. A. (1982). The drug abuse screening test. *Addictive Behaviors, 7*, 363–371.

Smail, P., Stockwell, T., Canter, S., & Hodgson, R. (1984). Alcohol dependence and phobic anxiety states I: A prevalence study. *British Journal of Psychiatry, 144*, 53–57.

Smith, S. S., O'Hara, B. F., Persico, A. M., Gorelick, D. A., Newlin, D. B., Vlahov, D., Solomon, L., Pickens, R., & Uhl, G. R. (1992). Genetic vulnerability to drug abuse: The D2 dopamine receptor Taq I B1 restriction fragment length polymorphism appears more frequently in polysubstance abusers. *Archives of General Psychiatry, 49*, 723–727.

Sobell, L. C. (1994). *Natural recovery: A major pathway to recovery from alcohol problems.* Paper presented at the 103rd annual meeting of the American Psychological Association, August 12–16, Los Angeles.

Speer, D. C., & Bates, K. (1992). Comorbid mental and substance disorders among older psychiatric patients. *Journal of the American Geriatrics Society, 40*(9), 886–890.

Spiegel, D., Hadley, P. A., & Hadley, R. G. (1970). Personality test patterns of rehabilitation center alcoholics, psychiatric inpatients and normals. *Journal of Clinical Psychology, 26*, 366–371.

Spielberger, C. D., Gorsuch, R. L., & Lushene, R. E. (1970). *STAI manual.* Palo Alto, CA: Consulting Psychologists Press.

Spilker, B., & Calaway, E. (1969). Augmenting and reducing in averaged visual evoked responses to sine wave light. *Psychophysiology, 6*, 49–57.

Spotts, J. V., & Shontz, F. C. (1983). Psychopathology and chronic drug use: A methodological paradigm. *International Journal of the Addictions, 5*, 633–680.

Stacy, A. W., Newcomb, M. D., & Bentler, P. M. (1991). Personality, problem drinking, and drunk driving: Mediating, moderating and direct-effect models. *Journal of Personality and Social Psychology, 60*(5), 795–811.

Stallings, M. C., Hewitt, J. K., Cloninger, C. R., Heath, A. C., & Eaves, L. J. (1994). *Factor structure of the Tridimensional Personality Questionnaire: Three or four primary temperament dimensions?* Unpublished manuscript.

Steele, C. M., & Josephs, R. A. (1988). Drinking your troubles away II: An attention-allocation model of alcohol's effect on psychological stress. *Journal of Abnormal Psychology, 97*(2), 196–205.

Steiger, H., Negrete, J. C., & Marcil, G. (1985). Field dependence in alcoholics: Relation to years of drinking, severity of alcohol dependence and emotional distress. *Journal of Studies on Alcohol, 46*(6), 486–489.

Strack, S., & Lorr, M. (Eds.). (1994). *Cluster analysis: Aims, methods, and problems.* New York: Springer Verlag.

Svanum, S., & McAdoo, W. G. (1991). Parental alcoholism: An examination of male and female alcoholics in treatment. *Journal of Studies on Alcohol, 52*(2), 127–132.

Svrakic, D. M., Whitehead, C., Przybeck, T. R., & Cloninger, C. R. (1993). Differential diagnosis of personality disorders by the Seven Factor Model of temperament and character. *Archives of General Psychiatry, 50*, 991–999.

Swan, G. E., Carmelli, D., & Cardon, L. R. (1997). Heavy consumption of cigarettes, alcohol and coffee in male twins. *Journal of Studies on Alcohol, 58*, 182–190.

Swartz, M., Blazer, D., George, L., & Winfield, I. (1990). Estimating the prevalence of borderline personality disorder in the community. *Journal of Personality Disorders, 4*, 257–272.

Tamkin, A. S., Carson, M. F., Nixon, D. H., & Hyer, L. A. (1987). A comparison among some measures of depression in male alcoholics. *Journal of Studies on Alcohol, 48*(2), 176–178.

Tamkin, A. S., & Klett, C. J. (1957). Barron's ego-strength scale: A replication of an evaluation of its construct validity. *Journal of Consulting Psychology, 21*(5), 412.

Tarter, R. E., Blackson, T., Martin, C., Loeber, R, . & Moss, H. B. (1993). Characteristics and correlates of child discipline practices in substance abuse and normal families. *The American Journal on Addictions, 2*(1), 18–25.

Tarter, R.E. & Edwards, K. (1986). Antecedents to alcoholism: Implications for prevention and treatment. *Behavior Therapy, 17*, 346-361.

Tarter, R. E., Hegedus, A. M., & Gavaler, J. S. (1985). Hyperactivity in sons of alcoholics. *Journal of Studies on Alcohol, 46*(3), 259–261.

Tarter, R. E., Hegedus, A. M., Goldstein, G., Shelly, C., & Alterman, A. (1984). Adolescent sons of alcoholics: Neuropsychological and personality characteristics. *Alcoholism: Clinical and Experimental Research, 8*, 216–222.

Tarter, R. E., Laird, S. B., Kabene, M., Bukstein, O., & Kaminer, Y. (1990). Drug use severity in adolescents is associated with magnitude of deviation in temperament traits. *British Journal of Addiction, 85*, 1501–1504.

Tarter, R. E., McBride, H., Buonpane, N., & Schneider, D. U. (1977). Differentiation of alcoholics-Childhood history of minimal brain dysfunction, family history, and drinking pattern. *Archives of General Psychiatry, 34*, 761–768.

Teasdale, J., Seagraves, R., & Zacune, J. (1971). Psychoticism in drug users. British *Journal of Social and Clinical Psychology, 10*, 160–171.

Teichman, M., Barnea, Z., & Ravav, G. (1989). Personality and substance use among adolescents: A longitudinal study. *British Journal of Addiction, 84*, 181–190.

Tein, J-Y., Roosa, M. W., & Michaels, M. (1994). Agreement between parent and child reports on parental behaviors. *Journal of Marriage and the Family, 56*(2), 341–355.

Thurstin, A. H. (1988). The association of alcoholic subtype with treatment outcome: An 18-month follow-up. *The International Journal of the Addictions, 23*, 321–330.

Thyer, B. A., & Curtis. G. C. (1984). The effects of ethanol intoxication on phobic anxiety. *Behavior Research and Therapy, 22*, 599–610.

Thyer, B. A., Parrish, R. T., Himle, J., Cameron, O. G., Curtis, G. C., & Nesse, R. M. (1986). Alcohol abuse among clinically anxious patients. *Behavior Research and Therapy, 24*, 357–359.

Trott, L., Barnes, G. E., & Dumoff, R. (1981). Ethnicity and other demographic characteristics as predictors of sudden drug-related deaths. *Journal of Studies on Alcohol, 42*(7), 564–578.

Tubman, J. G., & Windle, M. (1995). Continuity of difficult temperament in adolescence: Relations with depression, life events, family support, and substance use across a one-year period. *Journal of Youth and Adolescence, 24*(2), 133–153.

Turner, S. M., Beidel, D. C., Dancy, C. V., & Keys, D. J. (1986). Psychopathology of social phobia and comparison to avoidant personality disorder. *Journal of Abnormal Psychology, 95*, 389–394.

Uhl, G. R., Persico, A. M., & Smith, S. S. (1992). Current excitement with D_2 dopamine receptor gene alleles in substance abuse. *Archives of General Psychiatry, 49*, 157–160.

Ullman, J. (1996). Structural equation modeling. In B. G. Tabachnick & L. S. Fidell, *Using multivariate statistics* (3rd ed.) (pp. 709–811). New York: Harper Collins College Publishers.

Vaillant, G. (1983). *The natural history of alcoholism: Causes, patterns and paths to recovery.* Cambridge, MA: Harvard University Press.

Vaillant, G. E., & Milofsky, E. S. (1982). The etiology of alcoholism: A prospective viewpoint. *American Psychologist, 27*(5), 494–503.

Vaillant, G. E., & Milofsky, E. S. (1991). The etiology of alcoholism: A prospective viewpoint. In D. J. Pittman & H. R. White (Eds.), *Society, culture, and drinking patterns reexamined* (pp. 492–512). New Brunswick, NJ: Rutgers Center of Alcohol Studies.

Van Ammers, E. C., Sellman, J. D., & Mulder, R. T. (1997). Temperament and substance abuse in schizophrenia: Is there a relationship? *The Journal of Nervous and Mental Disease, 185*(5), 283–288.

Vando, A. (1969). A personality dimension related to pain tolerance. (Doctoral dissertation. Columbia University).

Verheul, R., van den Brink, W., & Hartgers, C. (1995). Prevalence of personality disorders among alcoholics and drug addicts: An overview. *European Addiction Research, 1*, 166–177.

Vogel, M. D. (1961). GSR conditioning and personality factors in alcoholics and normals. *Journal of Abnormal Psychology, 63*, 417–421.

von Knorring, L. (1976). Visual averaged evoked responses in patients suffering from alcoholism. *Neuropsychobiology*, 2, 233–238.

von Knorring, L., Oreland, L., & von Knorring, A-L. (1987). Personality traits and platelet MAO activity in alcohol and drug abusing teenage boys. *Acta Psychiatrica Scandinavica, 75,* 307–314.

von Knorring, L., Palm, U., & Andersson, H. (1985). Relationship between treatment outcome and subtype of alcoholism in men. *Journal of Studies on Alcohol, 46*(5), 388–391.

von Knorring, L., von Knorring, A., Smigan, L., Lindberg, U., & Eldholm, M. (1987). Personality traits in subtypes of alcoholics. *Journal of Studies on Alcohol, 48*(6), 523–527.

Vulcano, B. A., & Barnes, G. E. (1986). *Problem drinking among adolescents: Tests of a theoretical model.* Canadian Psychological Association Convention, Toronto.

Wachs, T. D. (1983). The use and abuse of environment in behavior-genetic research. *Child Development, 54,* 396–407.

Walfish, S., Massey, R., & Krone, A. (1990). MMPI Profiles of adolescent substance abusers in treatment. *Adolescence, 25*(99), 567–572.

Waller, N. G. (1995). *MicroFACT 1.0.* St Paul, MN: Assessment Systems.

Ward, J. H. (1963). Hierarchical grouping to optimize an objective function. *Journal of the American Statistical Association, 58,* 236–244.

Watson, D. (1989). Stranger's ratings of the five robust personality factors: Evidence of a surprising convergence with self-report. *Journal of Personality and Social Psychology, 57,* 120–128.

Watson, D., & Clark, L. A. (1993). Behavioral disinhibition versus constraint: A dispositional perspective. In D. M. Wegner & J. W. Pennebaker, *Handbook of mental control* (Century psychology series, pp. 506–527). Englewood Cliffs, NJ: Prentice-Hall.

Weiss, K. J., & Rosenberg, D. J. (1985). Prevalence of anxiety disorders among alcoholics. *Journal of Clinical Psychiatry, 46,* 3–5.

Weissman, M. M., & Myers, J. K. (1980). Clinical depression in alcoholism. *American Journal of Psychiatry, 137,* 372–373.

Werner, E. E. (1986). Resilient offspring of alcoholics: A longitudinal study from birth to age 18. *Journal of Studies on Alcohol, 47*(1), 34–40.

West, M. O., & Prinz, R. J. (1987). Parental alcoholism and childhood psychopathology. *Psychological Bulletin, 102*(2), 204–218.

Whalley, L. J. (1978). Sexual adjustment of male alcoholics. *Acta Psychiatrica Scandinavica, 58,* 281–289.

Whipple, S. C., & Noble, E. P. (1991). Personality characteristics of alcoholic fathers and their sons. *Journal of Studies on Alcohol, 52*(4), 331–337.

Whitbeck, L. B., Hoyt, D. R., Simons, R. L., Conger, R. D., Elder, G. H., Jr., Lorenz, F. O., & Huck, S. (1992). Intergenerational continuity of parental rejection and depressed affect. *Journal of Personality and Social Psychology, 63*(6), 1036–1045.

White, W., & Porter, T. L. (1966). Self-concept reports among hospitalized alcoholics during early periods of sobriety. *Journal of Counselling Psychology, 13*(3), 352–354.

Wills, T. A., Vaccaro, D.m & McNamara, G. (1994). Novelty seeking, risk taking , and related constructs as predictors of adolescent substance use: An application of Cloninger's theory. *Journal of Substance Abuse, 6,* 1–20.

Wilsnack, S. C. (1973). Sex role identity in female alcoholism. *Journal of Abnormal Psychology, 82,* 253–261.

Wilson, G. T. (1988). Alcohol and anxiety. *Behavior Research and Therapy, 26*(5), 369–381.

Witkin, H. A., Dyk, R. B., Faterson, H. F., Goodenough, D. R., & Karp, S. A. (1962). *Psychological differentiation.* New York: Wiley.

Witkin, H. A., Karp, S. A., & Goodenough, D. R. (1959). Dependence in alcoholics. *Quarterly Journal of Studies on Alcohol, 20,* 493–504.

314   References

Witkin, H. A., Oltman, P. K., Raskin, E., & Karp, S. A. (1971). *A manual for the Embedded Figures Test.* Palo Alto, CA: Consulting Psychologists Press.

Wolpaw, J. R., & Henry, J. K. (1978) Effects of ethanol, caffeine, and placebo on the auditory evoked response. *Electroencephalography and Clinical Neurophysiology, 44,* 568–574.

Wood, D., Wender, P. H., & Reimehr, F. W. (1983). The prevalence of attention deficit disorder, residual type, or minimal brain dysfunction, in a population of male alcoholic patients. *American Journal of Psychiatry, 140,* 95–98.

Workman-Daniels, K. L., & Hesselbrock, V. M. (1987). Childhood problem behavior and neuropsychological functioning in persons at risk for alcoholism. *Journal of Studies on Alcohol, 48,* 187–193.

Yanish, D. L., & Battle, J. (1985). Relationship between self-esteem, depression and alcohol consumption among adolescents. *Psychological Reports, 57,* 331–334.

Yeager, R. J., DiGiuseppe, R., Resweber, P. J., & Leaf, R. (1992). Comparison of Millon personality profiles of chronic residential substance abusers and a general outpatient population. *Psychological Reports, 71,* 71–79.

Yuan, K-H., & Bentler, P. M. (1996). Mean and covariance structure analysis with missing data. In A. Gupta & V. Girko (Eds.), *Multidimensional statistical analysis and theory of random matrices: Proceedings of Sixth Eugene Lukacs Symposium* (pp. 307–326). Netherlands: VSP.

Yuan, K.-H., & Bentler, P. M. (1997). Mean and covariance structure analysis: Theoretical and practical improvements. *Journal of the American Statistical Association, 92,* 767–774.

Yuan, K.-H., & Bentler, P. M. (in press). F-tests for mean and covariance structure analysis. *Journal of Educational and Behavioral Statistics.*

Zanarini, M. C., Gunderson, J. G., & Frankenburg, F. R. (1989). Axis I phenomenology of borderline personality disorder. *Comprehensive Psychiatry, 30,* 149–156.

Zaninelli, R. M., Porjesz, B., & Begleiter, H. (1992). The Tridimensional Personality Questionnaire in males at high and low risk for alcoholism. *Alcoholism Clinical and Experimental Research, 16*(1), 68–70.

Zivich, J. M. (1981). Alcoholic subtypes and treatment effectiveness. *Journal of Consulting and Clinical Psychology, 49,* 72–80.

Zucker, R. A. (1976). Parental influences on the drinking patterns of their children. In M. Greenblatt & M. A. Schucket (Eds.), *Alcoholism problems in women and children.* New York: Grune & Stratton.

Zucker, R. A. (1979). Developmental aspects of drinking through the young adult years. In H. T. Blane & M. E. Chafetz (Eds.), *Youth, alcohol and social policy.* New York: Plenum Publishing.

Zucker, R. A., & Barron, F. H. (1973). Parental behaviors associated with problem drinking and anti-social behavior among adolescent males. In M. Chafetz (Ed.), *Preceedings of the first annual alcoholism conference of the National Institute on Alcohol Abuse and Alcoholism, Research on alcoholism: Clinical problems and special populations.* Rockville, MD: NIAAA.

Zucker, R. A., Ellis, D. A., Bingham, C. R., Fitzgerald, H. E., & Sanford, K. (1996). Other evidence for at least two alcoholisms, II: Life course variation in antisociality and heterogeneity of alcoholic outcome. *Development and Psychopathology, 8,* 831–848.

Zucker, R. A., Fitzgerald, H. E., & Moses, H. D. (1995). Emergence of alcohol problems and the several alcoholisms: A developmental perspective on etiologic theory and life course trajectory. In C. Cicchetti & D. J. Cohen (Eds.), *Development and psychopathology, Vol. 2: Risk, disorder and adaptation* (pp. 677–711). New York: Wiley.

Zucker, R. A., & Lisansky Gomberg, E. S. (1986). Etiology of alcoholism reconsidered: The case for a biolpsychosocial process. *American Psychologist, 41*(7), 783–793.

Zuckerman, M. (1983). A biological theory of sensation seeking. In M. Zuckerman (Ed.), *Biological bases of sensation seeking, impulsivity and anxiety.* Hillsdale, NJ: Erlbaum.

Zuckerman, M. (1987) Biological connection between sensation seeking and drug abuse. In J. Engel & L. Oreland (Eds.), *Brain reward systems and abuse*. New York: Raven Press.

Zuckerman, M. (1989). Personality in the third dimension: A psychobiological approach. *Personality and Individual Differences, 10*, 391–418.

Zuckerman, M. (1994). *Behavioral expressions and biosocial bases of sensation seeking*. New York: Cambridge University Press.

Zuckerman, M., Kuhlman, M., & Camac, C. (1988). What lies beyond N and E? Factor analysis of scales believed to measure basic dimensions of personality. *Journal of Personality and Social Psychology, 54*, 96–107.

Zuckerman, M., Murtaugh, T., & Siegel, J. (1974). Sensation seeking and cortical augmenting-reducing. *Psychophysiology, 11*(5), 535–542.

Index

317

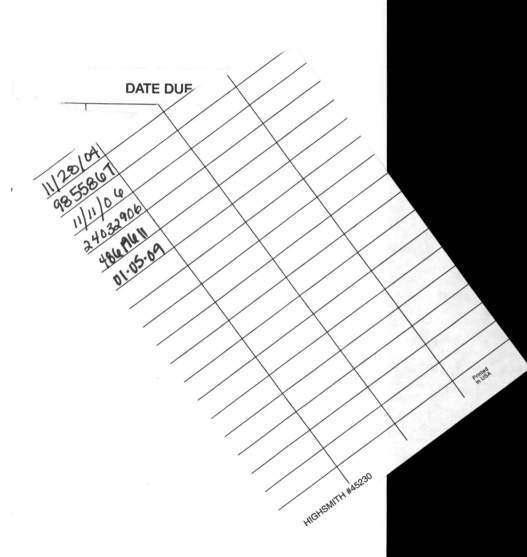

DATE DUE

11/20/04
98 55861
11/11/06
24032906
486 M6 11
01-05-09

HIGHSMITH #45230

Printed
In USA